# STOP!

## This is the back of the book.
## You wouldn't want to spoil a great ending!

This book is printed "manga-style," in the authentic Japanese right-to-left format. Since none of the artwork has been flipped or altered, readers get to experience the story just as the creator intended. You've been ~~as~~king for it, so TOKYOPOP® delivered: authentic, hot-off-the-press, ~~an~~d far more fun!

# DIRECTIONS

If this is your first time reading manga-style, here's a quick guide to help you understand how it works.

It's easy... just start in the top right panel and follow the numbers. Have fun, and look for more 100% authentic manga from TOKYOPOP®!

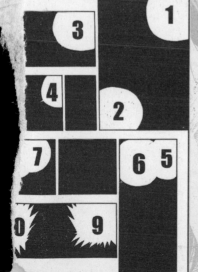

NOV 09

# BIZENGHAST

*Dear Diary,*
*I'm starting to feel*

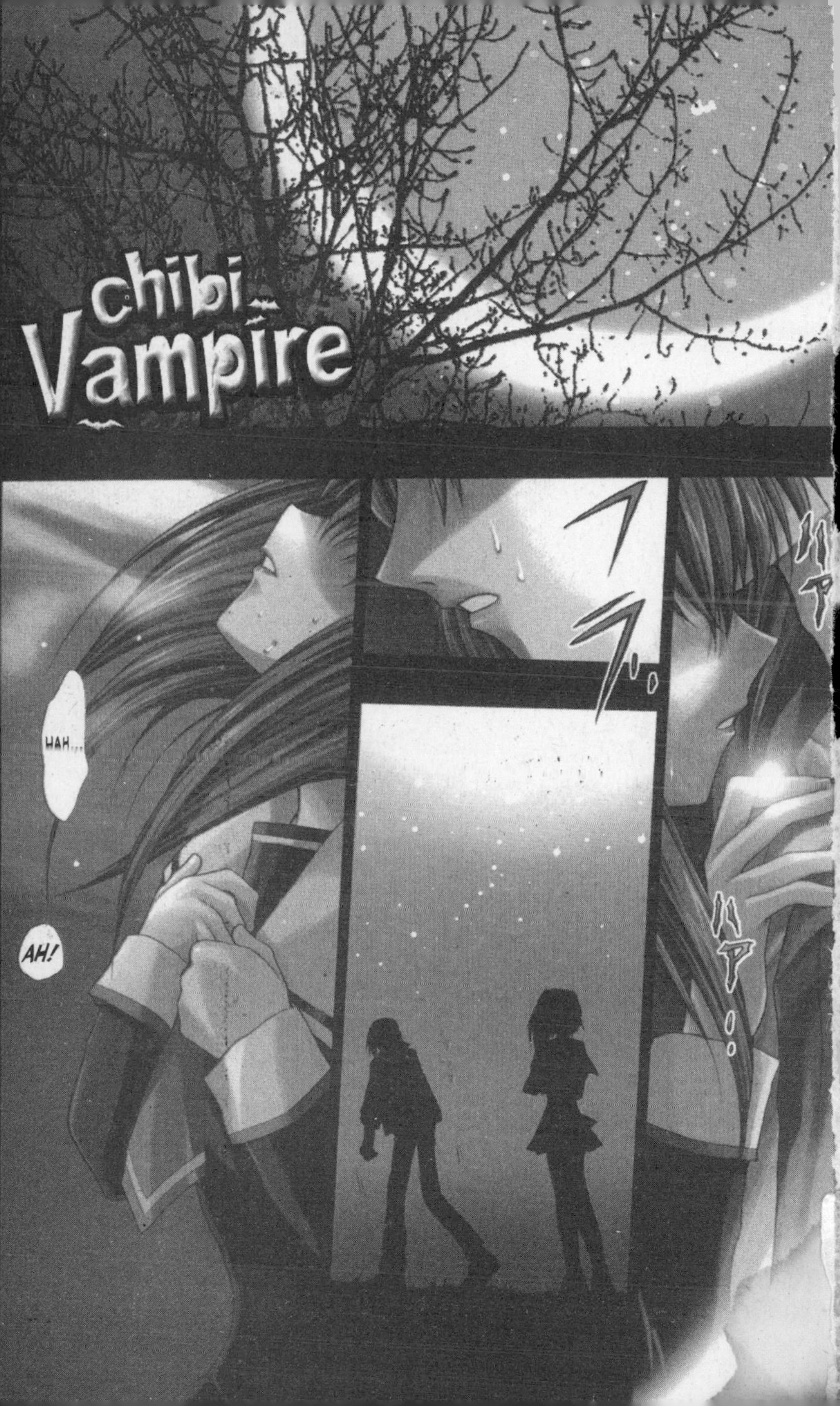
chibi Vampire
ハァ
ハァ・・
HAH...
AH!

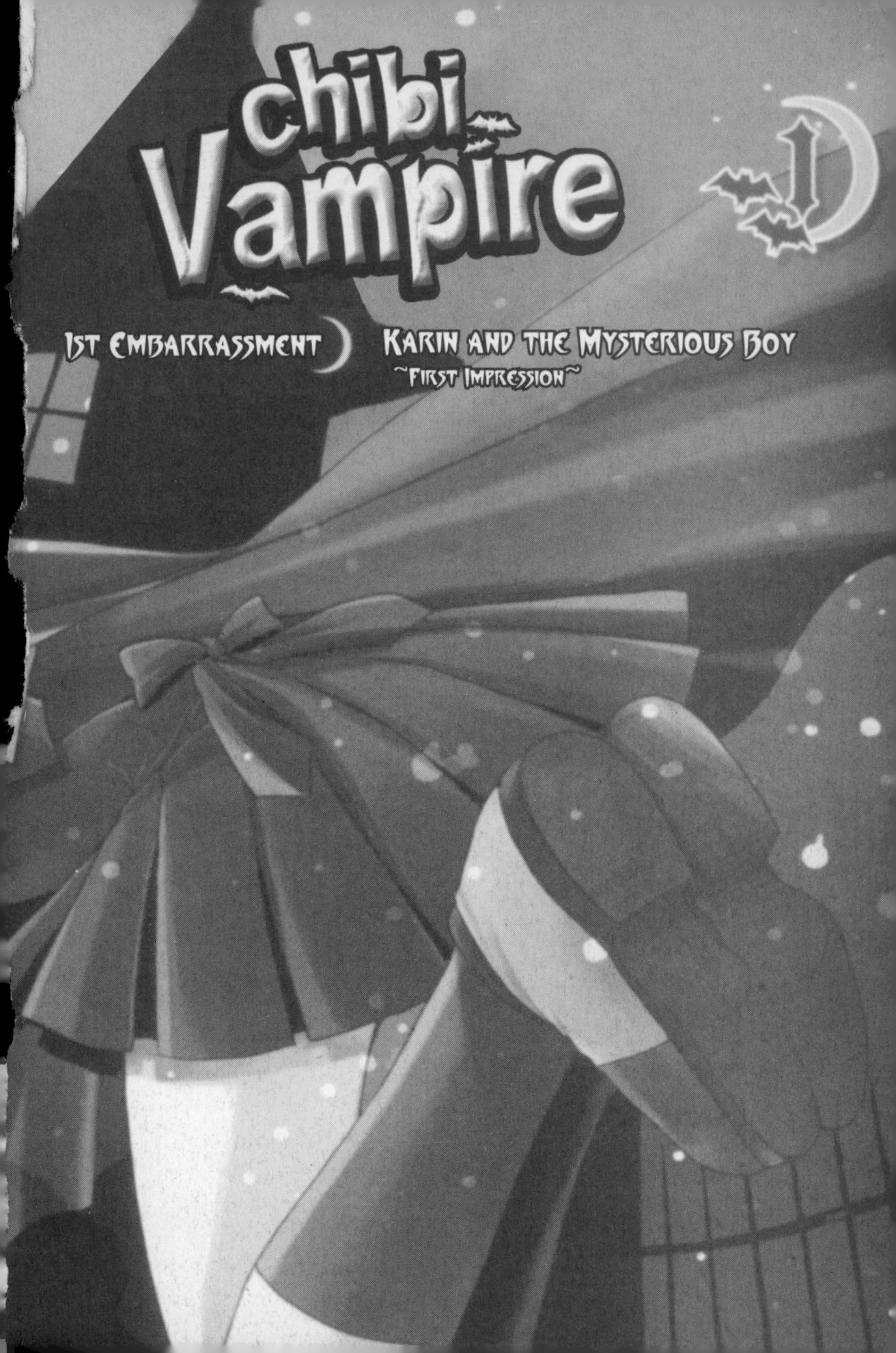
chibi Vampire
1
1st Embarrassment
Karin and the Mysterious Boy
~First Impression~

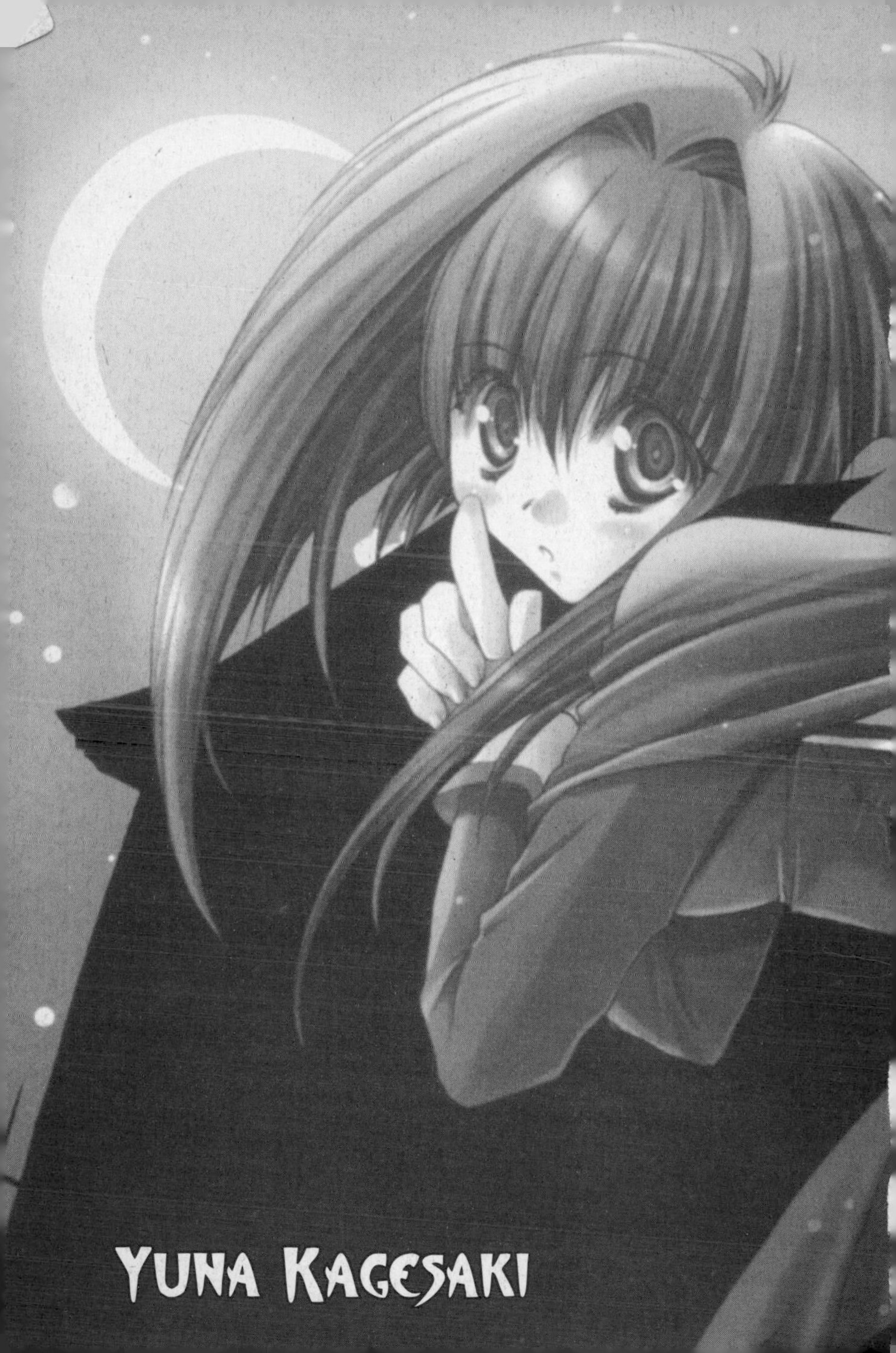
YUNA KAGESAKI

# C☾NTENTS

⟨ 1st Embarrassment:
Karin and the Mysterious Boy
.................................................. 1

⟨ 2nd Embarrassment:
Karin's Family and the Dangerous Afternoon
.................................................. 41

⟨ 3rd Embarrassment:
Karin's Face and the Mask Removed
.................................................. 71

⟨ 4th Embarrassment:
Karin's Worries and Kenta's Distress
.................................................. 101

⟨ 5th Embarrassment:
Karin's Preference and the Charming Woman
.................................................. 131

# Chibi Vampire

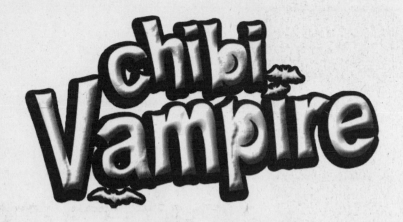

## Volume 1

Created by
Yuna Kagesaki

TOKYOPOP®

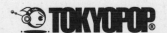

HAMBURG // LONDON // LOS ANGELES // TOKYO

## *Chibi Vampire Vol. 1*
### Created by Yuna Kagesaki

---

Translation - Alexis Kirsch
English Adaptation - Christine Boylan
Copy Editor - Hope Donovan
Layout and Lettering - Vincente Rivera, Jr.
Production Artist - Jennifer Carbajal
Cover Layout - Kyle Plummer

Editor - Tim Beedle
Digital Imaging Manager - Chris Buford
Production Manager - Jennifer Miller
Managing Editor - Lindsey Johnston
Editorial Director - Jeremy Ross
VP of Production - Ron Klamert
Publisher and E.I.C. - Mike Kiley
President and C.O.O. - John Parker
C.E.O. and Chief Creative Officer - Stuart Levy

A  Manga

TOKYOPOP Inc.
5900 Wilshire Blvd. Suite 2000
Los Angeles, CA 90036

E-mail: info@TOKYOPOP.com
Come visit us online at www.TOKYOPOP.com

ISBN: 1-59816-322-1

First TOKYOPOP printing: April 2006
20  19  18  17  16
Printed in the USA

# THE MAAKA FAMILY

## CALERA MARKER

Karin's overbearing mother. While Calera resents that Karin wasn't born a normal vampire, she does love her daughter in her own obnoxious way. Calera has chosen to keep her European last name.

## HENRY MARKER

Karin's father. In general, Henry treats Karin a lot better than she's treated by her mother, but the pants in this particular family are worn by Calera. Henry has also chosen to keep his European last name.

## KARIN MAAKA

Our little heroine. Karin is a vampire living in Japan, but instead of sucking blood from her victims, she actually GIVES them some of her blood. She's a vampire in reverse!

## REN MAAKA

Karin's older brother. Ren milks the "sexy creature of the night" thing for all it's worth, and spends his nights in the arms (and beds) of attractive young women.

## ANJU MAAKA

Karin's little sister. Anju has not yet awoken as a full vampire, but she can control bats and is usually the one who cleans up after Karin's messes. Rarely seen without her "talking" doll, Boogie.

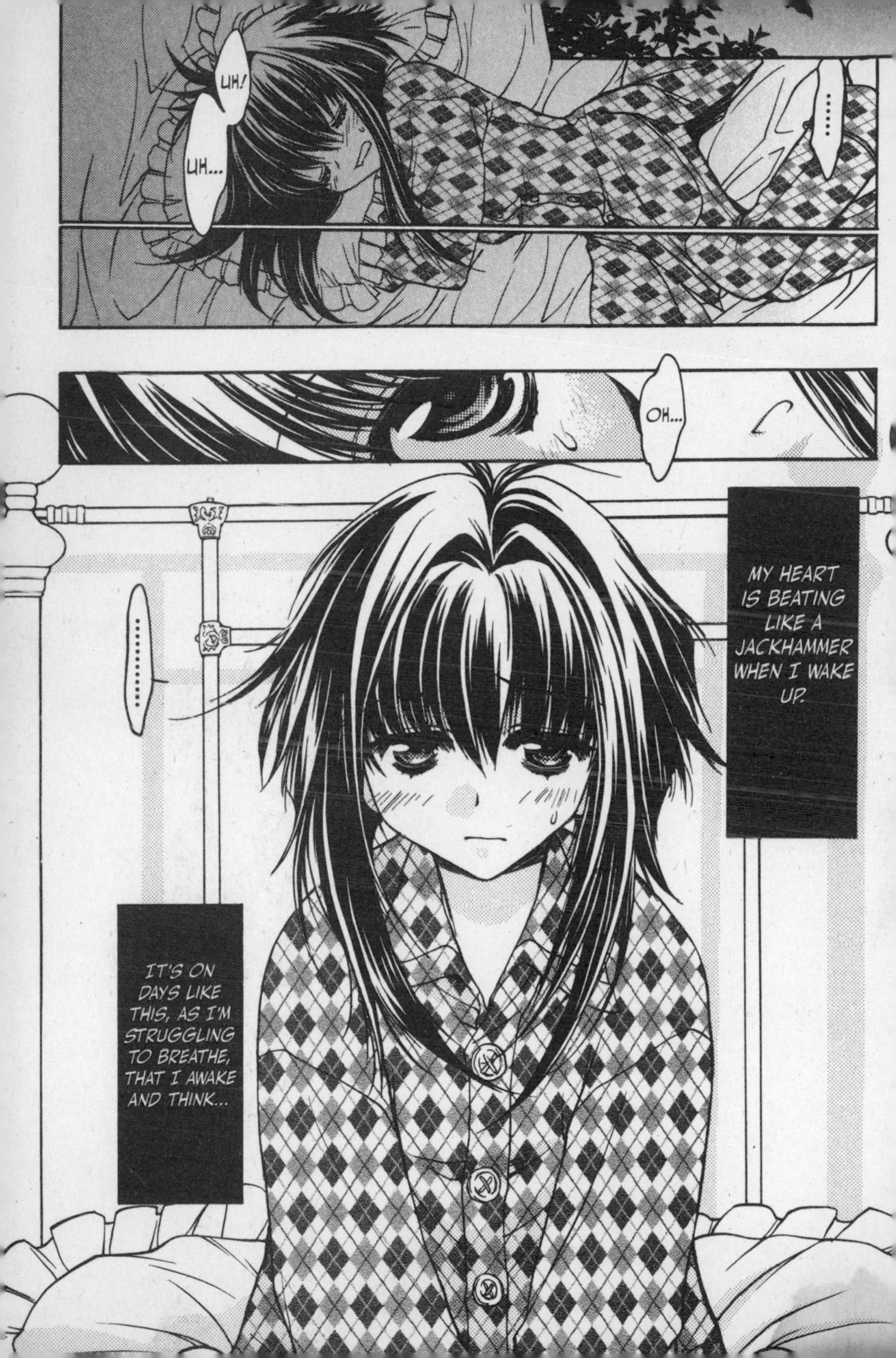
......
UH!
UH...
OH...
MY HEART IS BEATING LIKE A JACKHAMMER WHEN I WAKE UP.
.........
IT'S ON DAYS LIKE THIS, AS I'M STRUGGLING TO BREATHE, THAT I AWAKE AND THINK...

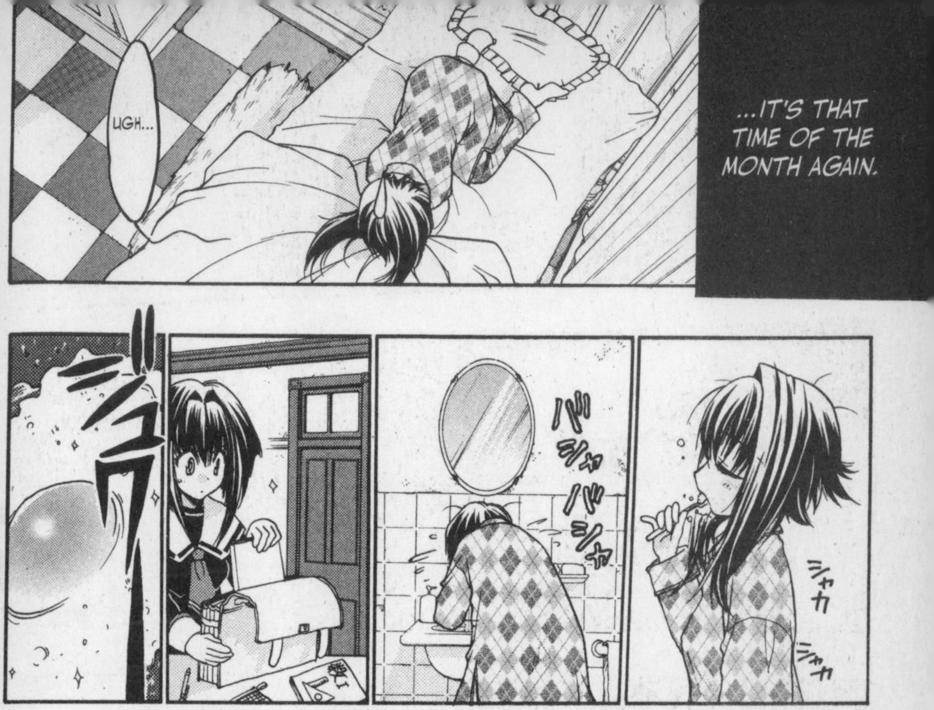
...IT'S THAT TIME OF THE MONTH AGAIN.
UGH...
シャカ
シャカ
バシャバシャ

*That's pronounced Ma-Aka!!

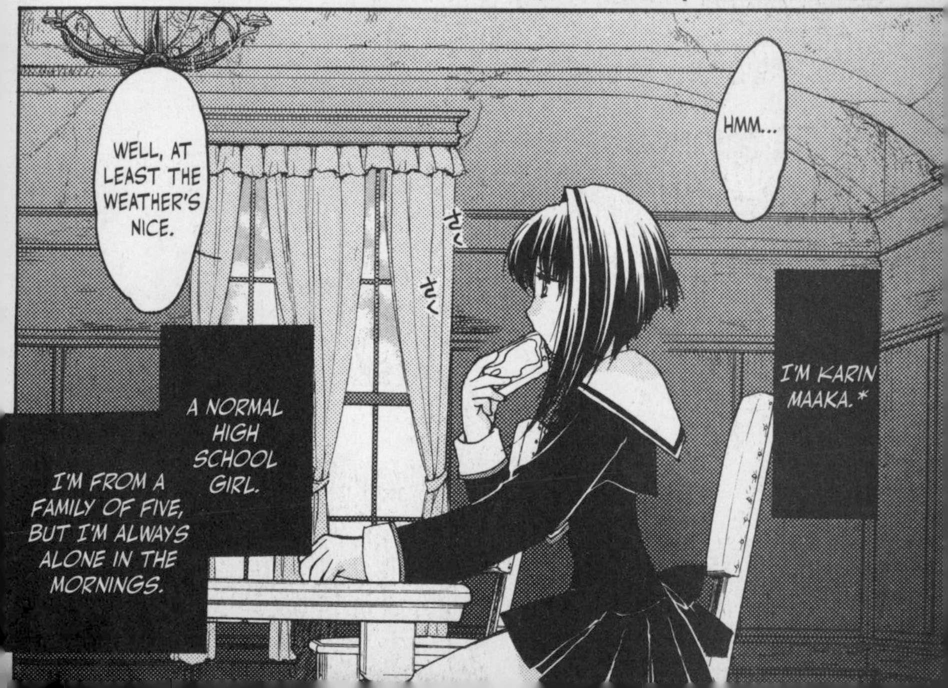
HMM...
WELL, AT LEAST THE WEATHER'S NICE.
さく
さく
I'M KARIN MAAKA.*
A NORMAL HIGH SCHOOL GIRL.
I'M FROM A FAMILY OF FIVE, BUT I'M ALWAYS ALONE IN THE MORNINGS.

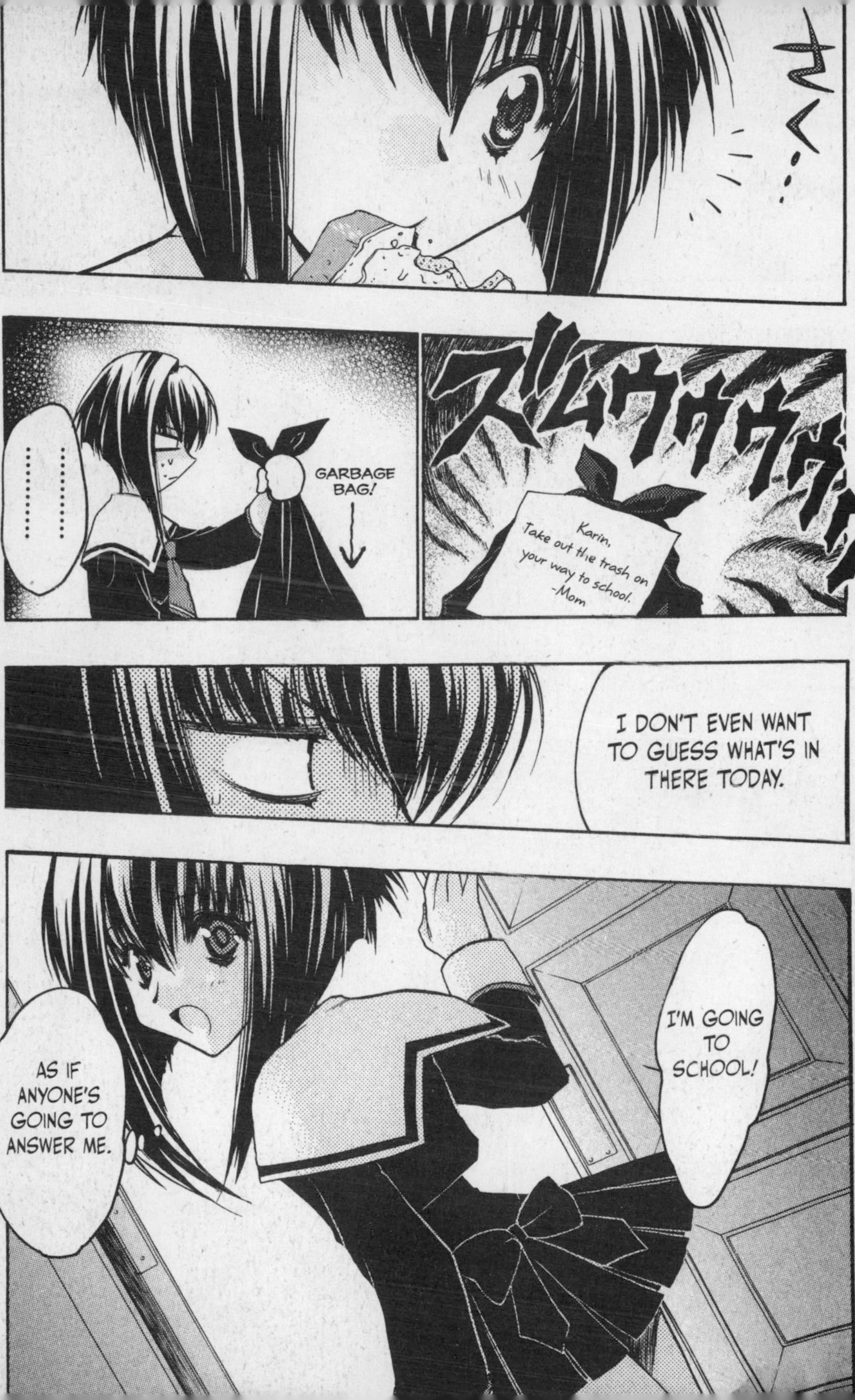
さく…
Karin,
Take out the trash on your way to school.
-Mom
……
GARBAGE BAG!
I DON'T EVEN WANT TO GUESS WHAT'S IN THERE TODAY.
I'M GOING TO SCHOOL!
AS IF ANYONE'S GOING TO ANSWER ME.

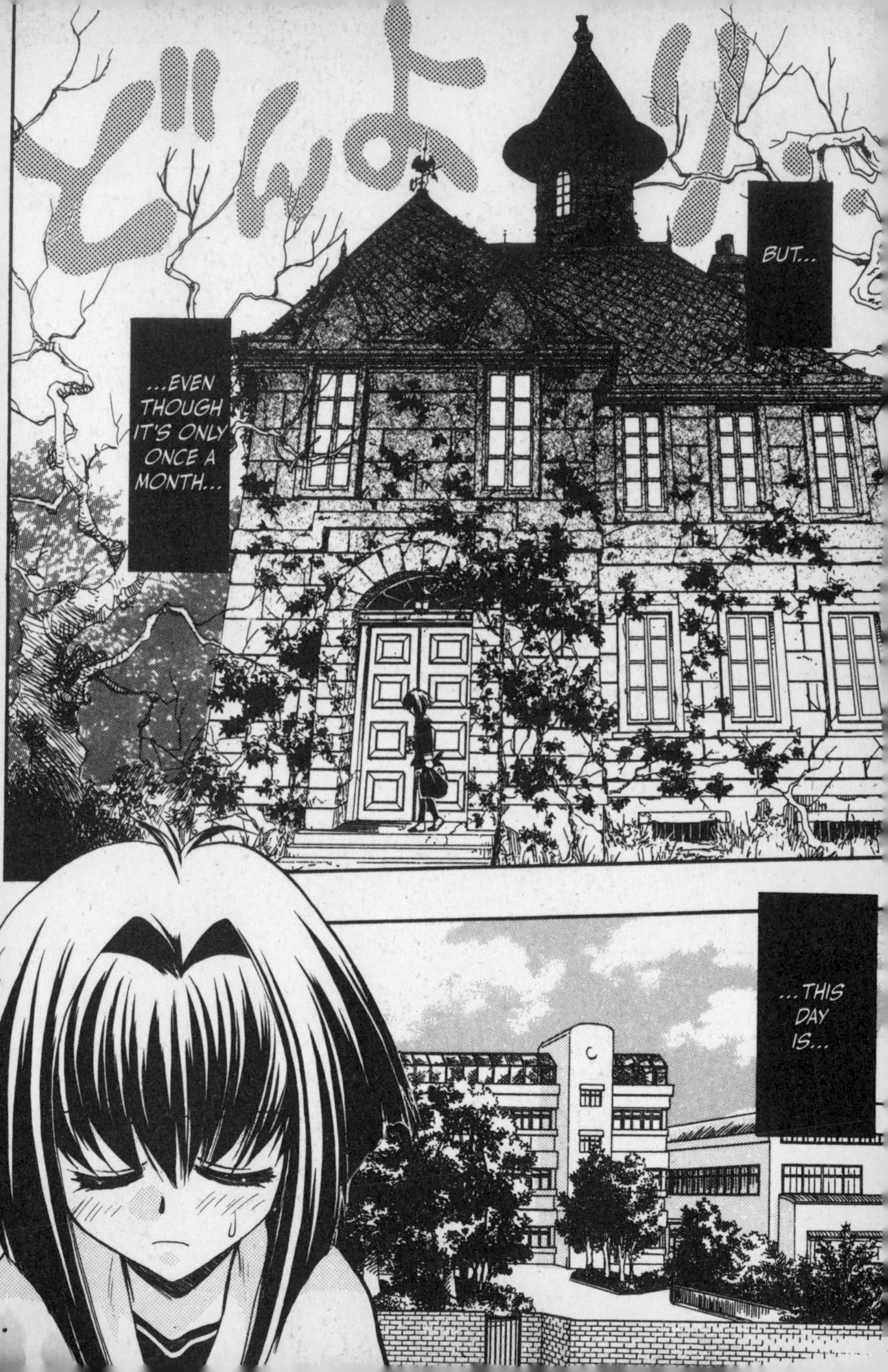
どんより…
BUT...
...EVEN THOUGH IT'S ONLY ONCE A MONTH...
...THIS DAY IS...

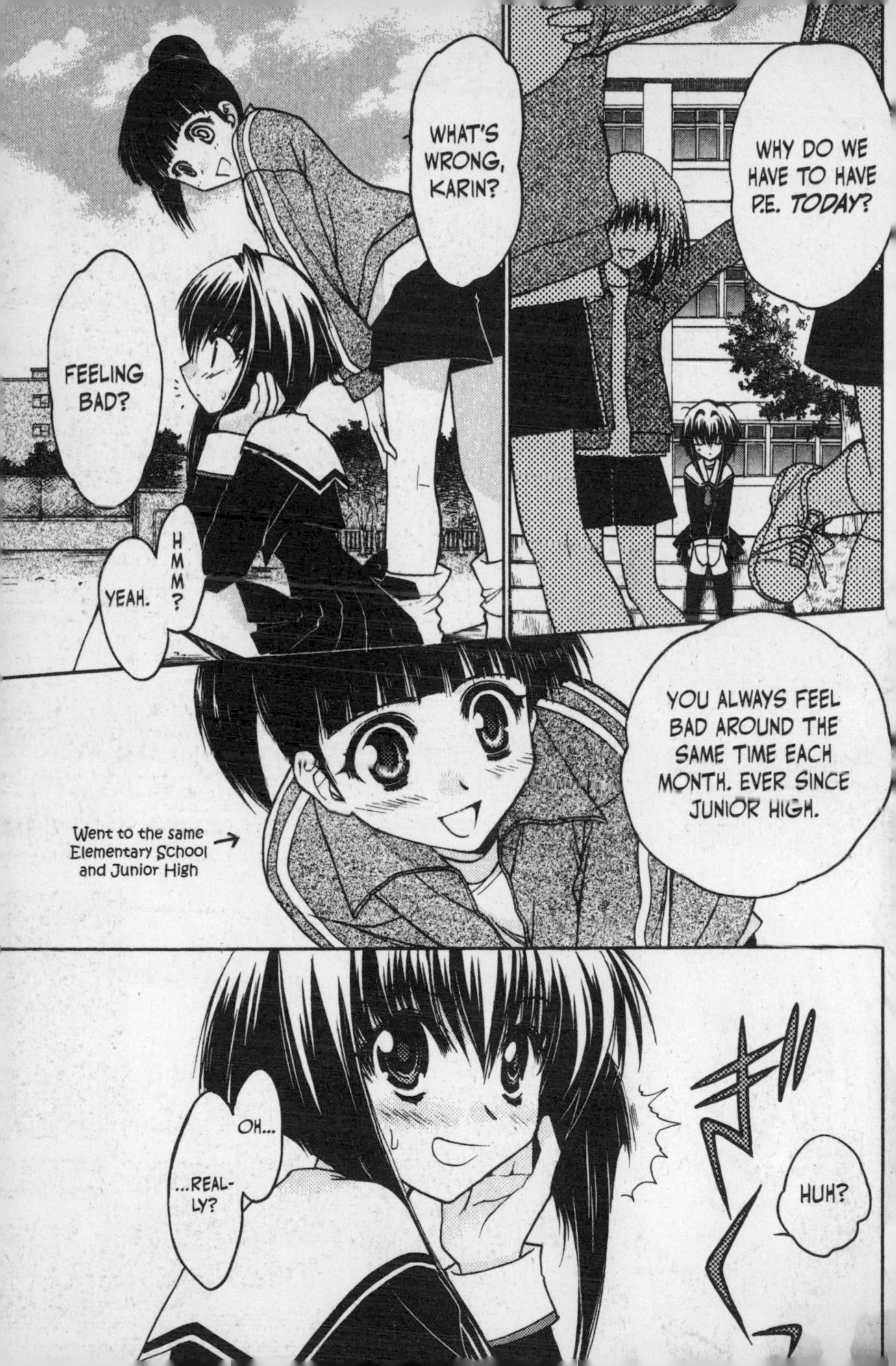
WHY DO WE HAVE TO HAVE P.E. *TODAY*?
WHAT'S WRONG, KARIN?
FEELING BAD?
HMM?
YEAH.
YOU ALWAYS FEEL BAD AROUND THE SAME TIME EACH MONTH. EVER SINCE JUNIOR HIGH.
Went to the same Elementary School and Junior High
HUH?
OH...
...REAL-LY?

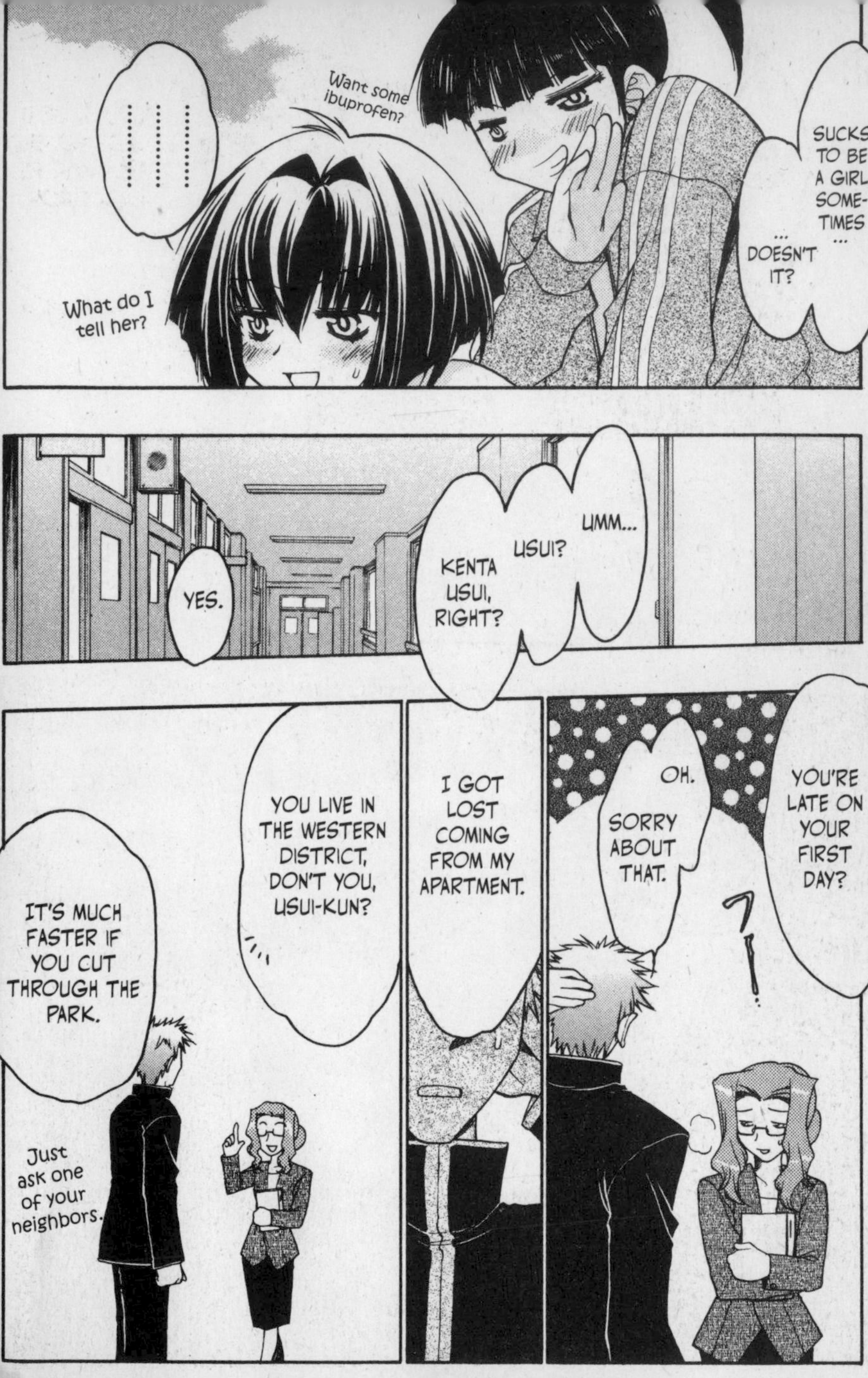
SUCKS TO BE A GIRL SOME-TIMES ... ... DOESN'T IT?
Want some ibuprofen?
......
What do I tell her?
UMM...
USUI?
KENTA USUI, RIGHT?
YES.
YOU'RE LATE ON YOUR FIRST DAY?
OH.
SORRY ABOUT THAT.
I GOT LOST COMING FROM MY APARTMENT.
YOU LIVE IN THE WESTERN DISTRICT, DON'T YOU, USUI-KUN?
IT'S MUCH FASTER IF YOU CUT THROUGH THE PARK.
Just ask one of your neighbors.

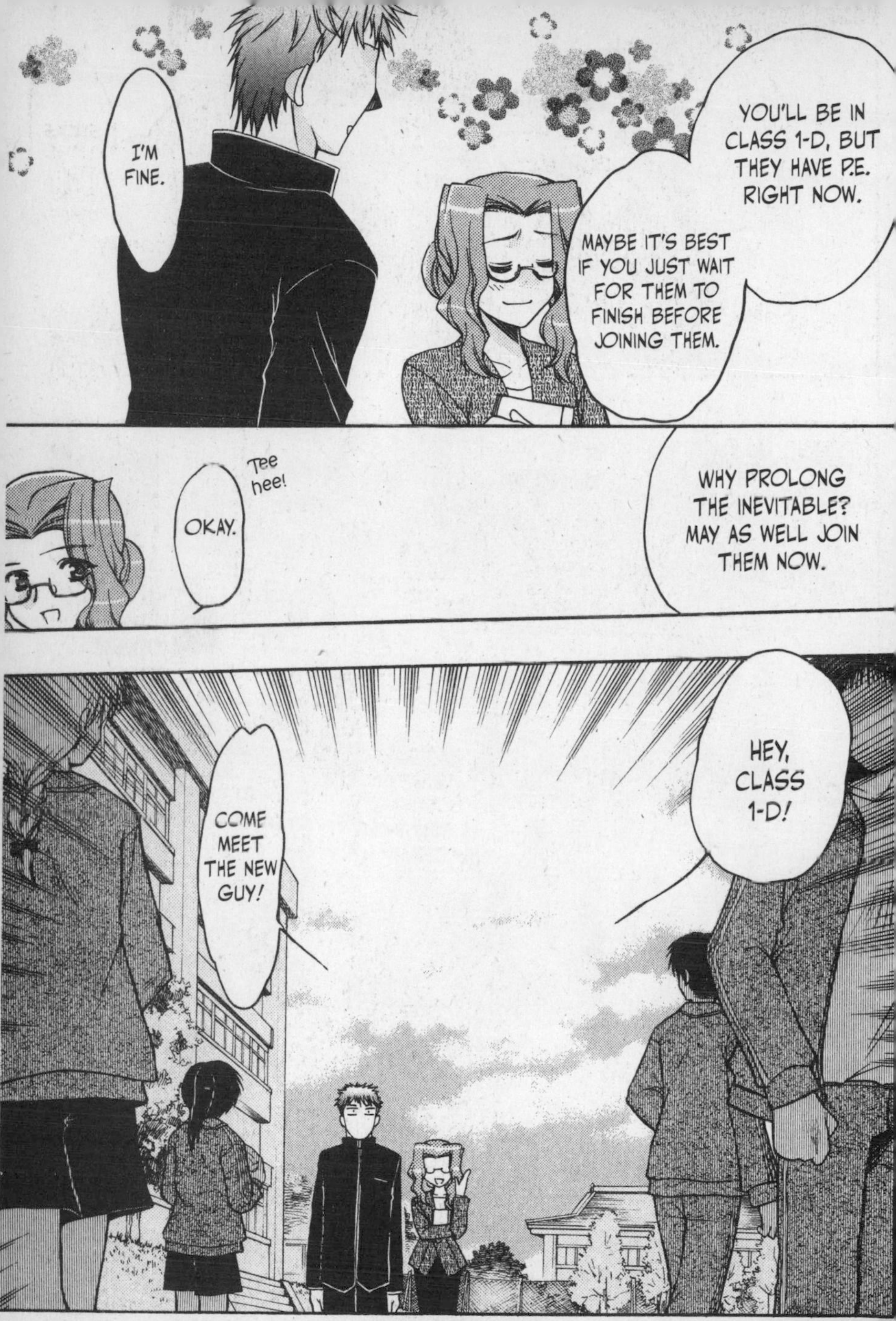
YOU'LL BE IN CLASS 1-D, BUT THEY HAVE P.E. RIGHT NOW.
MAYBE IT'S BEST IF YOU JUST WAIT FOR THEM TO FINISH BEFORE JOINING THEM.
I'M FINE.
WHY PROLONG THE INEVITABLE? MAY AS WELL JOIN THEM NOW.
OKAY.
Tee hee!
HEY, CLASS 1-D!
COME MEET THE NEW GUY!

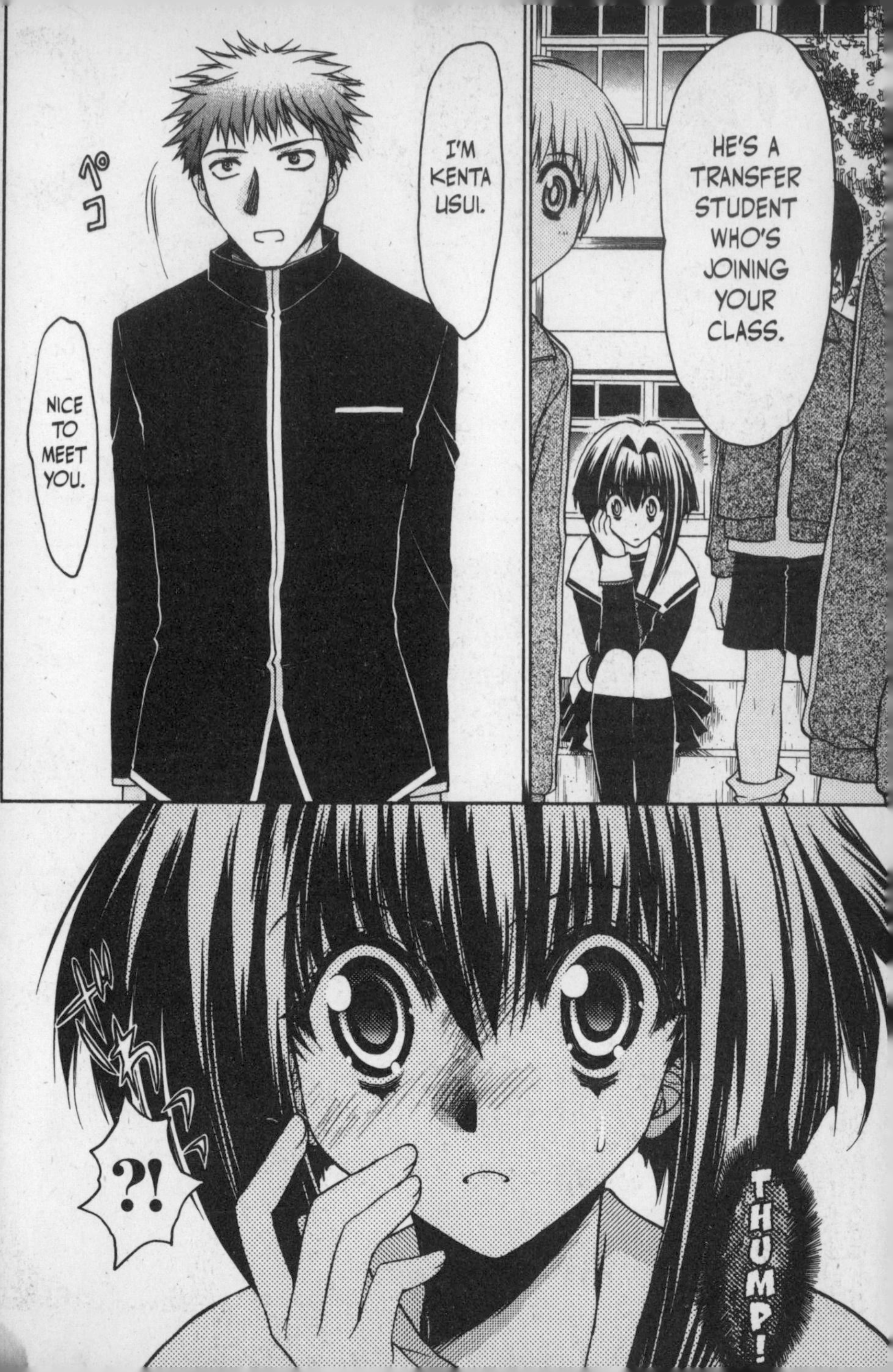
HE'S A TRANSFER STUDENT WHO'S JOINING YOUR CLASS.
I'M KENTA USUI.
ペコ
NICE TO MEET YOU.
THUMP!
?!

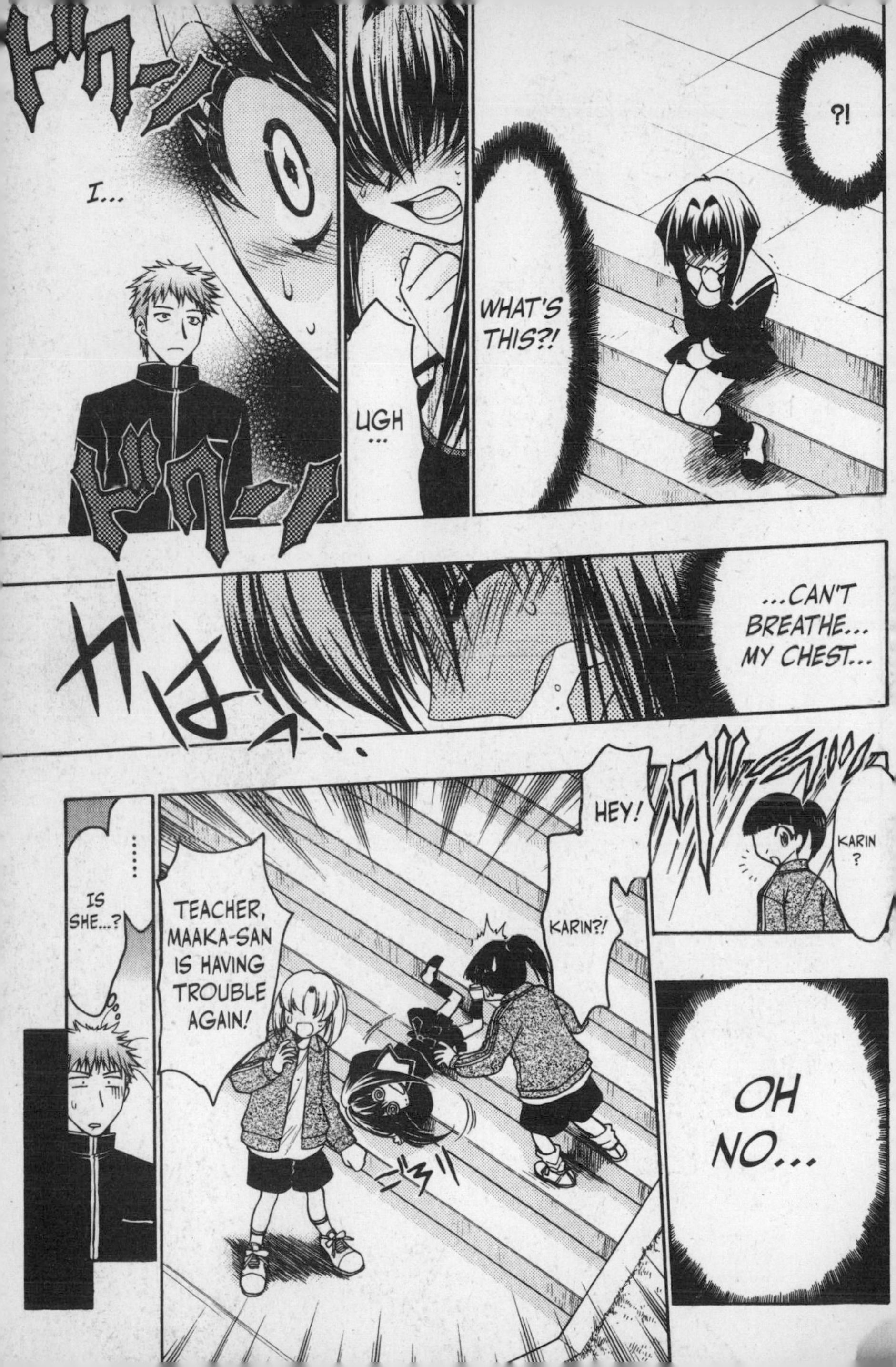
?!
WHAT'S THIS?!
UGH ...
I...
...CAN'T BREATHE... MY CHEST...
KARIN ?
HEY!
OH NO...
KARIN?!
TEACHER, MAAKA-SAN IS HAVING TROUBLE AGAIN!
......
IS SHE...?

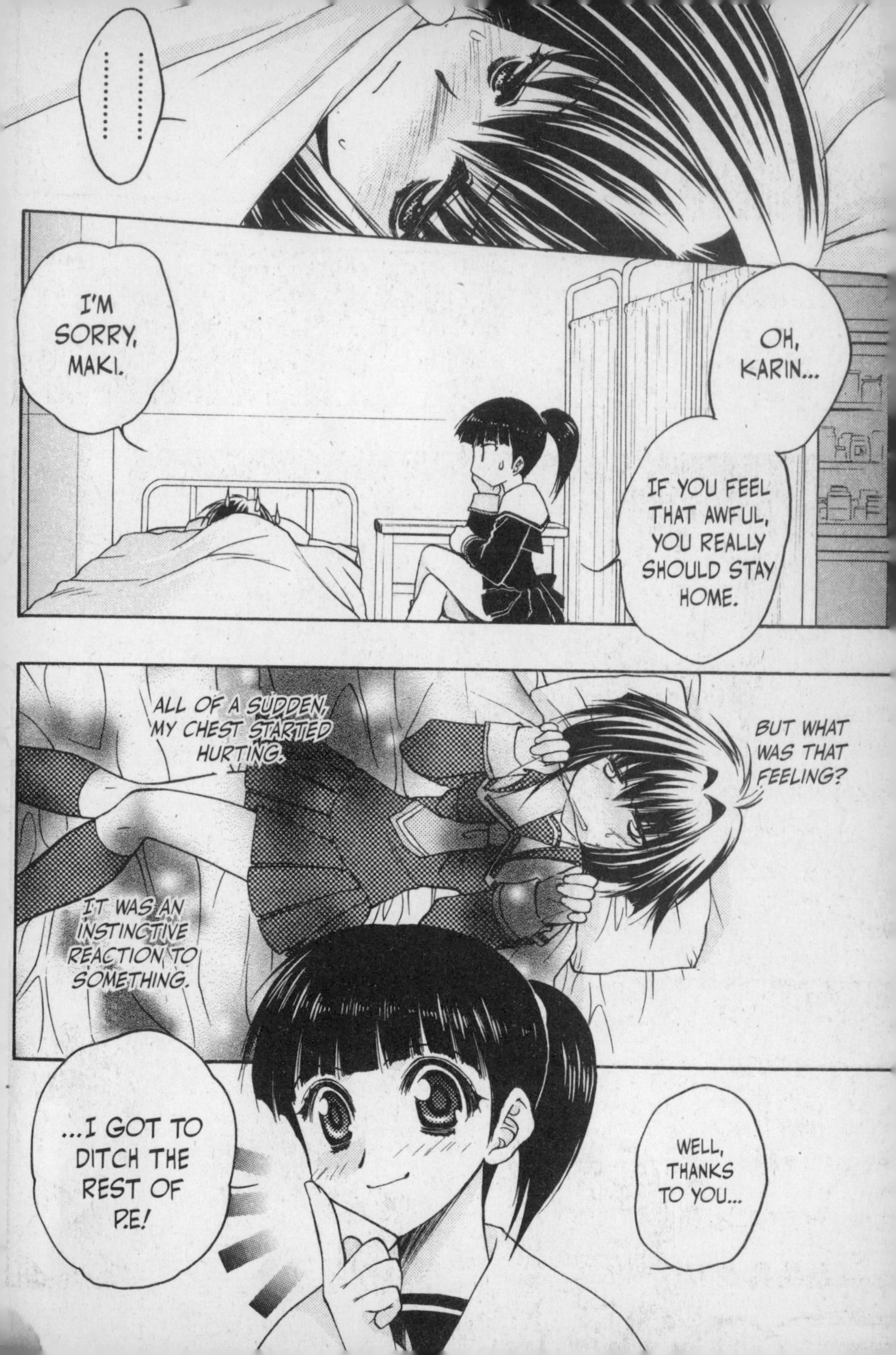
......
OH, KARIN...
IF YOU FEEL THAT AWFUL, YOU REALLY SHOULD STAY HOME.
I'M SORRY, MAKI.
BUT WHAT WAS THAT FEELING?
ALL OF A SUDDEN, MY CHEST STARTED HURTING.
IT WAS AN INSTINCTIVE REACTION TO SOMETHING.
WELL, THANKS TO YOU...
...I GOT TO DITCH THE REST OF P.E!

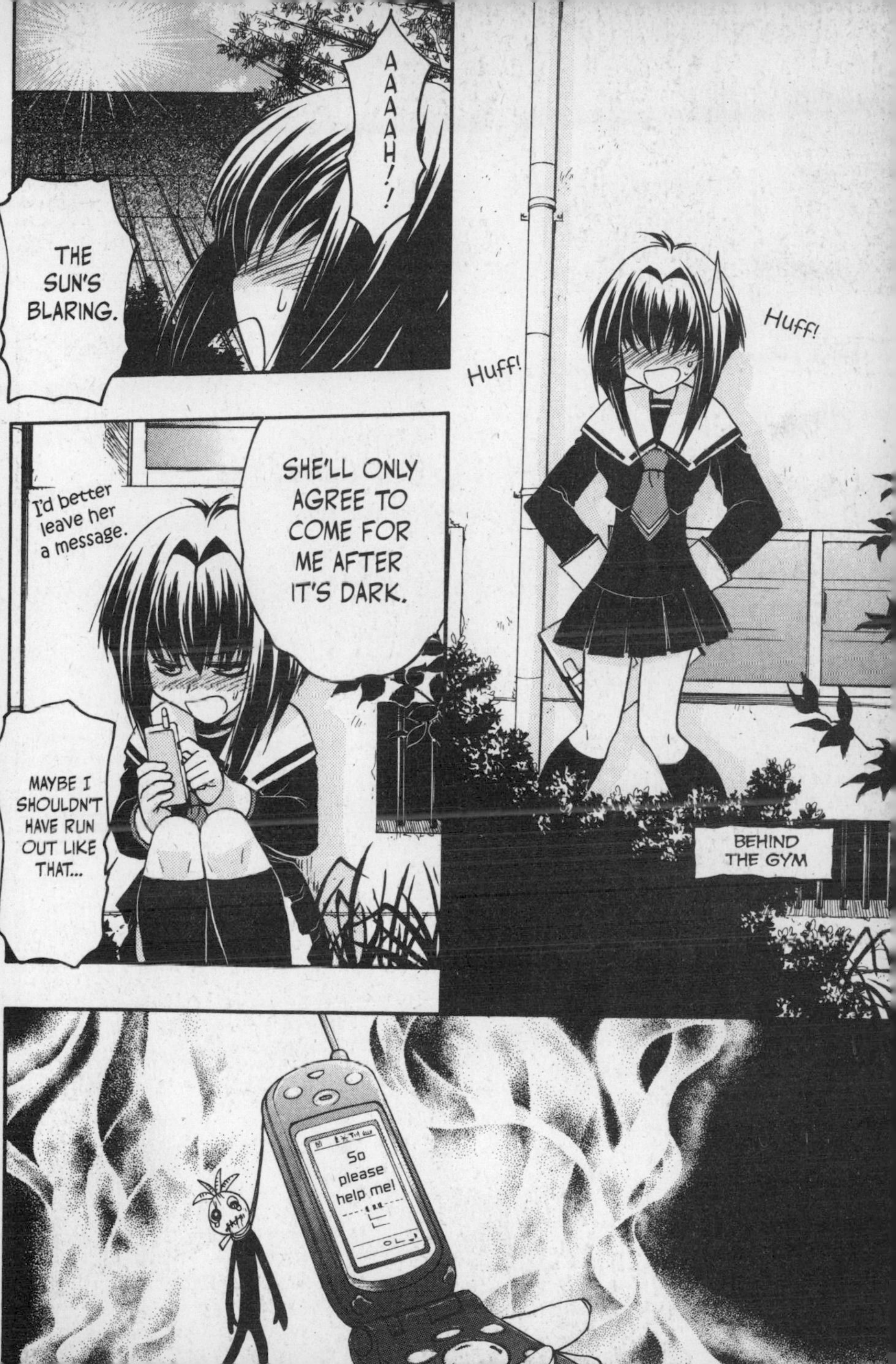
Huff!
Huff!
BEHIND THE GYM
AAAAH!!
THE SUN'S BLARING.
SHE'LL ONLY AGREE TO COME FOR ME AFTER IT'S DARK.
I'd better leave her a message.
MAYBE I SHOULDN'T HAVE RUN OUT LIKE THAT...
So please help me!

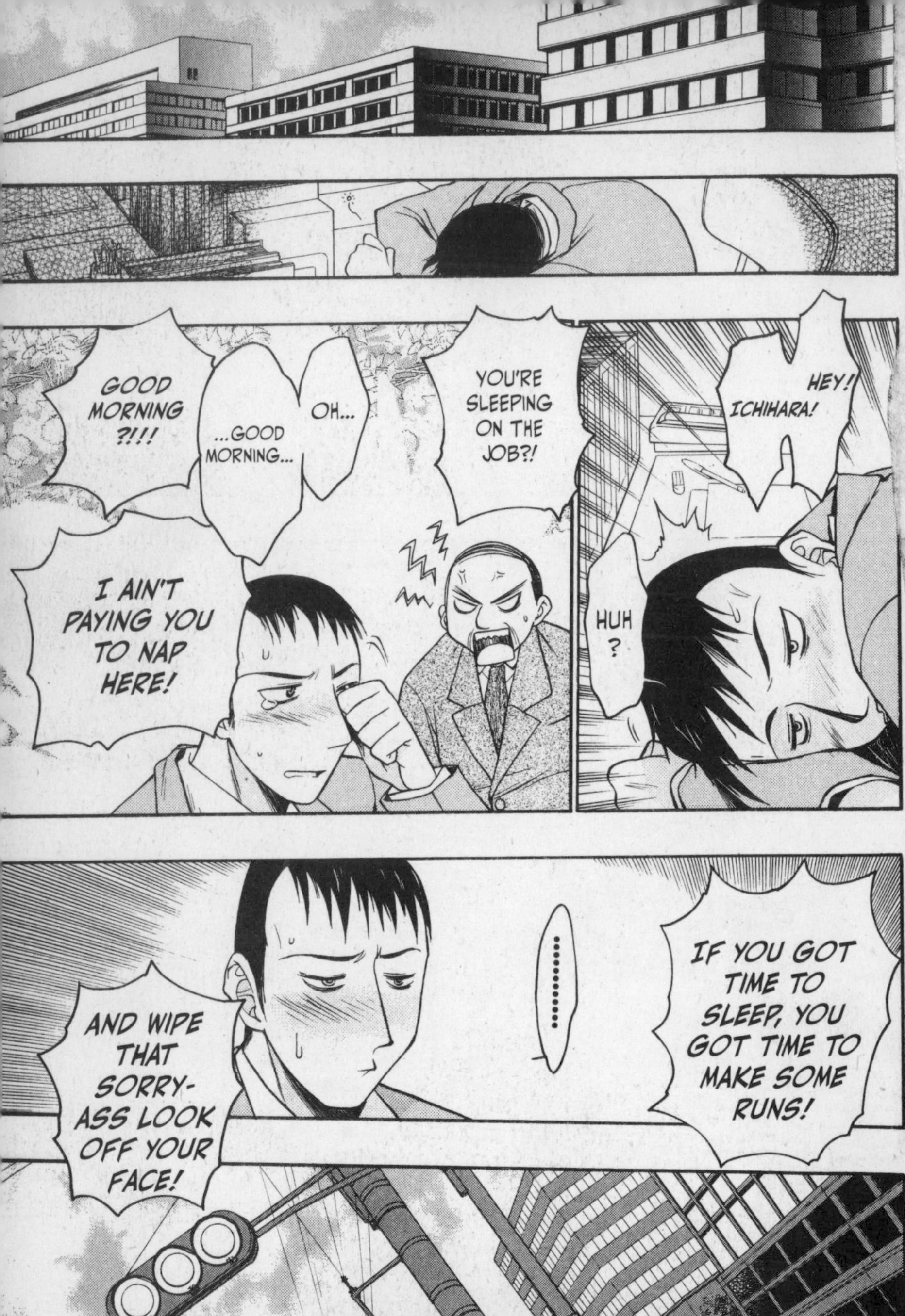
HEY! ICHIHARA!
HUH ?
YOU'RE SLEEPING ON THE JOB?!
OH...
...GOOD MORNING...
GOOD MORNING ?!!!
I AIN'T PAYING YOU TO NAP HERE!
IF YOU GOT TIME TO SLEEP, YOU GOT TIME TO MAKE SOME RUNS!
......
AND WIPE THAT SORRY-ASS LOOK OFF YOUR FACE!

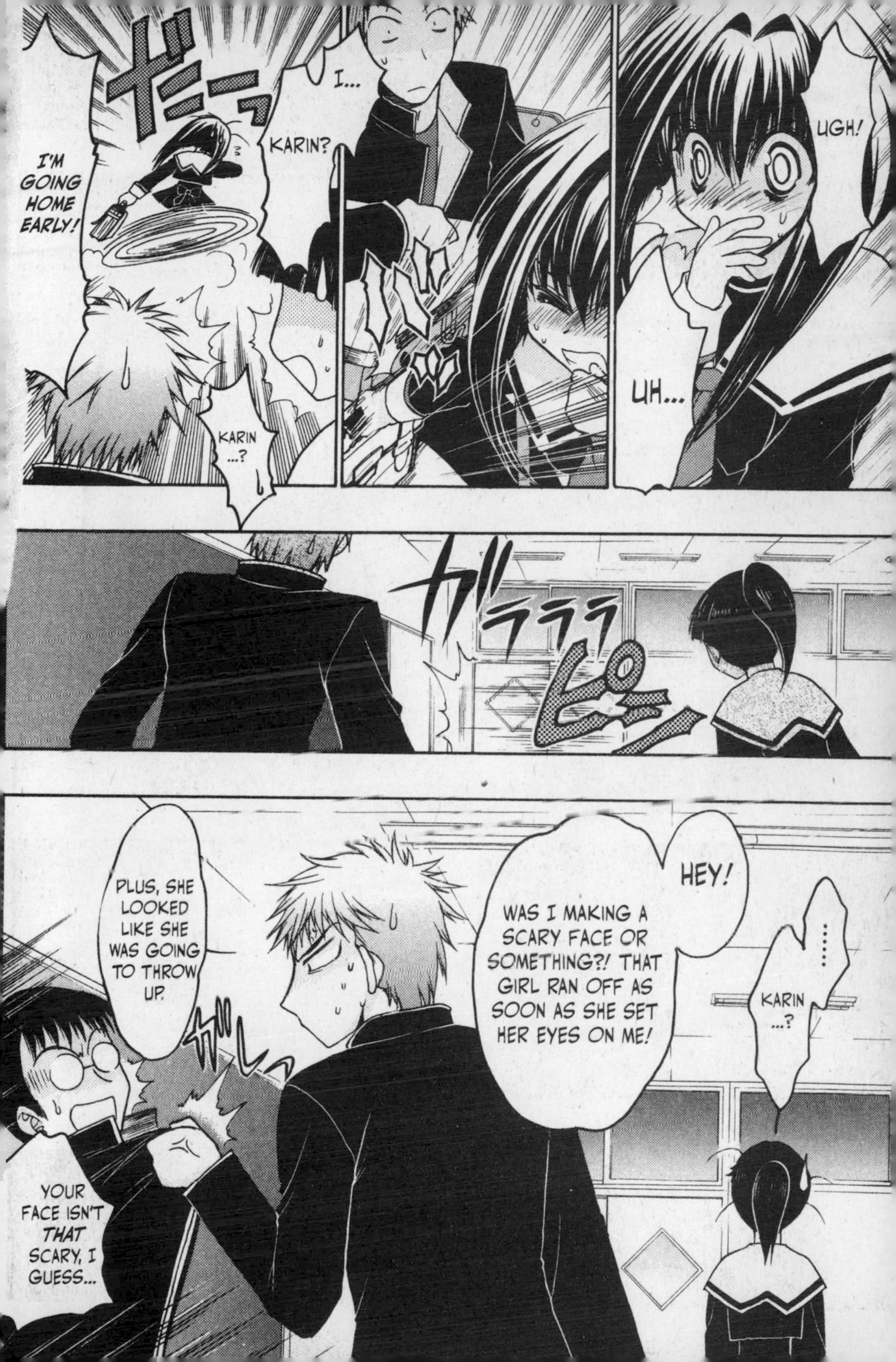
UGH!
UH...
I...
KARIN?
I'M GOING HOME EARLY!
KARIN ...?
HEY!
......
KARIN ...?
WAS I MAKING A SCARY FACE OR SOMETHING?! THAT GIRL RAN OFF AS SOON AS SHE SET HER EYES ON ME!
PLUS, SHE LOOKED LIKE SHE WAS GOING TO THROW UP.
YOUR FACE ISN'T *THAT* SCARY, I GUESS...

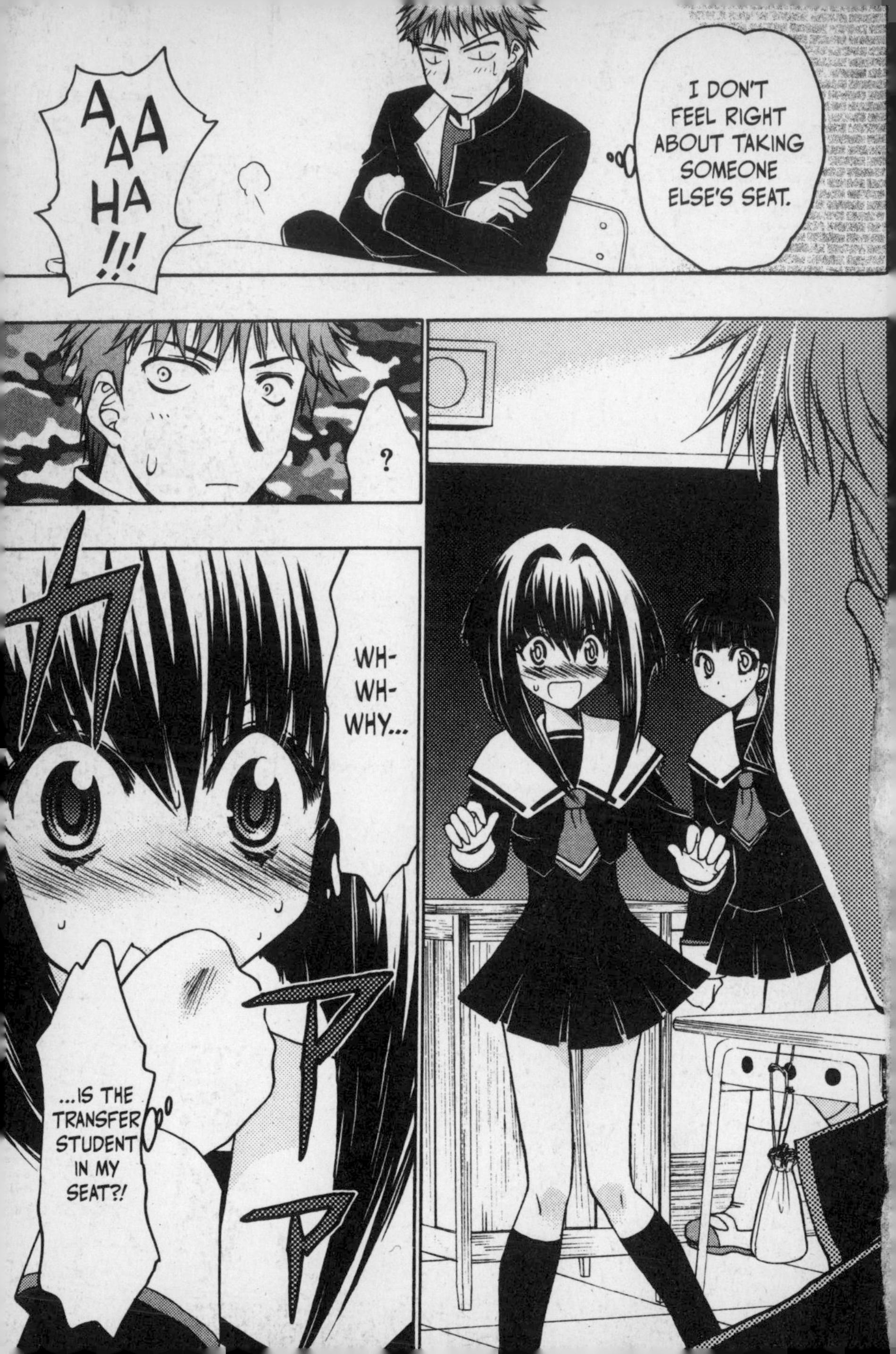

I DON'T FEEL RIGHT ABOUT TAKING SOMEONE ELSE'S SEAT.
AAAHA!!!
?
WH-WH-WHY...
...IS THE TRANSFER STUDENT IN MY SEAT?!

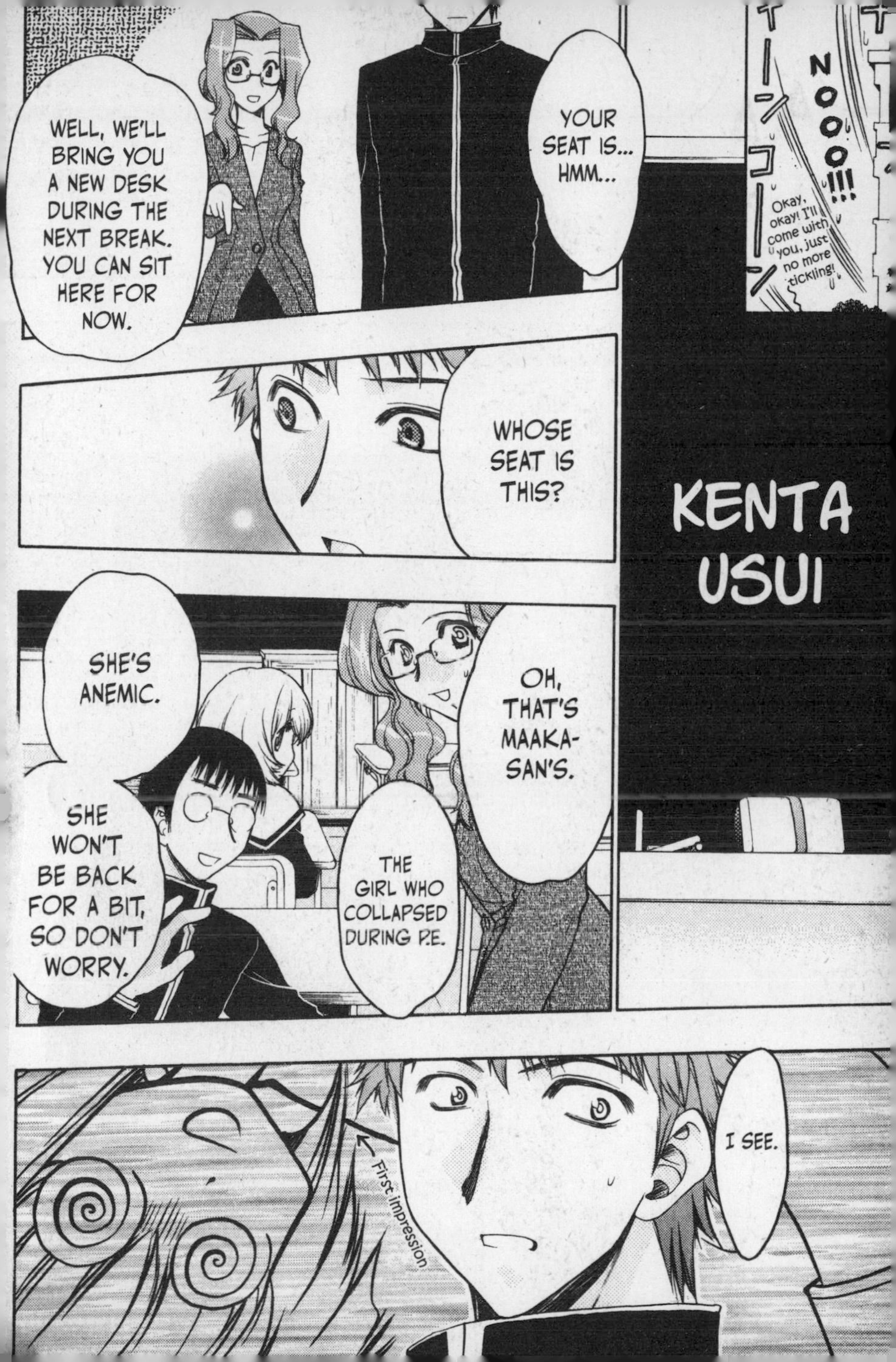
NOOO!!!
Okay, okay! I'll come with you, just no more tickling!
KENTA USUI
YOUR SEAT IS... HMM...
WELL, WE'LL BRING YOU A NEW DESK DURING THE NEXT BREAK. YOU CAN SIT HERE FOR NOW.
WHOSE SEAT IS THIS?
OH, THAT'S MAAKA-SAN'S.
THE GIRL WHO COLLAPSED DURING P.E.
SHE'S ANEMIC.
SHE WON'T BE BACK FOR A BIT, SO DON'T WORRY.
I SEE.
First impression

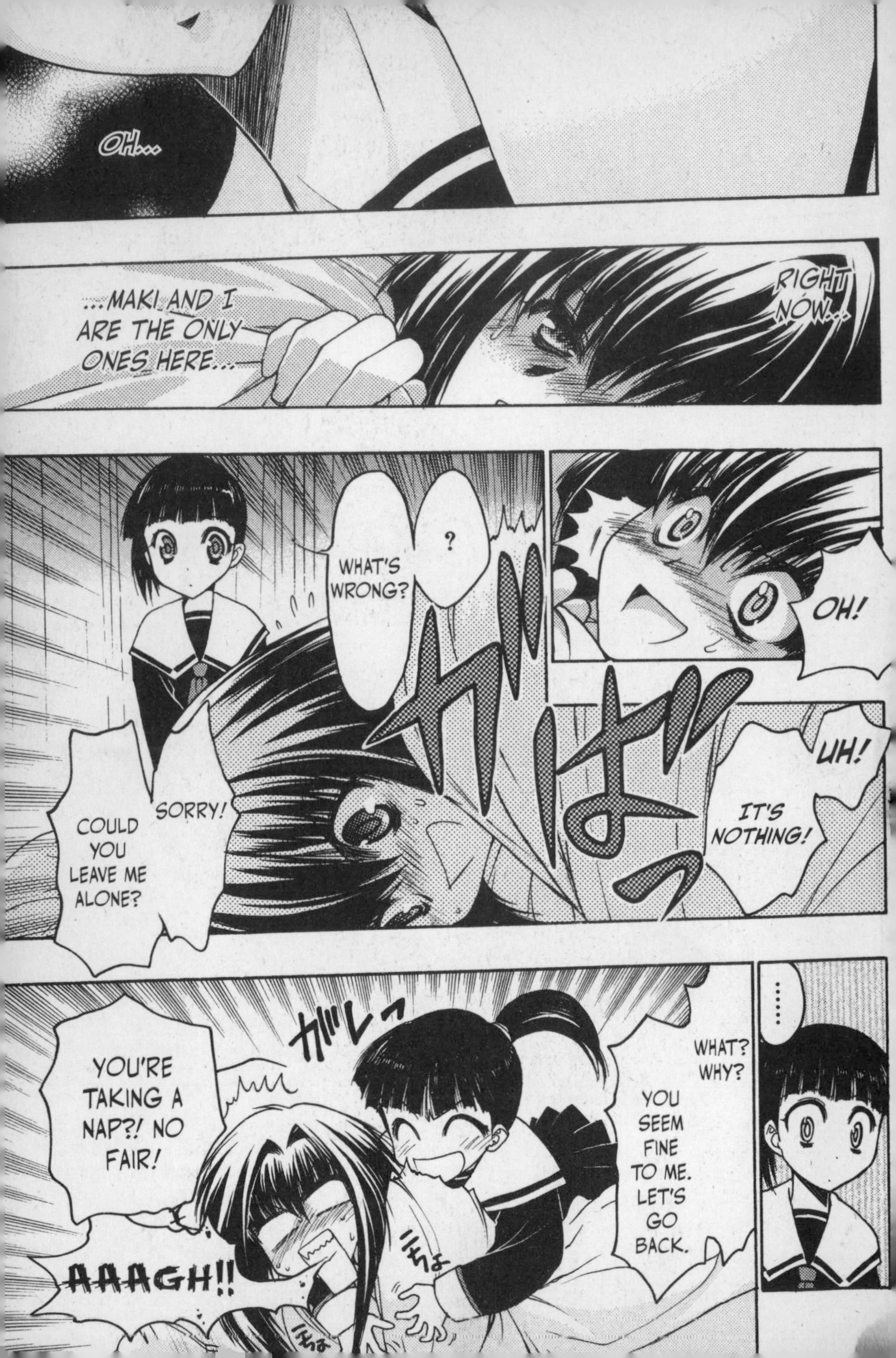
OH...
RIGHT NOW...
...MAKI AND I ARE THE ONLY ONES HERE...
OH!
?
WHAT'S WRONG?
UH!
IT'S NOTHING!
SORRY!
COULD YOU LEAVE ME ALONE?
......
WHAT? WHY?
YOU SEEM FINE TO ME. LET'S GO BACK.
YOU'RE TAKING A NAP?! NO FAIR!
AAAGH!!

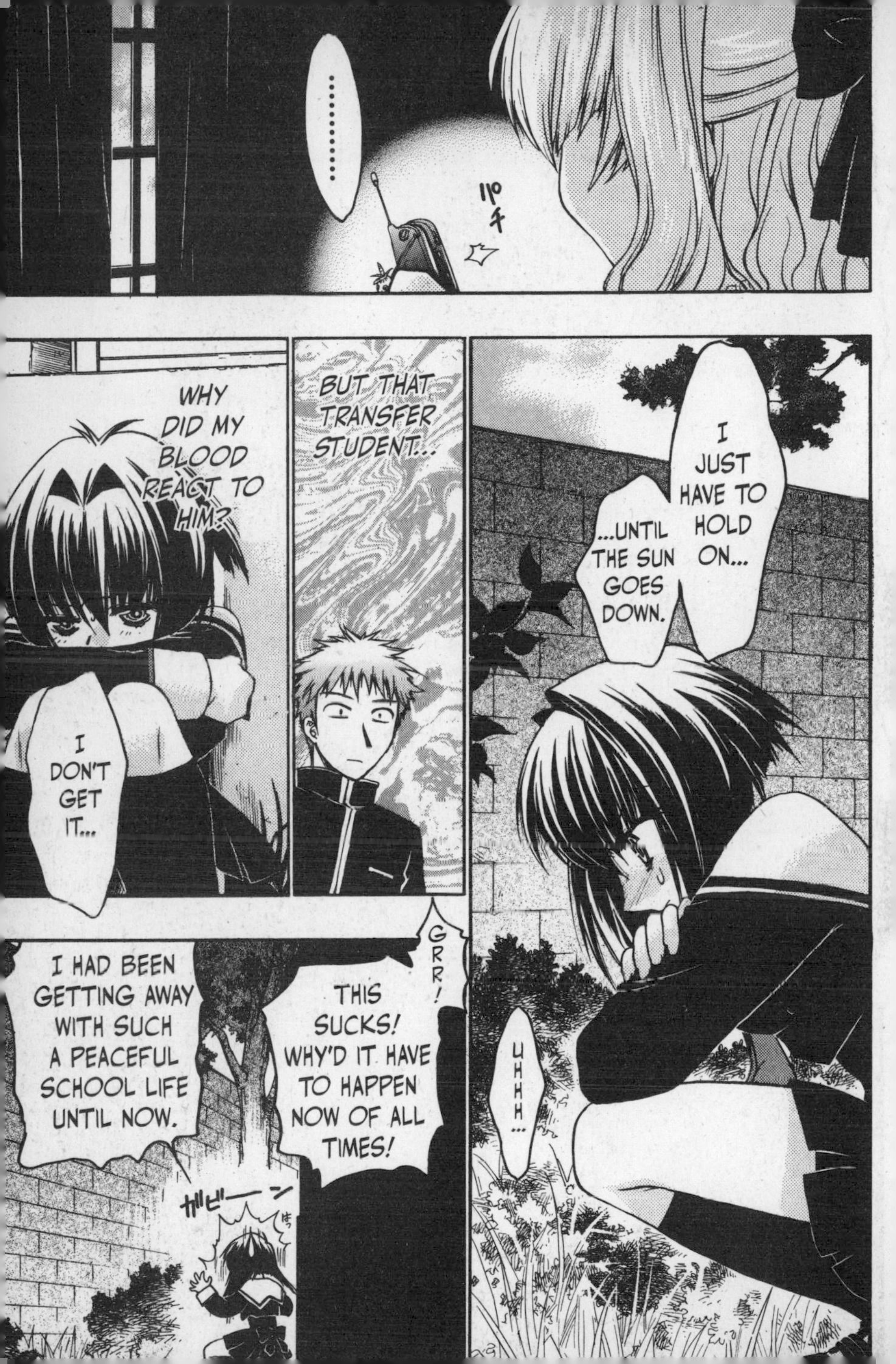

......
パチ
I JUST HAVE TO HOLD ON...
...UNTIL THE SUN GOES DOWN.
UHHH...
BUT THAT TRANSFER STUDENT...
WHY DID MY BLOOD REACT TO HIM?
I DON'T GET IT...
GRR!
THIS SUCKS! WHY'D IT HAVE TO HAPPEN NOW OF ALL TIMES!
I HAD BEEN GETTING AWAY WITH SUCH A PEACEFUL SCHOOL LIFE UNTIL NOW.
ガビーン

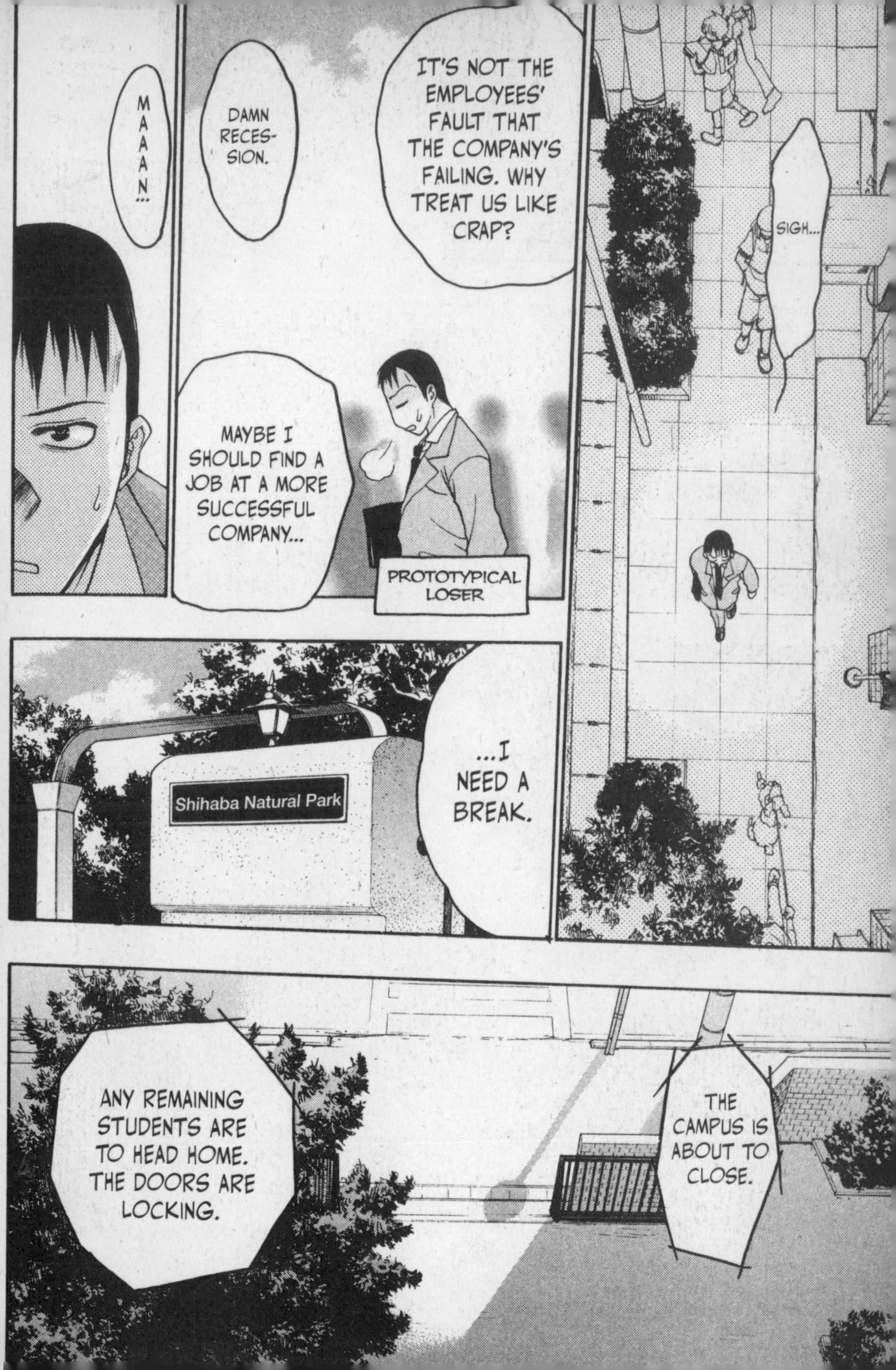
SIGH...
IT'S NOT THE EMPLOYEES' FAULT THAT THE COMPANY'S FAILING. WHY TREAT US LIKE CRAP?
DAMN RECES-SION.
MAYBE I SHOULD FIND A JOB AT A MORE SUCCESSFUL COMPANY...
PROTOTYPICAL LOSER
MAAAAN...
...I NEED A BREAK.
Shihaba Natural Park
THE CAMPUS IS ABOUT TO CLOSE.
ANY REMAINING STUDENTS ARE TO HEAD HOME. THE DOORS ARE LOCKING.

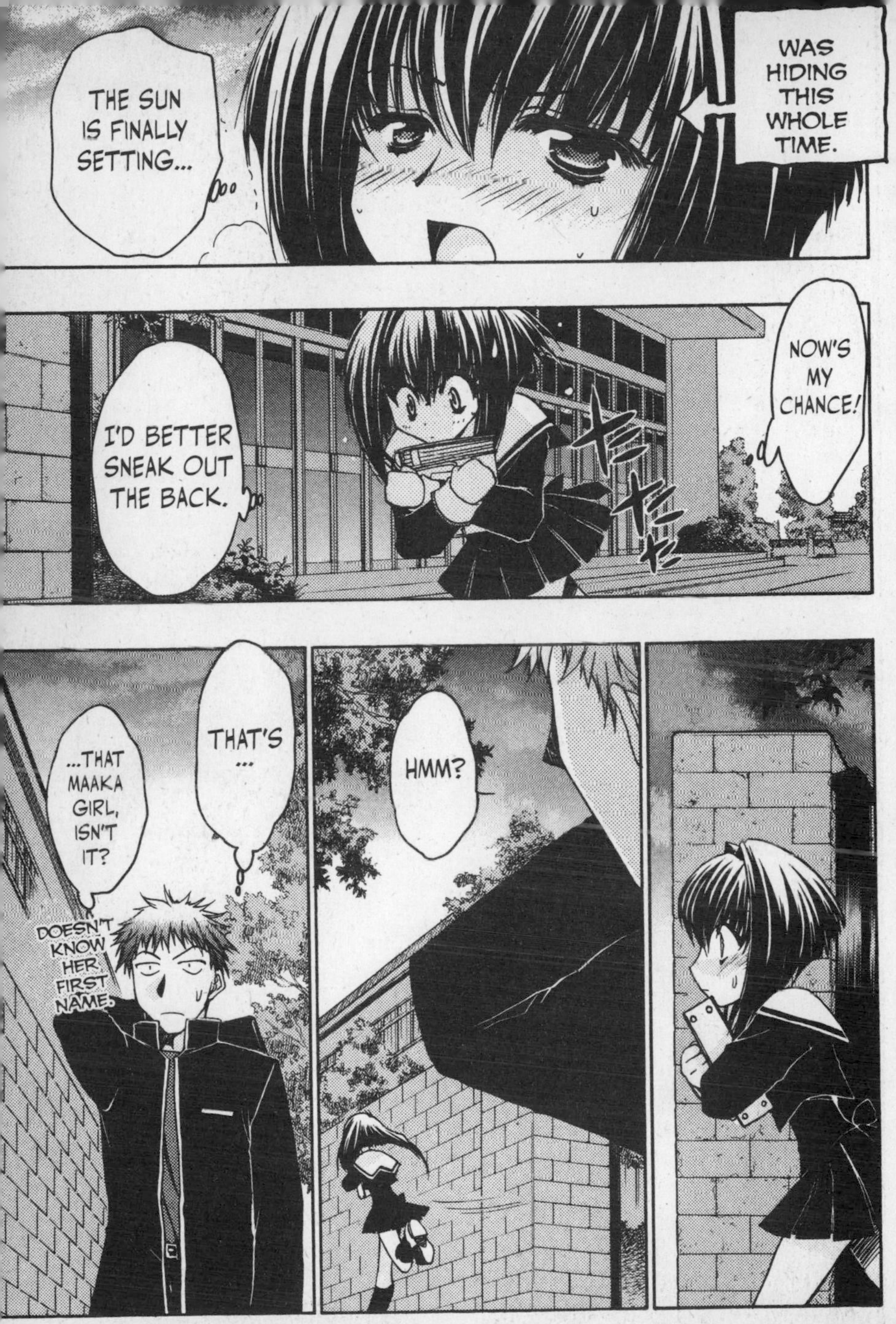
WAS HIDING THIS WHOLE TIME.
THE SUN IS FINALLY SETTING...
NOW'S MY CHANCE!
I'D BETTER SNEAK OUT THE BACK.
HMM?
THAT'S ...
...THAT MAAKA GIRL, ISN'T IT?
DOESN'T KNOW HER FIRST NAME.

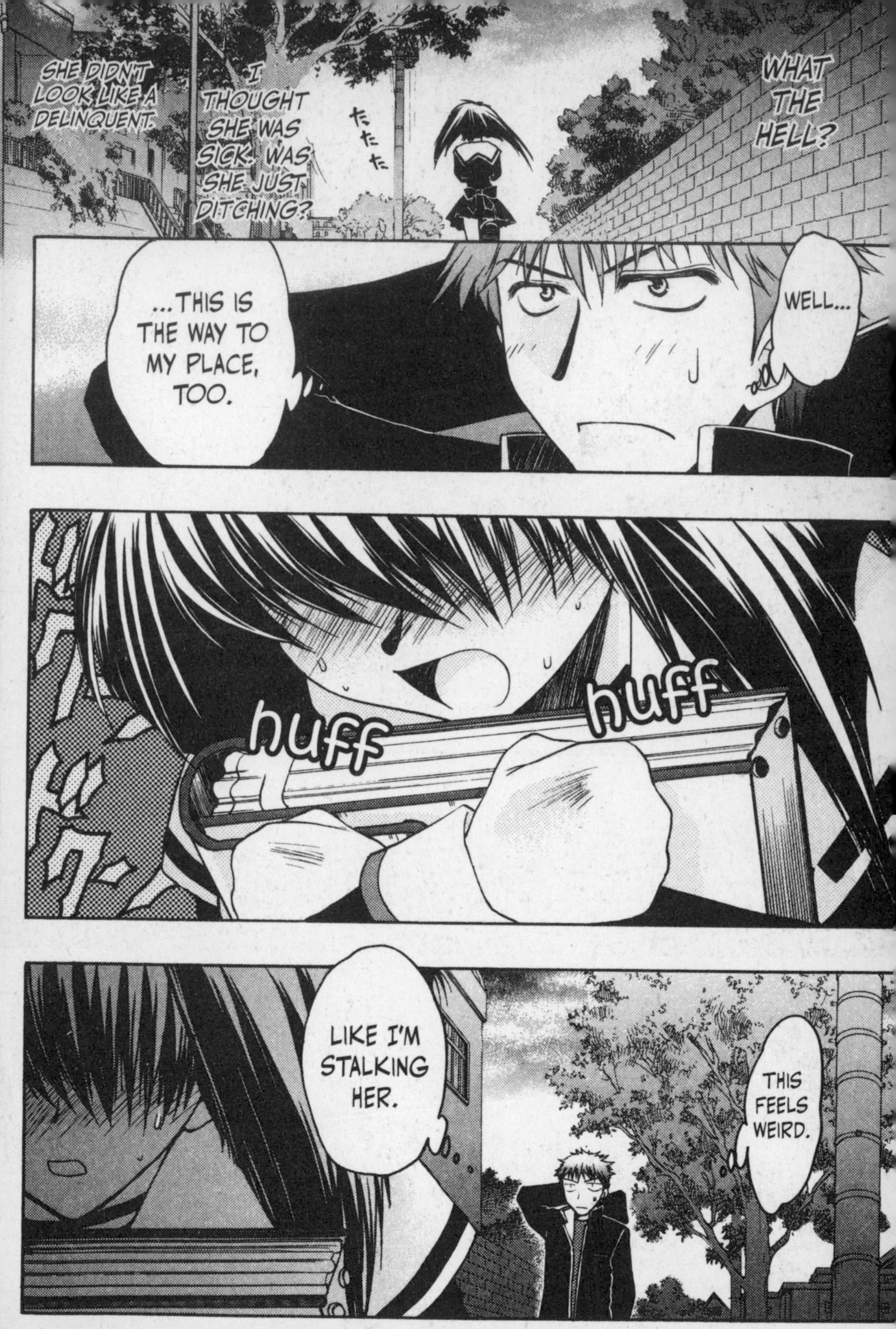
WHAT THE HELL?
たたた
I THOUGHT SHE WAS SICK. WAS SHE JUST DITCHING?
SHE DIDN'T LOOK LIKE A DELINQUENT.
WELL...
...THIS IS THE WAY TO MY PLACE, TOO.
huff
huff
THIS FEELS WEIRD.
LIKE I'M STALKING HER.

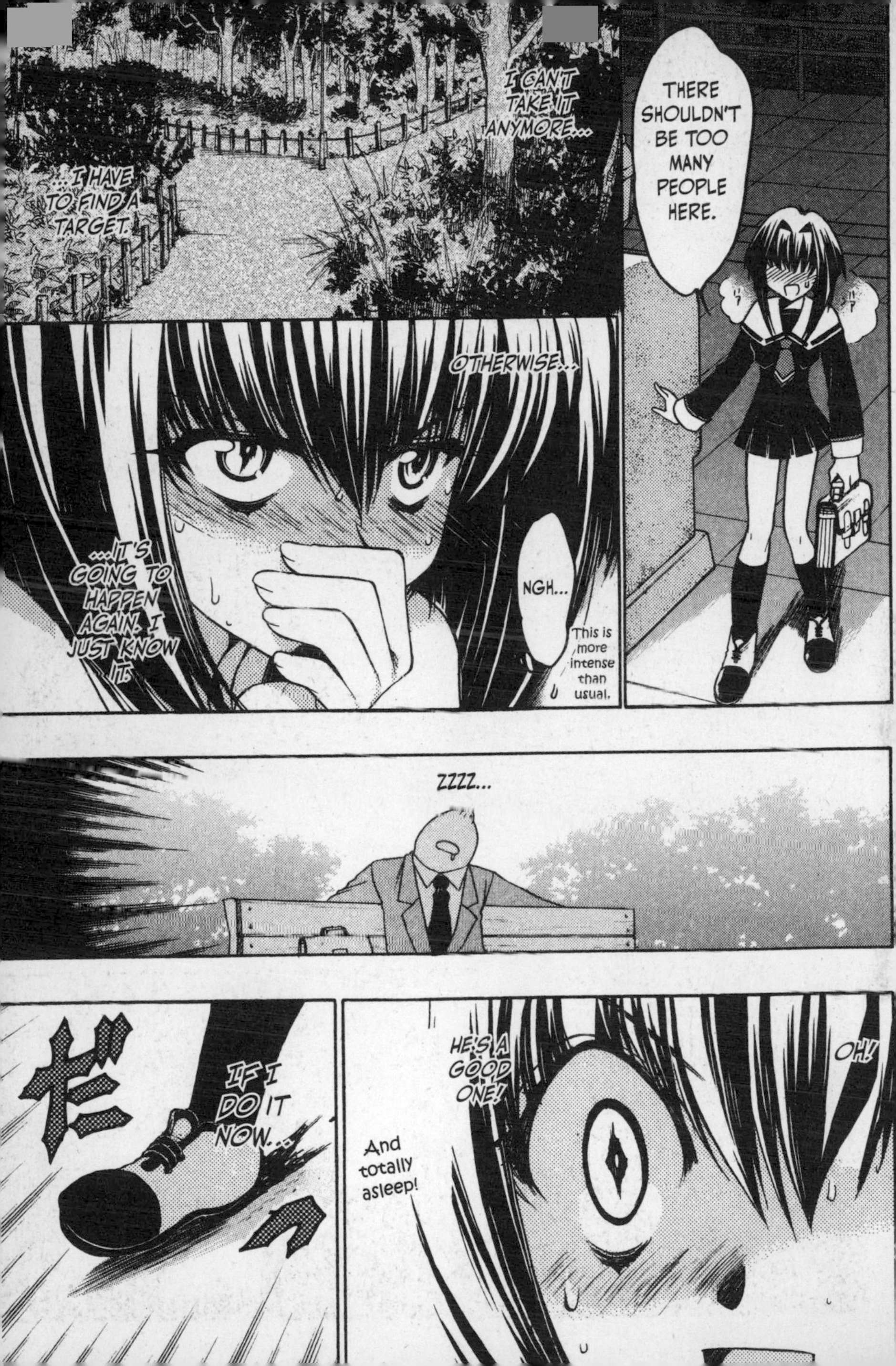
THERE SHOULDN'T BE TOO MANY PEOPLE HERE.
I CAN'T TAKE IT ANYMORE...
...I HAVE TO FIND A TARGET.
OTHERWISE...
NGH...
This is more intense than usual.
...IT'S GOING TO HAPPEN AGAIN. I JUST KNOW IT.
ZZZZ...
OH!
HE'S A GOOD ONE!
And totally asleep!
ダ
IF I DO IT NOW...

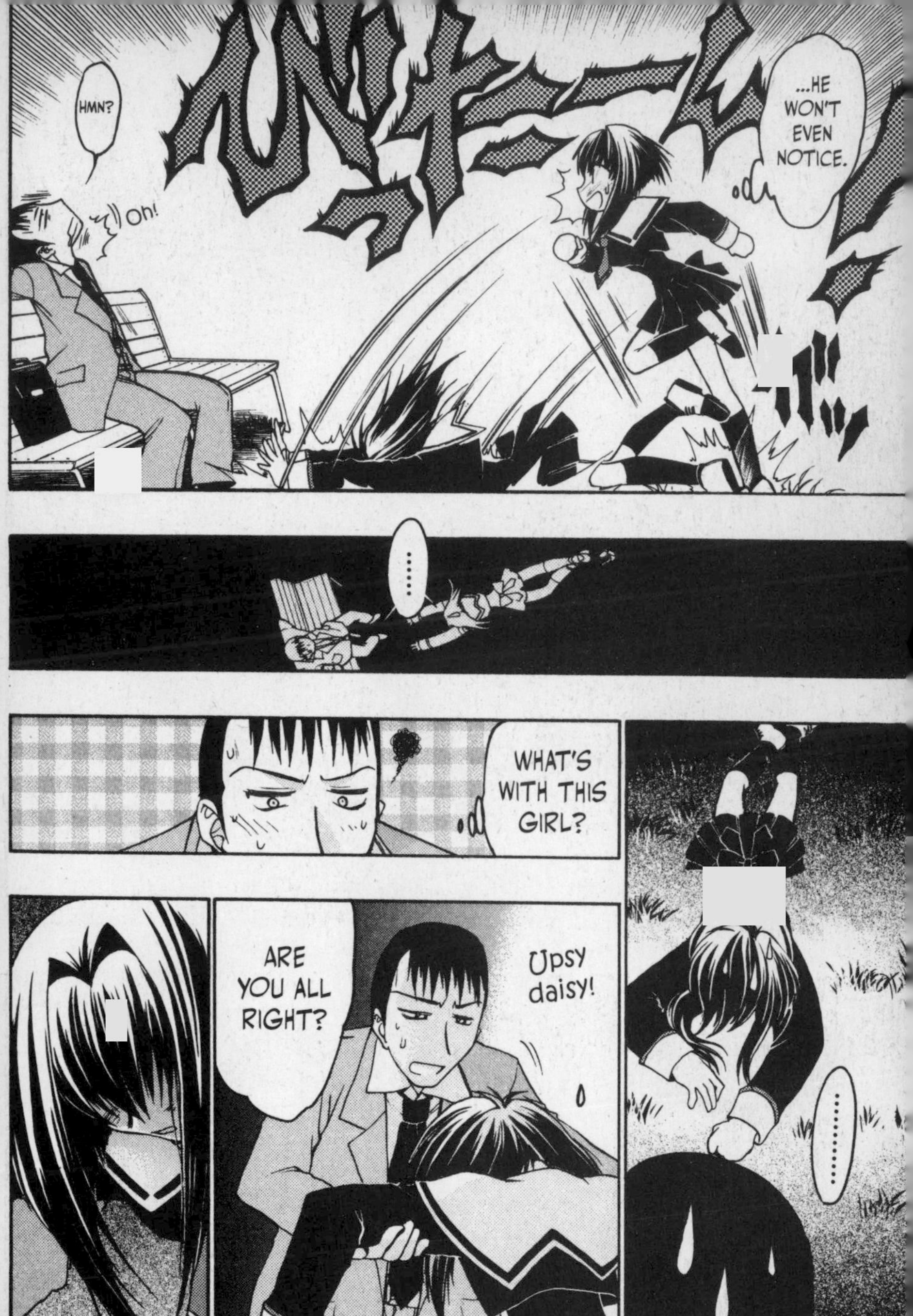
...HE WON'T EVEN NOTICE.
HMN?
Oh!
......
......
WHAT'S WITH THIS GIRL?
Upsy daisy!
ARE YOU ALL RIGHT?

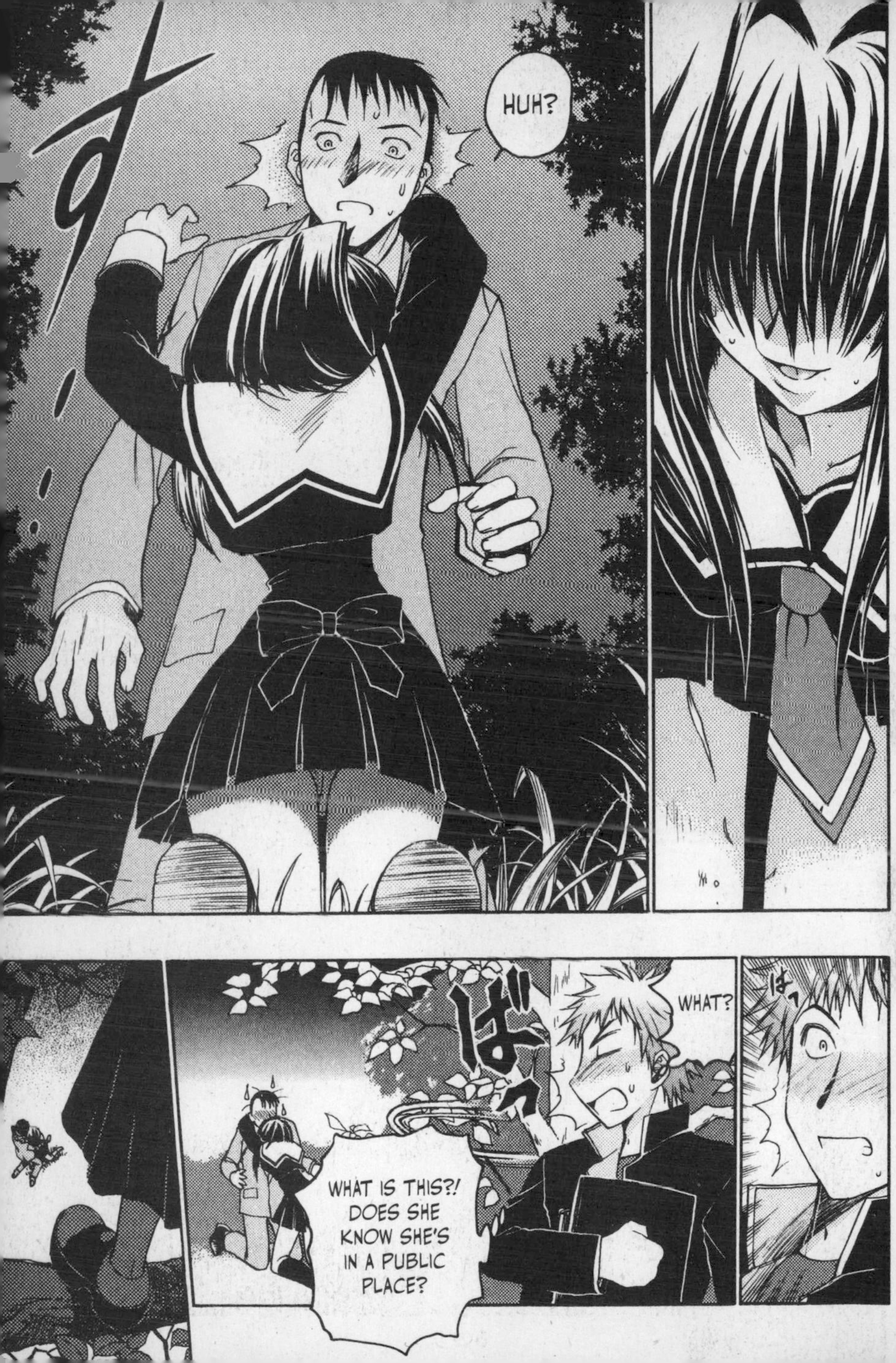
す
HUH?
はっ
ばっ
WHAT?
WHAT IS THIS?! DOES SHE KNOW SHE'S IN A PUBLIC PLACE?

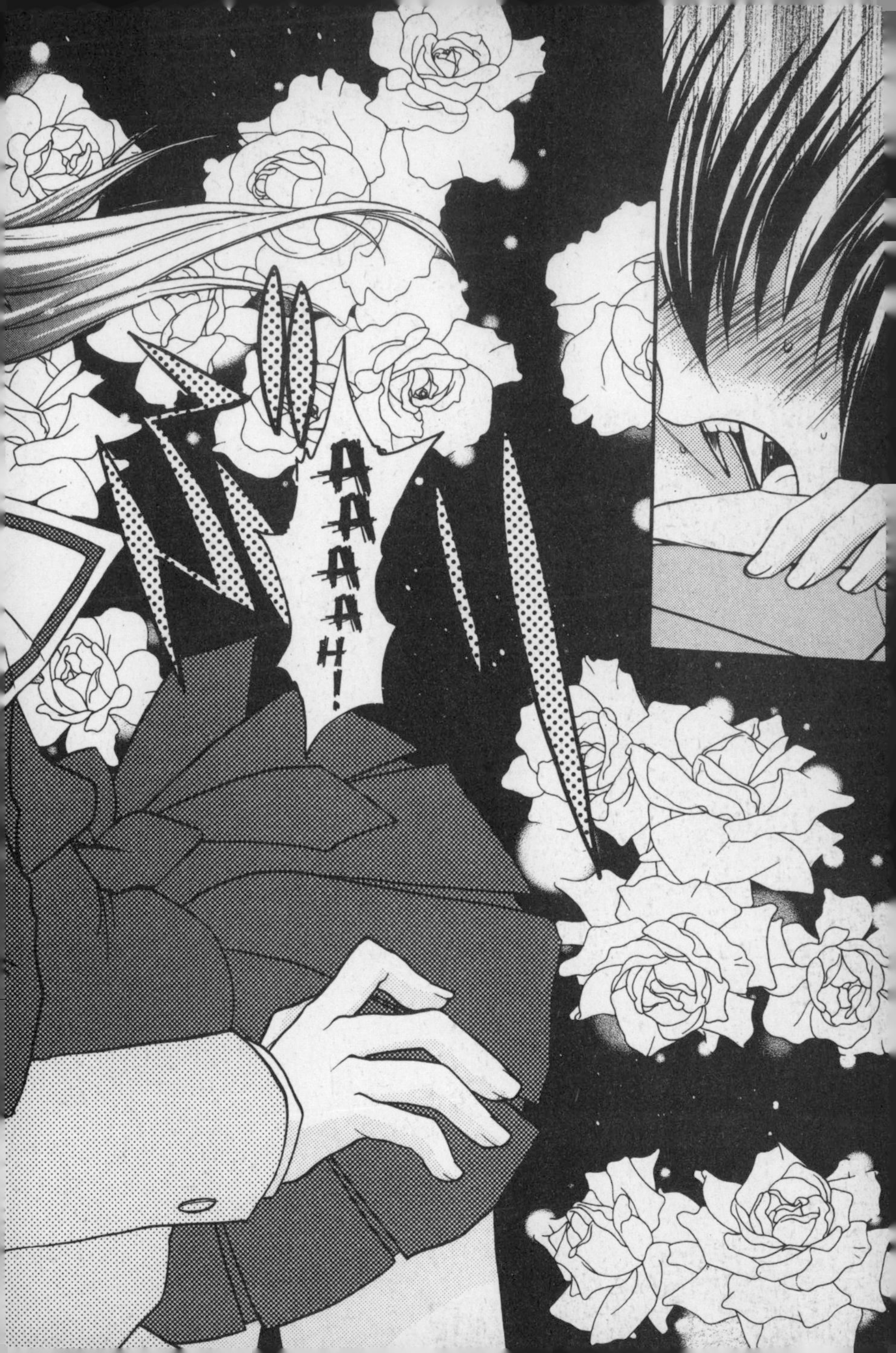
AAAAAH!

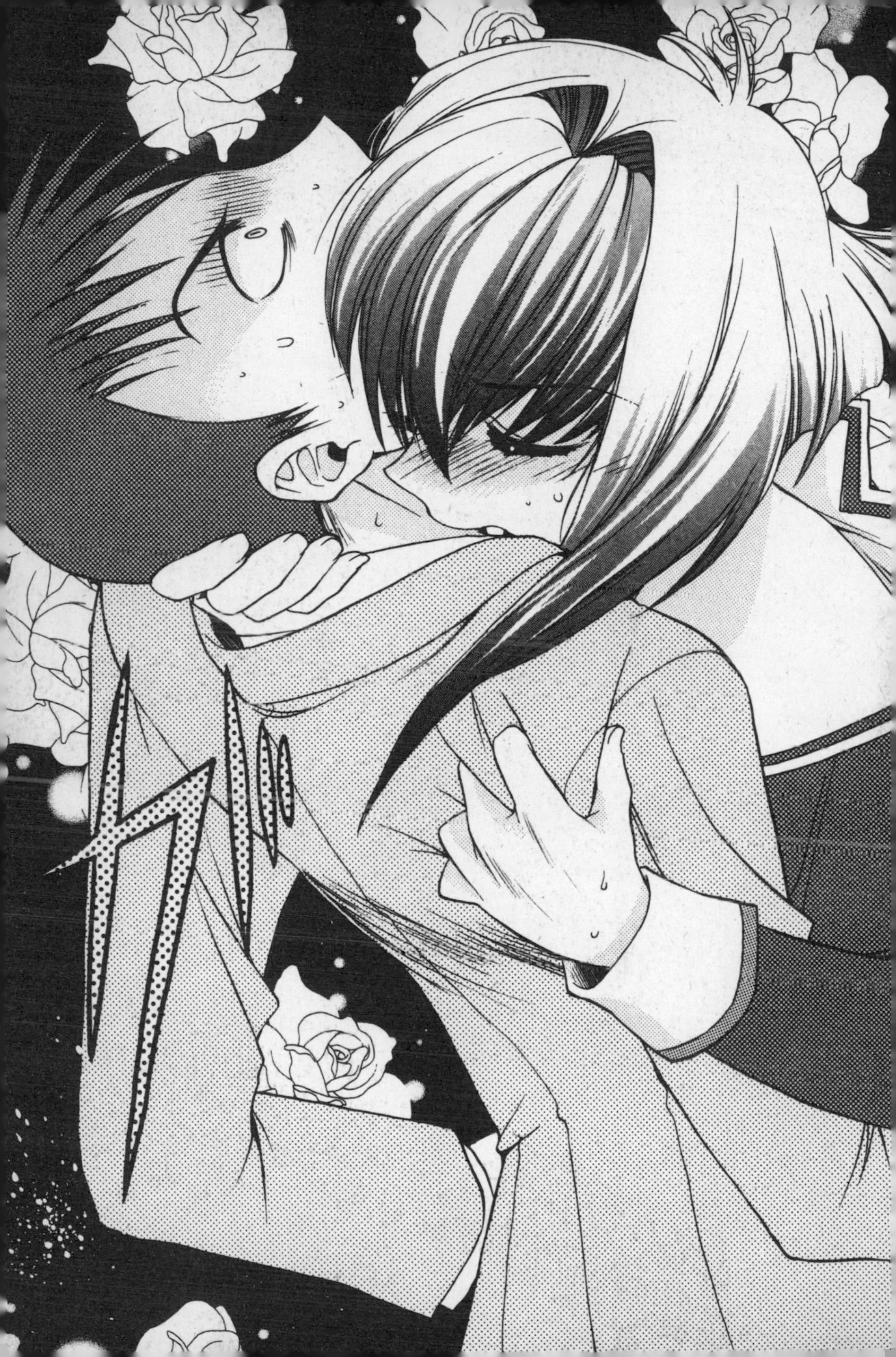

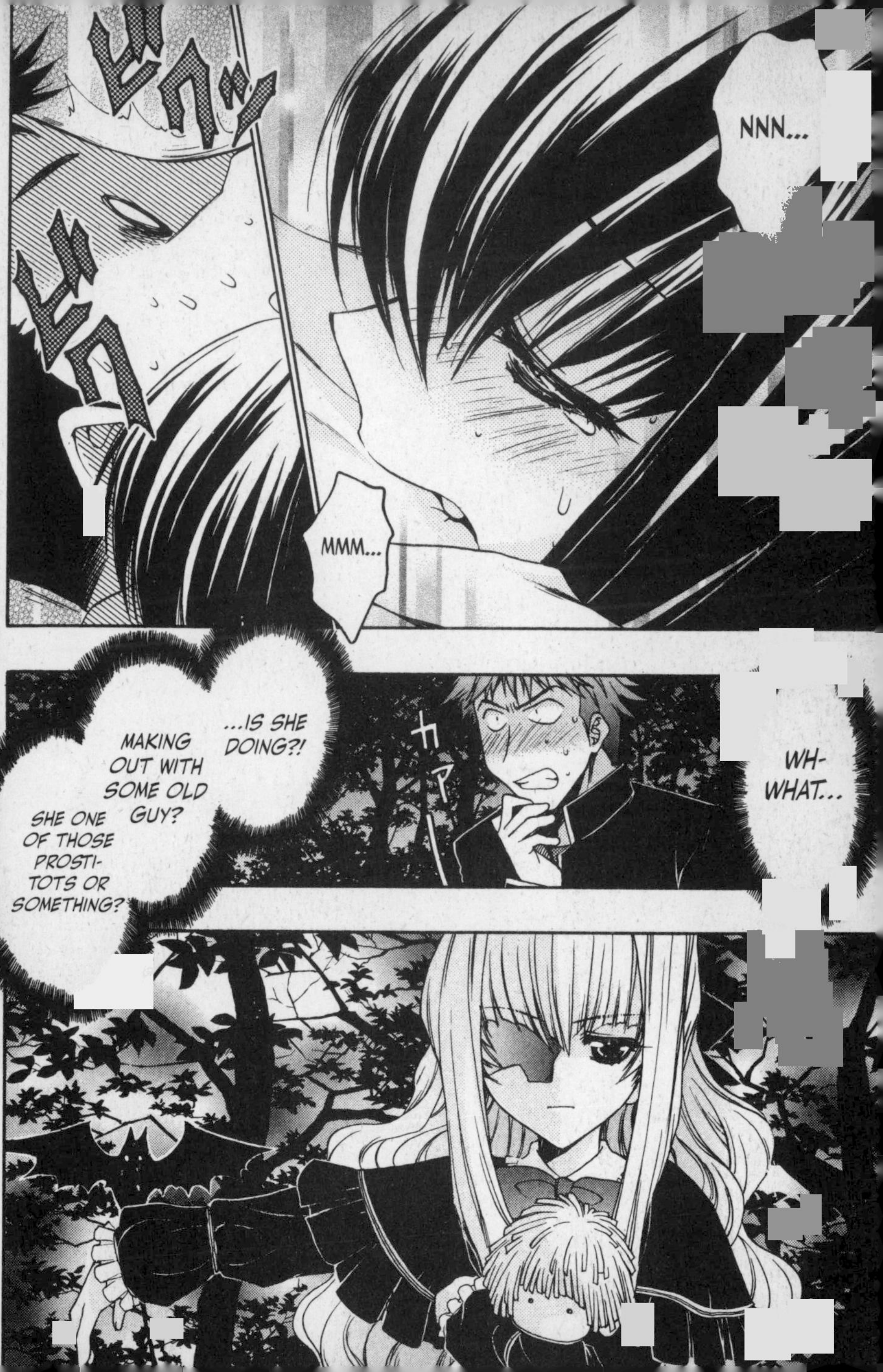
NNN...
MMM...
WH-WHAT...
...IS SHE DOING?!
MAKING OUT WITH SOME OLD GUY?
SHE ONE OF THOSE PROSTI-TOTS OR SOMETHING?

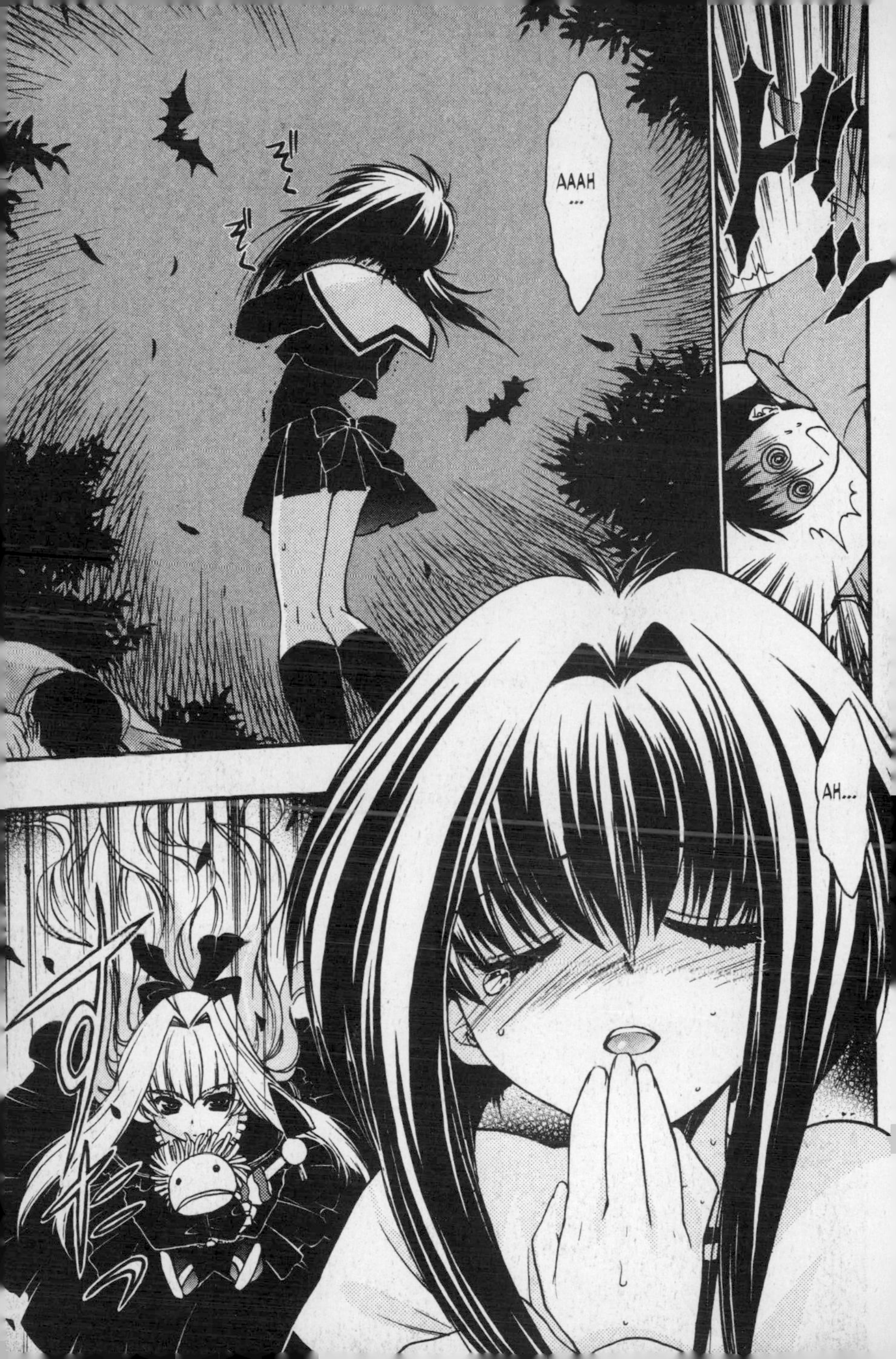
AAAH ...
ぞく
ぞく
AH...

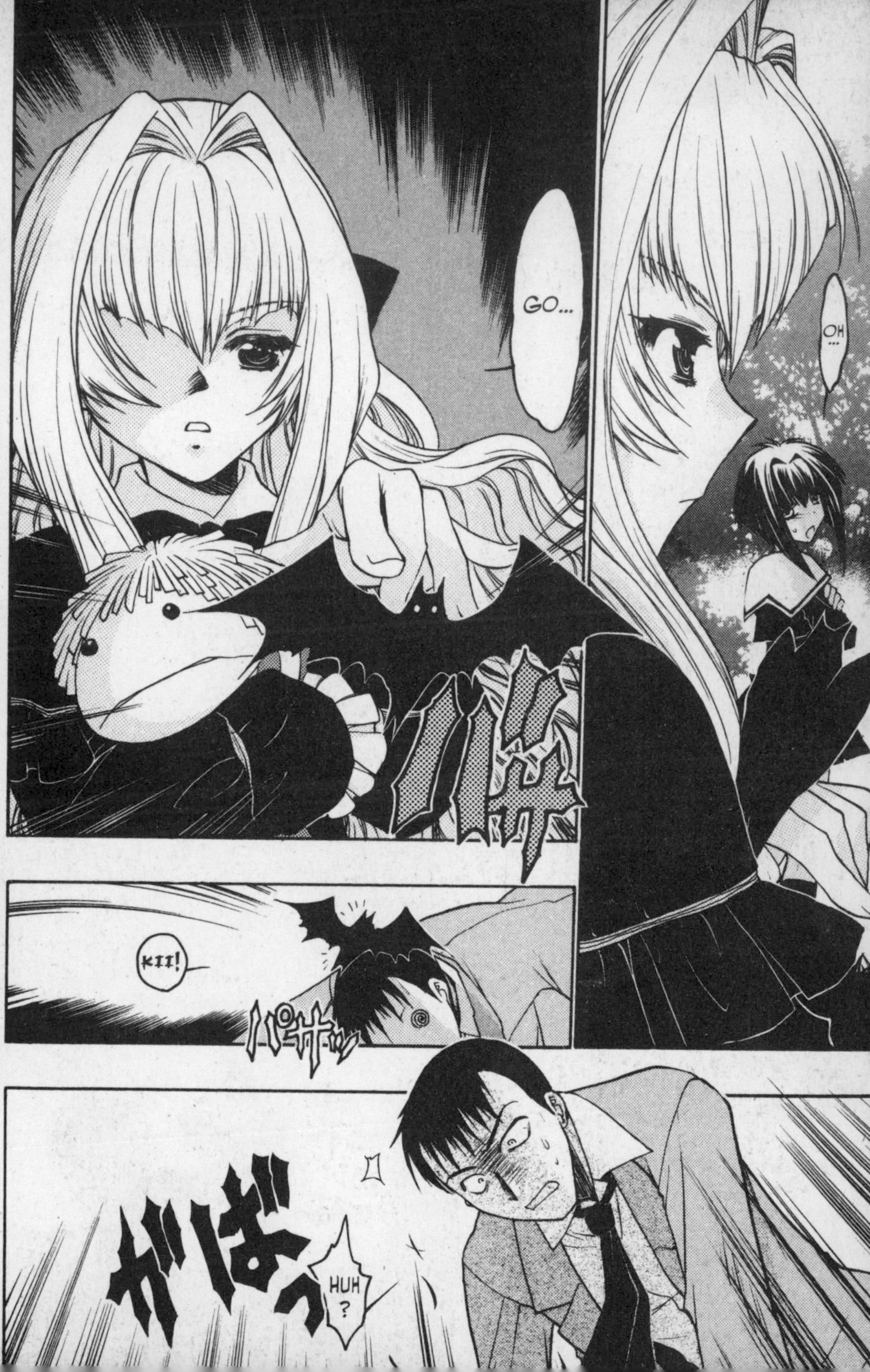

OH...
GO...
KII!
パサッ
がばっ
HUH?

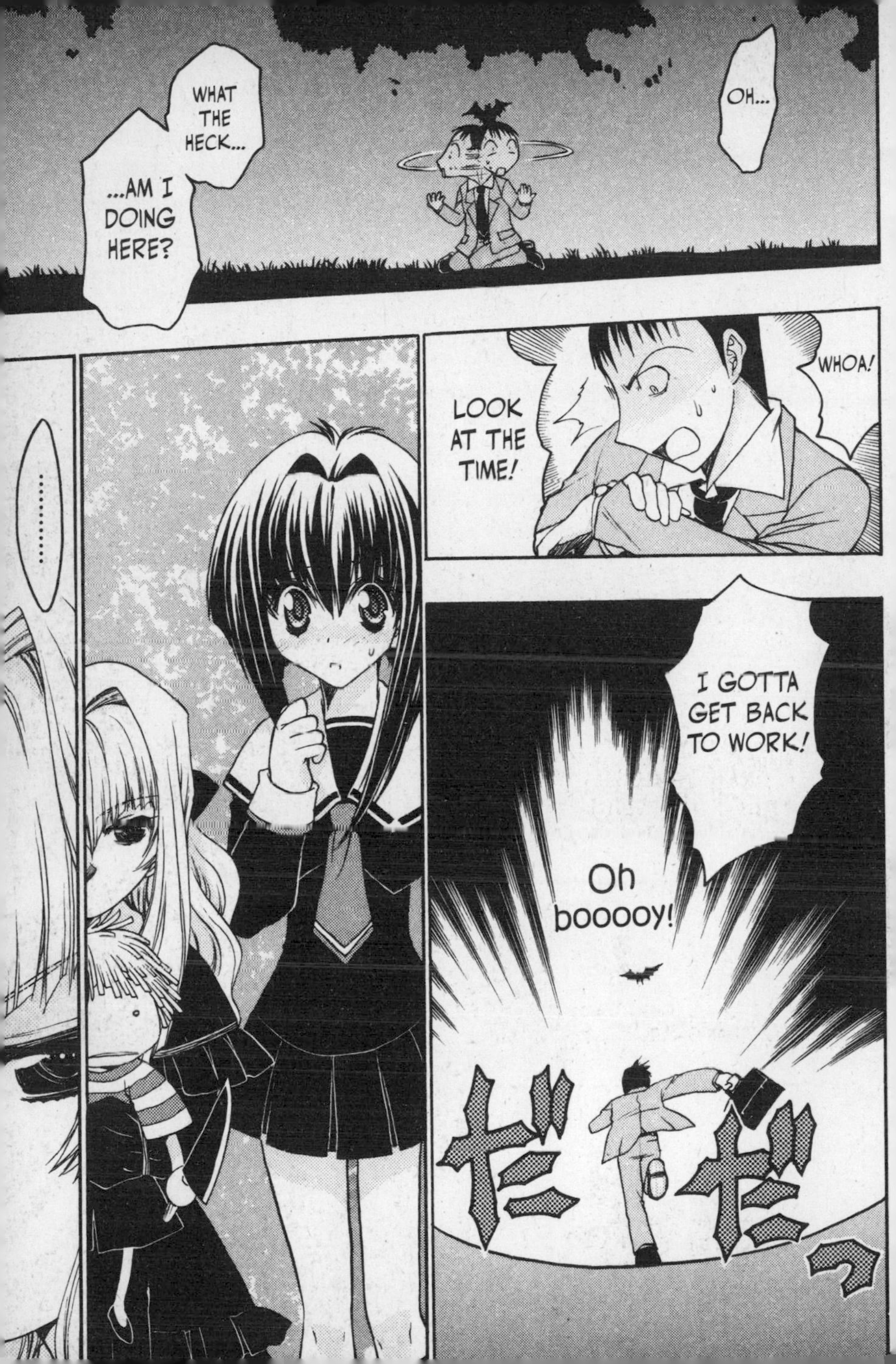
OH...
WHAT THE HECK...
...AM I DOING HERE?
WHOA!
LOOK AT THE TIME!
I GOTTA GET BACK TO WORK!
Oh booooy!
だだっ
......

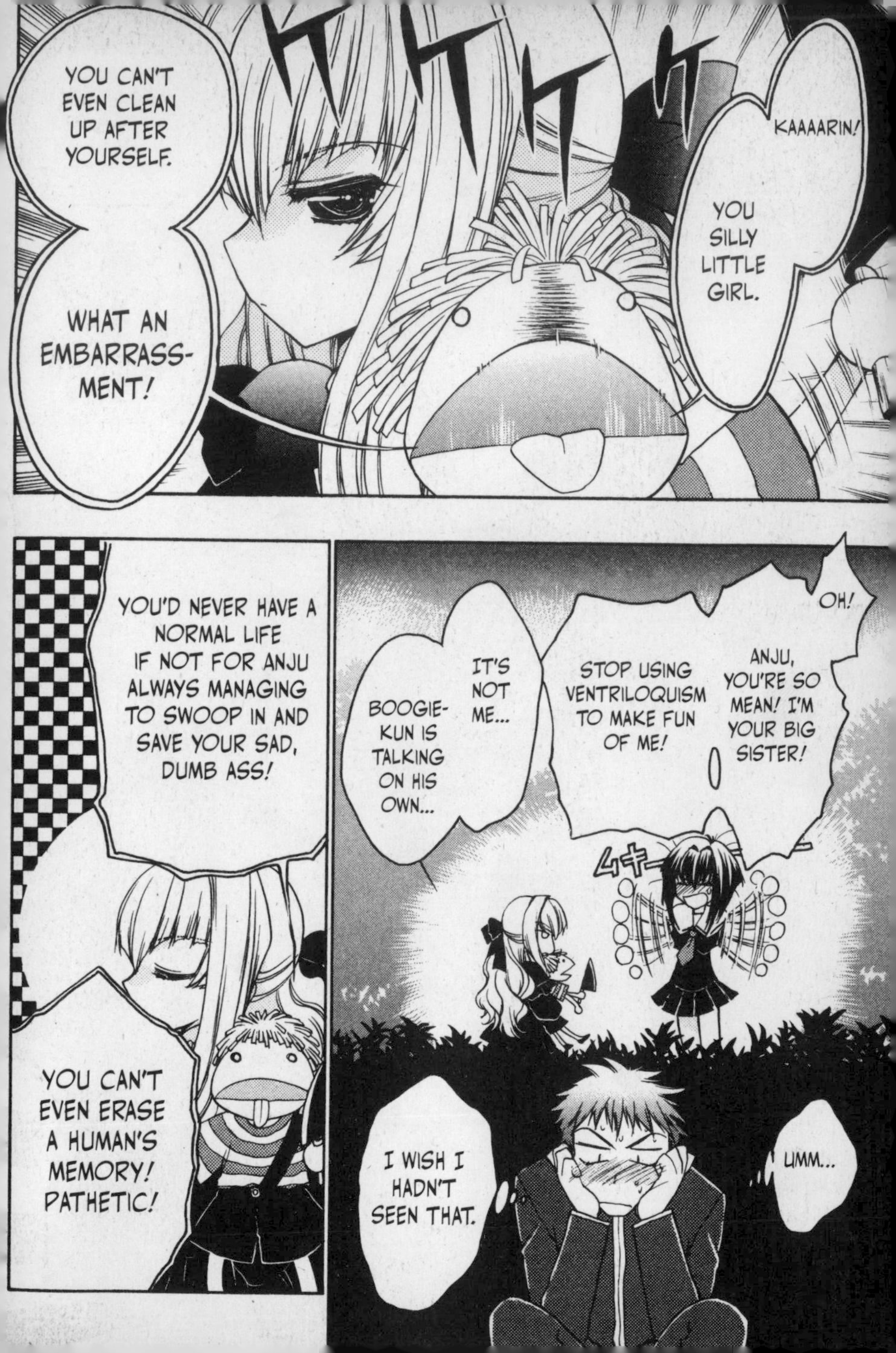
KAAAARIN!
YOU SILLY LITTLE GIRL.
YOU CAN'T EVEN CLEAN UP AFTER YOURSELF.
WHAT AN EMBARRASS- MENT!
OH!
ANJU, YOU'RE SO MEAN! I'M YOUR BIG SISTER!
STOP USING VENTRILOQUISM TO MAKE FUN OF ME!
IT'S NOT ME...
BOOGIE- KUN IS TALKING ON HIS OWN...
ムキー
UMM...
I WISH I HADN'T SEEN THAT.
YOU'D NEVER HAVE A NORMAL LIFE IF NOT FOR ANJU ALWAYS MANAGING TO SWOOP IN AND SAVE YOUR SAD, DUMB ASS!
YOU CAN'T EVEN ERASE A HUMAN'S MEMORY! PATHETIC!

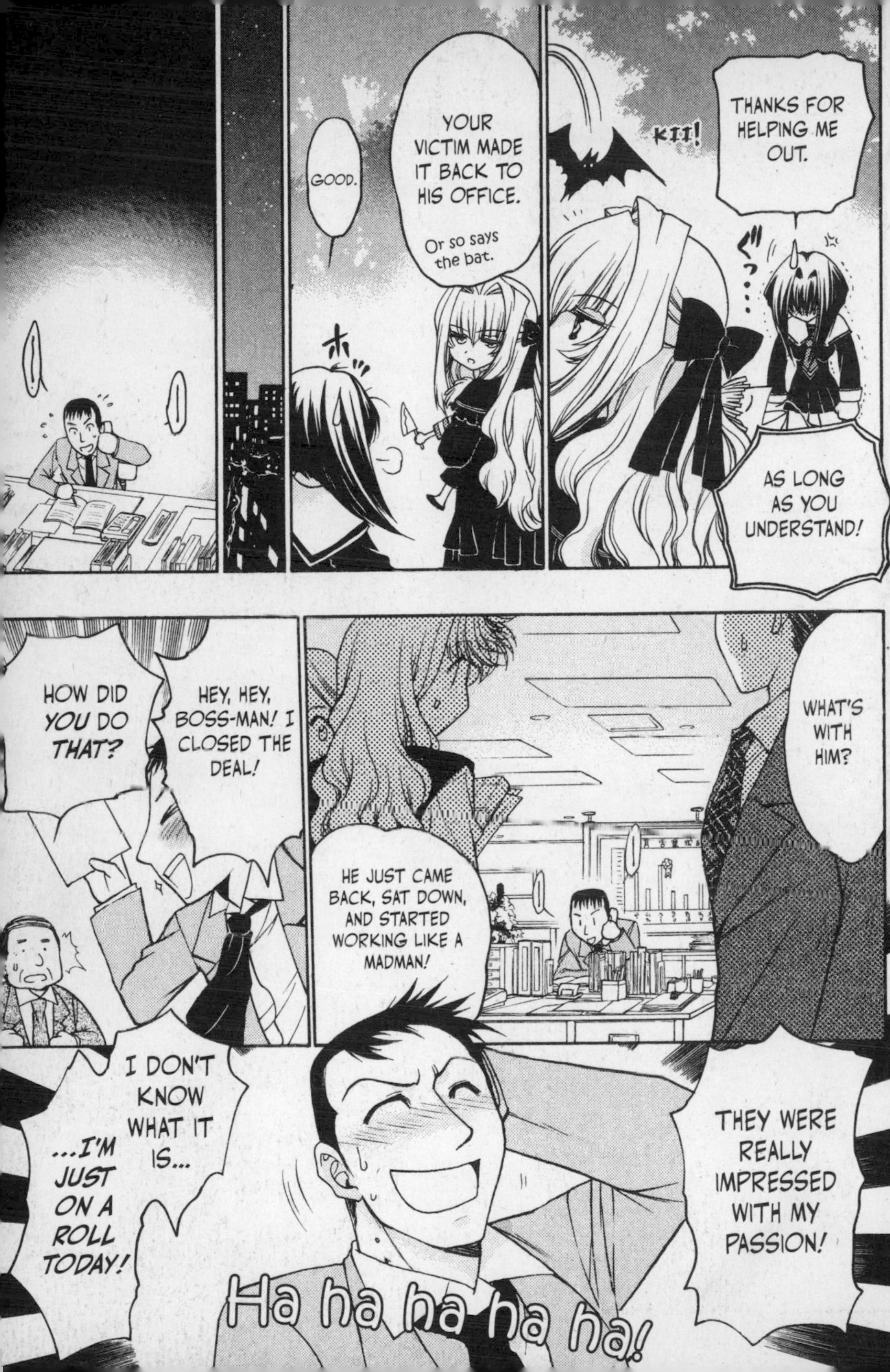
THANKS FOR HELPING ME OUT.
KII!
ぐっ…
AS LONG AS YOU UNDERSTAND!
YOUR VICTIM MADE IT BACK TO HIS OFFICE.
Or so says the bat.
GOOD.
ホ
WHAT'S WITH HIM?
HE JUST CAME BACK, SAT DOWN, AND STARTED WORKING LIKE A MADMAN!
HEY, HEY, BOSS-MAN! I CLOSED THE DEAL!
HOW DID *YOU* DO *THAT?*
THEY WERE REALLY IMPRESSED WITH MY PASSION!
I DON'T KNOW WHAT IT IS...
...I'M JUST ON A ROLL TODAY!
Ha ha ha ha ha!

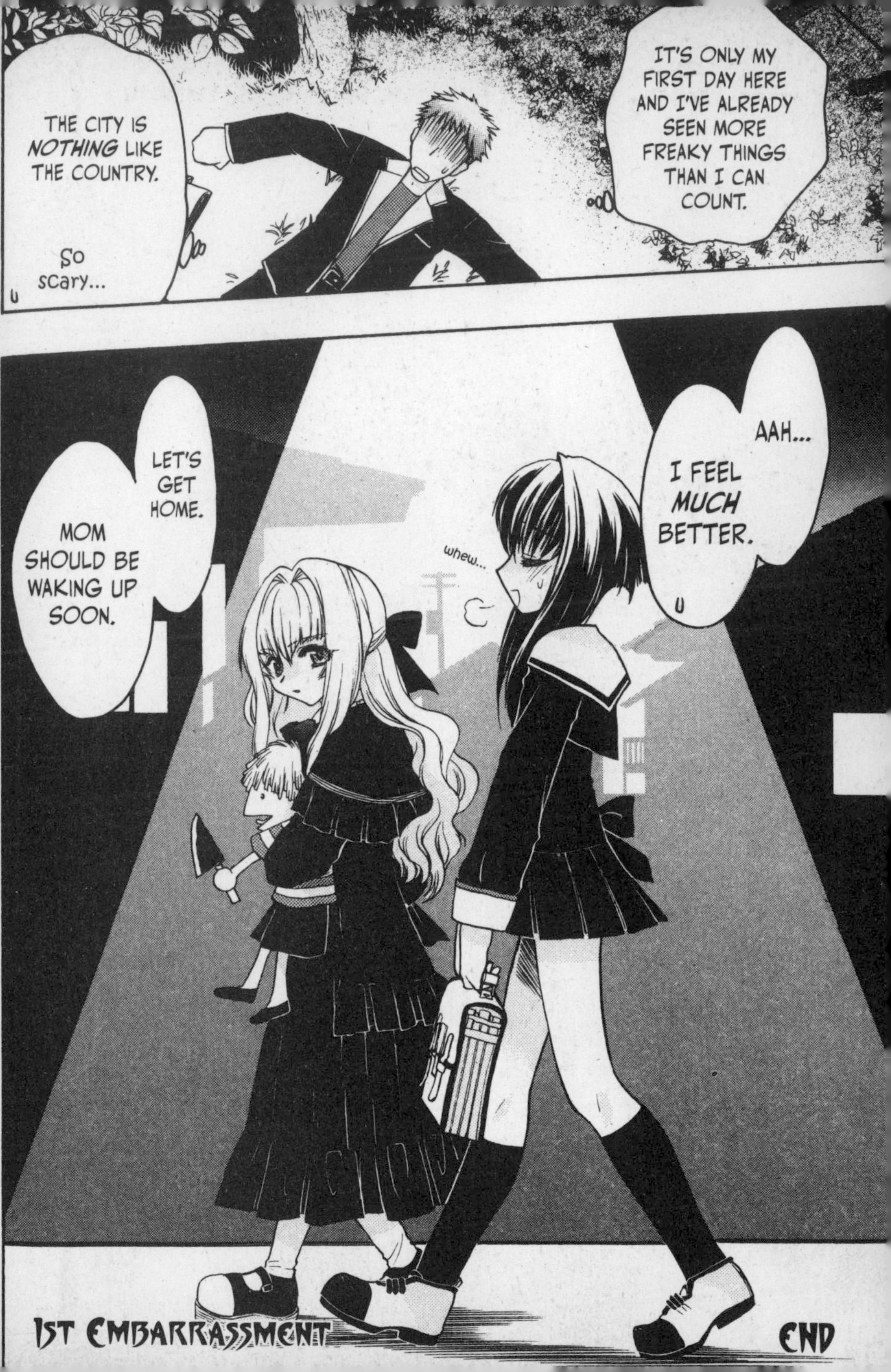
IT'S ONLY MY FIRST DAY HERE AND I'VE ALREADY SEEN MORE FREAKY THINGS THAN I CAN COUNT.
THE CITY IS *NOTHING* LIKE THE COUNTRY.
So scary...
AAH...
I FEEL *MUCH* BETTER.
whew...
LET'S GET HOME.
MOM SHOULD BE WAKING UP SOON.
1ST EMBARRASSMENT
END

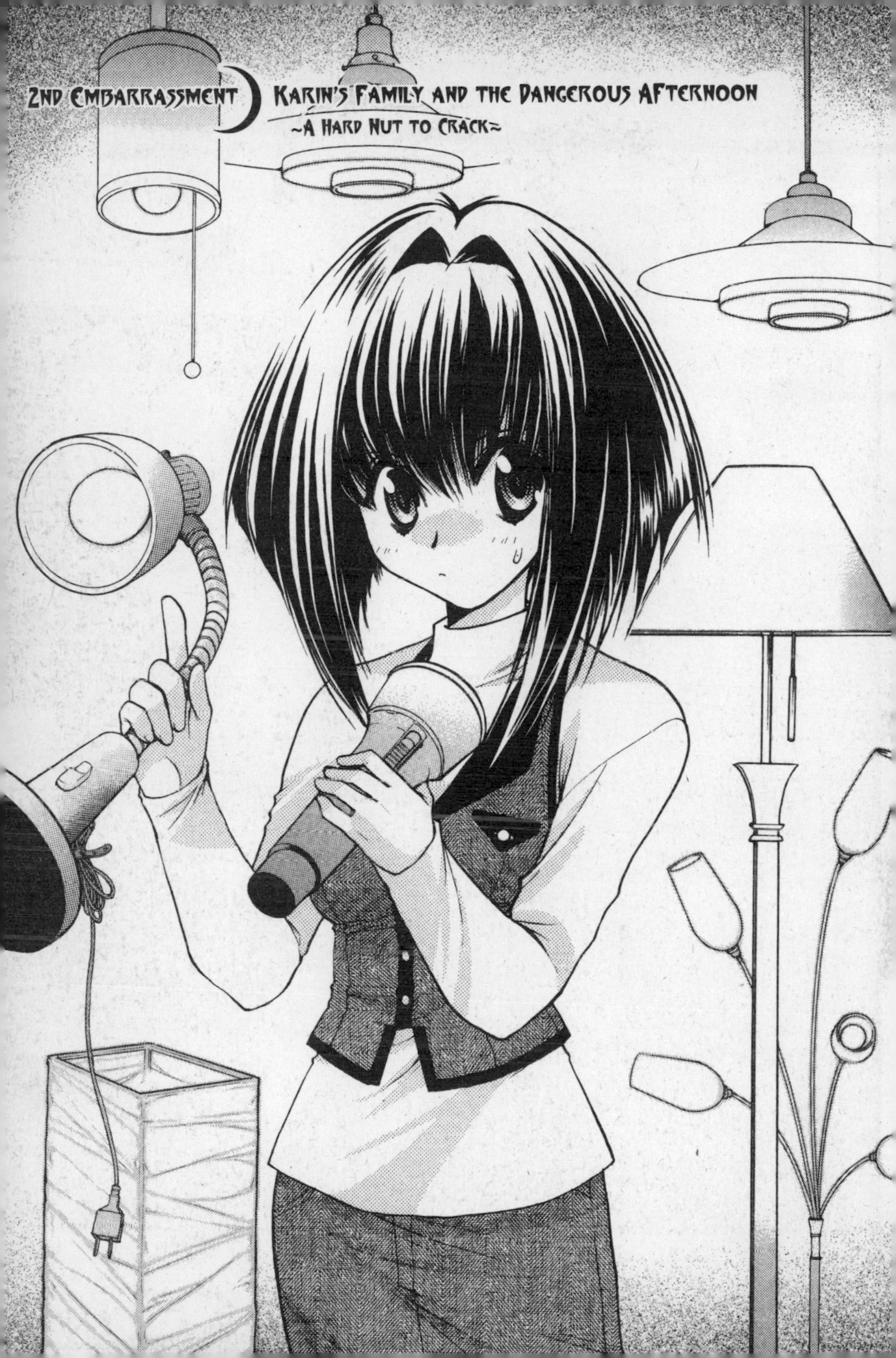
2nd Embarrassment
Karin's Family and the Dangerous Afternoon
~A Hard Nut to Crack~

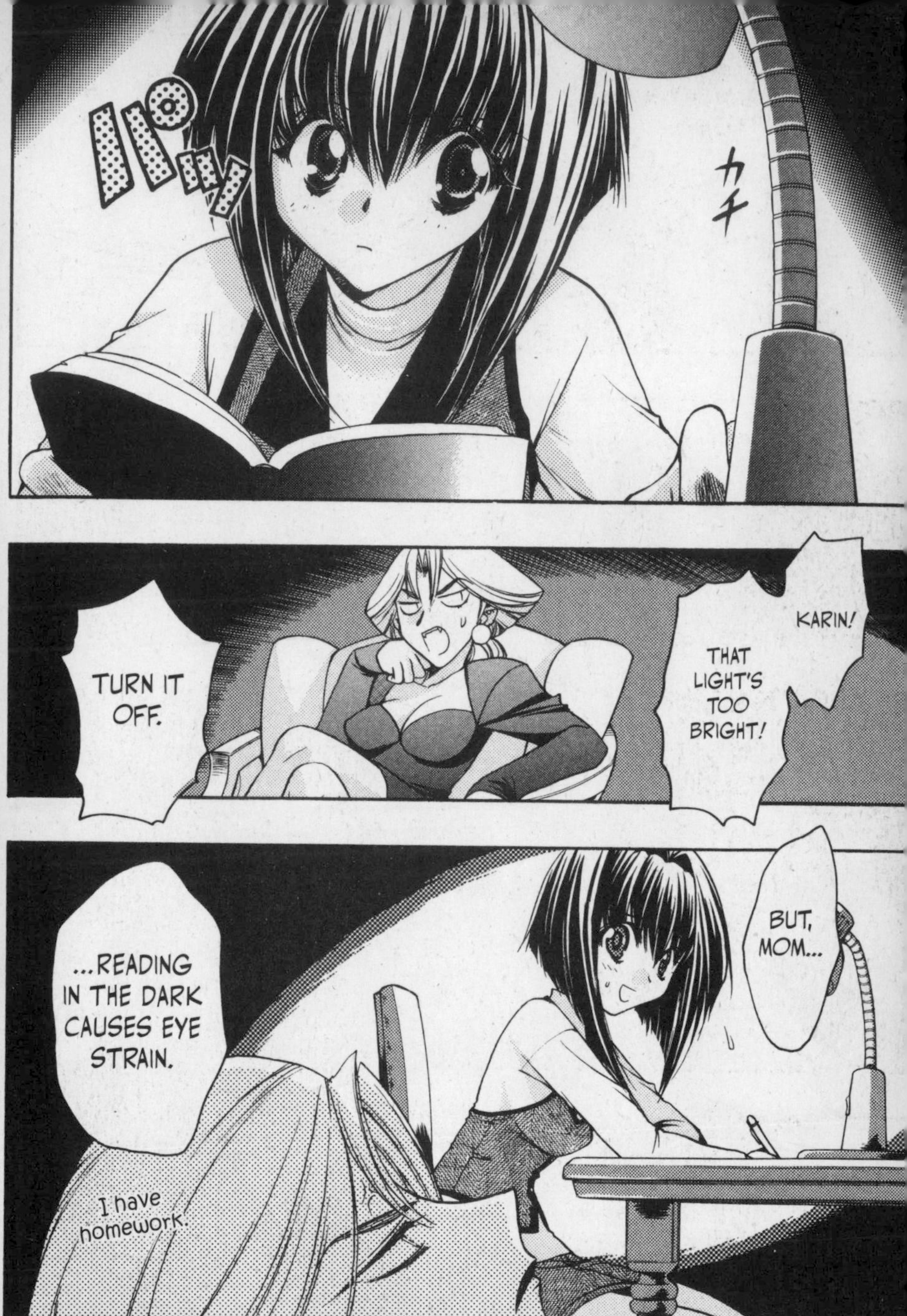
パッ
カチ
KARIN!
THAT LIGHT'S TOO BRIGHT!
TURN IT OFF.
BUT, MOM...
...READING IN THE DARK CAUSES EYE STRAIN.
I have homework.

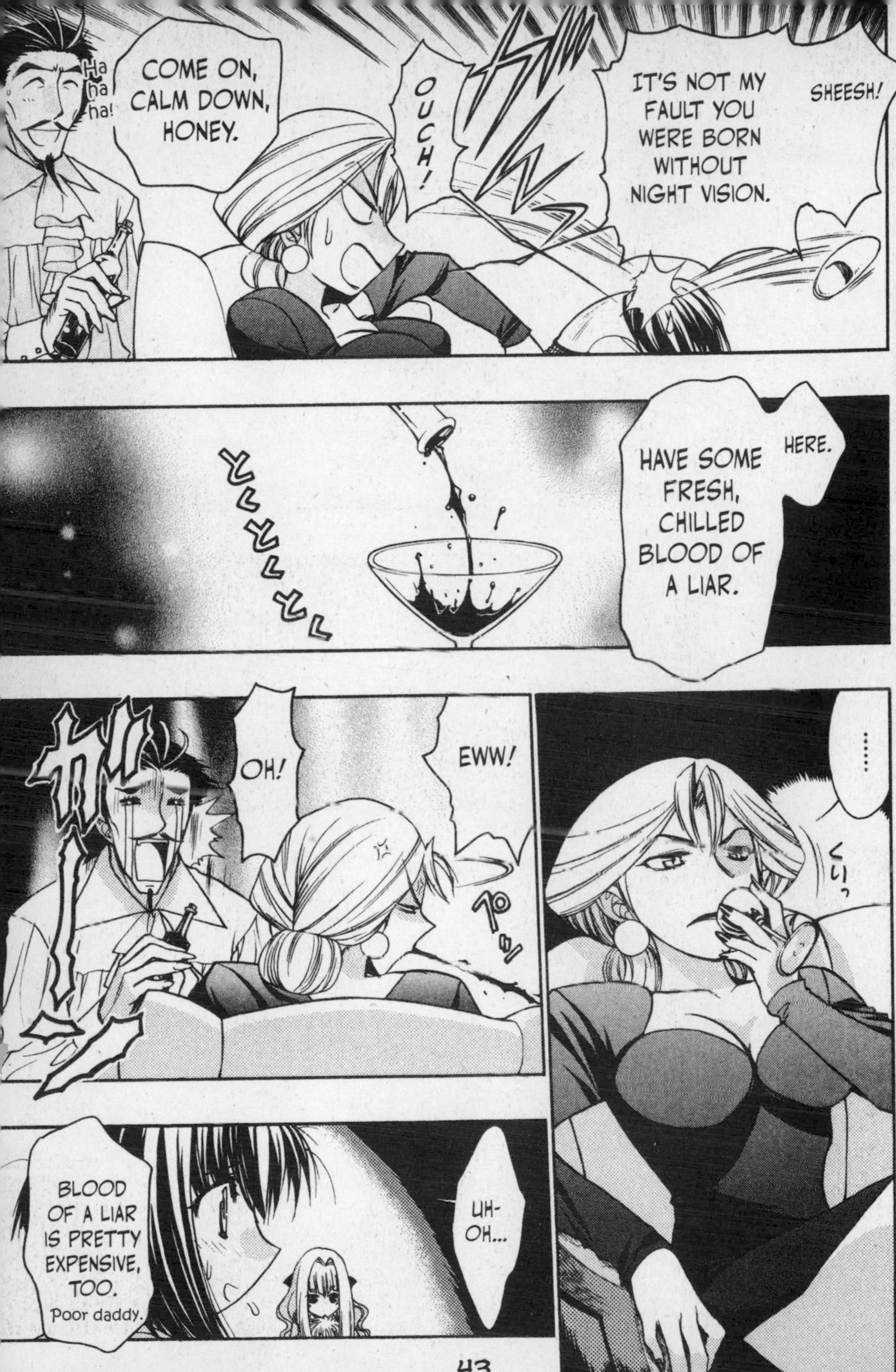
SHEESH!
IT'S NOT MY FAULT YOU WERE BORN WITHOUT NIGHT VISION.
OUCH!
COME ON, CALM DOWN, HONEY.
Ha ha ha!
HERE.
HAVE SOME FRESH, CHILLED BLOOD OF A LIAR.
......
EWW!
OH!
UH-OH...
BLOOD OF A LIAR IS PRETTY EXPENSIVE, TOO.
Poor daddy.

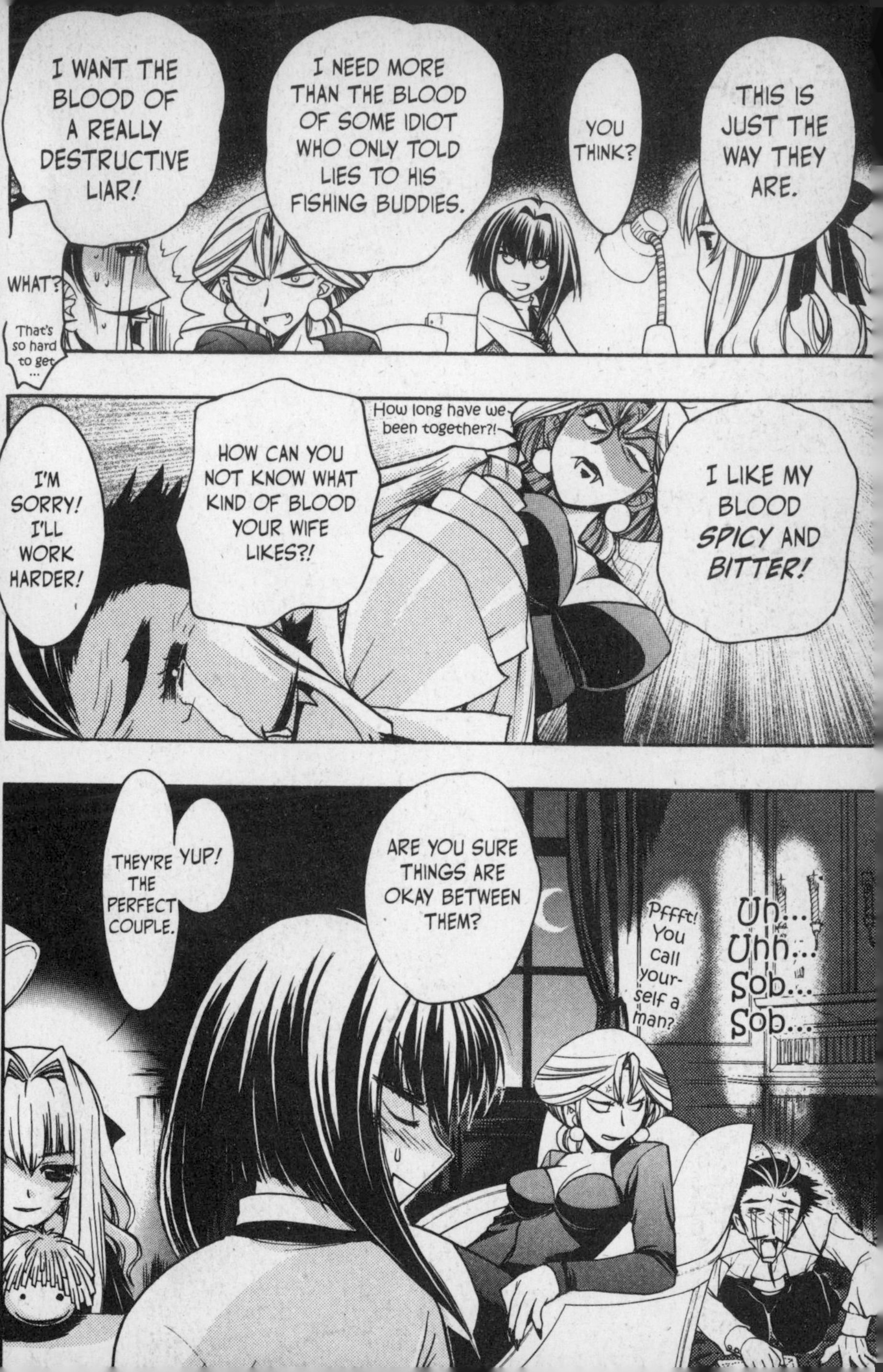
THIS IS JUST THE WAY THEY ARE.
YOU THINK?
I NEED MORE THAN THE BLOOD OF SOME IDIOT WHO ONLY TOLD LIES TO HIS FISHING BUDDIES.
I WANT THE BLOOD OF A REALLY DESTRUCTIVE LIAR!
WHAT?
That's so hard to get...
I LIKE MY BLOOD SPICY AND BITTER!
How long have we been together?!
HOW CAN YOU NOT KNOW WHAT KIND OF BLOOD YOUR WIFE LIKES?!
I'M SORRY! I'LL WORK HARDER!
Uh... Uhh... Sob... Sob...
Pffft! You call your-self a man?
ARE YOU SURE THINGS ARE OKAY BETWEEN THEM?
YUP! THEY'RE THE PERFECT COUPLE.

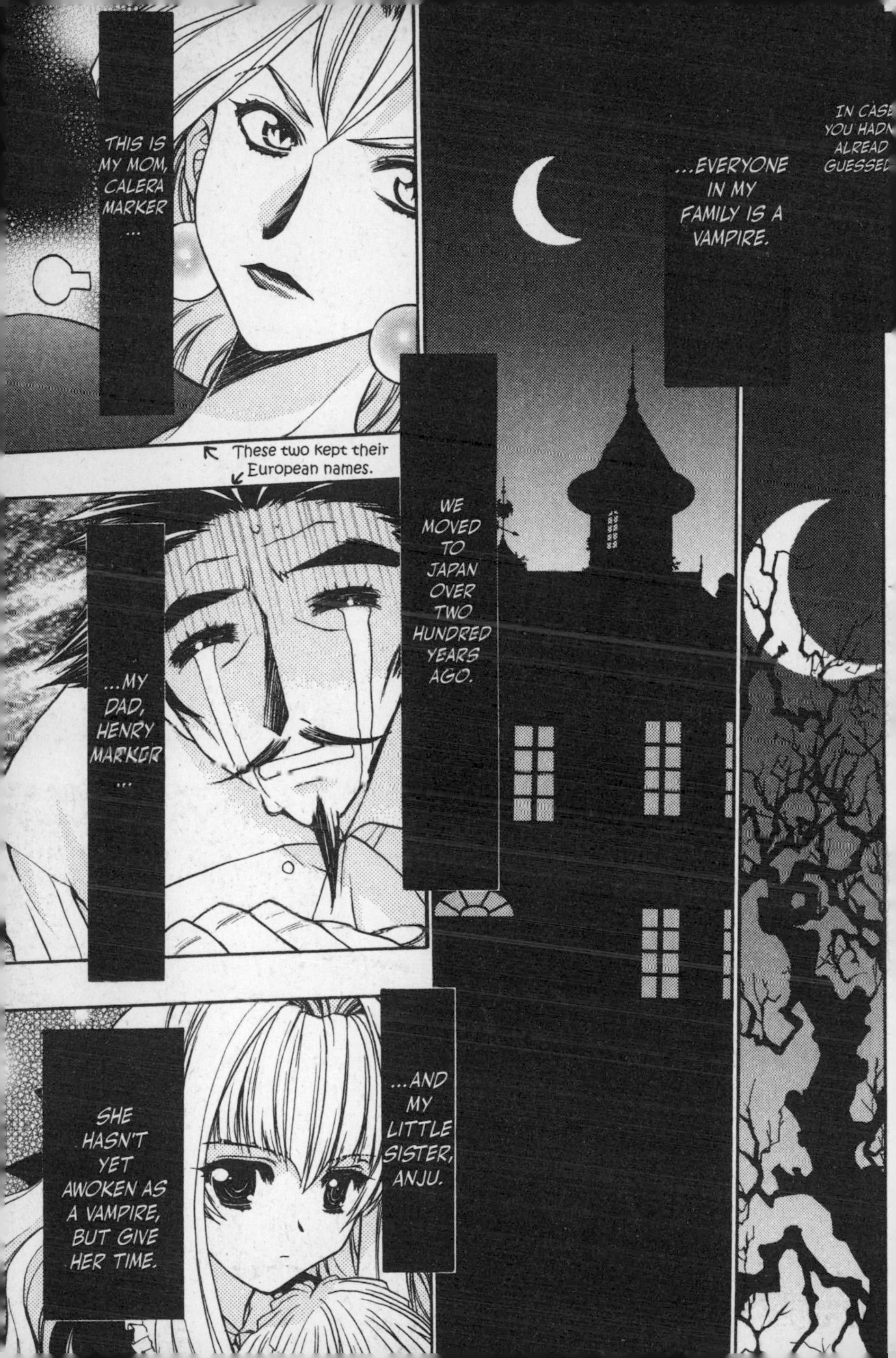
IN CASE YOU HADN ALREAD GUESSED
...EVERYONE IN MY FAMILY IS A VAMPIRE.
WE MOVED TO JAPAN OVER TWO HUNDRED YEARS AGO.
THIS IS MY MOM, CALERA MARKER ...
These two kept their European names.
...MY DAD, HENRY MARKER ...
...AND MY LITTLE SISTER, ANJU.
SHE HASN'T YET AWOKEN AS A VAMPIRE, BUT GIVE HER TIME.

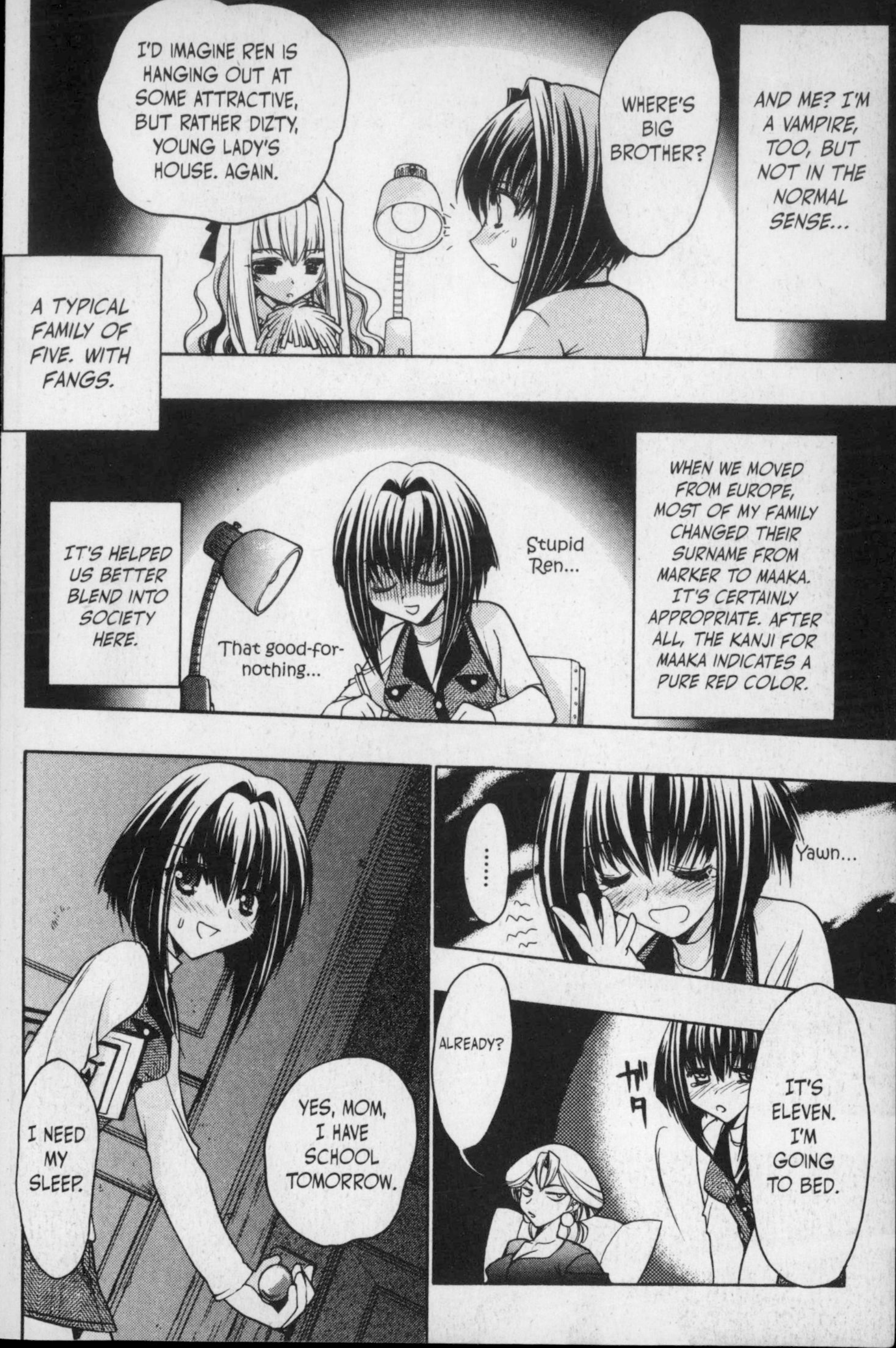
AND ME? I'M A VAMPIRE, TOO, BUT NOT IN THE NORMAL SENSE...
WHERE'S BIG BROTHER?
I'D IMAGINE REN IS HANGING OUT AT SOME ATTRACTIVE, BUT RATHER DIZTY, YOUNG LADY'S HOUSE. AGAIN.
A TYPICAL FAMILY OF FIVE. WITH FANGS.
WHEN WE MOVED FROM EUROPE, MOST OF MY FAMILY CHANGED THEIR SURNAME FROM MARKER TO MAAKA. IT'S CERTAINLY APPROPRIATE. AFTER ALL, THE KANJI FOR MAAKA INDICATES A PURE RED COLOR.
Stupid Ren...
That good-for-nothing...
IT'S HELPED US BETTER BLEND INTO SOCIETY HERE.
Yawn...
......
IT'S ELEVEN. I'M GOING TO BED.
ガタ
ALREADY?
YES, MOM, I HAVE SCHOOL TOMORROW.
I NEED MY SLEEP.

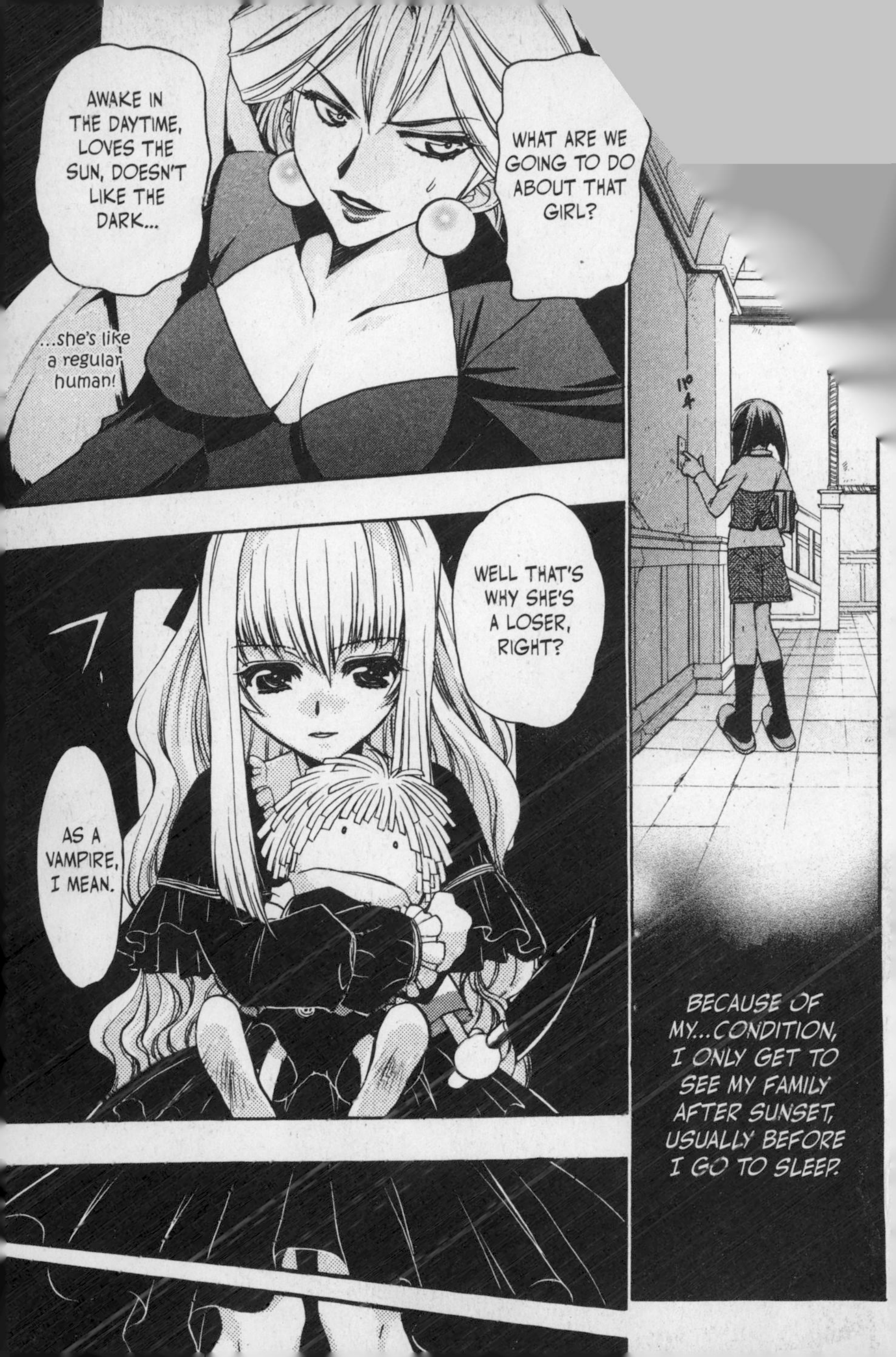
BECAUSE OF MY...CONDITION, I ONLY GET TO SEE MY FAMILY AFTER SUNSET, USUALLY BEFORE I GO TO SLEEP.
WHAT ARE WE GOING TO DO ABOUT THAT GIRL?
AWAKE IN THE DAYTIME, LOVES THE SUN, DOESN'T LIKE THE DARK...
...she's like a regular human!
WELL THAT'S WHY SHE'S A LOSER, RIGHT?
AS A VAMPIRE, I MEAN.

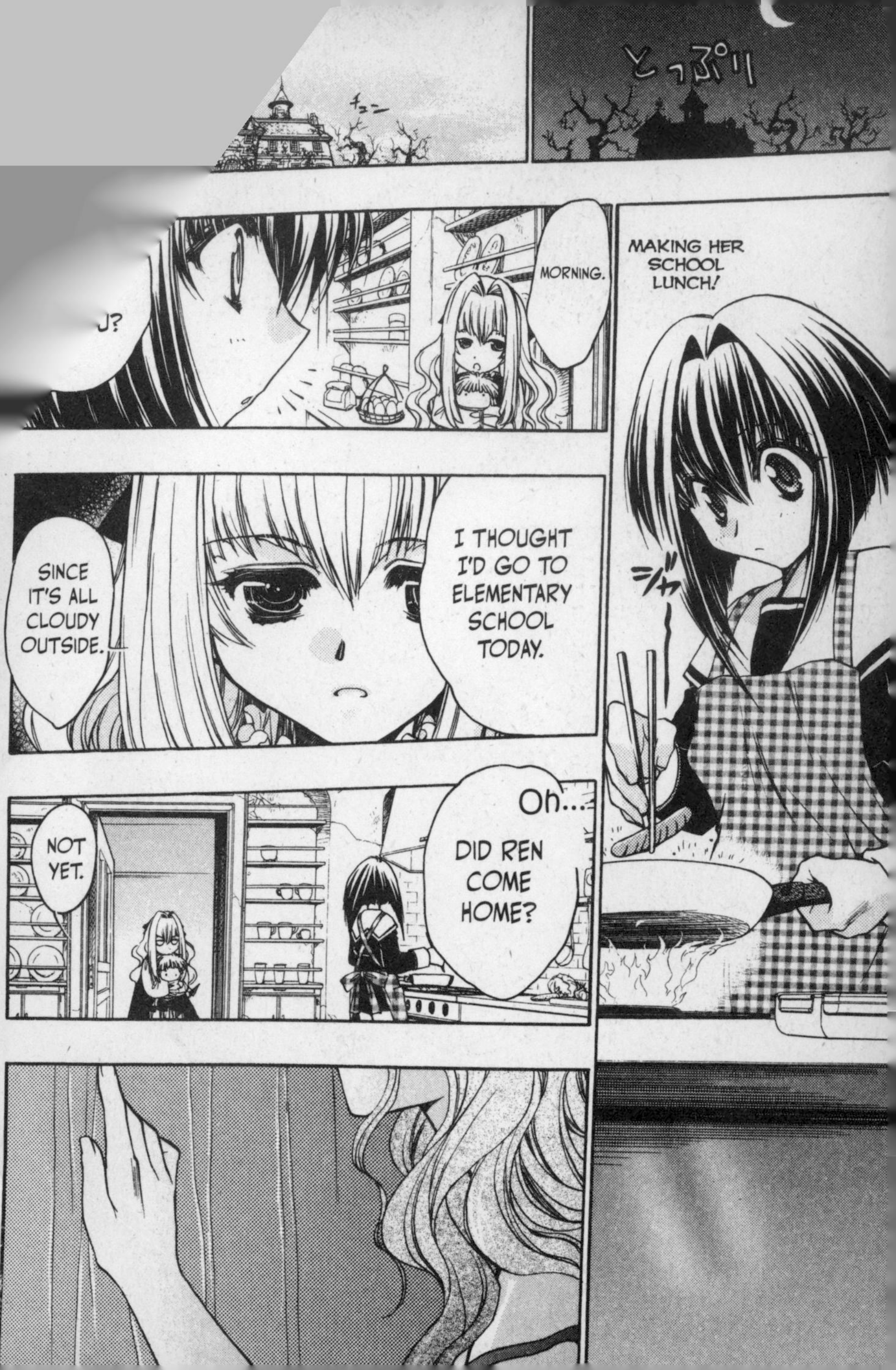
とっぷり
チュン
MAKING HER SCHOOL LUNCH!
MORNING.
I THOUGHT I'D GO TO ELEMENTARY SCHOOL TODAY.
SINCE IT'S ALL CLOUDY OUTSIDE.
Oh...
DID REN COME HOME?
NOT YET.

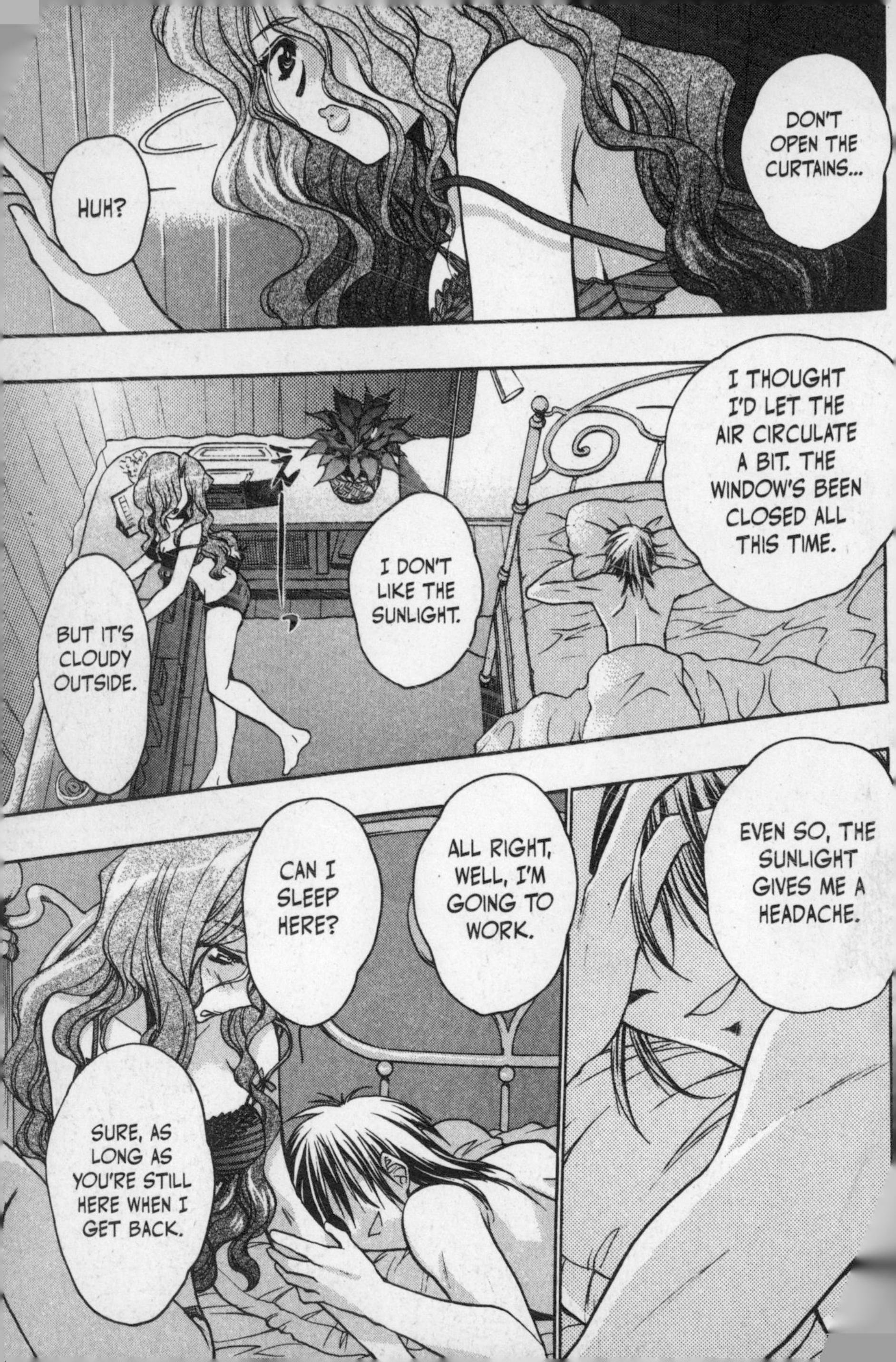
DON'T OPEN THE CURTAINS...
HUH?
I THOUGHT I'D LET THE AIR CIRCULATE A BIT. THE WINDOW'S BEEN CLOSED ALL THIS TIME.
I DON'T LIKE THE SUNLIGHT.
BUT IT'S CLOUDY OUTSIDE.
EVEN SO, THE SUNLIGHT GIVES ME A HEADACHE.
ALL RIGHT, WELL, I'M GOING TO WORK.
CAN I SLEEP HERE?
SURE, AS LONG AS YOU'RE STILL HERE WHEN I GET BACK.

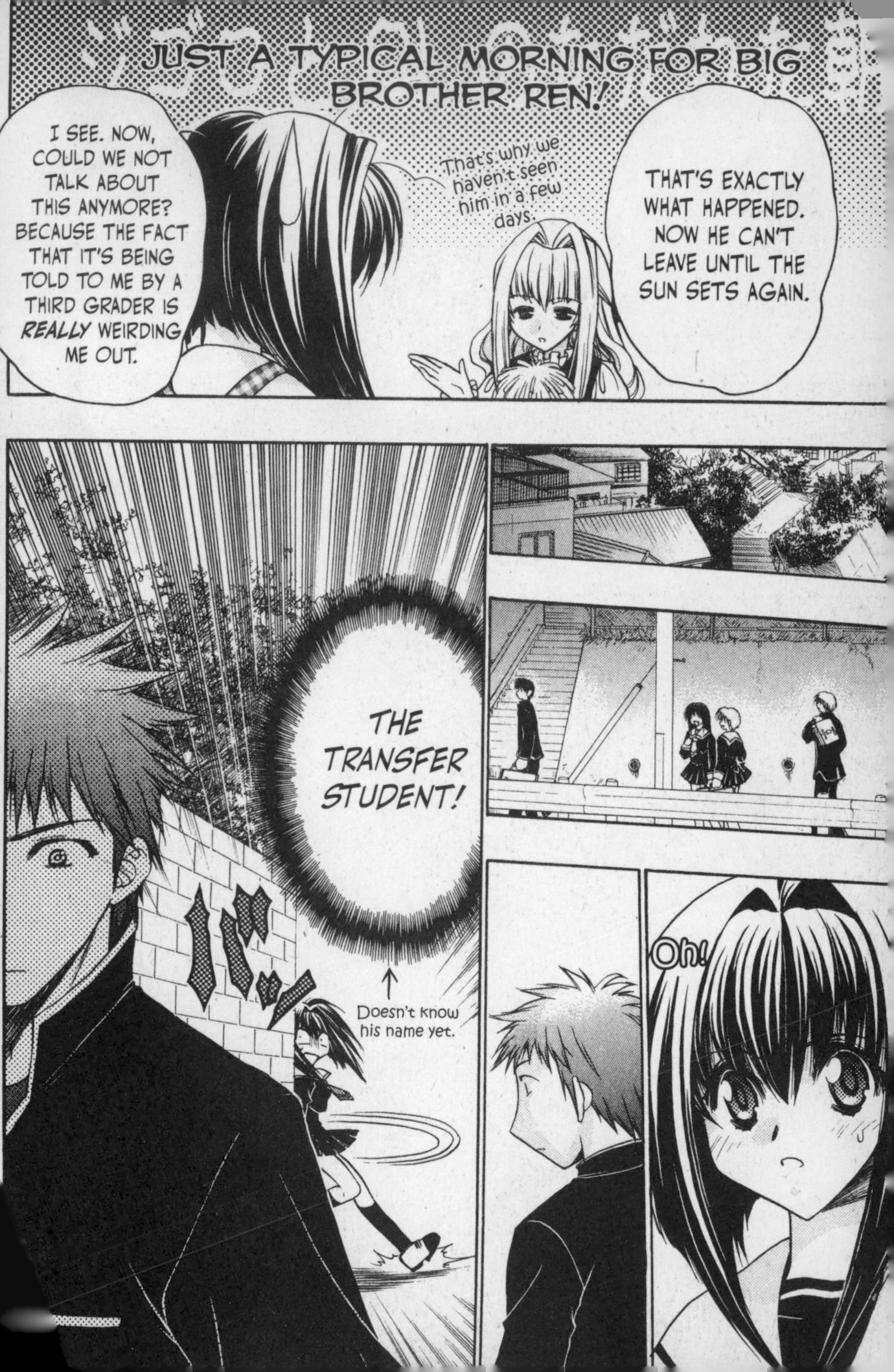
JUST A TYPICAL MORNING FOR BIG BROTHER REN!
THAT'S EXACTLY WHAT HAPPENED. NOW HE CAN'T LEAVE UNTIL THE SUN SETS AGAIN.
That's why we haven't seen him in a few days.
I SEE. NOW, COULD WE NOT TALK ABOUT THIS ANYMORE? BECAUSE THE FACT THAT IT'S BEING TOLD TO ME BY A THIRD GRADER IS *REALLY* WEIRDING ME OUT.
Oh!
THE TRANSFER STUDENT!
Doesn't know his name yet.

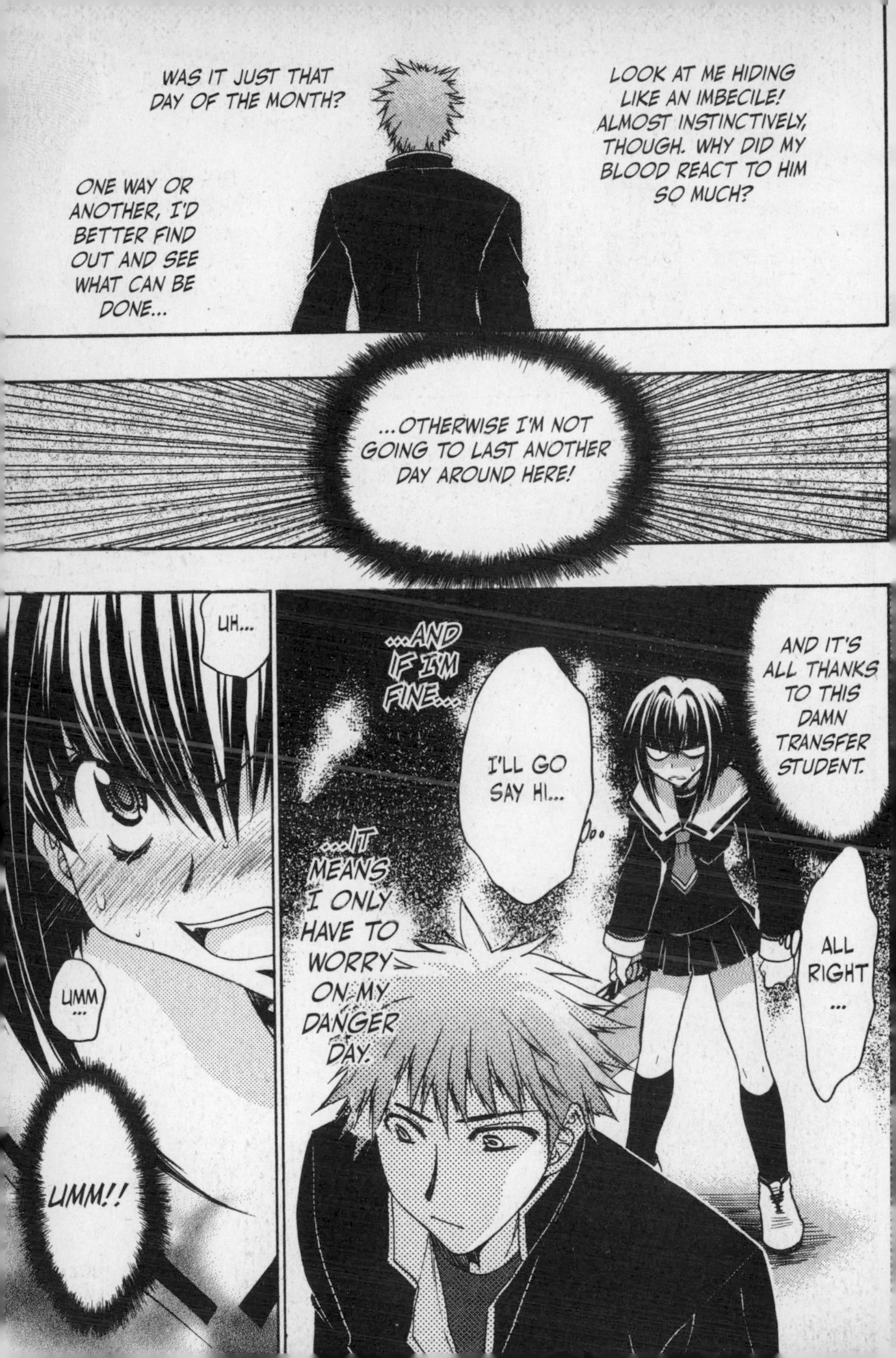
LOOK AT ME HIDING LIKE AN IMBECILE! ALMOST INSTINCTIVELY, THOUGH. WHY DID MY BLOOD REACT TO HIM SO MUCH?
WAS IT JUST THAT DAY OF THE MONTH?
ONE WAY OR ANOTHER, I'D BETTER FIND OUT AND SEE WHAT CAN BE DONE...
...OTHERWISE I'M NOT GOING TO LAST ANOTHER DAY AROUND HERE!
AND IT'S ALL THANKS TO THIS DAMN TRANSFER STUDENT.
...AND IF I'M FINE...
...IT MEANS I ONLY HAVE TO WORRY ON MY DANGER DAY.
ALL RIGHT...
I'LL GO SAY HI...
UH...
UMM...
UMM!!

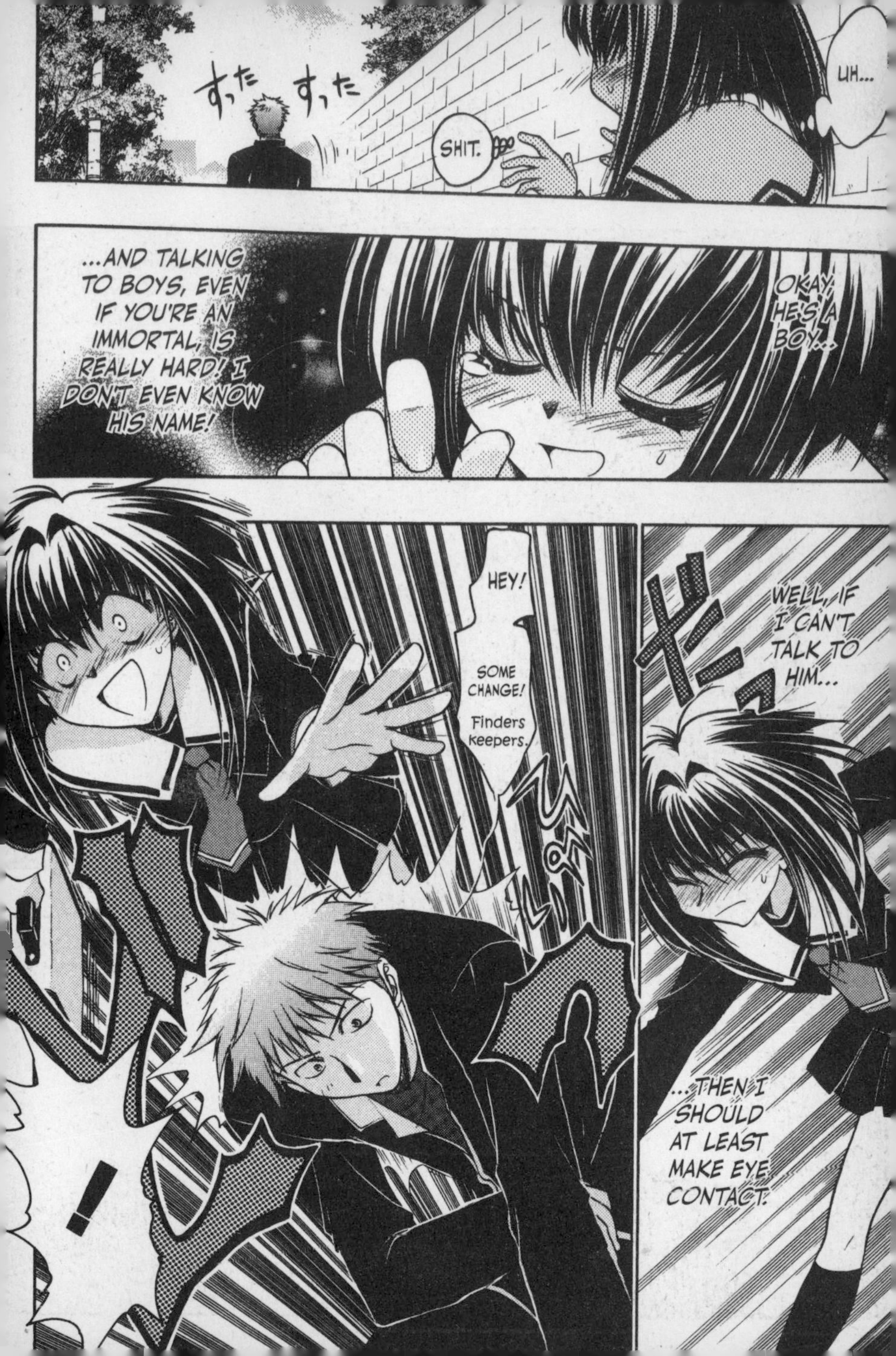
UH...
すった すった
SHIT.
OKAY, HE'S A BOY...
...AND TALKING TO BOYS, EVEN IF YOU'RE AN IMMORTAL, IS REALLY HARD! I DON'T EVEN KNOW HIS NAME!
WELL, IF I CAN'T TALK TO HIM...
...THEN I SHOULD AT LEAST MAKE EYE CONTACT.
HEY!
SOME CHANGE!
Finders keepers.
!

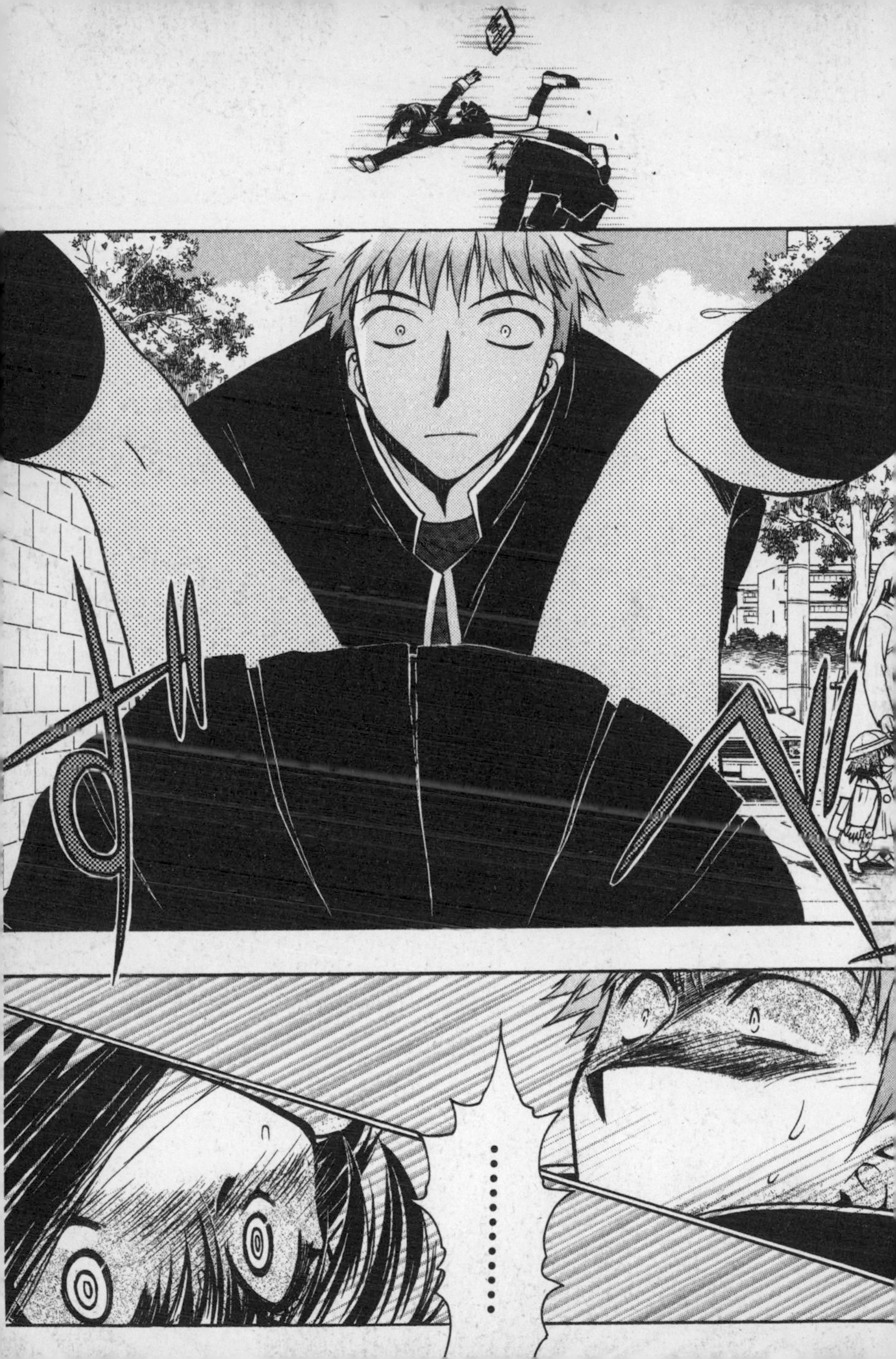
........

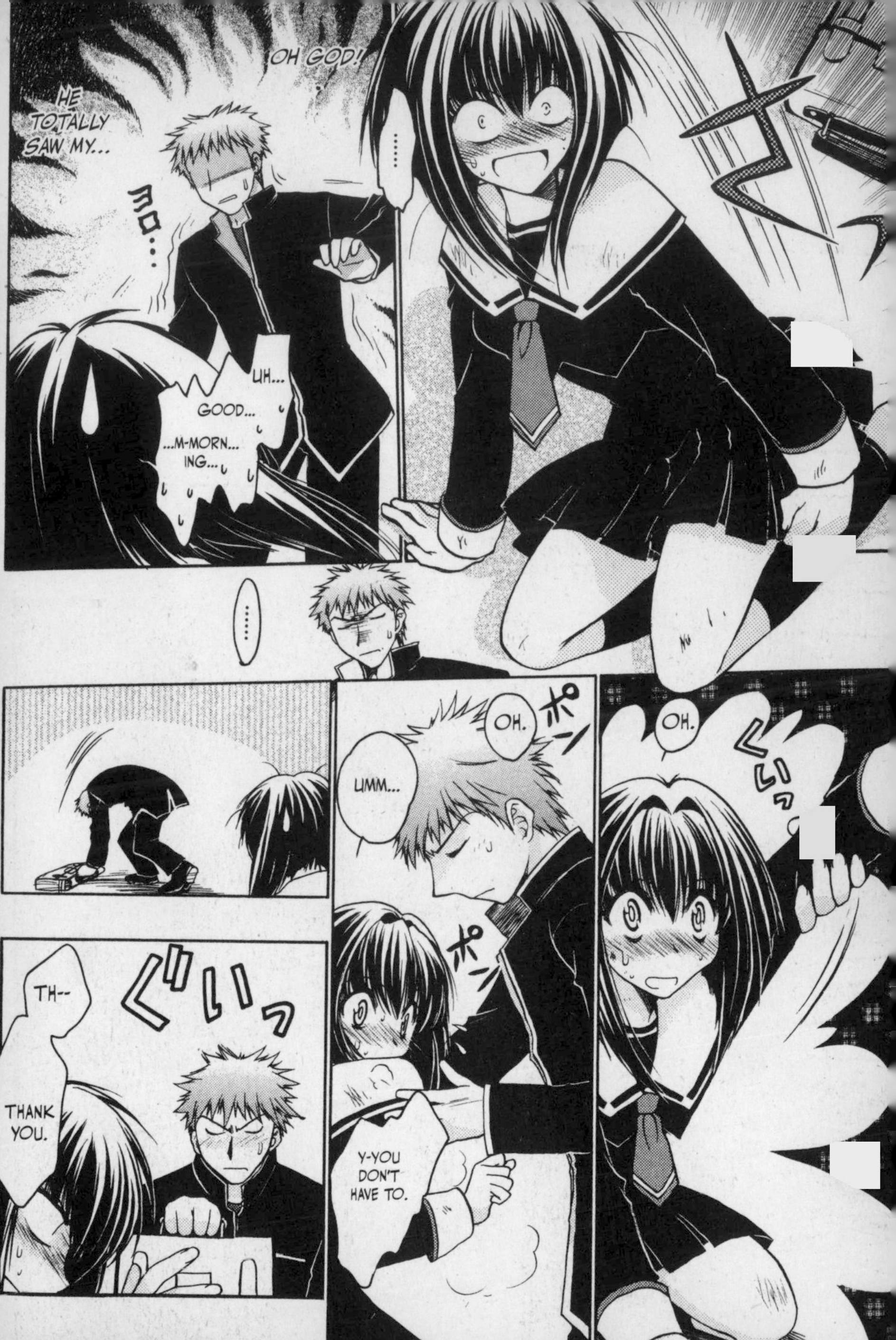
......
OH GOD!
HE TOTALLY SAW MY...
ヨロ...
UH...
GOOD...
...M-MORN... ING...
......
OH.
くいっ
OH.
ポン
UMM...
ポン
Y-YOU DON'T HAVE TO.
TH--
ぐいーっ
THANK YOU.

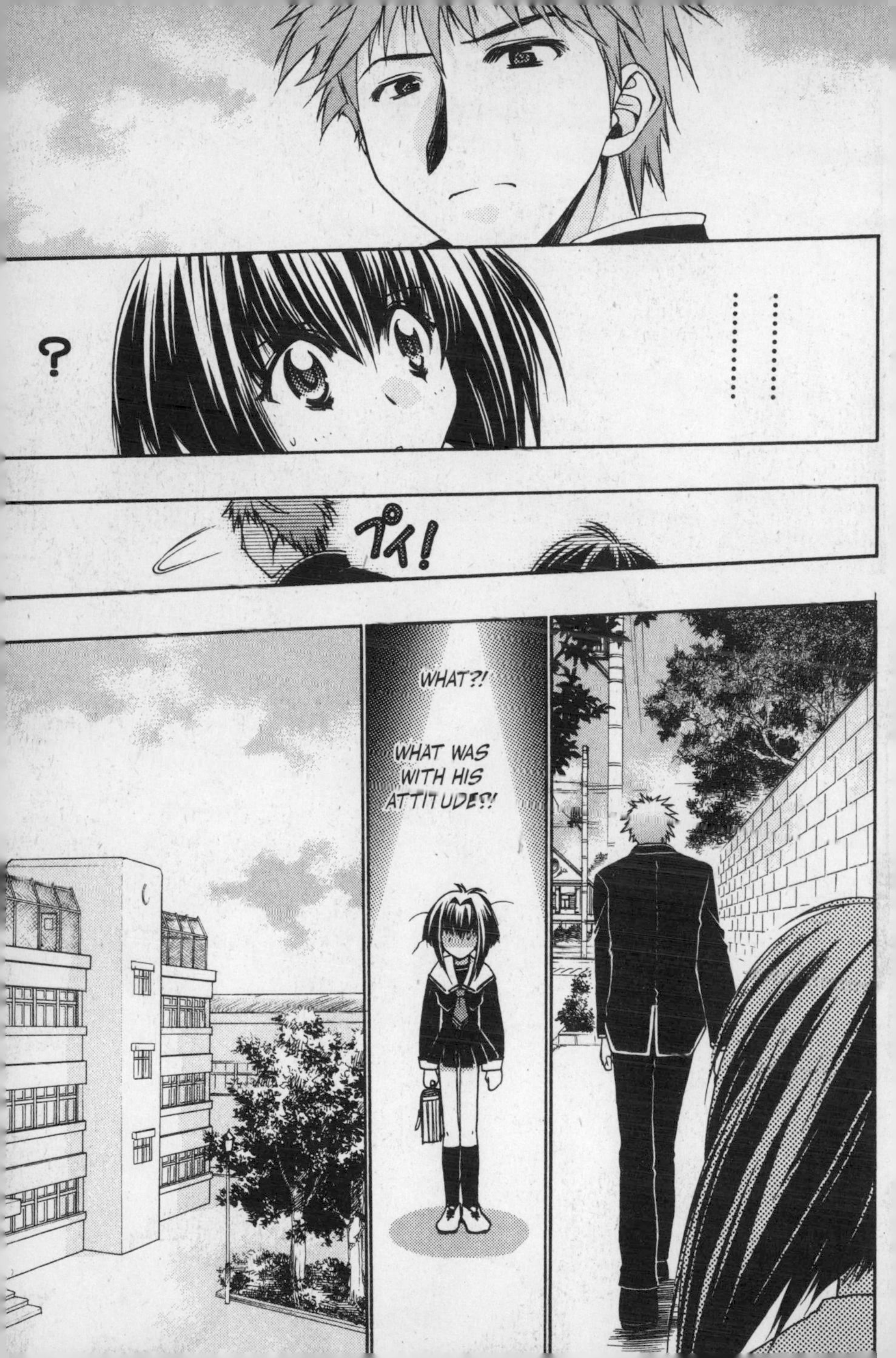

......
?
ピィ!
WHAT?!
WHAT WAS WITH HIS ATTITUDE?!

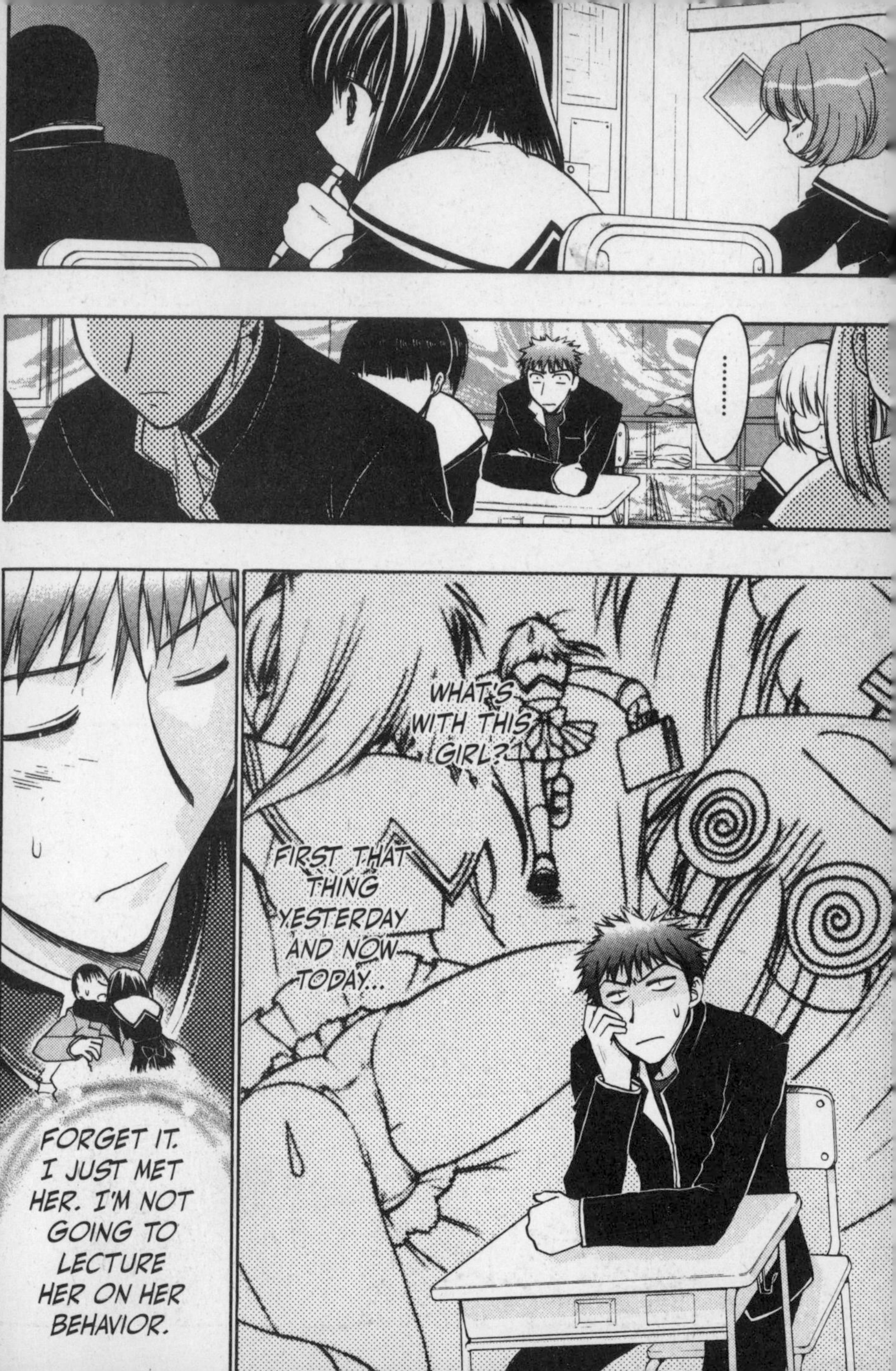
......
WHAT'S WITH THIS GIRL?
FIRST THAT THING YESTERDAY AND NOW TODAY...
FORGET IT. I JUST MET HER. I'M NOT GOING TO LECTURE HER ON HER BEHAVIOR.

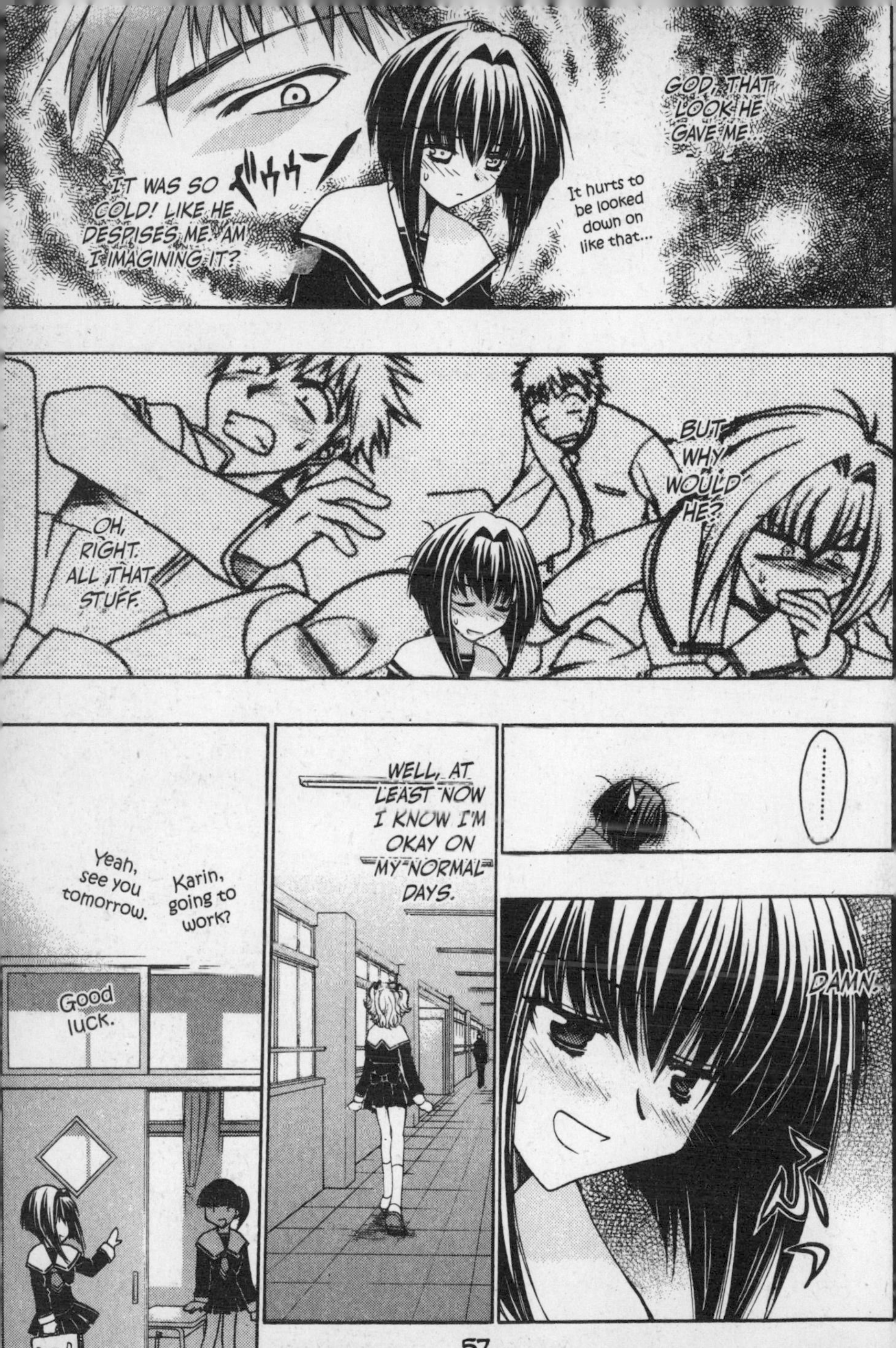
GOD, THAT LOOK HE GAVE ME
It hurts to be looked down on like that...
IT WAS SO COLD! LIKE HE DESPISES ME. AM I IMAGINING IT?
BUT WHY WOULD HE?
OH, RIGHT. ALL THAT STUFF.
......
DAMN.
WELL, AT LEAST NOW I KNOW I'M OKAY ON MY NORMAL DAYS.
Karin, going to work?
Yeah, see you tomorrow.
Good luck.

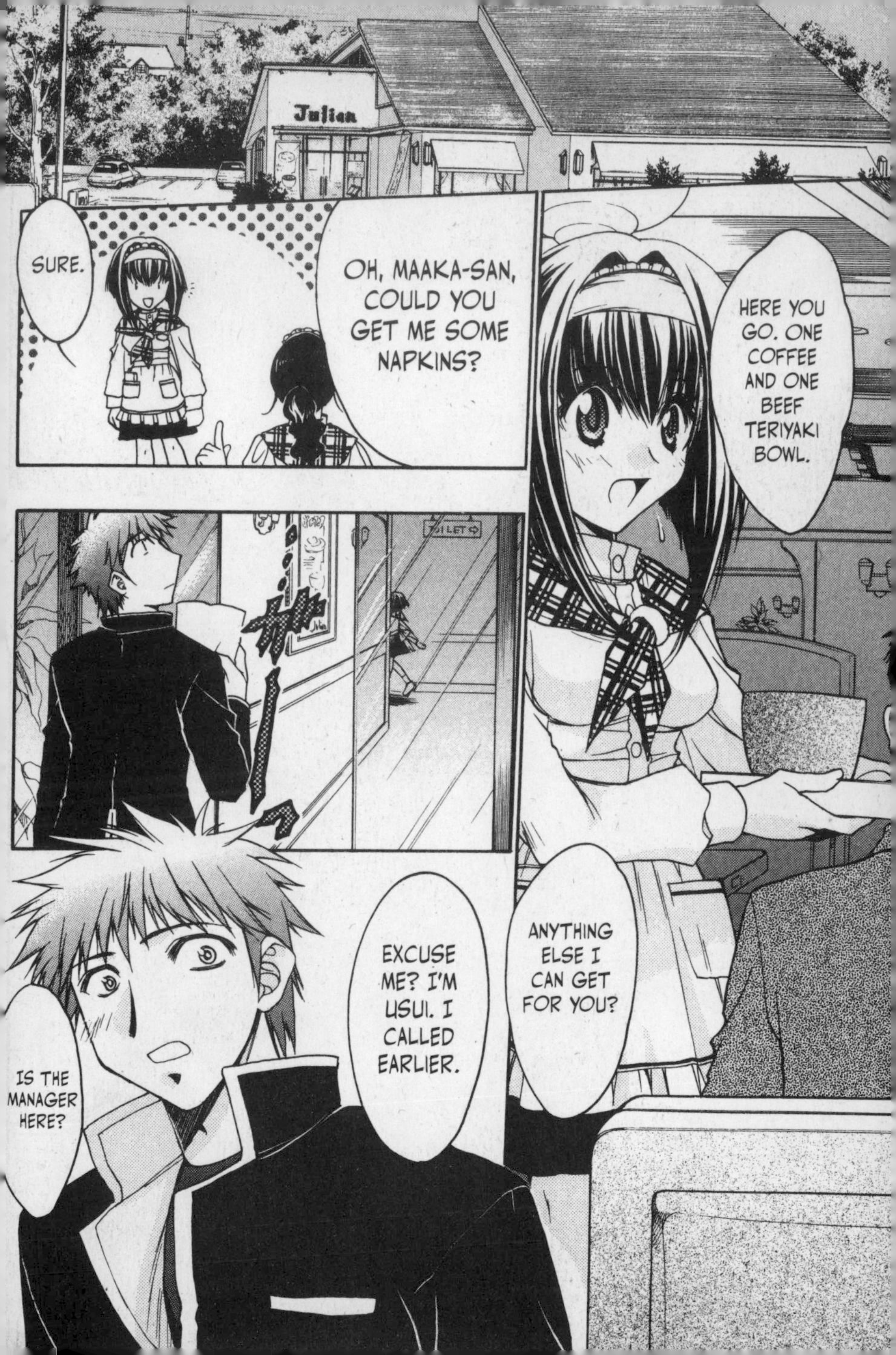
Julian
HERE YOU GO. ONE COFFEE AND ONE BEEF TERIYAKI BOWL.
OH, MAAKA-SAN, COULD YOU GET ME SOME NAPKINS?
SURE.
TOILET
ANYTHING ELSE I CAN GET FOR YOU?
EXCUSE ME? I'M USUI. I CALLED EARLIER.
IS THE MANAGER HERE?

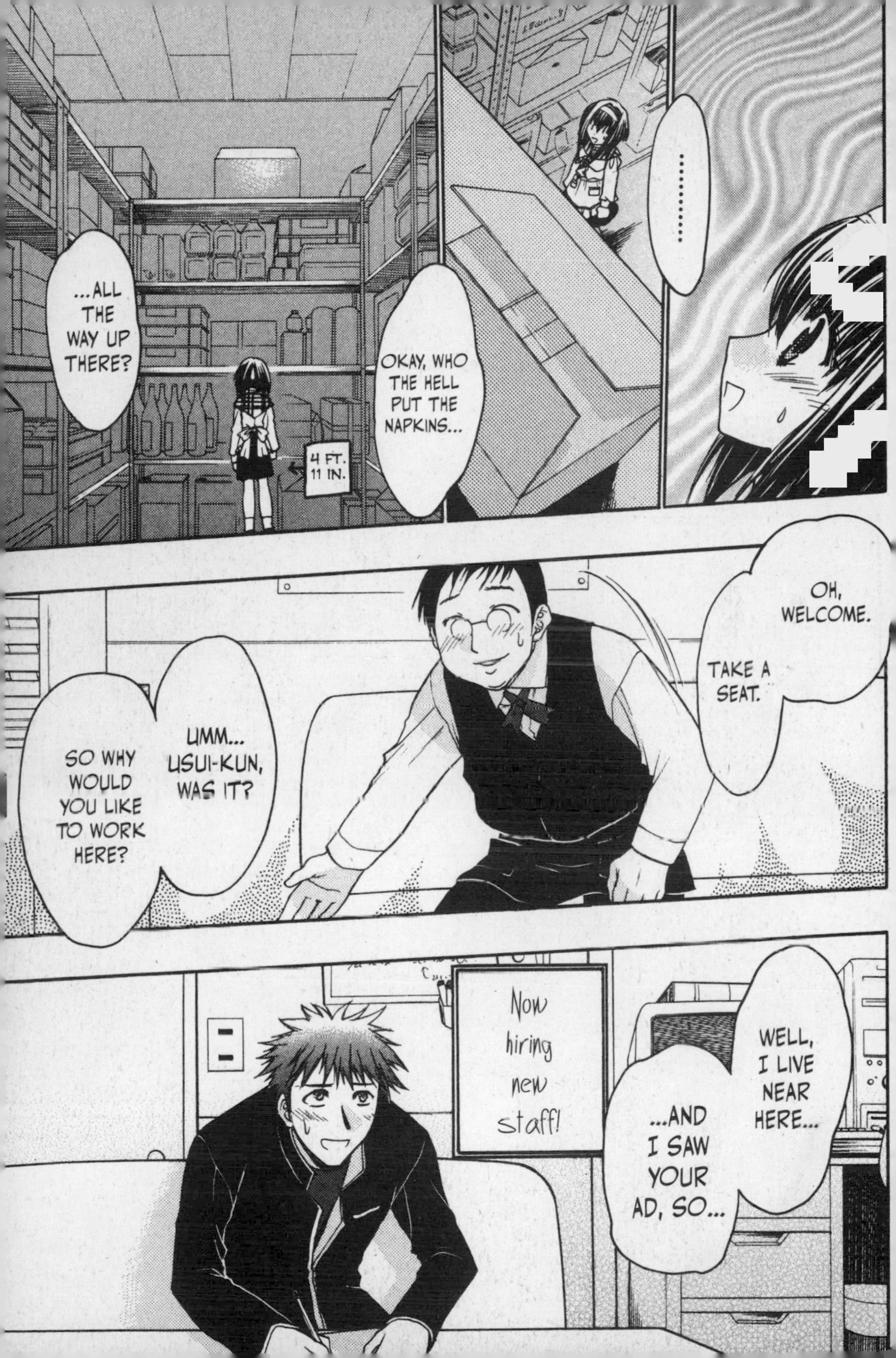
......
OKAY, WHO THE HELL PUT THE NAPKINS...
...ALL THE WAY UP THERE?
4 FT. 11 IN.
OH, WELCOME.
TAKE A SEAT.
UMM... USUI-KUN, WAS IT?
SO WHY WOULD YOU LIKE TO WORK HERE?
WELL, I LIVE NEAR HERE...
...AND I SAW YOUR AD, SO...
Now hiring new staff!

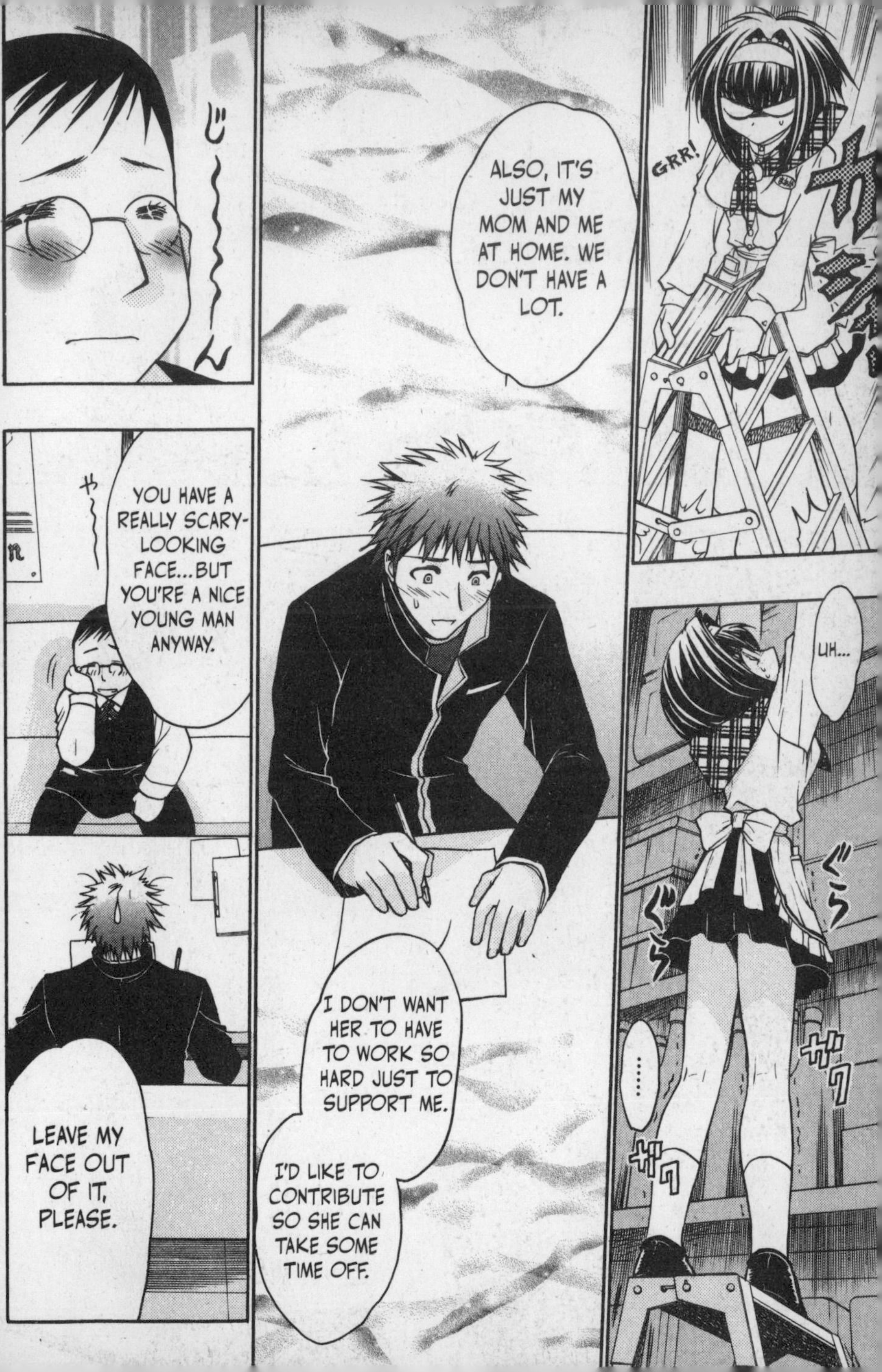
GRR!
UH...
......
ALSO, IT'S JUST MY MOM AND ME AT HOME. WE DON'T HAVE A LOT.
I DON'T WANT HER TO HAVE TO WORK SO HARD JUST TO SUPPORT ME.
I'D LIKE TO CONTRIBUTE SO SHE CAN TAKE SOME TIME OFF.
YOU HAVE A REALLY SCARY-LOOKING FACE...BUT YOU'RE A NICE YOUNG MAN ANYWAY.
LEAVE MY FACE OUT OF IT, PLEASE.

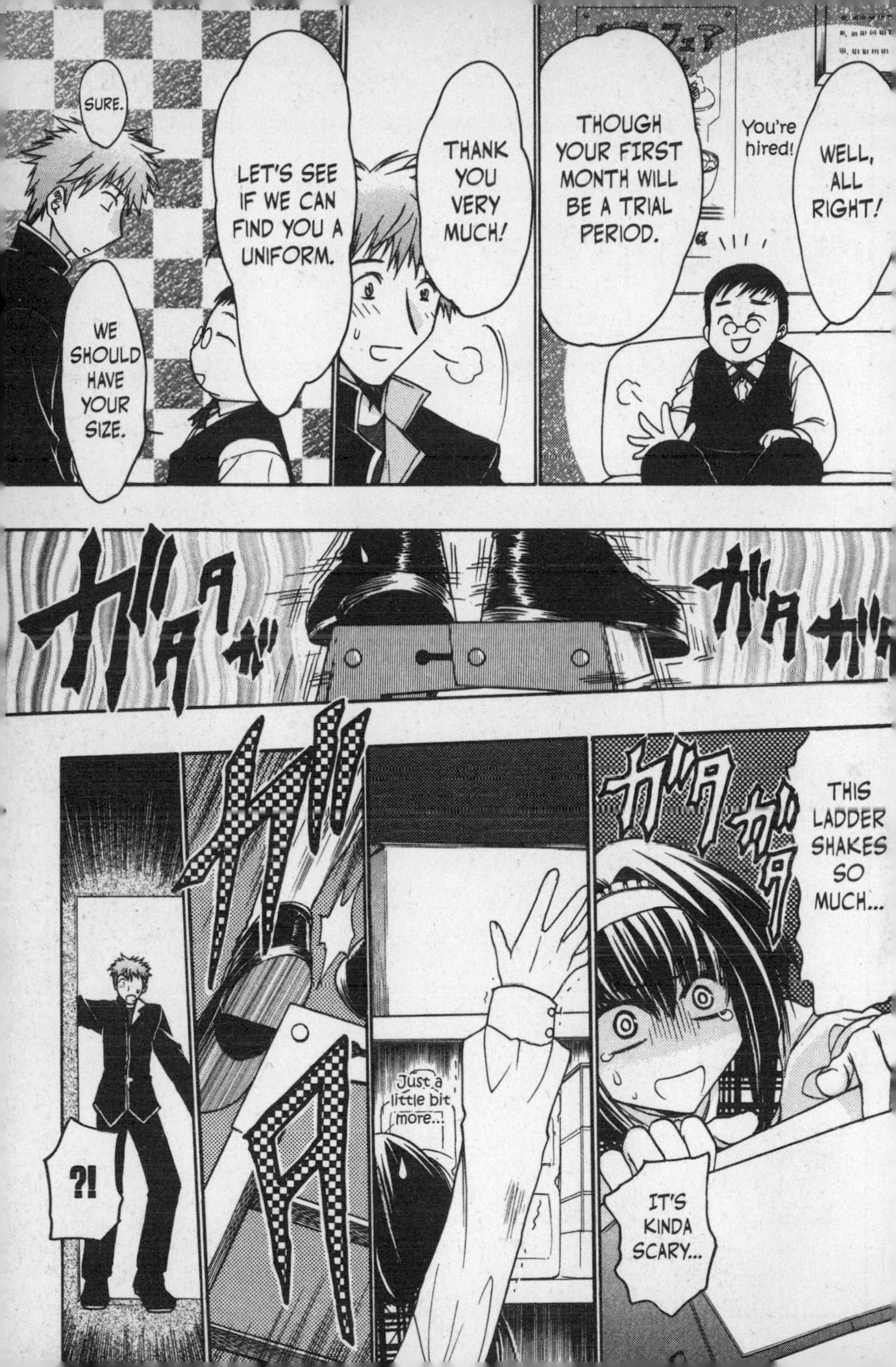
WELL, ALL RIGHT!
You're hired!
THOUGH YOUR FIRST MONTH WILL BE A TRIAL PERIOD.
THANK YOU VERY MUCH!
LET'S SEE IF WE CAN FIND YOU A UNIFORM.
SURE.
WE SHOULD HAVE YOUR SIZE.
THIS LADDER SHAKES SO MUCH...
IT'S KINDA SCARY...
Just a little bit more...
?!

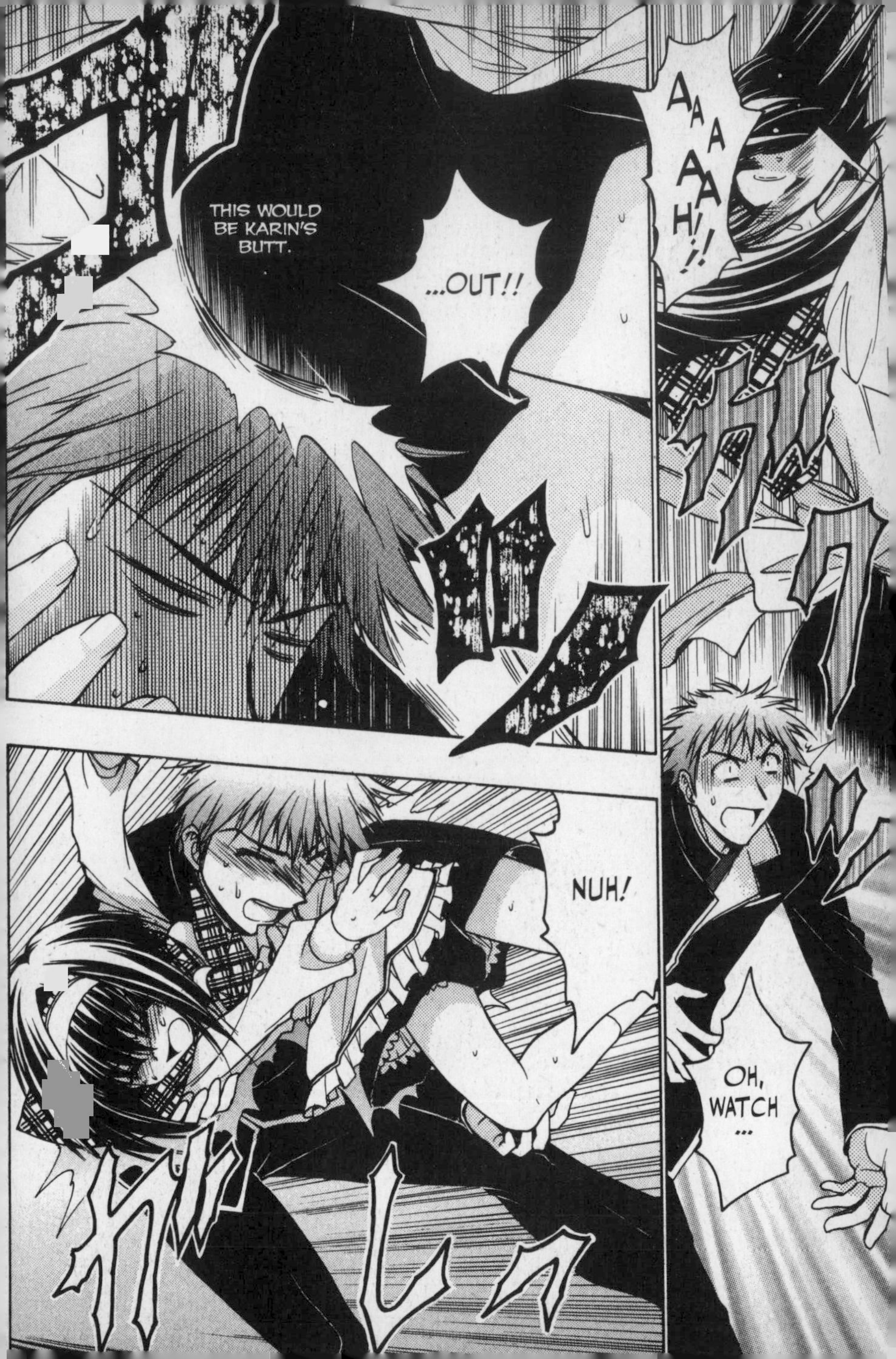
AAAAAH!!!
...OUT!!
THIS WOULD BE KARIN'S BUTT.
OH, WATCH ...
NUH!

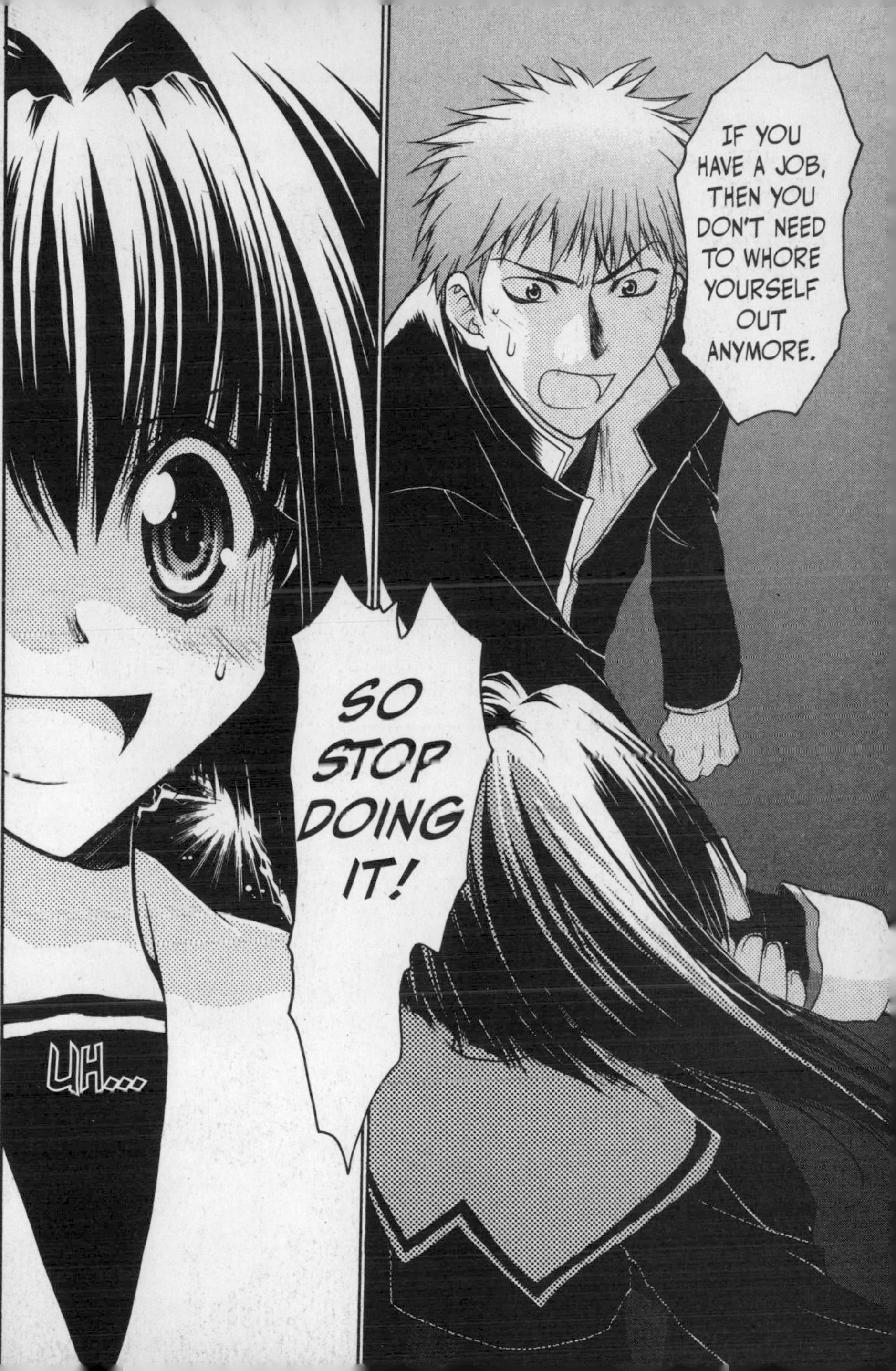
IF YOU HAVE A JOB, THEN YOU DON'T NEED TO WHORE YOURSELF OUT ANYMORE.
SO STOP DOING IT!
UH...

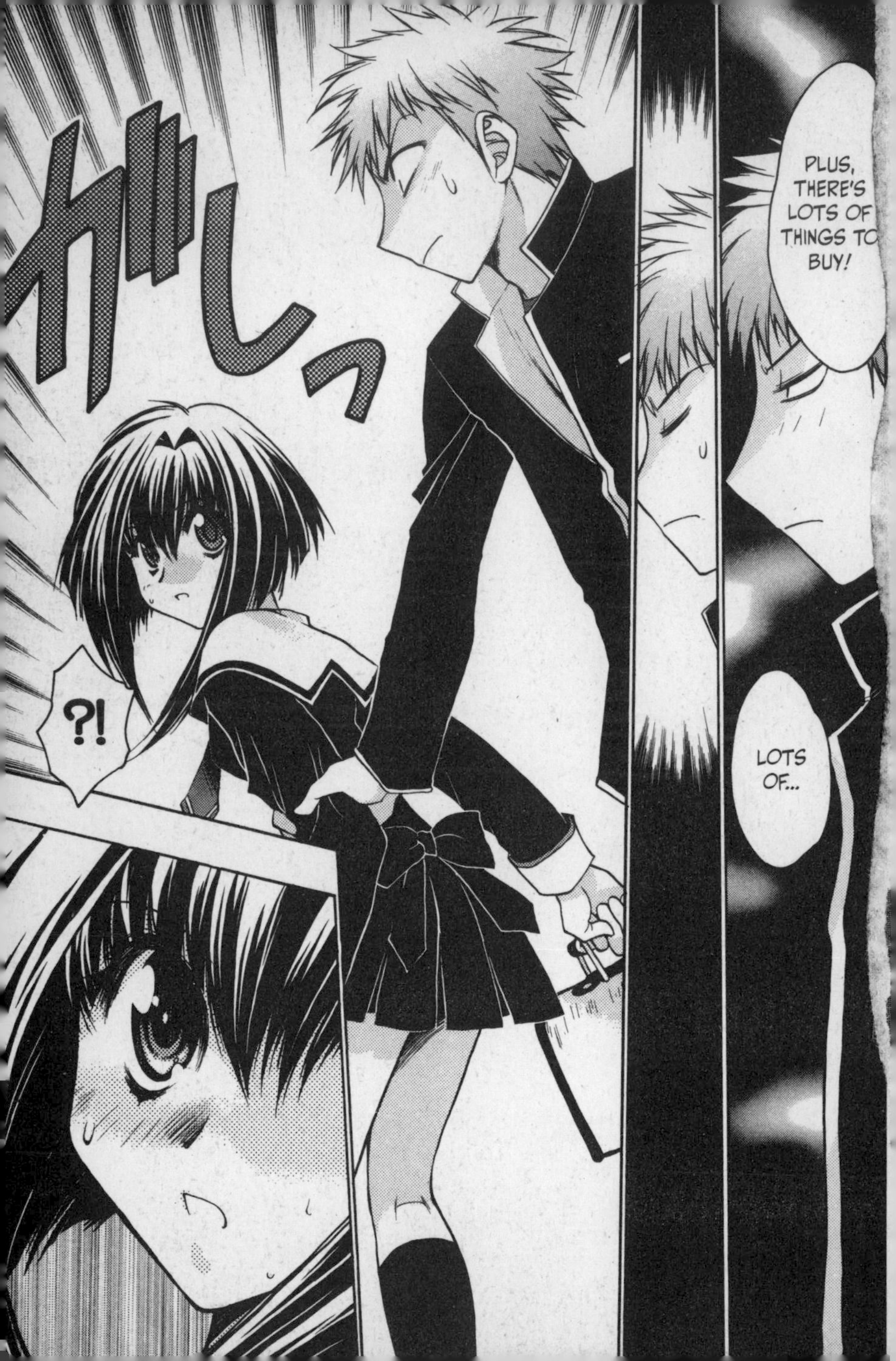
PLUS, THERE'S LOTS OF THINGS TO BUY!
LOTS OF...
ガしっ
?!

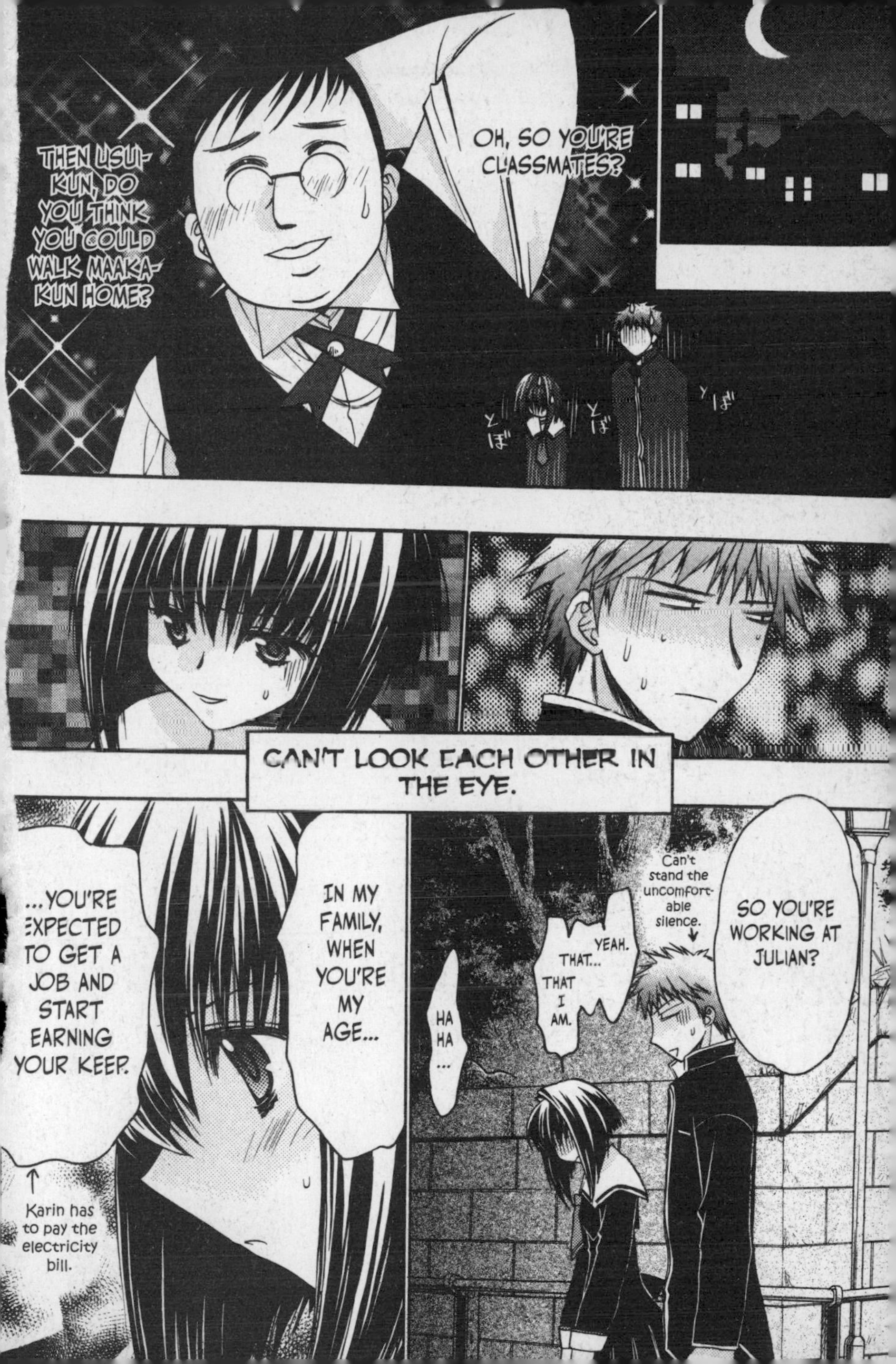
OH, SO YOU'RE CLASSMATES?
THEN USUI-KUN, DO YOU THINK YOU COULD WALK MAAKA-KUN HOME?
とぼ
とぼ
とぼ
CAN'T LOOK EACH OTHER IN THE EYE.
SO YOU'RE WORKING AT JULIAN?
Can't stand the uncomfortable silence.
YEAH. THAT... THAT I AM.
HA HA ...
IN MY FAMILY, WHEN YOU'RE MY AGE...
...YOU'RE EXPECTED TO GET A JOB AND START EARNING YOUR KEEP.
Karin has to pay the electricity bill.

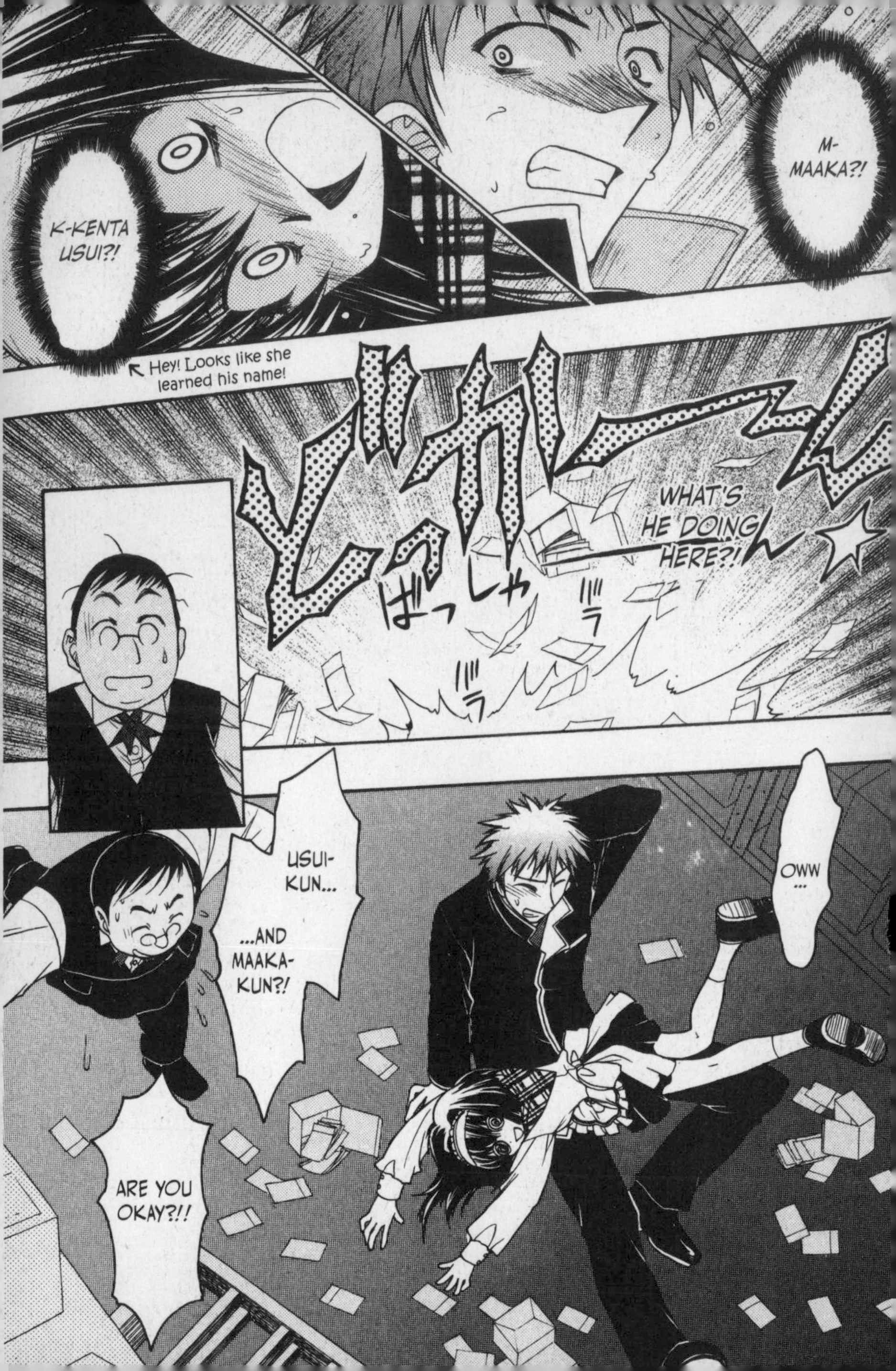
M-MAAKA?!
K-KENTA USUI?!
↖ Hey! Looks like she learned his name!
どっカーん
WHAT'S HE DOING HERE?!
ばっしゃ
ガラ
ガラ
OWW ...
USUI-KUN...
...AND MAAKA-KUN?!
ARE YOU OKAY?!!

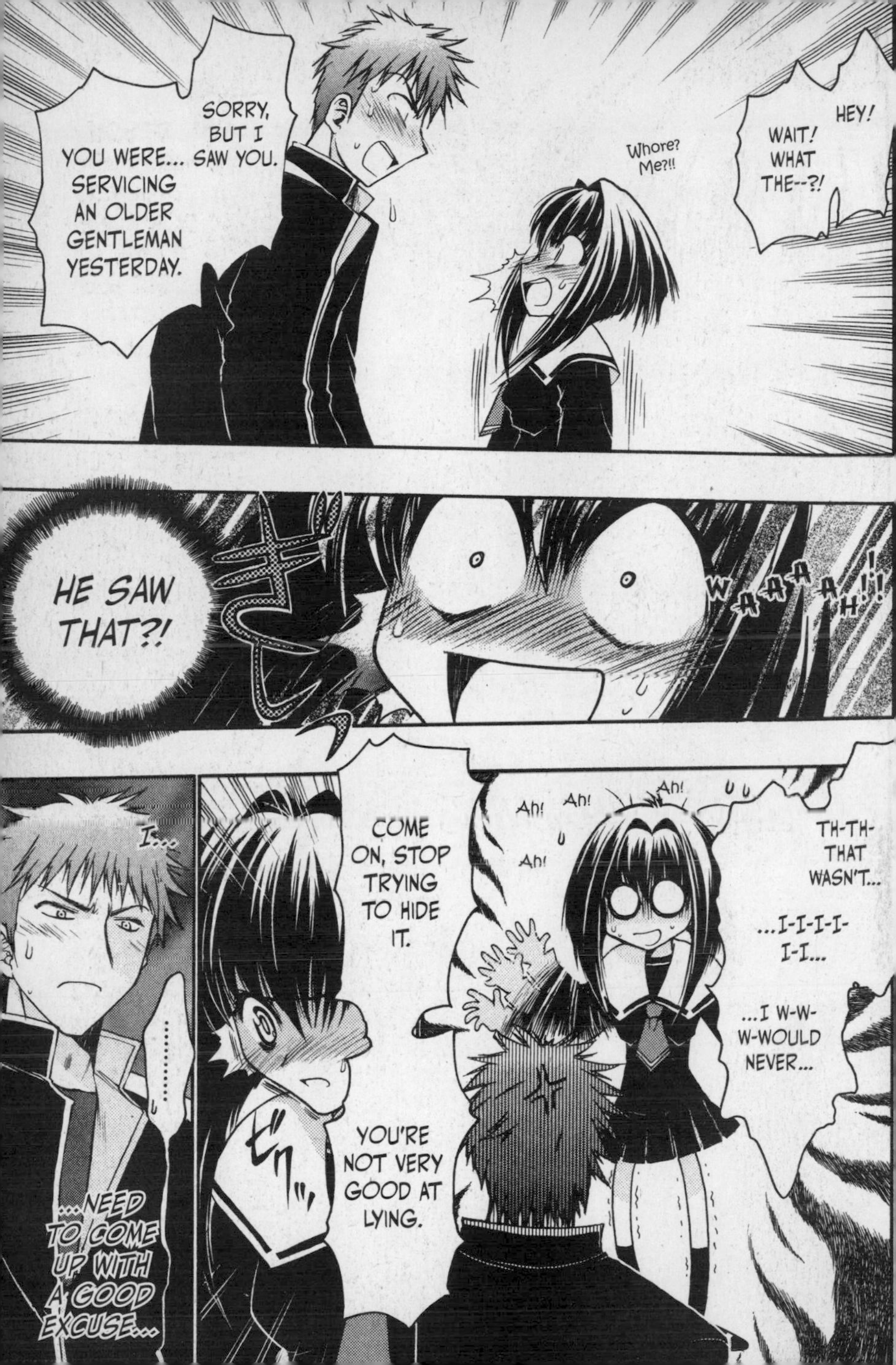
HEY! WAIT! WHAT THE--?!
Whore? Me?!!
SORRY, BUT I SAW YOU.
YOU WERE... SERVICING AN OLDER GENTLEMAN YESTERDAY.
WAAAAAH!!!
HE SAW THAT?!
TH-TH-THAT WASN'T...
...I-I-I-I-I-I...
...I W-W-W-WOULD NEVER...
Ah!
Ah!
Ah!
Ah!
COME ON, STOP TRYING TO HIDE IT.
YOU'RE NOT VERY GOOD AT LYING.
I...
......
...NEED TO COME UP WITH A GOOD EXCUSE...

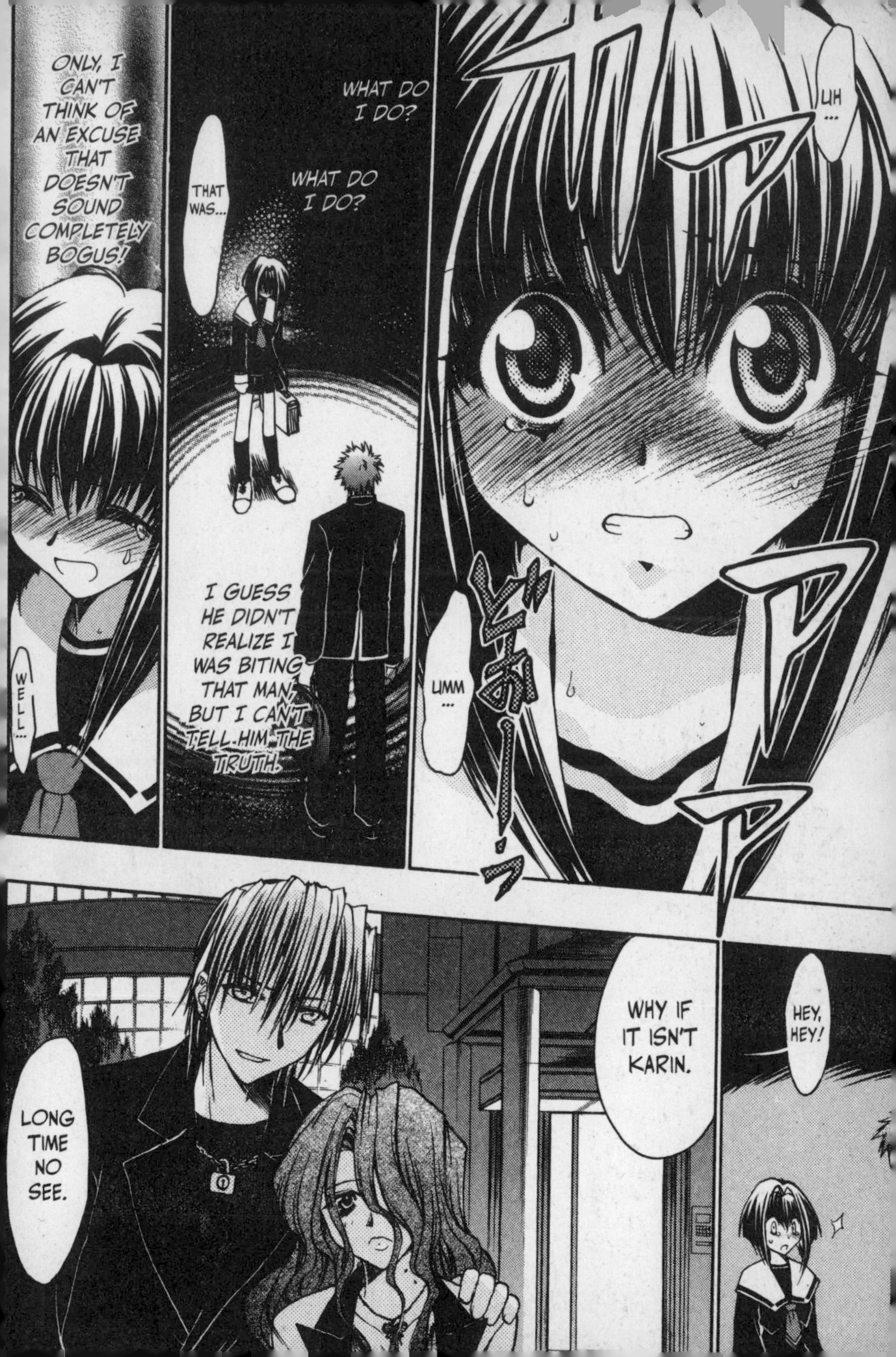
UH ...
UMM ...
WHAT DO I DO?
WHAT DO I DO?
THAT WAS...
I GUESS HE DIDN'T REALIZE I WAS BITING THAT MAN, BUT I CAN'T TELL HIM THE TRUTH.
ONLY, I CAN'T THINK OF AN EXCUSE THAT DOESN'T SOUND COMPLETELY BOGUS!
WELL...
HEY, HEY!
WHY IF IT ISN'T KARIN.
LONG TIME NO SEE.

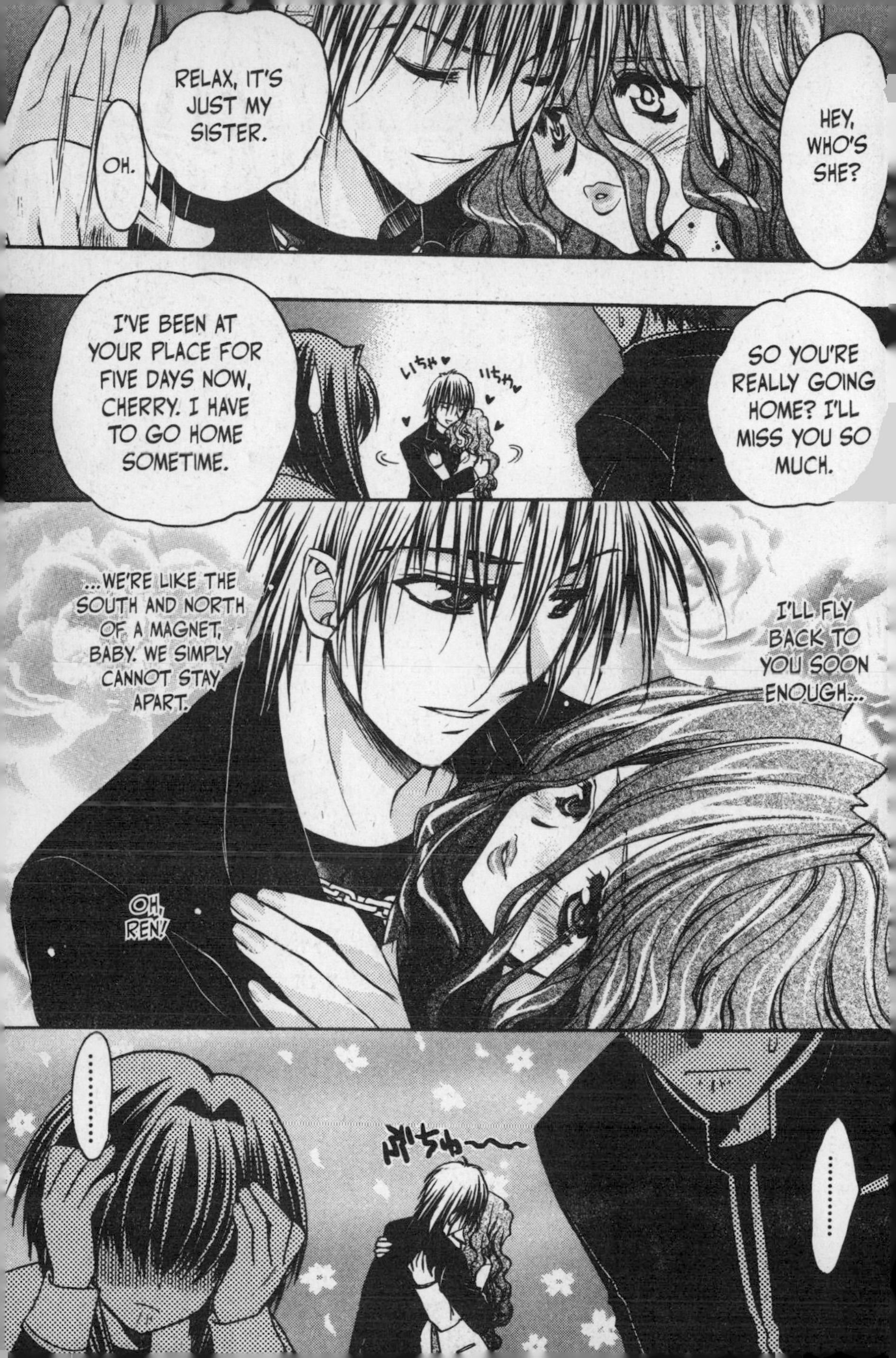
HEY, WHO'S SHE?
RELAX, IT'S JUST MY SISTER.
OH.
SO YOU'RE REALLY GOING HOME? I'LL MISS YOU SO MUCH.
いちゃ
いちゃ
I'VE BEEN AT YOUR PLACE FOR FIVE DAYS NOW, CHERRY. I HAVE TO GO HOME SOMETIME.
I'LL FLY BACK TO YOU SOON ENOUGH...
...WE'RE LIKE THE SOUTH AND NORTH OF A MAGNET, BABY. WE SIMPLY CANNOT STAY APART.
OH, REN!
......
......

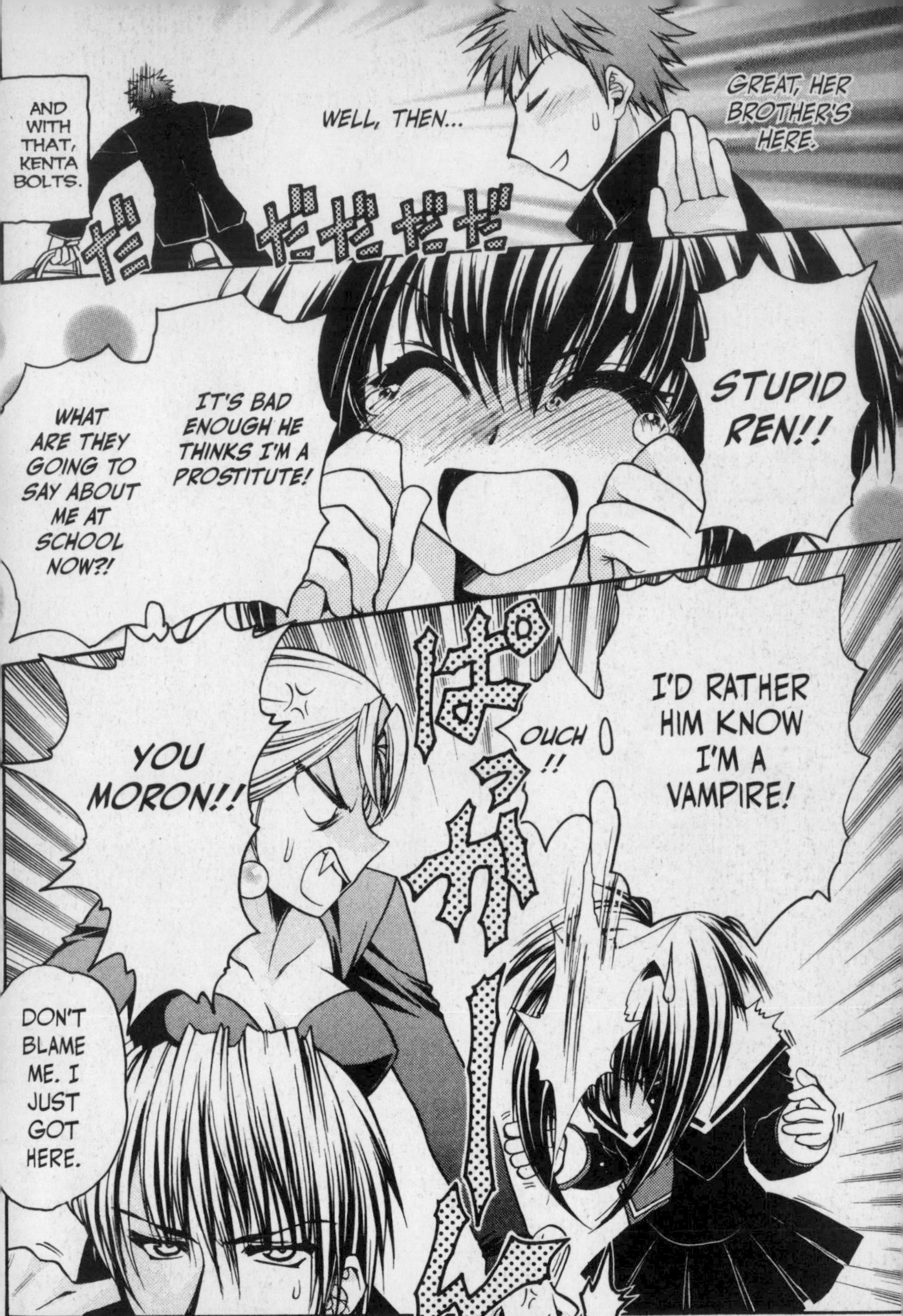
GREAT, HER BROTHER'S HERE.
WELL, THEN...
AND WITH THAT, KENTA BOLTS.
STUPID REN!!
IT'S BAD ENOUGH HE THINKS I'M A PROSTITUTE!
WHAT ARE THEY GOING TO SAY ABOUT ME AT SCHOOL NOW?!
I'D RATHER HIM KNOW I'M A VAMPIRE!
OUCH!!
YOU MORON!!
DON'T BLAME ME. I JUST GOT HERE.

2ND EMBARRASSMENT END

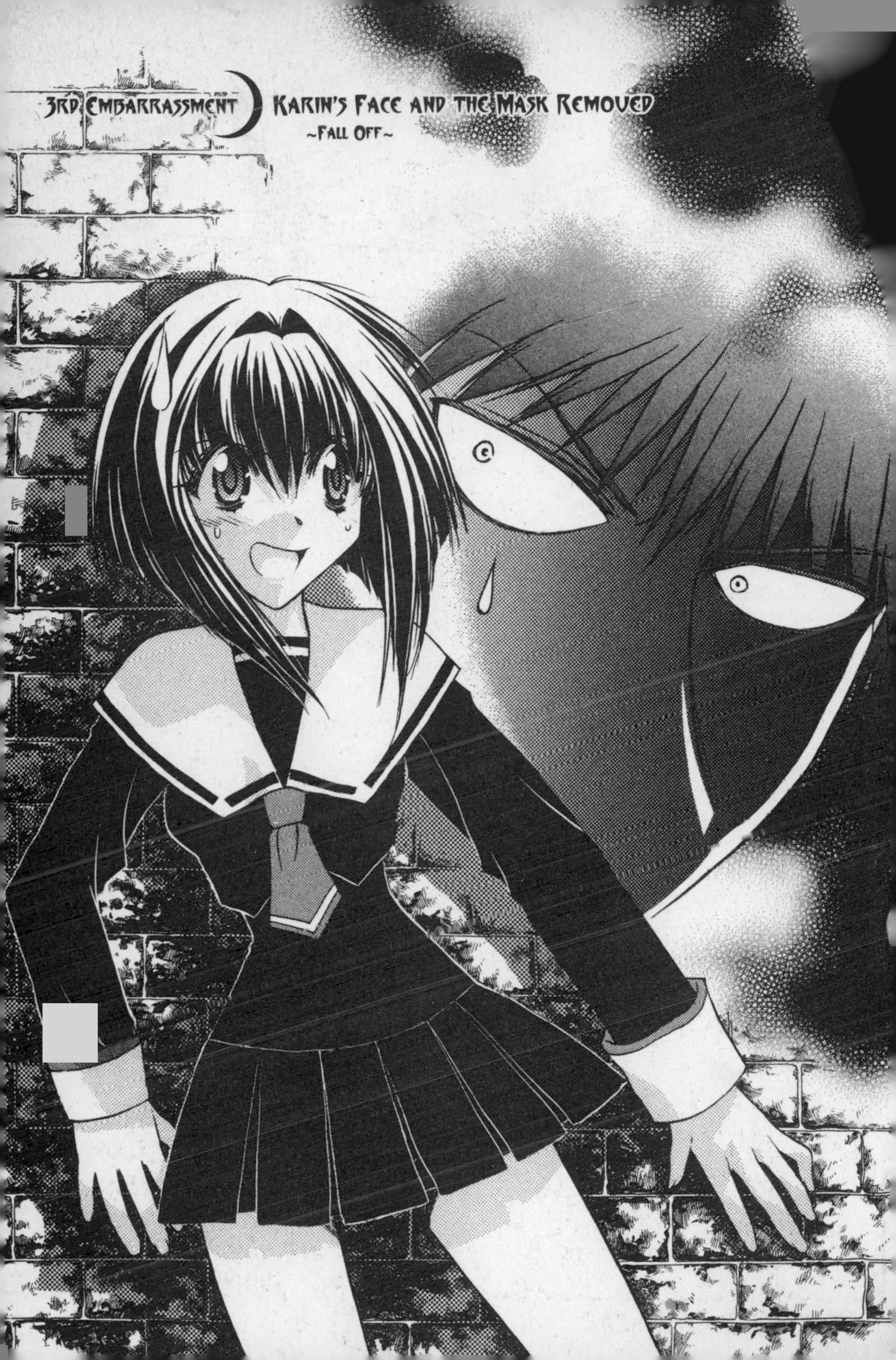
3rd Embarrassment
Karin's Face and the Mask Removed
~Fall Off~

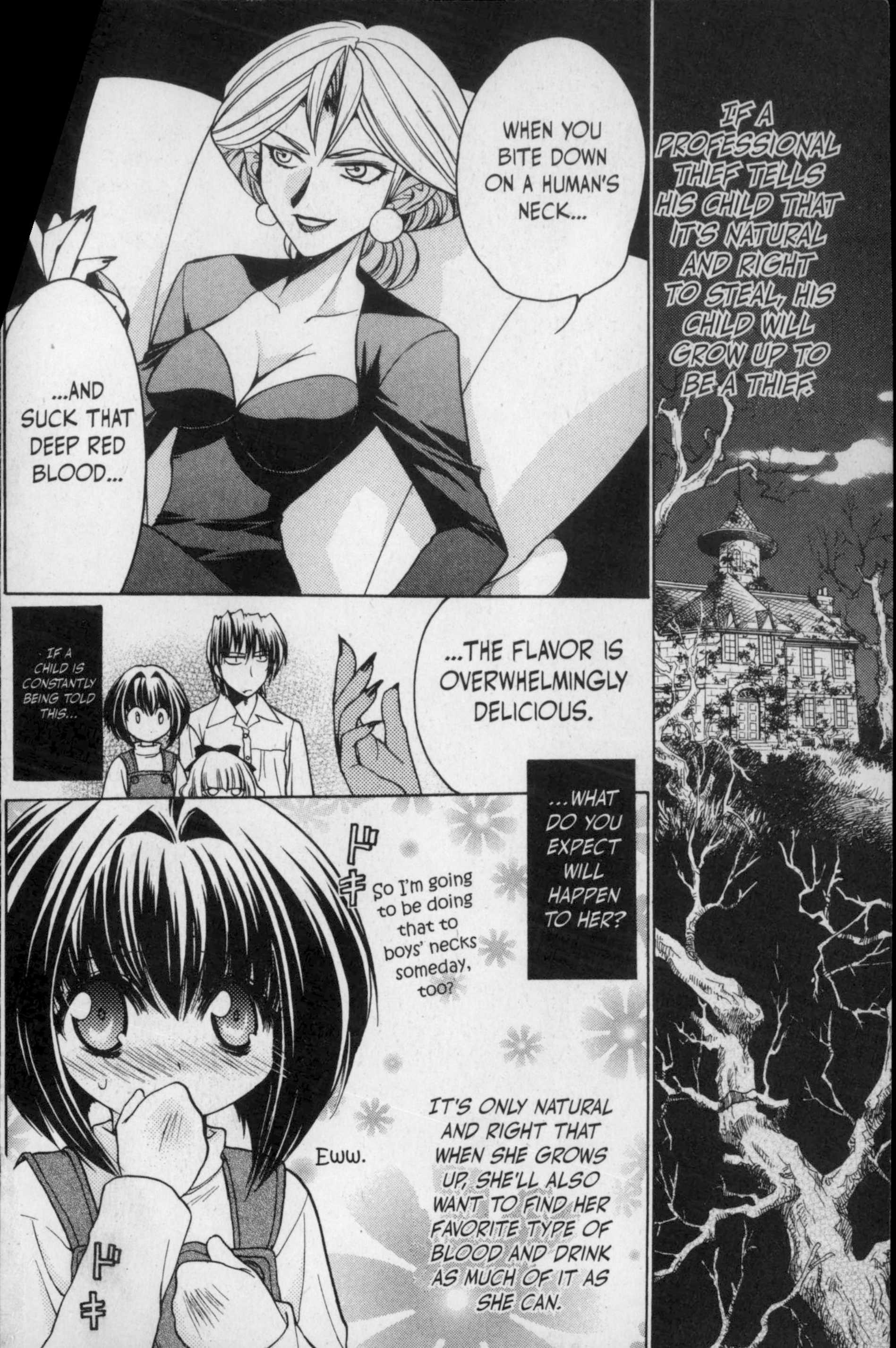
IF A PROFESSIONAL THIEF TELLS HIS CHILD THAT IT'S NATURAL AND RIGHT TO STEAL, HIS CHILD WILL GROW UP TO BE A THIEF.
WHEN YOU BITE DOWN ON A HUMAN'S NECK...
...AND SUCK THAT DEEP RED BLOOD...
...THE FLAVOR IS OVERWHELMINGLY DELICIOUS.
IF A CHILD IS CONSTANTLY BEING TOLD THIS...
...WHAT DO YOU EXPECT WILL HAPPEN TO HER?
ドキ
So I'm going to be doing that to boys' necks someday, too?
IT'S ONLY NATURAL AND RIGHT THAT WHEN SHE GROWS UP, SHE'LL ALSO WANT TO FIND HER FAVORITE TYPE OF BLOOD AND DRINK AS MUCH OF IT AS SHE CAN.
Eww.
ドキ

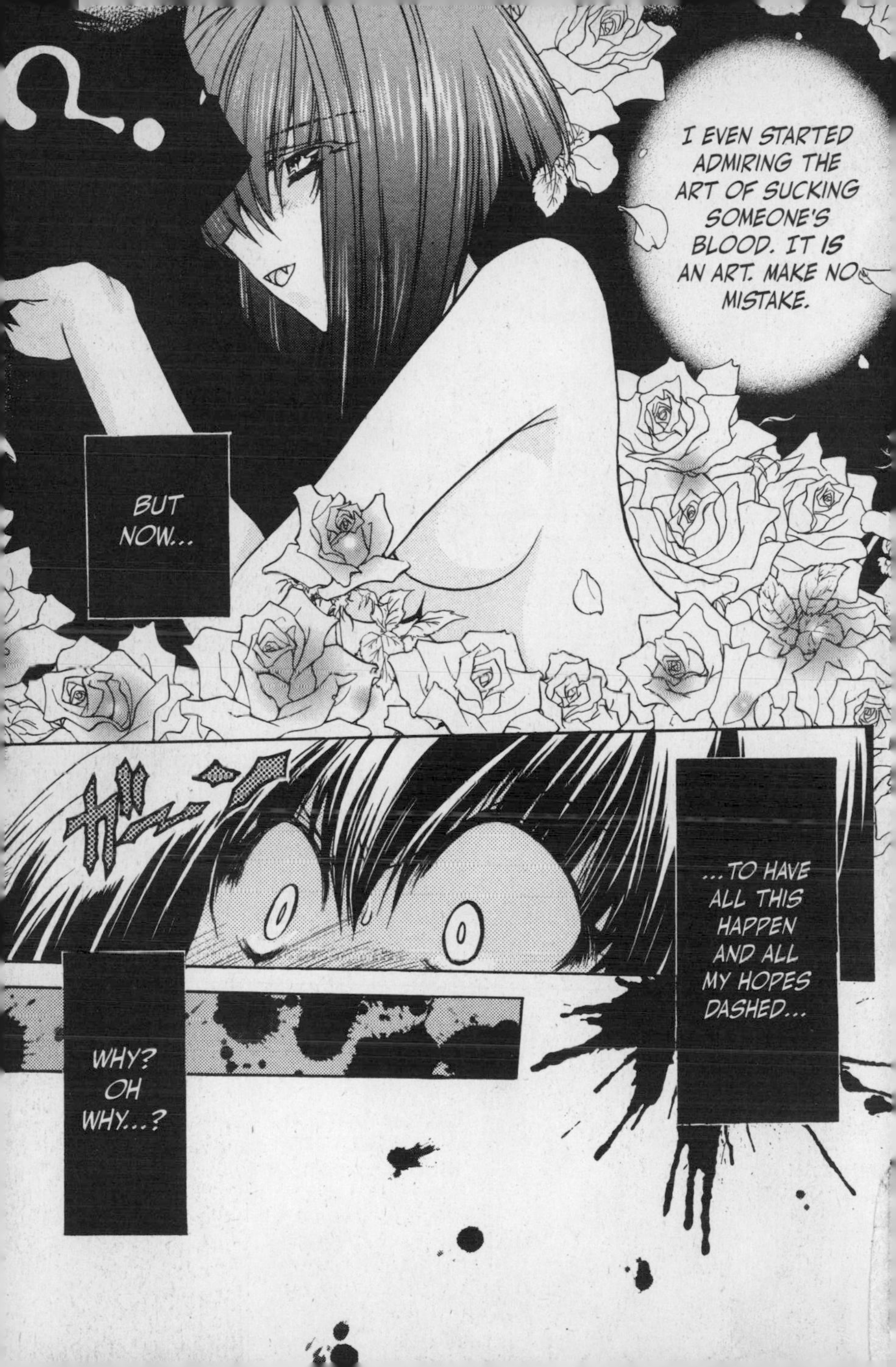
I EVEN STARTED ADMIRING THE ART OF SUCKING SOMEONE'S BLOOD. IT IS AN ART. MAKE NO MISTAKE.
BUT NOW...
...TO HAVE ALL THIS HAPPEN AND ALL MY HOPES DASHED...
WHY? OH WHY...?

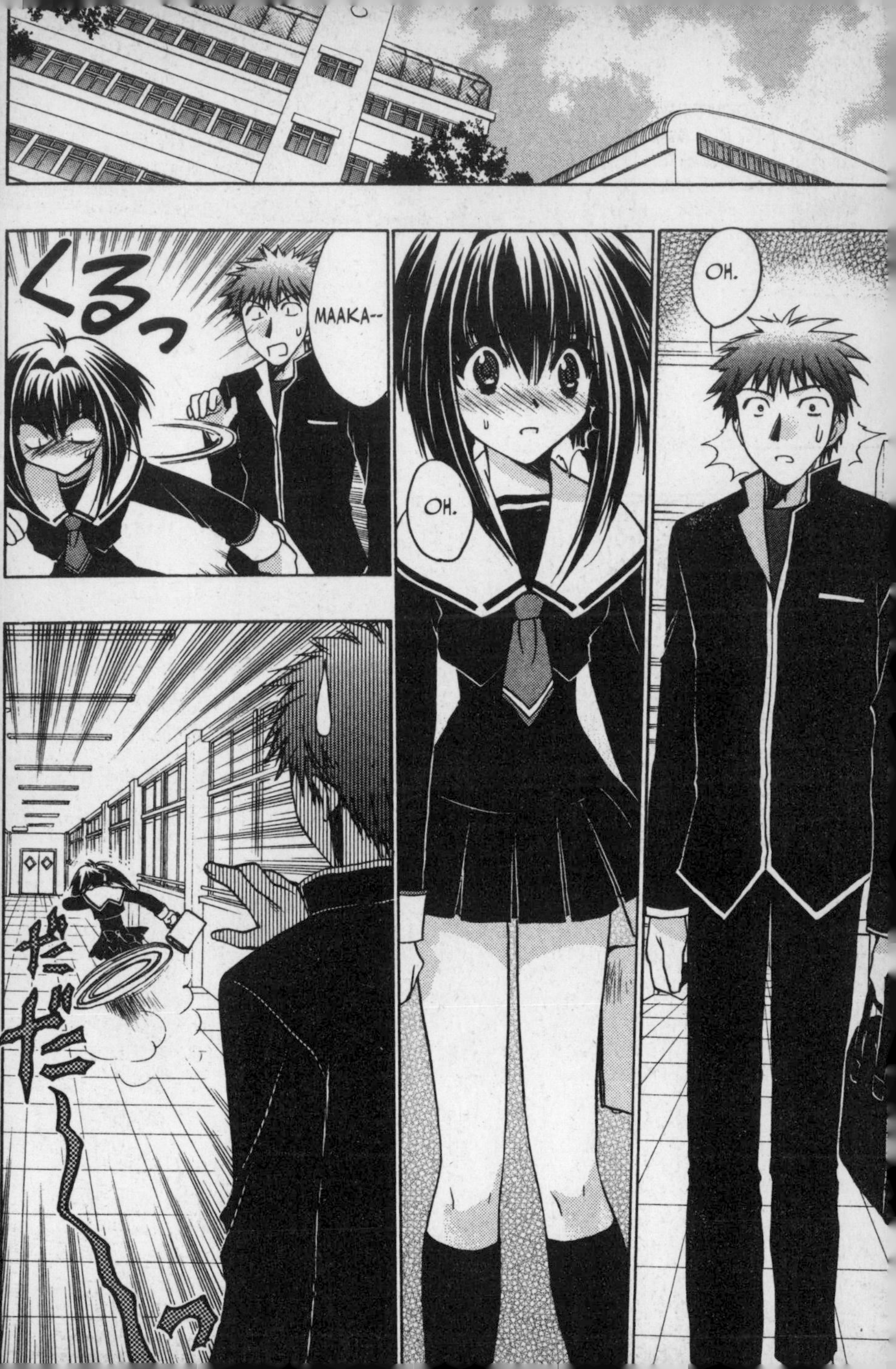
OH.
OH.
くるっ
MAAKA--
ダダーっ

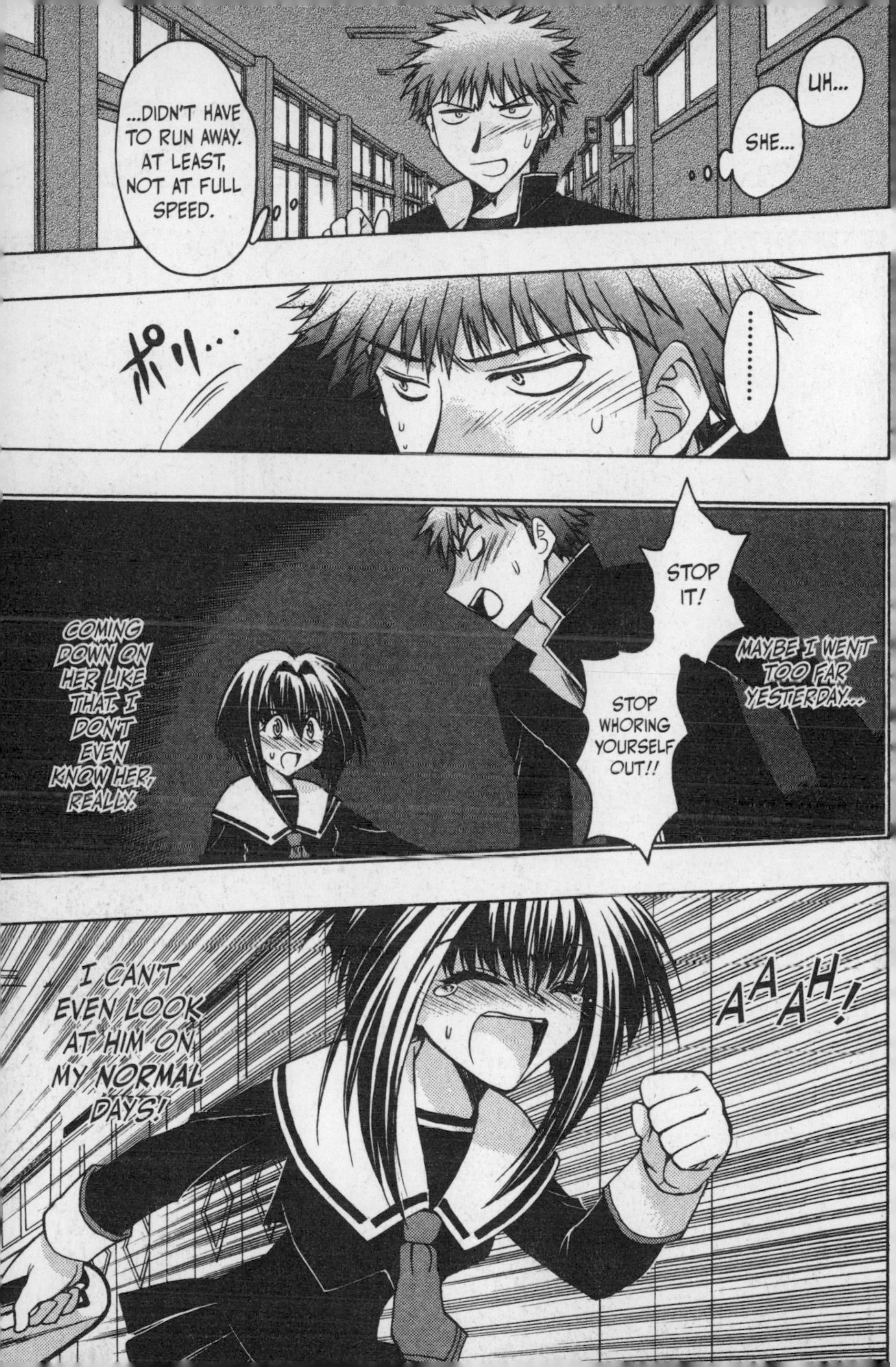
UH...
SHE...
...DIDN'T HAVE TO RUN AWAY. AT LEAST, NOT AT FULL SPEED.
......
ポリ…
MAYBE I WENT TOO FAR YESTERDAY...
STOP IT!
STOP WHORING YOURSELF OUT!!
COMING DOWN ON HER LIKE THAT. I DON'T EVEN KNOW HER, REALLY.
AAAH!
I CAN'T EVEN LOOK AT HIM ON MY NORMAL DAYS!

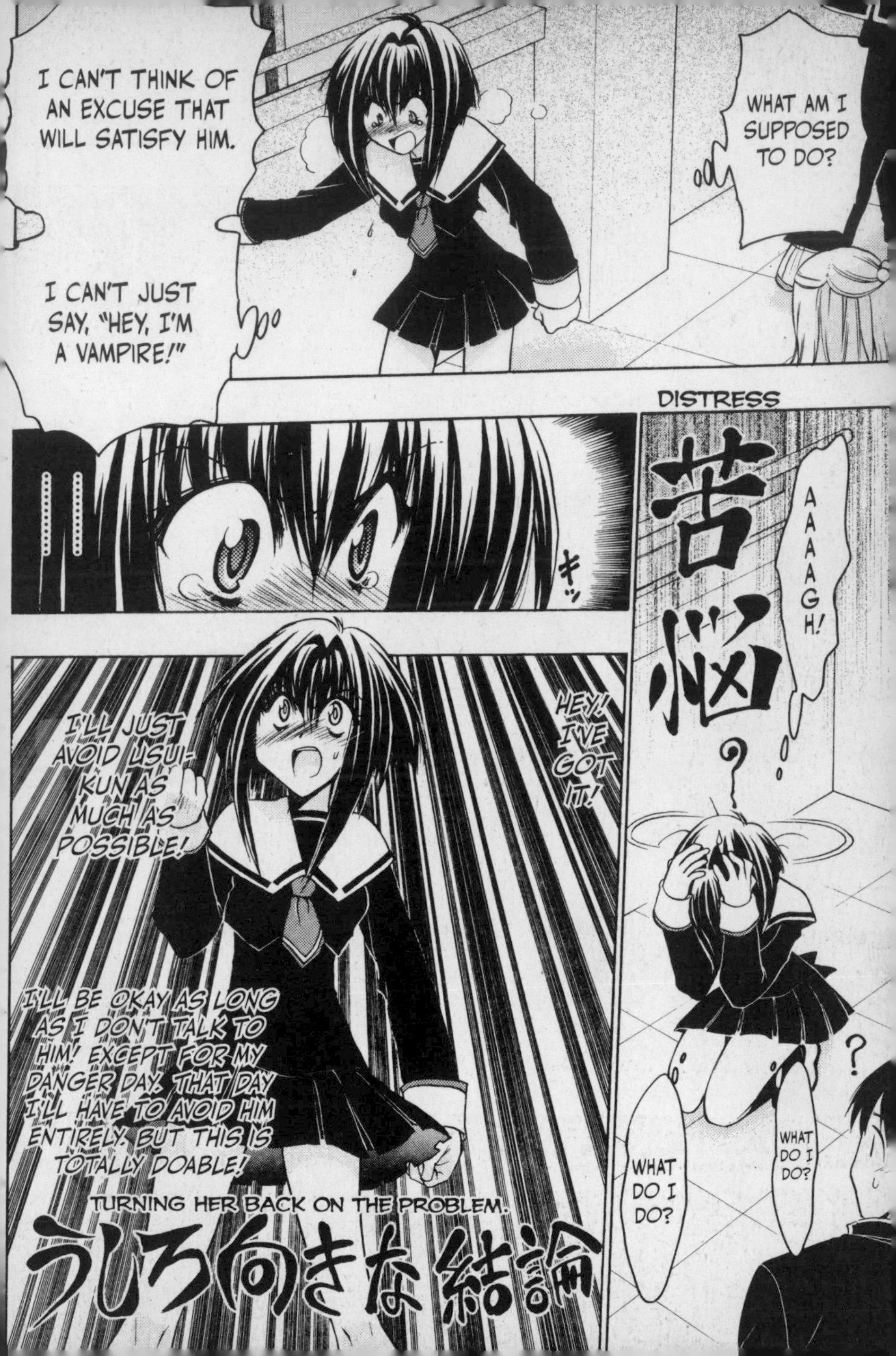
WHAT AM I SUPPOSED TO DO?
I CAN'T THINK OF AN EXCUSE THAT WILL SATISFY HIM.
I CAN'T JUST SAY, "HEY, I'M A VAMPIRE!"
DISTRESS
苦悩
AAAAGH!
?
WHAT DO I DO?
WHAT DO I DO?
?
キッ
HEY! I'VE GOT IT!
I'LL JUST AVOID USUI-KUN AS MUCH AS POSSIBLE!
I'LL BE OKAY AS LONG AS I DON'T TALK TO HIM! EXCEPT FOR MY DANGER DAY. THAT DAY I'LL HAVE TO AVOID HIM ENTIRELY. BUT THIS IS TOTALLY DOABLE!
TURNING HER BACK ON THE PROBLEM.
うしろ向きな結論

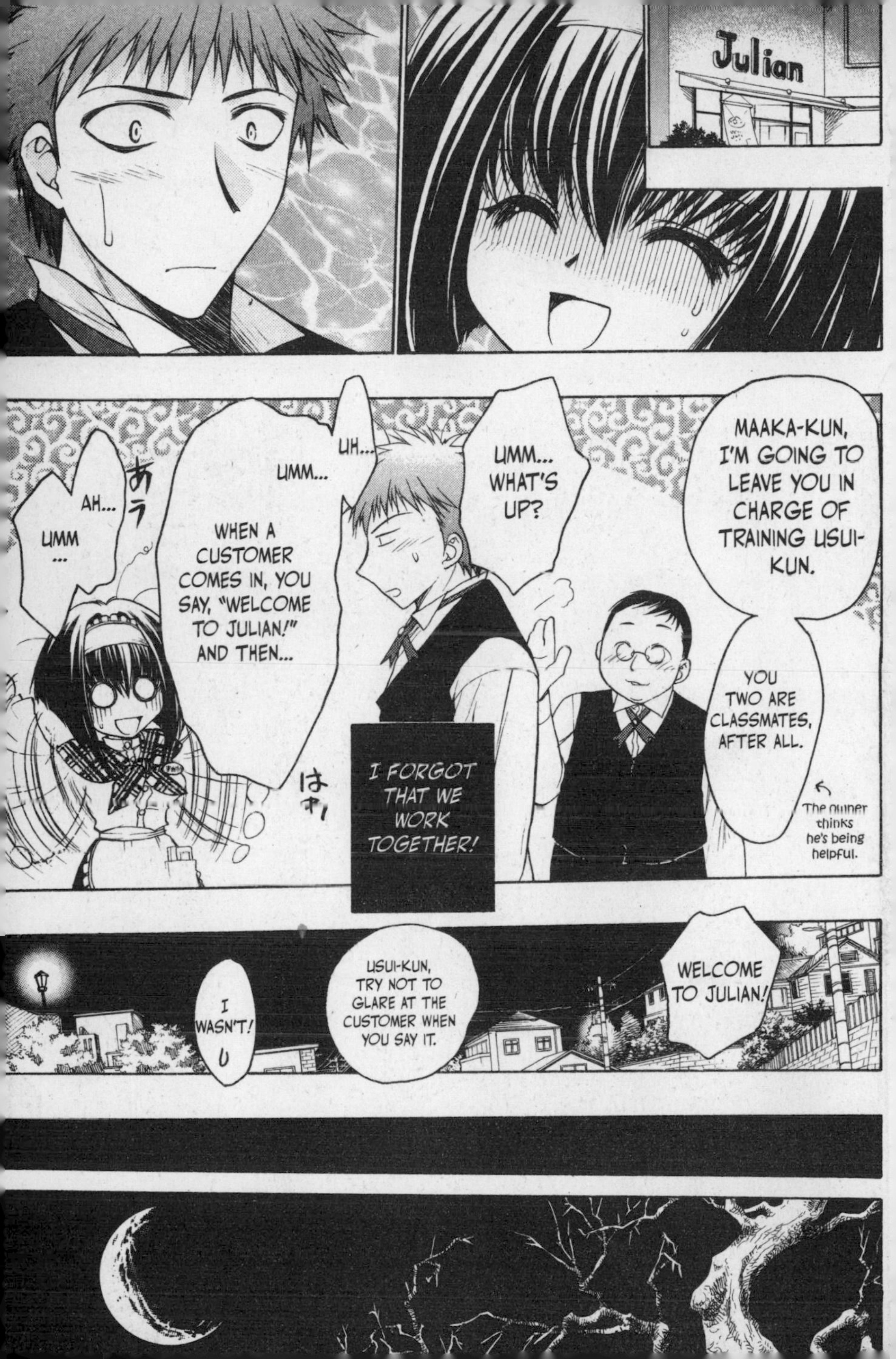
Julian
MAAKA-KUN, I'M GOING TO LEAVE YOU IN CHARGE OF TRAINING USUI-KUN.
YOU TWO ARE CLASSMATES, AFTER ALL.
The owner thinks he's being helpful.
UMM... WHAT'S UP?
UH...
UMM...
WHEN A CUSTOMER COMES IN, YOU SAY, "WELCOME TO JULIAN!" AND THEN...
AH... UMM...
あラ
I FORGOT THAT WE WORK TOGETHER!
はッ
WELCOME TO JULIAN!
USUI-KUN, TRY NOT TO GLARE AT THE CUSTOMER WHEN YOU SAY IT.
I WASN'T!

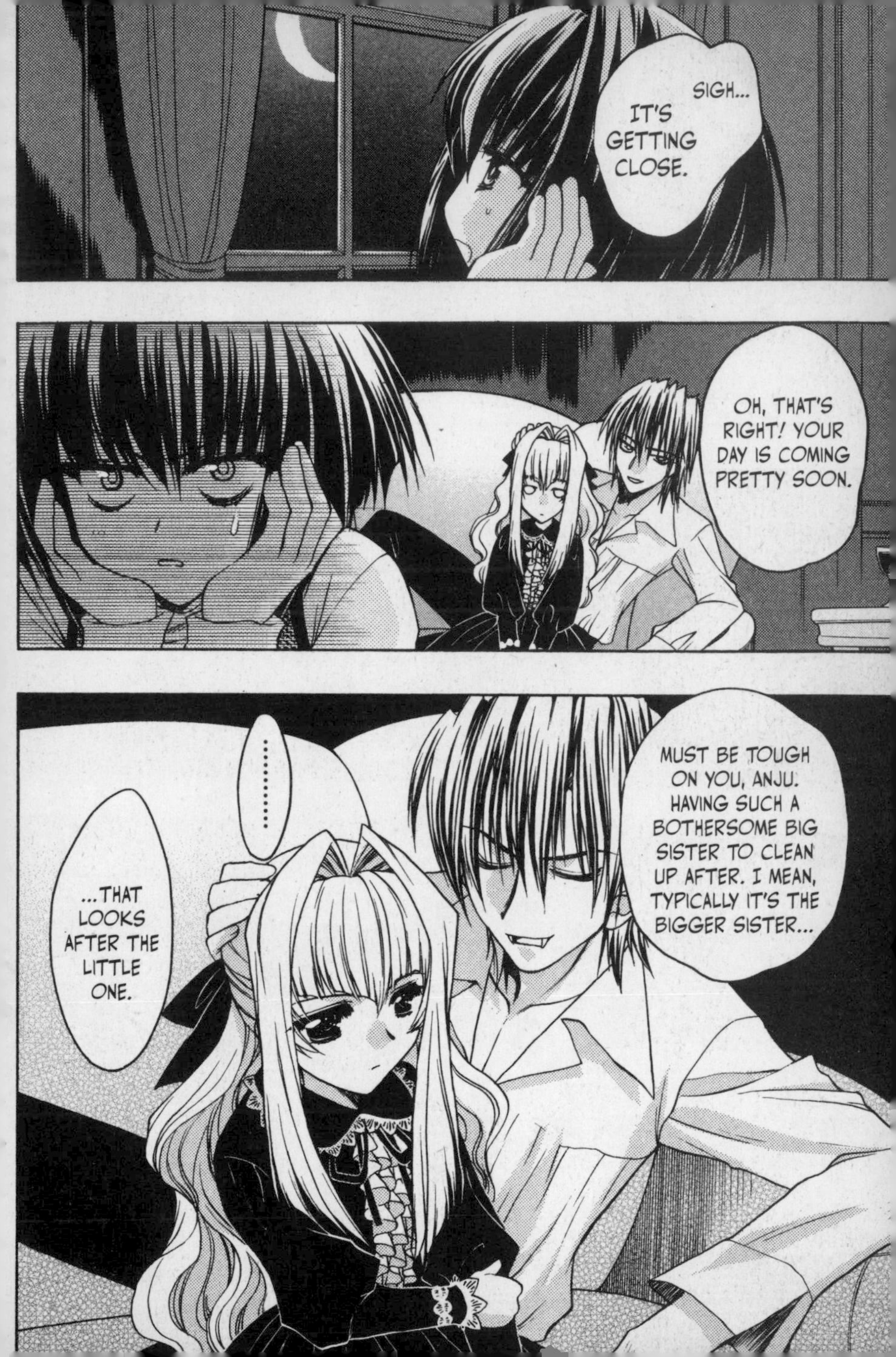
SIGH... IT'S GETTING CLOSE.
OH, THAT'S RIGHT! YOUR DAY IS COMING PRETTY SOON.
MUST BE TOUGH ON YOU, ANJU. HAVING SUCH A BOTHERSOME BIG SISTER TO CLEAN UP AFTER. I MEAN, TYPICALLY IT'S THE BIGGER SISTER...
.........
...THAT LOOKS AFTER THE LITTLE ONE.

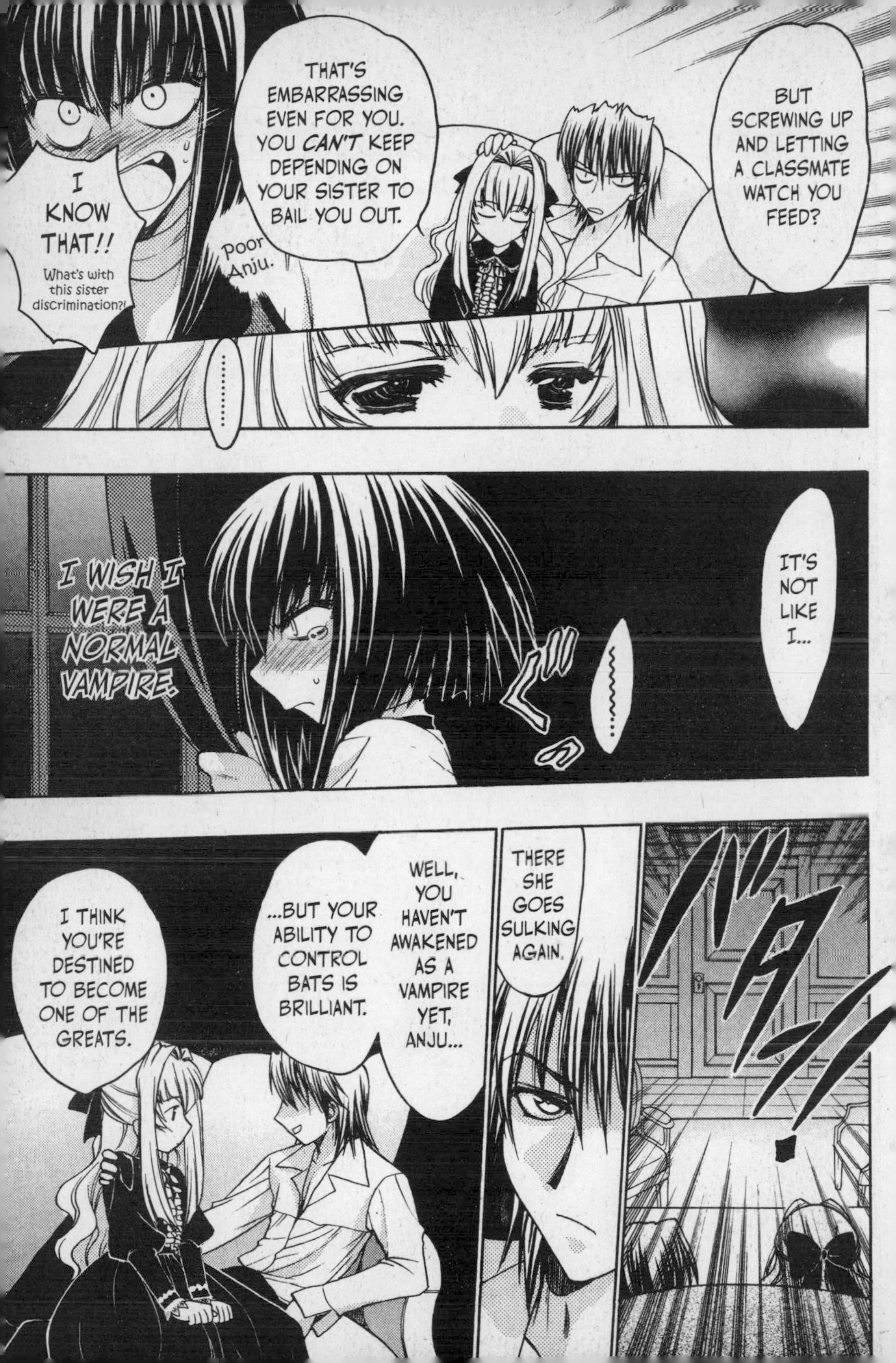
BUT SCREWING UP AND LETTING A CLASSMATE WATCH YOU FEED?
THAT'S EMBARRASSING EVEN FOR YOU. YOU *CAN'T* KEEP DEPENDING ON YOUR SISTER TO BAIL YOU OUT.
Poor Anju.
I KNOW THAT!!
What's with this sister discrimination?!
......
IT'S NOT LIKE I...
......
I WISH I WERE A NORMAL VAMPIRE.
THERE SHE GOES SULKING AGAIN.
WELL, YOU HAVEN'T AWAKENED AS A VAMPIRE YET, ANJU...
...BUT YOUR ABILITY TO CONTROL BATS IS BRILLIANT.
I THINK YOU'RE DESTINED TO BECOME ONE OF THE GREATS.

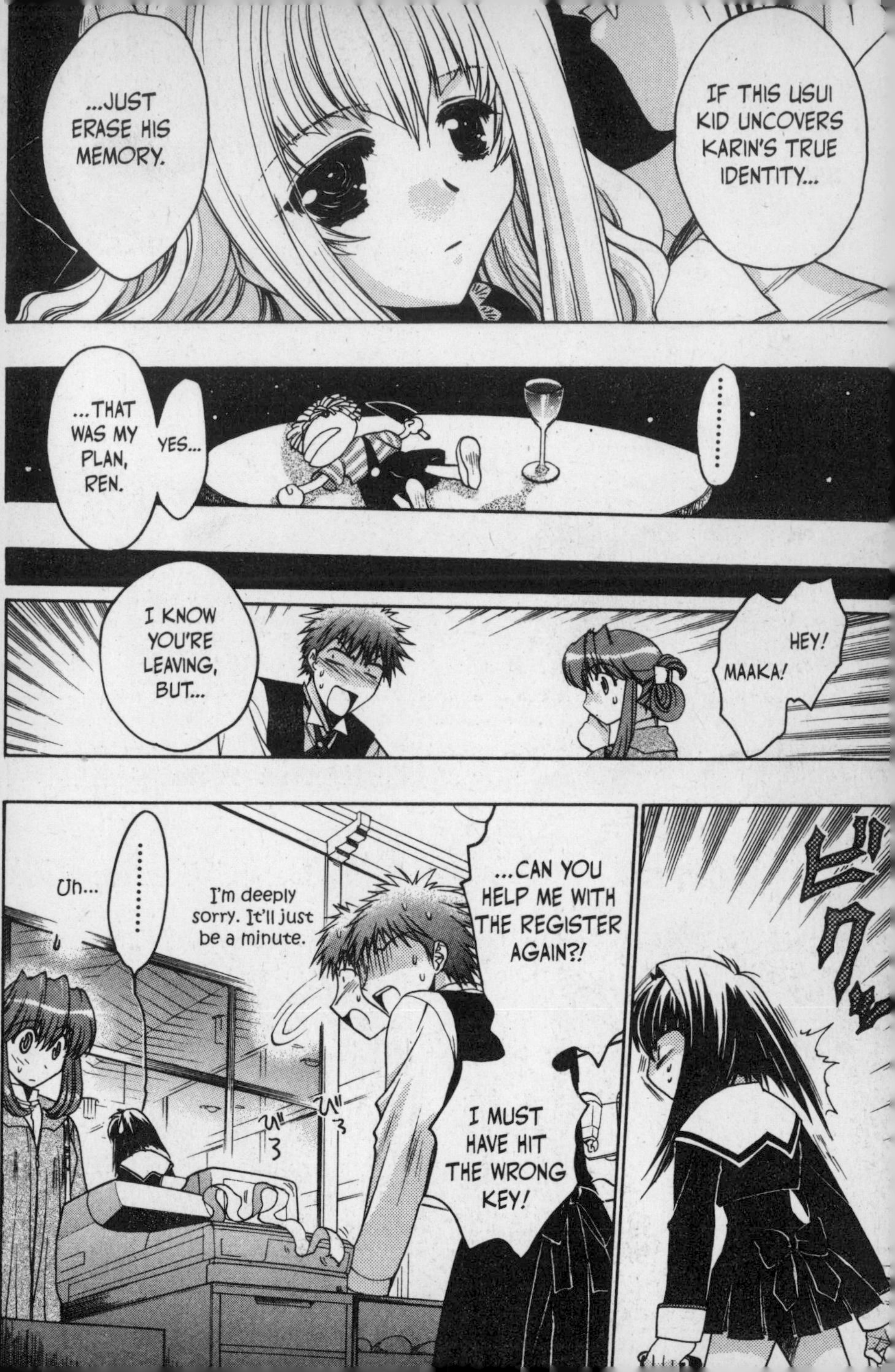

IF THIS USUI KID UNCOVERS KARIN'S TRUE IDENTITY...
...JUST ERASE HIS MEMORY.
........
YES...
...THAT WAS MY PLAN, REN.
HEY! MAAKA!
I KNOW YOU'RE LEAVING, BUT...
ビクッ
...CAN YOU HELP ME WITH THE REGISTER AGAIN?!
I MUST HAVE HIT THE WRONG KEY!
I'm deeply sorry. It'll just be a minute.
........
Uh...

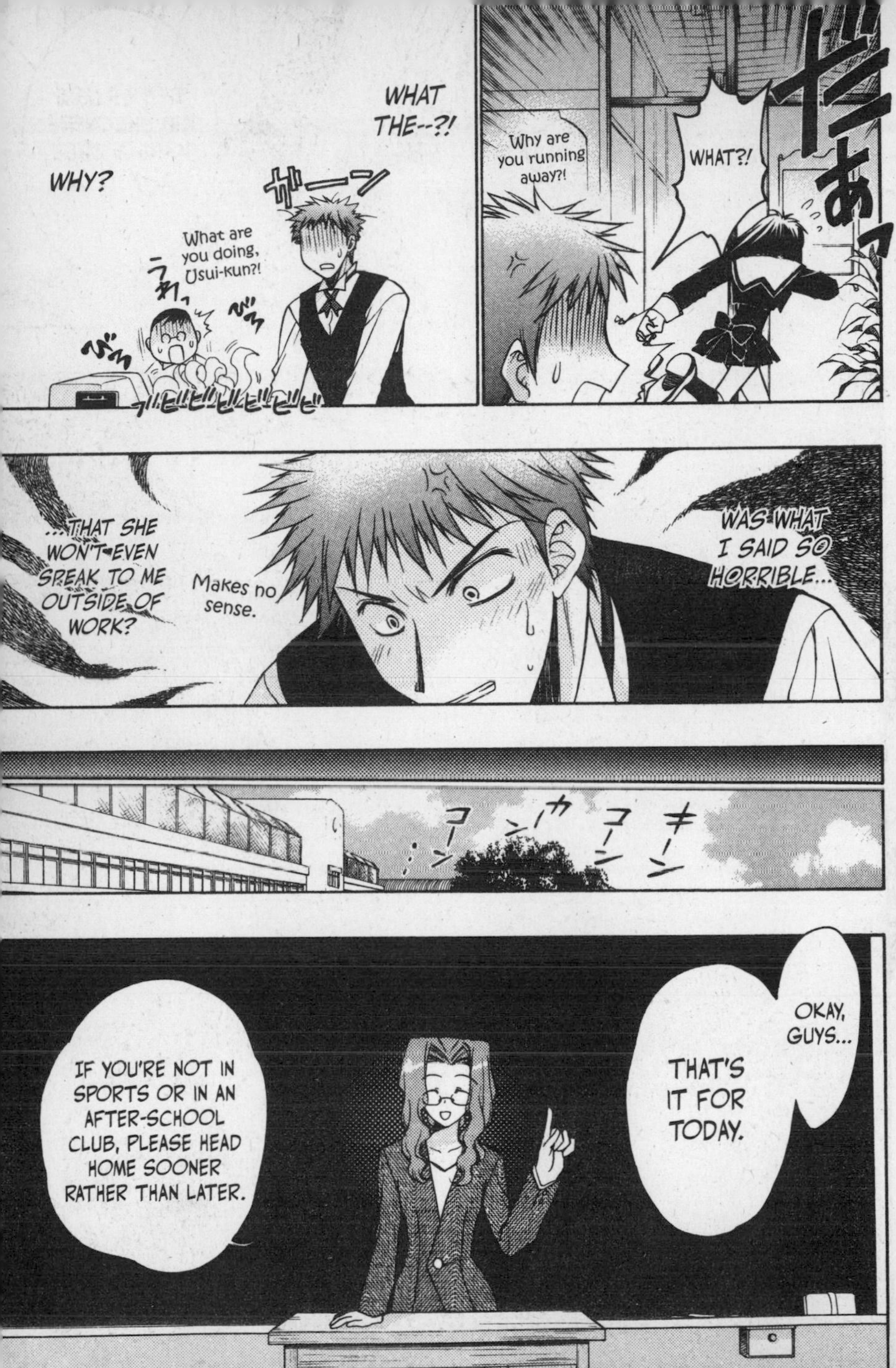
WHAT?!
Why are you running away?!
What are you doing, Usui-kun?!
WHAT THE--?!
WHY?
WAS WHAT I SAID SO HORRIBLE...
Makes no sense.
...THAT SHE WON'T EVEN SPEAK TO ME OUTSIDE OF WORK?
OKAY, GUYS...
THAT'S IT FOR TODAY.
IF YOU'RE NOT IN SPORTS OR IN AN AFTER-SCHOOL CLUB, PLEASE HEAD HOME SOONER RATHER THAN LATER.

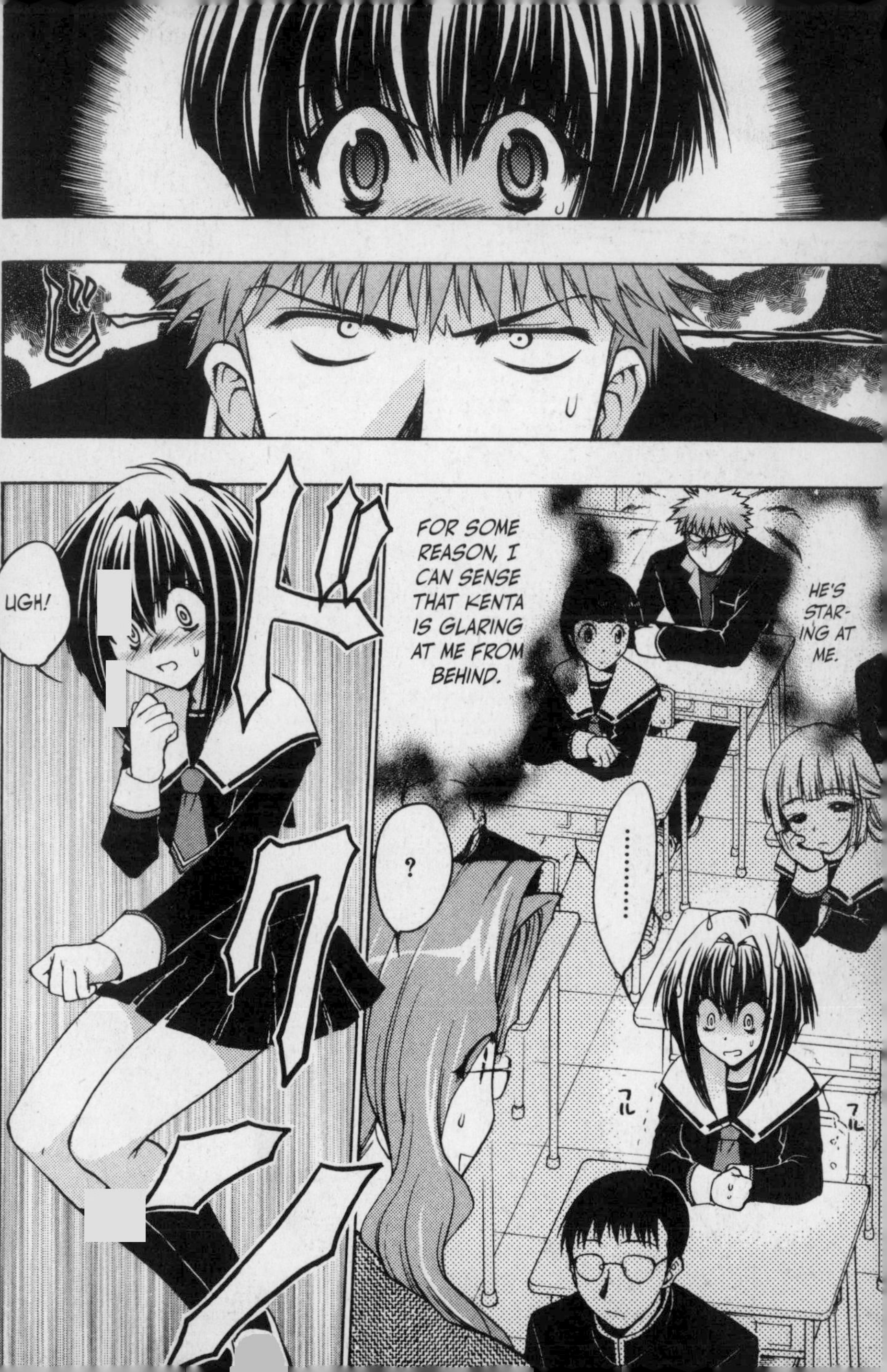
HE'S STARING AT ME.
FOR SOME REASON, I CAN SENSE THAT KENTA IS GLARING AT ME FROM BEHIND.
UGH!
......
?

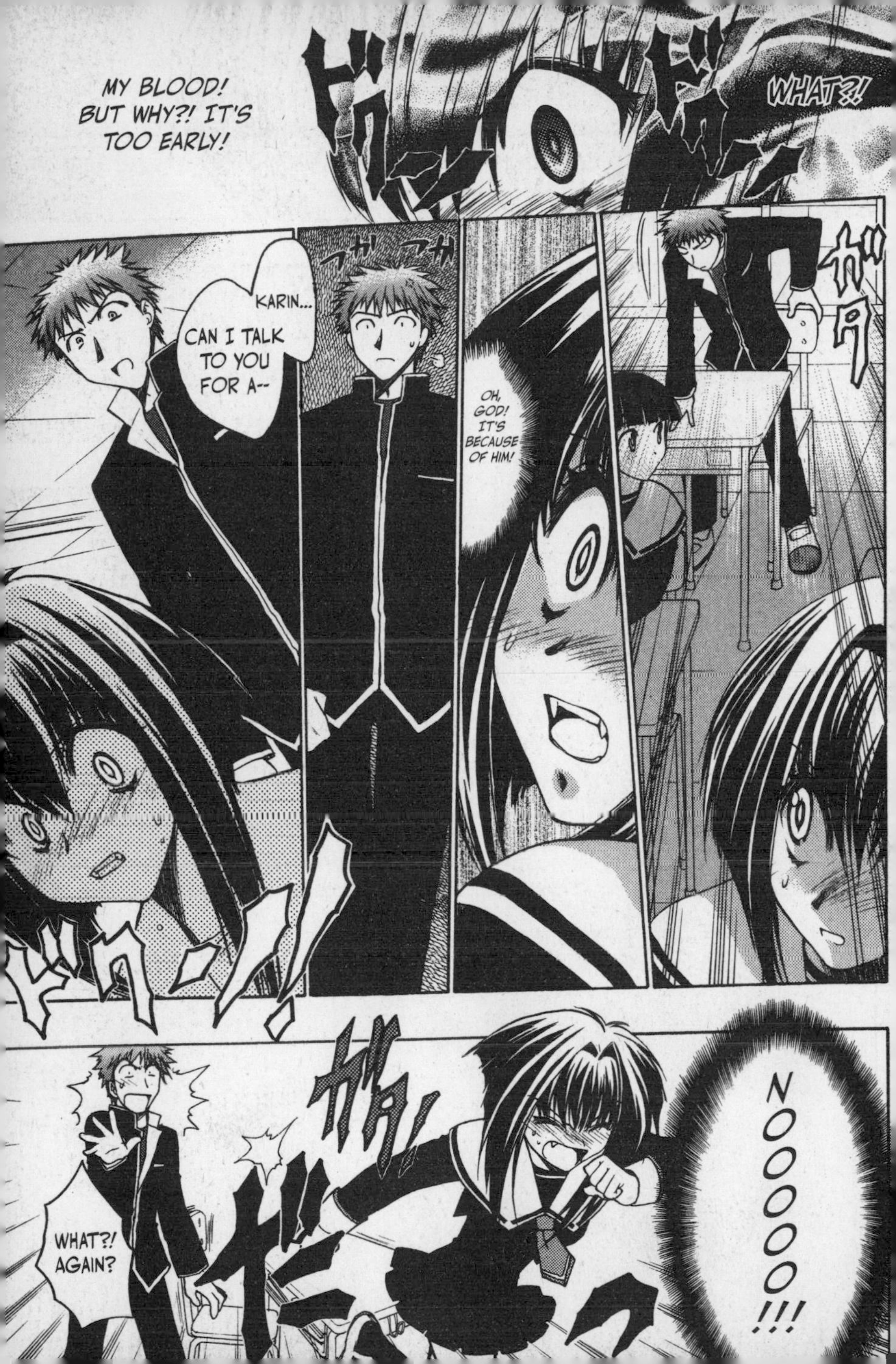
WHAT?!
MY BLOOD! BUT WHY?! IT'S TOO EARLY!
OH, GOD! IT'S BECAUSE OF HIM!
KARIN...
CAN I TALK TO YOU FOR A--
NOOOOOO!!!
WHAT?! AGAIN?

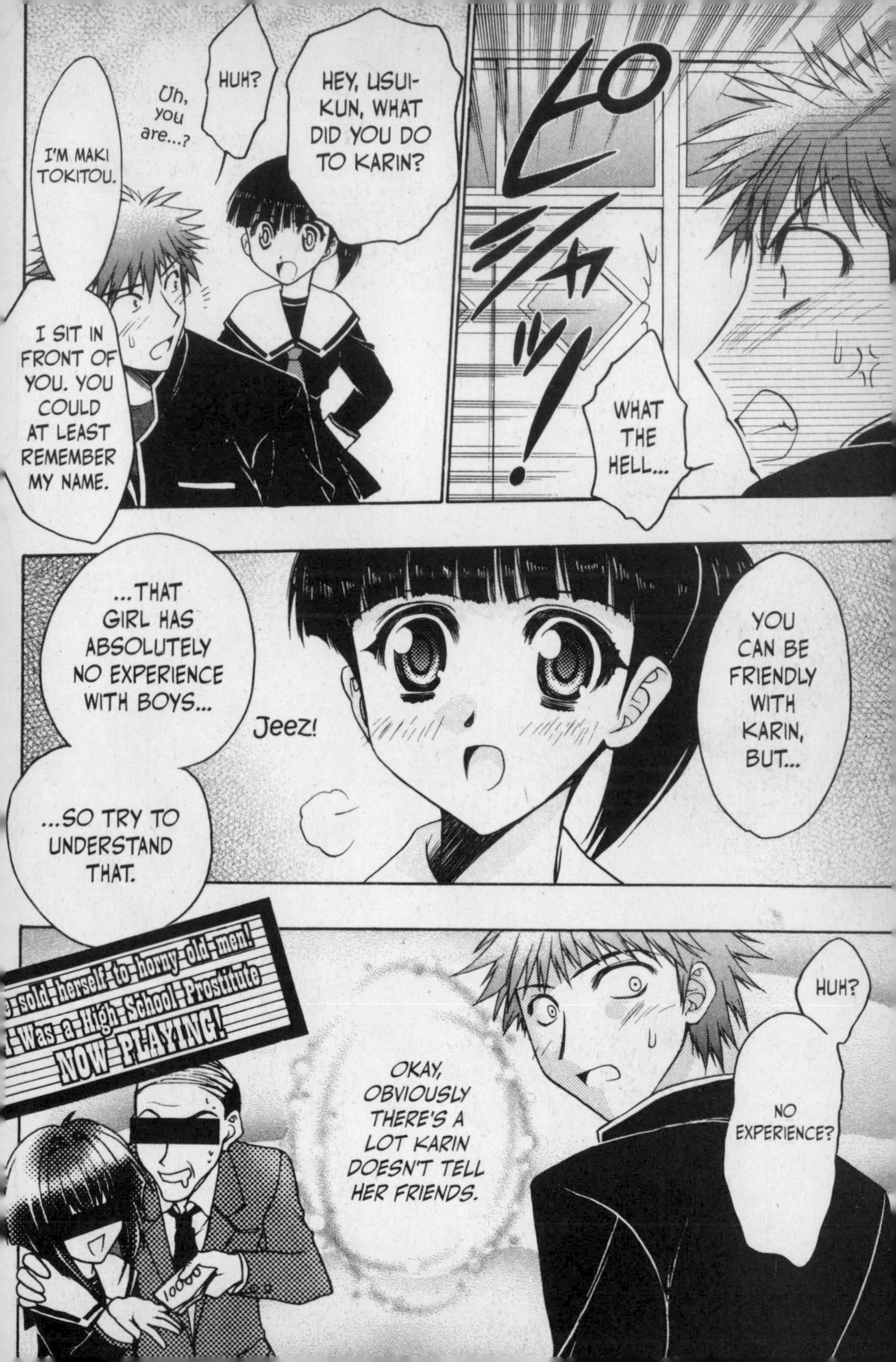
ピシャッ!
WHAT THE HELL...
HEY, USUI-KUN, WHAT DID YOU DO TO KARIN?
HUH?
Uh, you are...?
I'M MAKI TOKITOU.
I SIT IN FRONT OF YOU. YOU COULD AT LEAST REMEMBER MY NAME.
YOU CAN BE FRIENDLY WITH KARIN, BUT...
...THAT GIRL HAS ABSOLUTELY NO EXPERIENCE WITH BOYS...
Jeez!
...SO TRY TO UNDERSTAND THAT.
HUH?
NO EXPERIENCE?
OKAY, OBVIOUSLY THERE'S A LOT KARIN DOESN'T TELL HER FRIENDS.
sold herself to horny old men!
Was a High School Prostitute
NOW PLAYING!

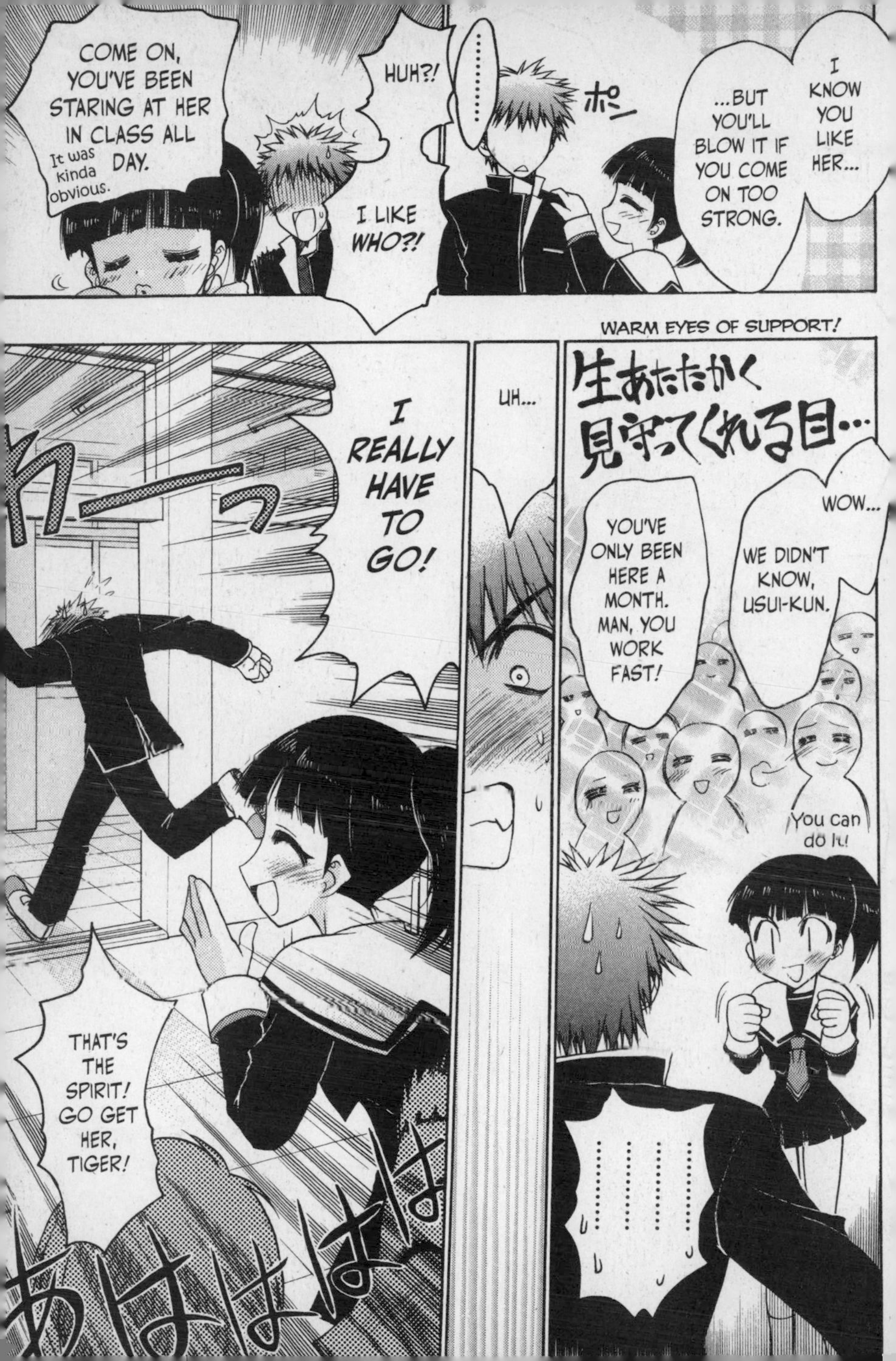
I KNOW YOU LIKE HER...
...BUT YOU'LL BLOW IT IF YOU COME ON TOO STRONG.
ポン
......
HUH?!
I LIKE WHO?!
COME ON, YOU'VE BEEN STARING AT HER IN CLASS ALL DAY.
It was kinda obvious.
WARM EYES OF SUPPORT!
生あたたかく見守ってくれる目…
WOW...
WE DIDN'T KNOW, USUI-KUN.
YOU'VE ONLY BEEN HERE A MONTH. MAN, YOU WORK FAST!
You can do it!
............
UH...
I REALLY HAVE TO GO!
わーっ
THAT'S THE SPIRIT! GO GET HER, TIGER!
あははは

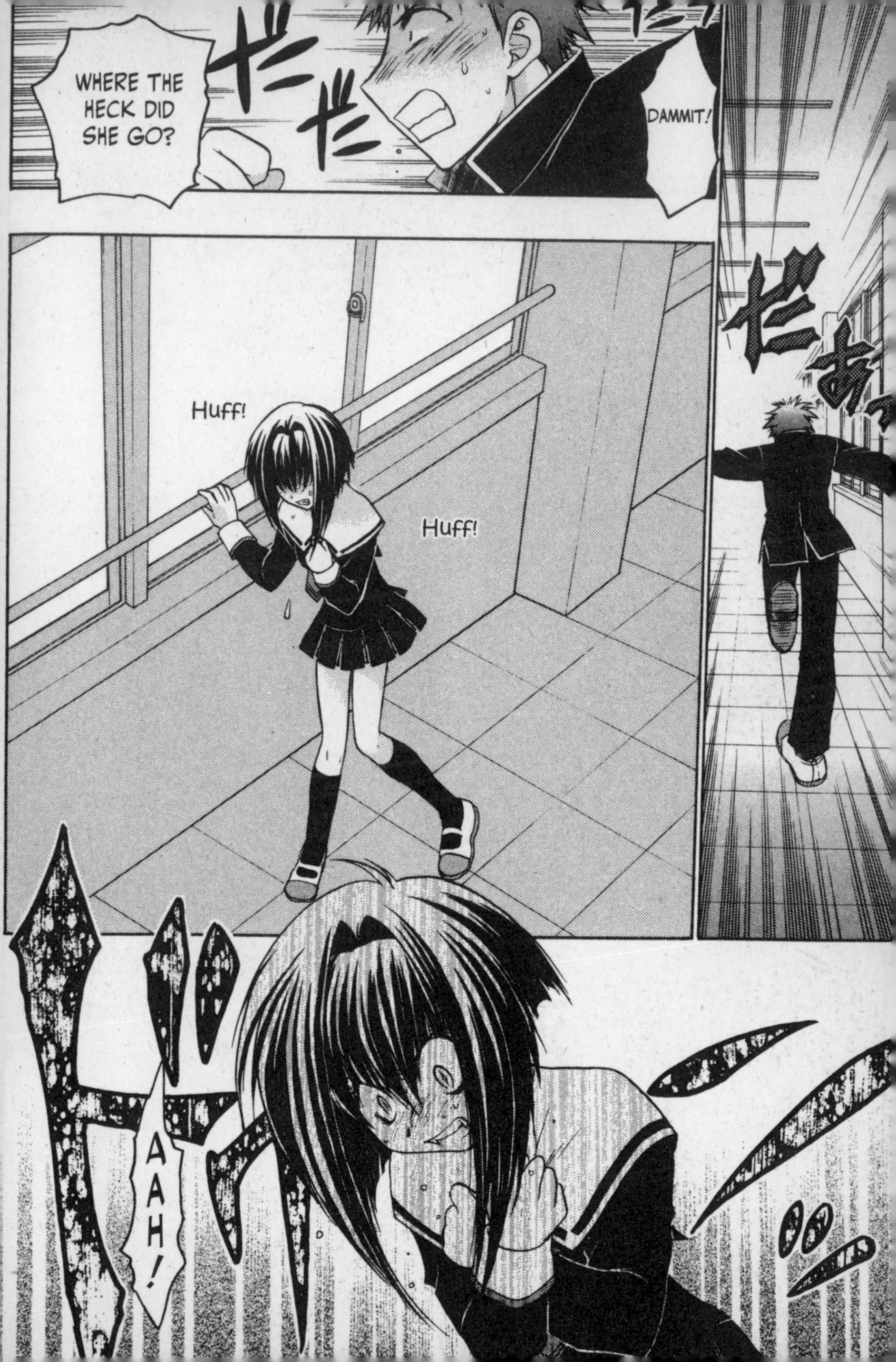
DAMMIT!
WHERE THE HECK DID SHE GO?
Huff!
Huff!
AAH!

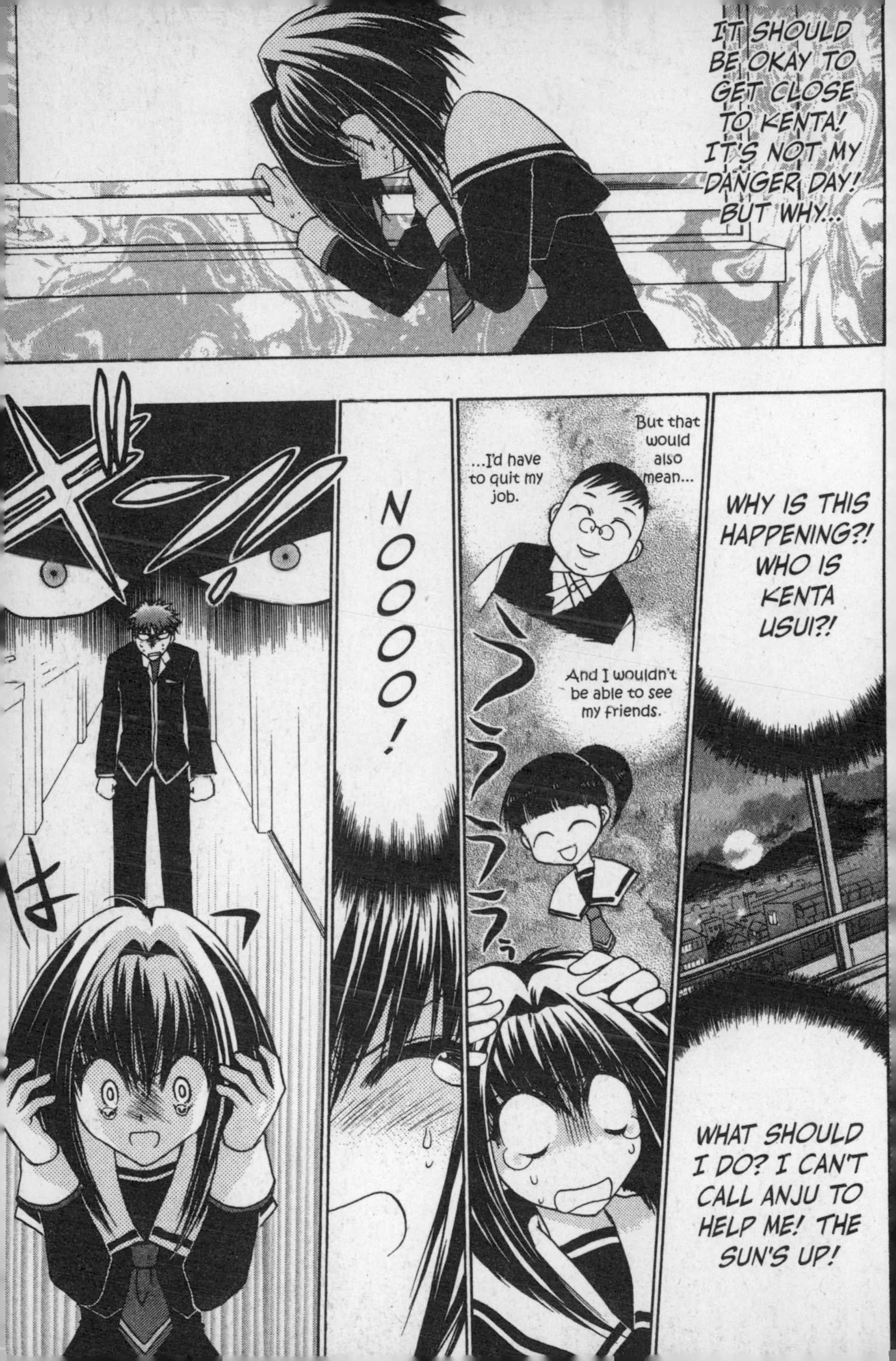
IT SHOULD BE OKAY TO GET CLOSE TO KENTA! IT'S NOT MY DANGER DAY! BUT WHY...
WHY IS THIS HAPPENING?! WHO IS KENTA USUI?!
WHAT SHOULD I DO? I CAN'T CALL ANJU TO HELP ME! THE SUN'S UP!
But that would also mean...
...I'd have to quit my job.
And I wouldn't be able to see my friends.
NOOOOO!

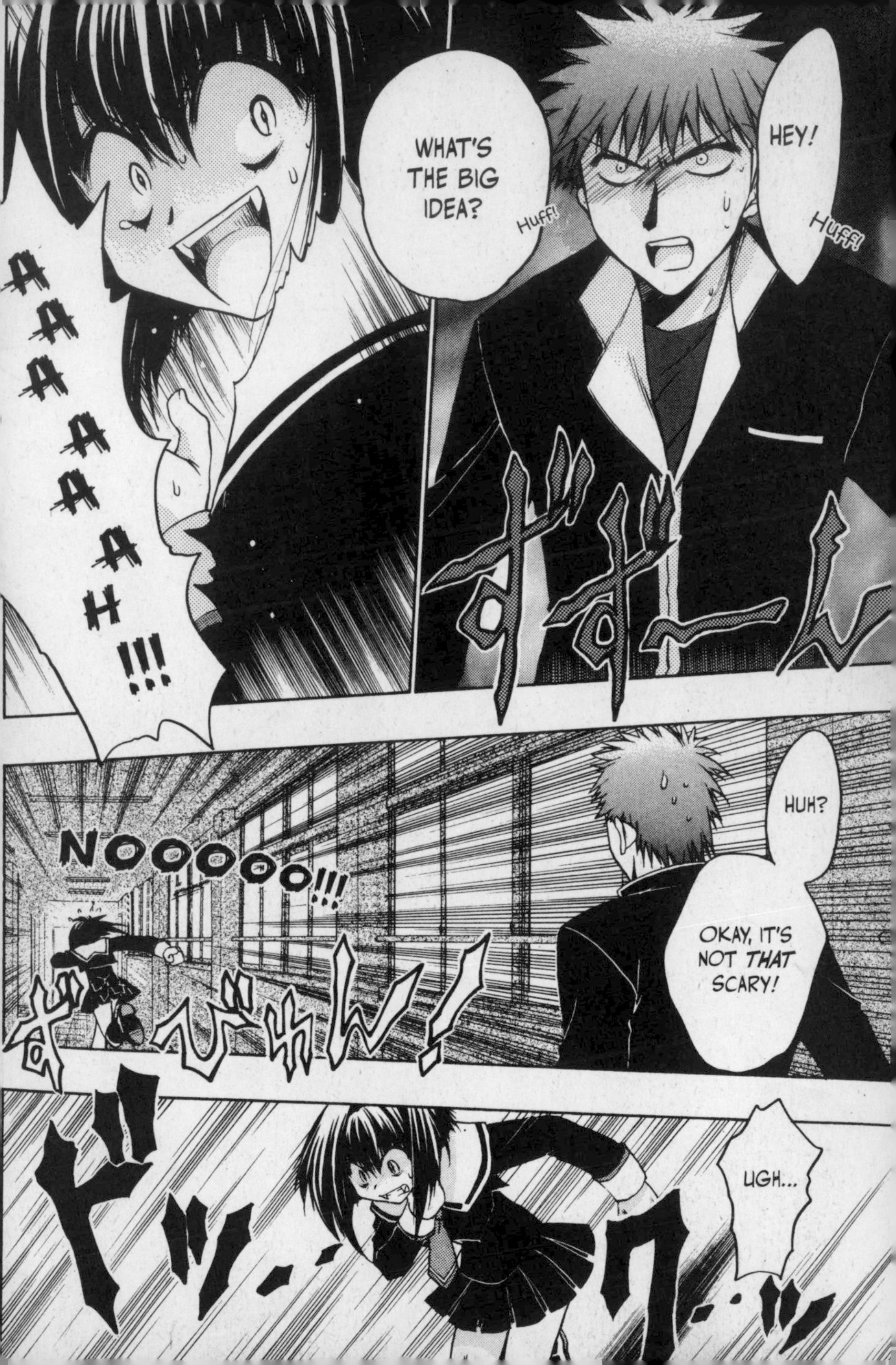
HEY!
Huff!
Huff!
WHAT'S THE BIG IDEA?
ずず〜ん
AAAAAAH!!!
HUH?
OKAY, IT'S NOT *THAT* SCARY!
NOOOOOO!!!
ずびゅん!
UGH...

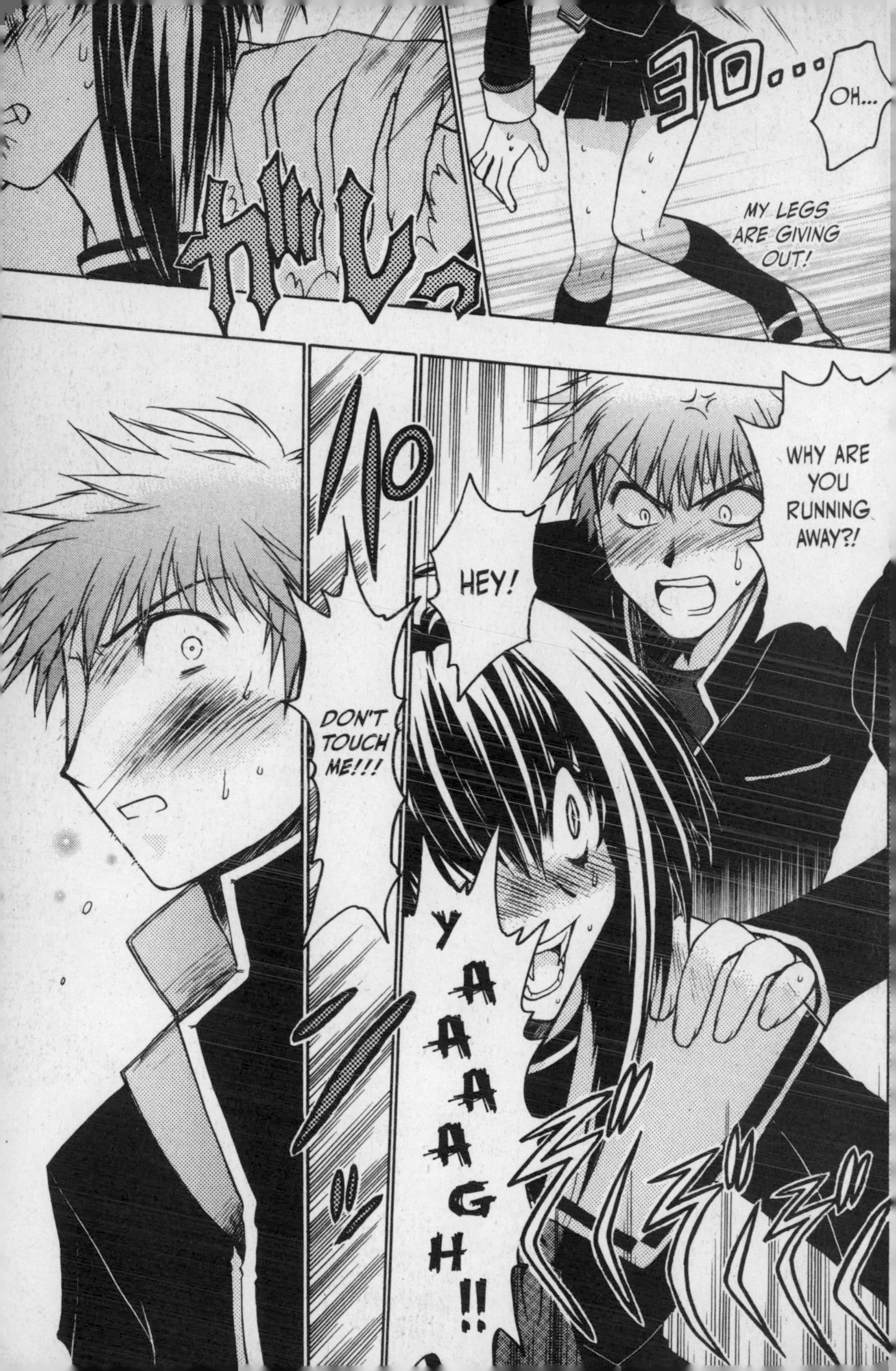
OH...
MY LEGS ARE GIVING OUT!
WHY ARE YOU RUNNING AWAY?!
HEY!
DON'T TOUCH ME!!!
YAAAAAGH!!

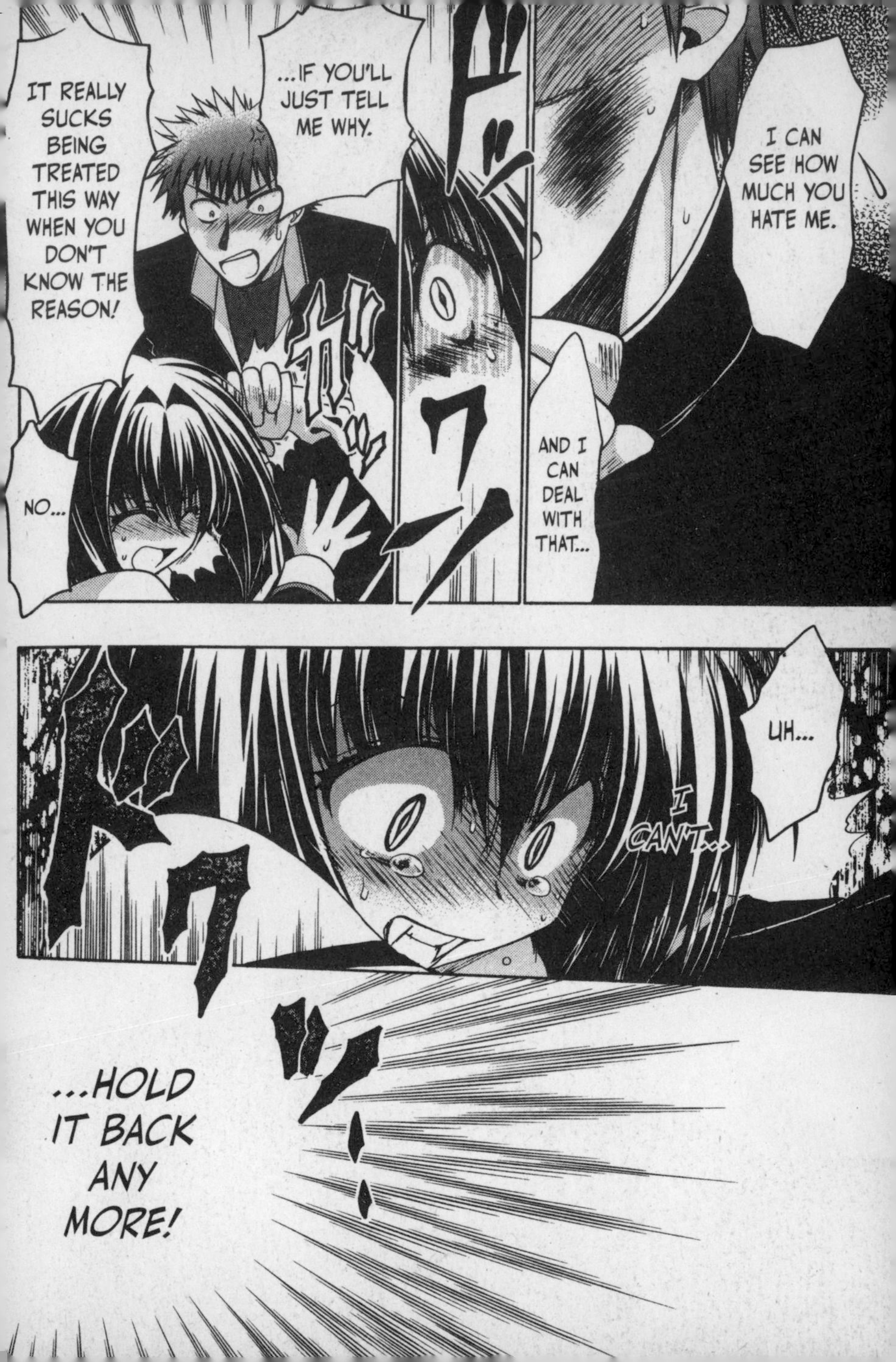
I CAN SEE HOW MUCH YOU HATE ME.
AND I CAN DEAL WITH THAT...
...IF YOU'LL JUST TELL ME WHY.
IT REALLY SUCKS BEING TREATED THIS WAY WHEN YOU DON'T KNOW THE REASON!
NO...
UH...
I CAN'T...
...HOLD IT BACK ANY MORE!

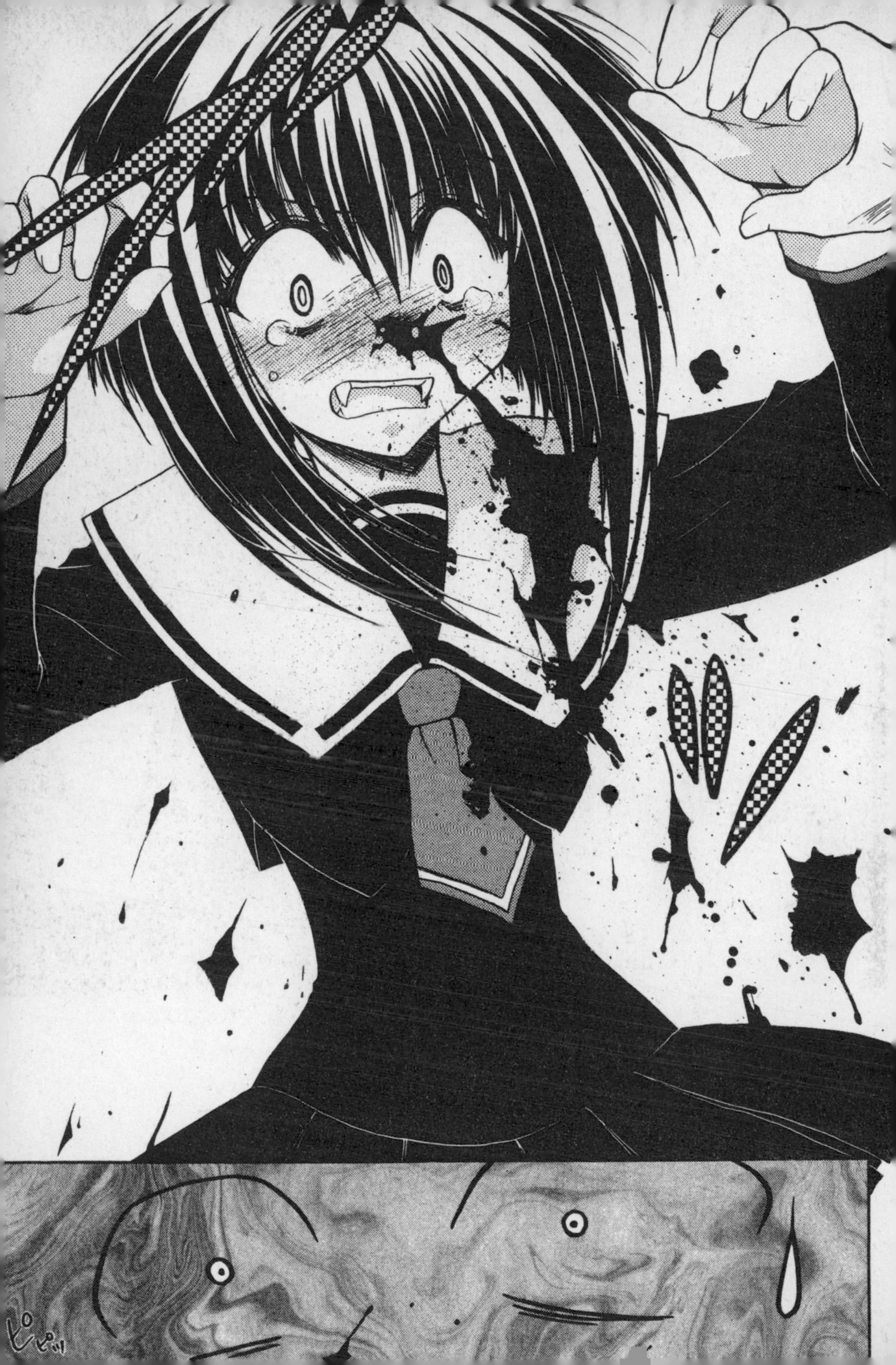
ピピッ

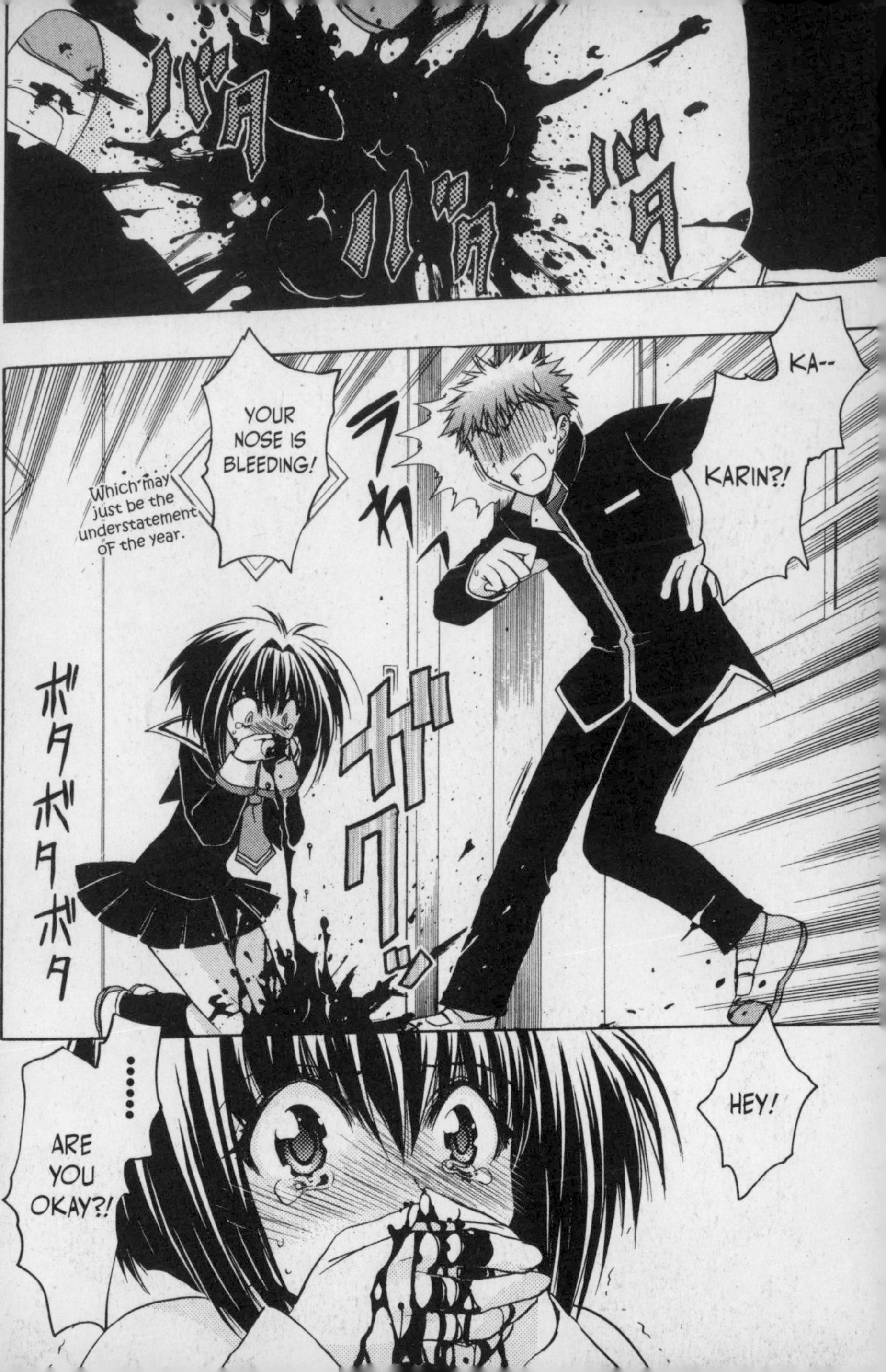
KA-- KARIN?!
YOUR NOSE IS BLEEDING!
Which may just be the understatement of the year.
HEY!
...... ARE YOU OKAY?!

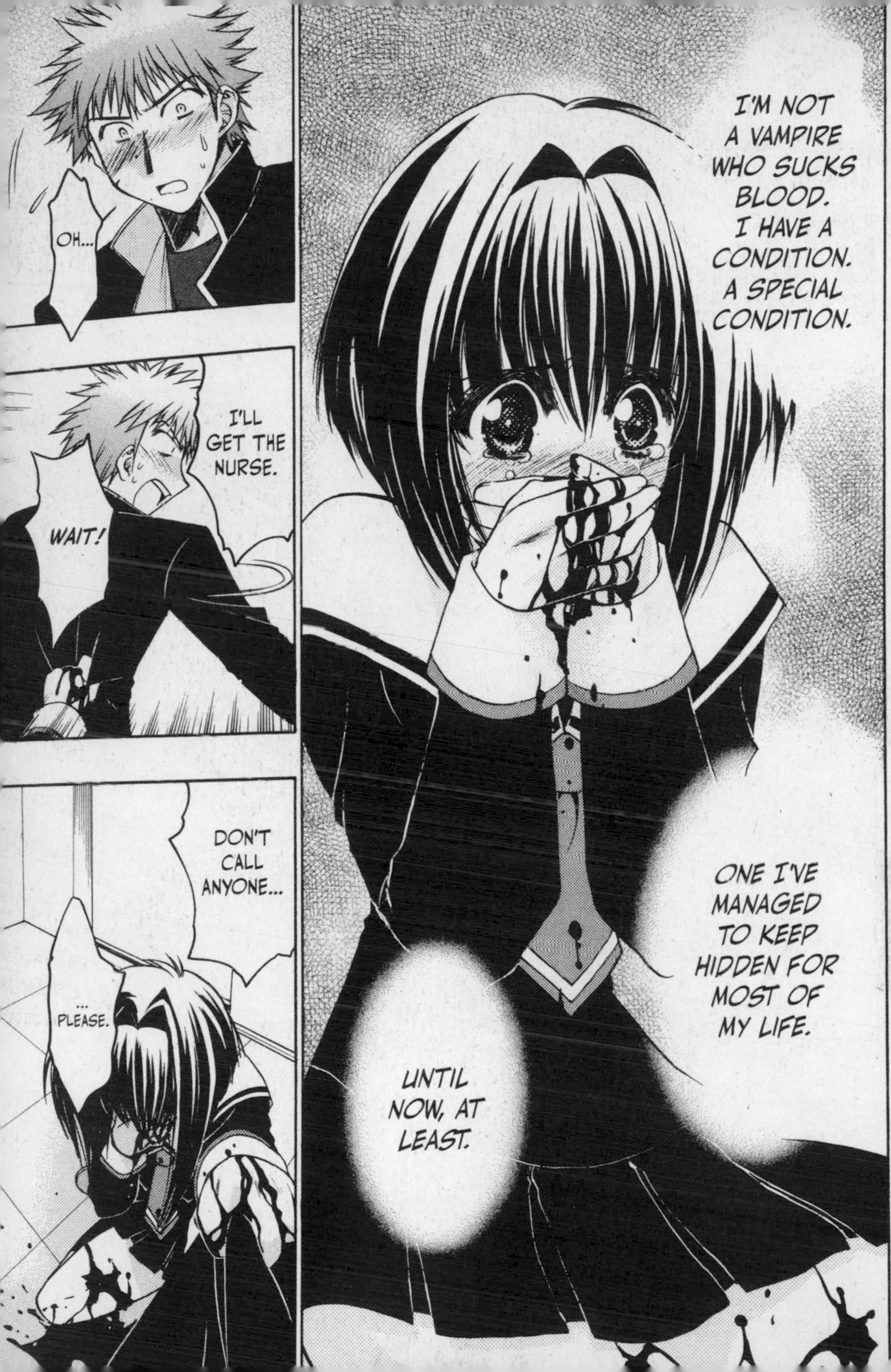
I'M NOT A VAMPIRE WHO SUCKS BLOOD. I HAVE A CONDITION. A SPECIAL CONDITION.
ONE I'VE MANAGED TO KEEP HIDDEN FOR MOST OF MY LIFE.
UNTIL NOW, AT LEAST.
OH...
I'LL GET THE NURSE.
WAIT!
DON'T CALL ANYONE...
... PLEASE.

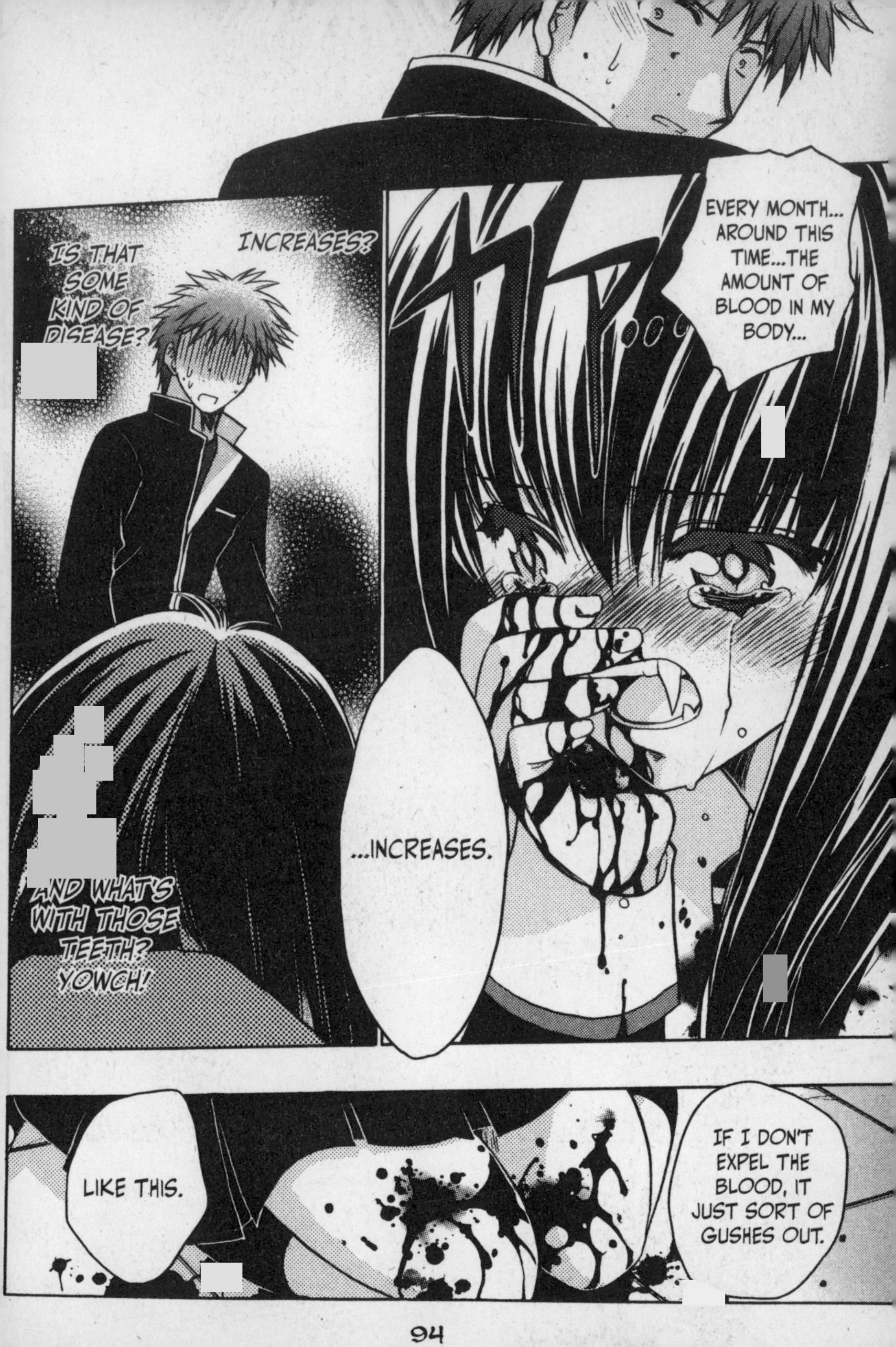
EVERY MONTH... AROUND THIS TIME...THE AMOUNT OF BLOOD IN MY BODY...
...INCREASES.
INCREASES?
IS THAT SOME KIND OF DISEASE?
AND WHAT'S WITH THOSE TEETH? YOWCH!
IF I DON'T EXPEL THE BLOOD, IT JUST SORT OF GUSHES OUT.
LIKE THIS.

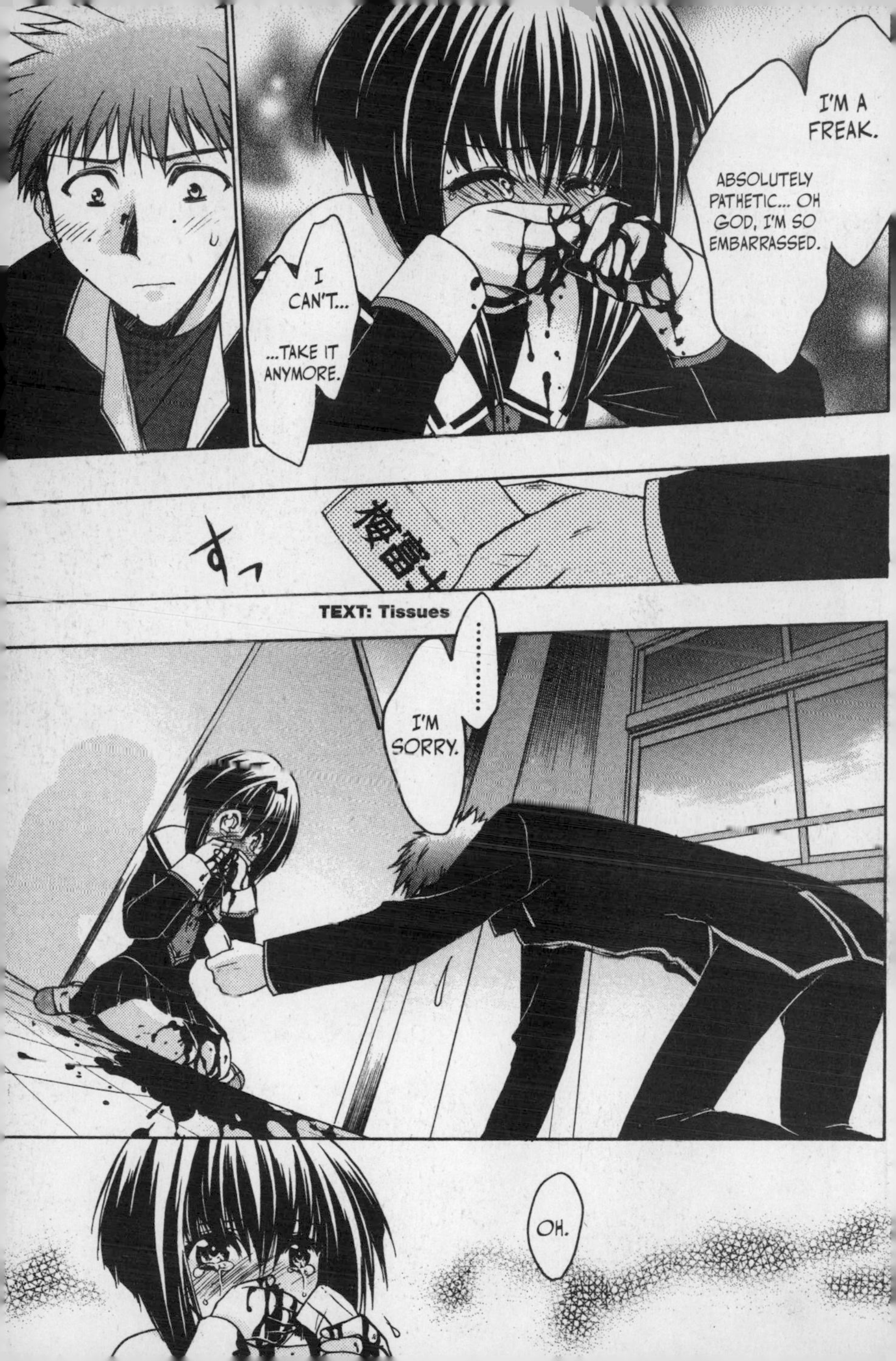
I'M A FREAK.
ABSOLUTELY PATHETIC... OH GOD, I'M SO EMBARRASSED.
I CAN'T...
...TAKE IT ANYMORE.
すっ
TEXT: Tissues
......
I'M SORRY.
OH.

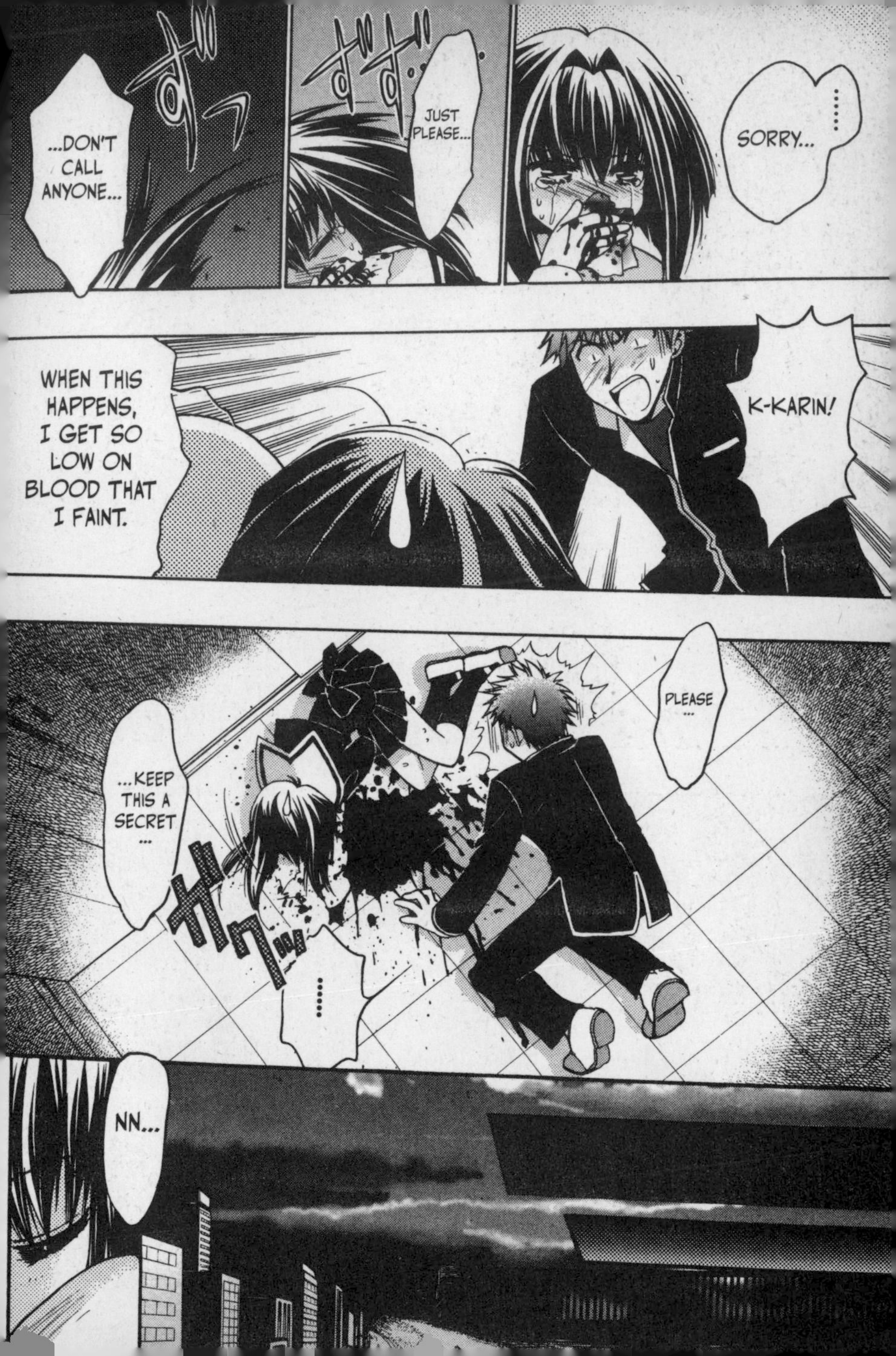
......
SORRY...
JUST PLEASE...
...DON'T CALL ANYONE...
K-KARIN!
WHEN THIS HAPPENS, I GET SO LOW ON BLOOD THAT I FAINT.
PLEASE...
...KEEP THIS A SECRET...
......
NN...

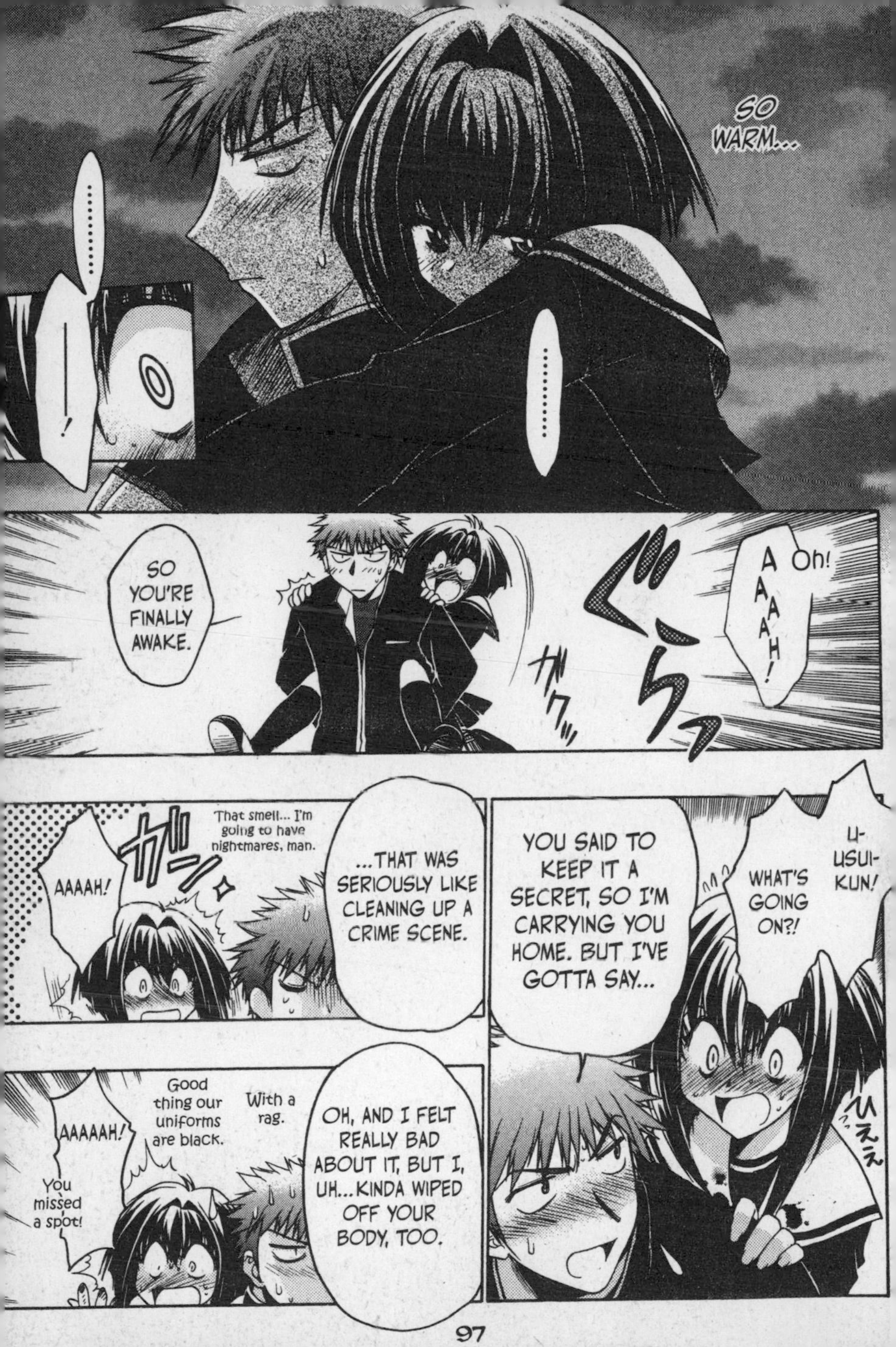
SO WARM...
......
......
—!
Oh!
AAAAH!
ぐらっ
SO YOU'RE FINALLY AWAKE.
U-USUI-KUN!
WHAT'S GOING ON?!
YOU SAID TO KEEP IT A SECRET, SO I'M CARRYING YOU HOME. BUT I'VE GOTTA SAY...
ひぇぇ
...THAT WAS SERIOUSLY LIKE CLEANING UP A CRIME SCENE.
That smell... I'm going to have nightmares, man.
AAAAH!
OH, AND I FELT REALLY BAD ABOUT IT, BUT I, UH...KINDA WIPED OFF YOUR BODY, TOO.
With a rag.
Good thing our uniforms are black.
AAAAAH!
You missed a spot!

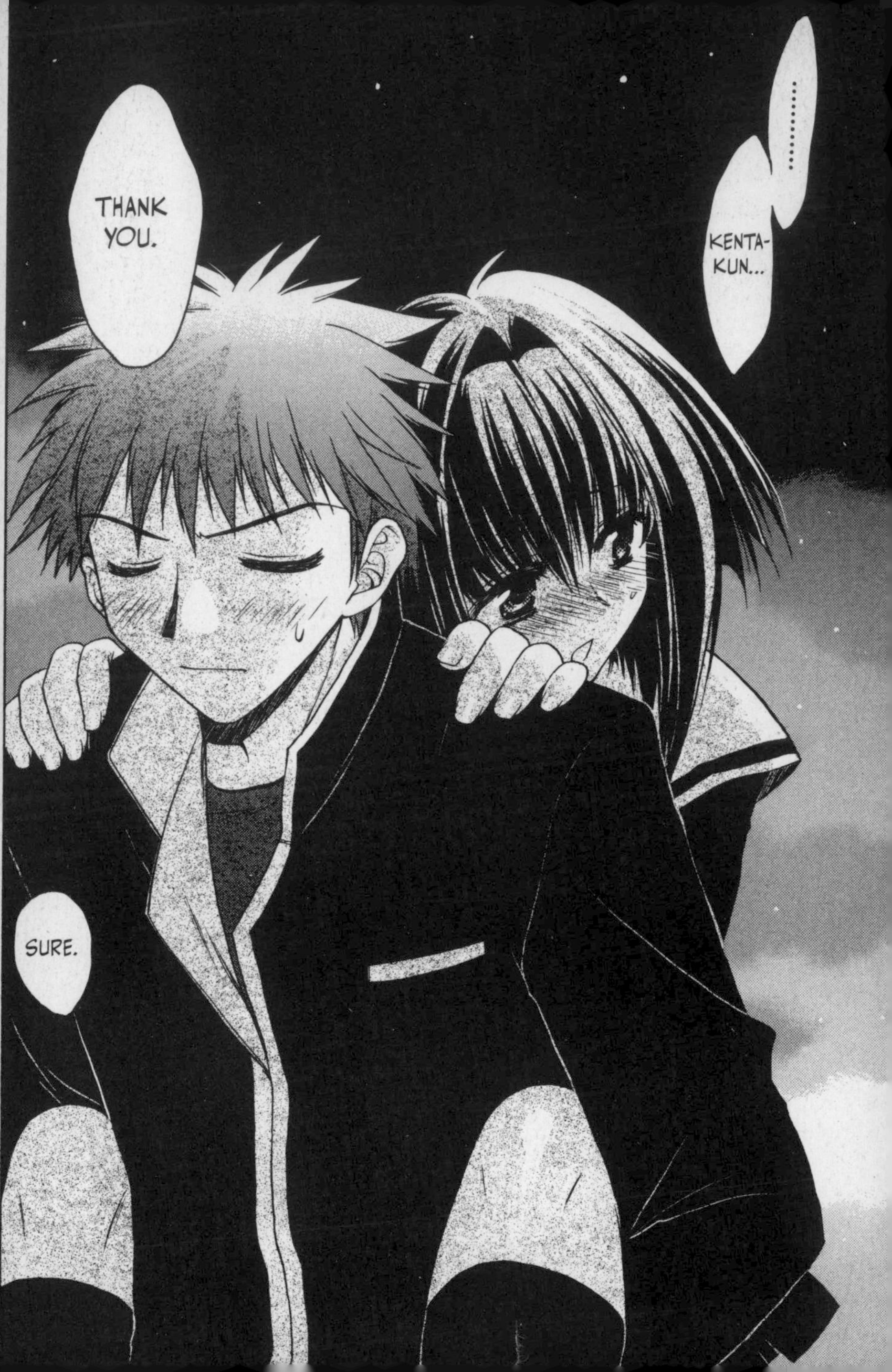
......
KENTA-KUN...
THANK YOU.
SURE.

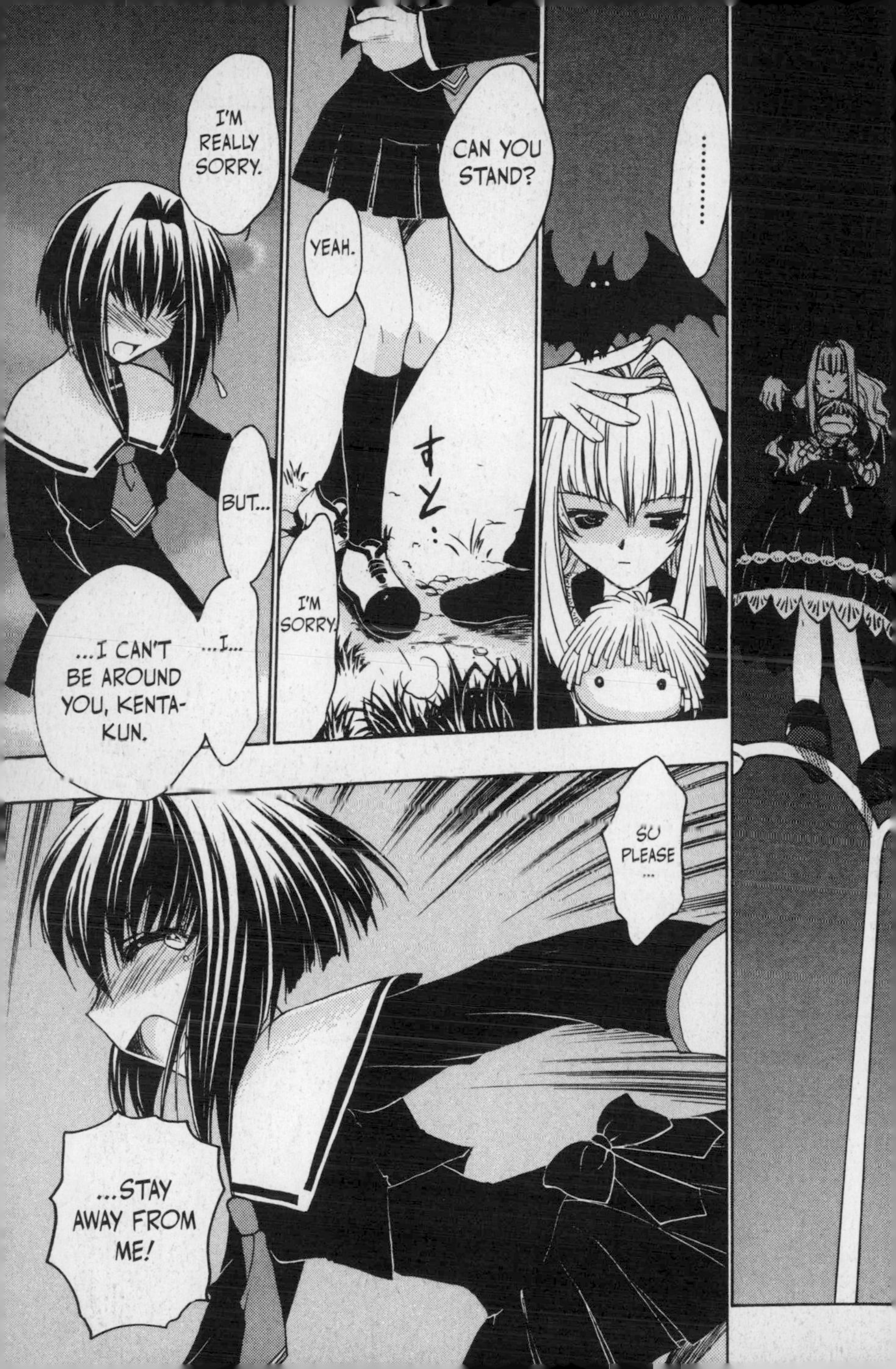
......
CAN YOU STAND?
YEAH.
すと…
I'M SORRY.
I'M REALLY SORRY.
BUT...
...I...
...I CAN'T BE AROUND YOU, KENTA-KUN.
SO PLEASE ...
...STAY AWAY FROM ME!

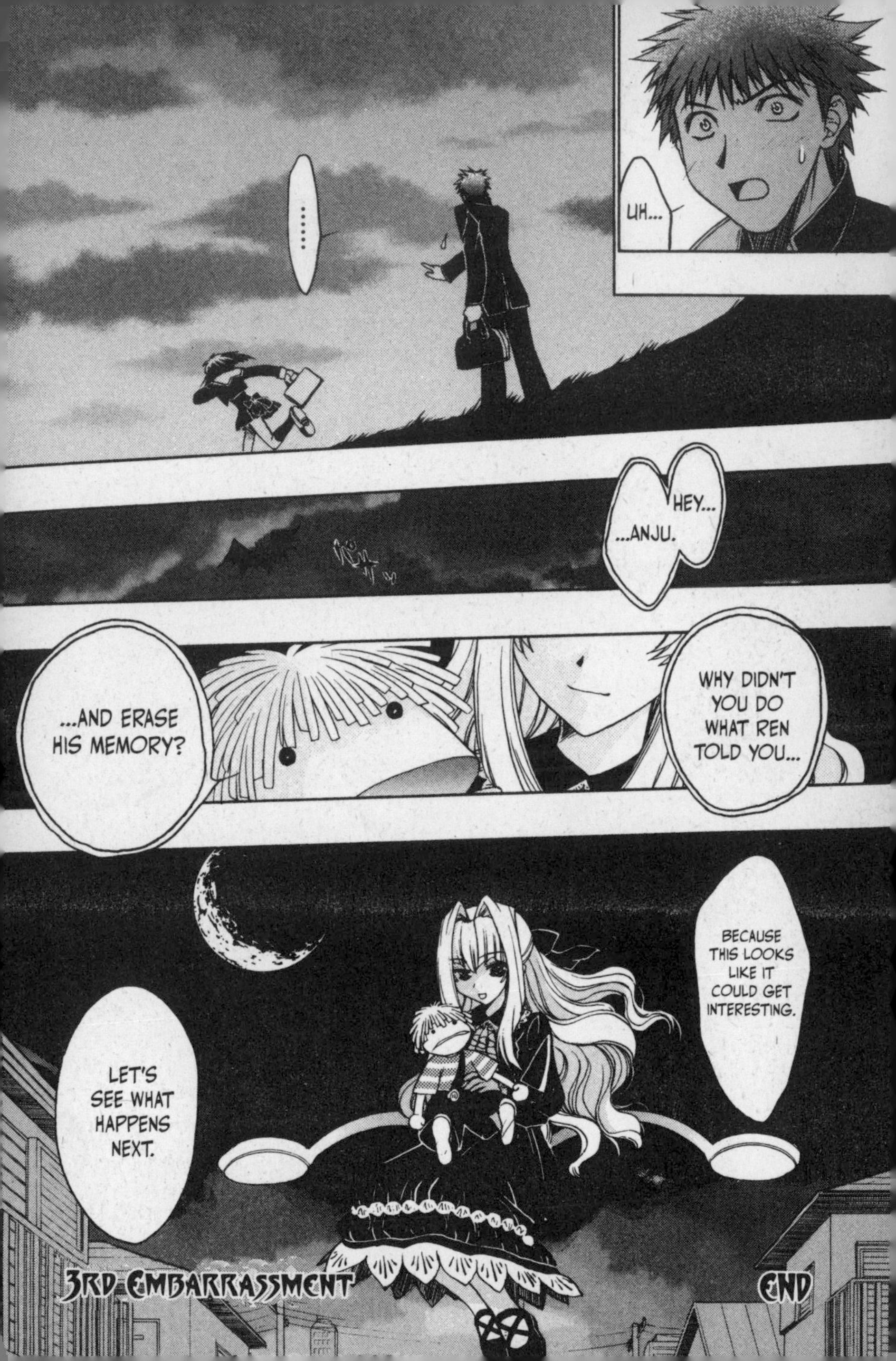
UH...
......
HEY...
...ANJU.
WHY DIDN'T YOU DO WHAT REN TOLD YOU...
...AND ERASE HIS MEMORY?
BECAUSE THIS LOOKS LIKE IT COULD GET INTERESTING.
LET'S SEE WHAT HAPPENS NEXT.
3RD EMBARRASSMENT
END

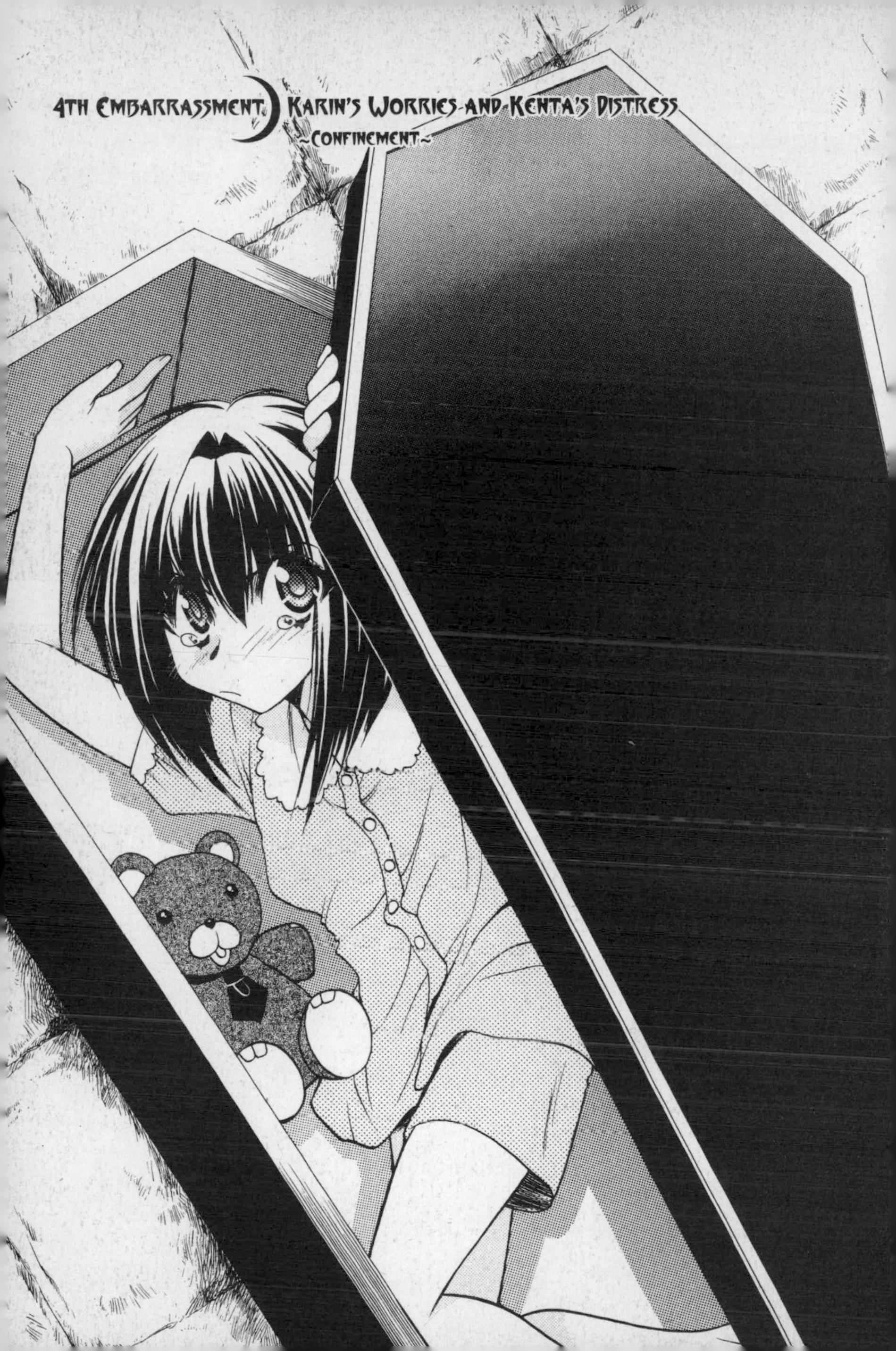
4th Embarrassment Karin's Worries and Kenta's Distress
~Confinement~

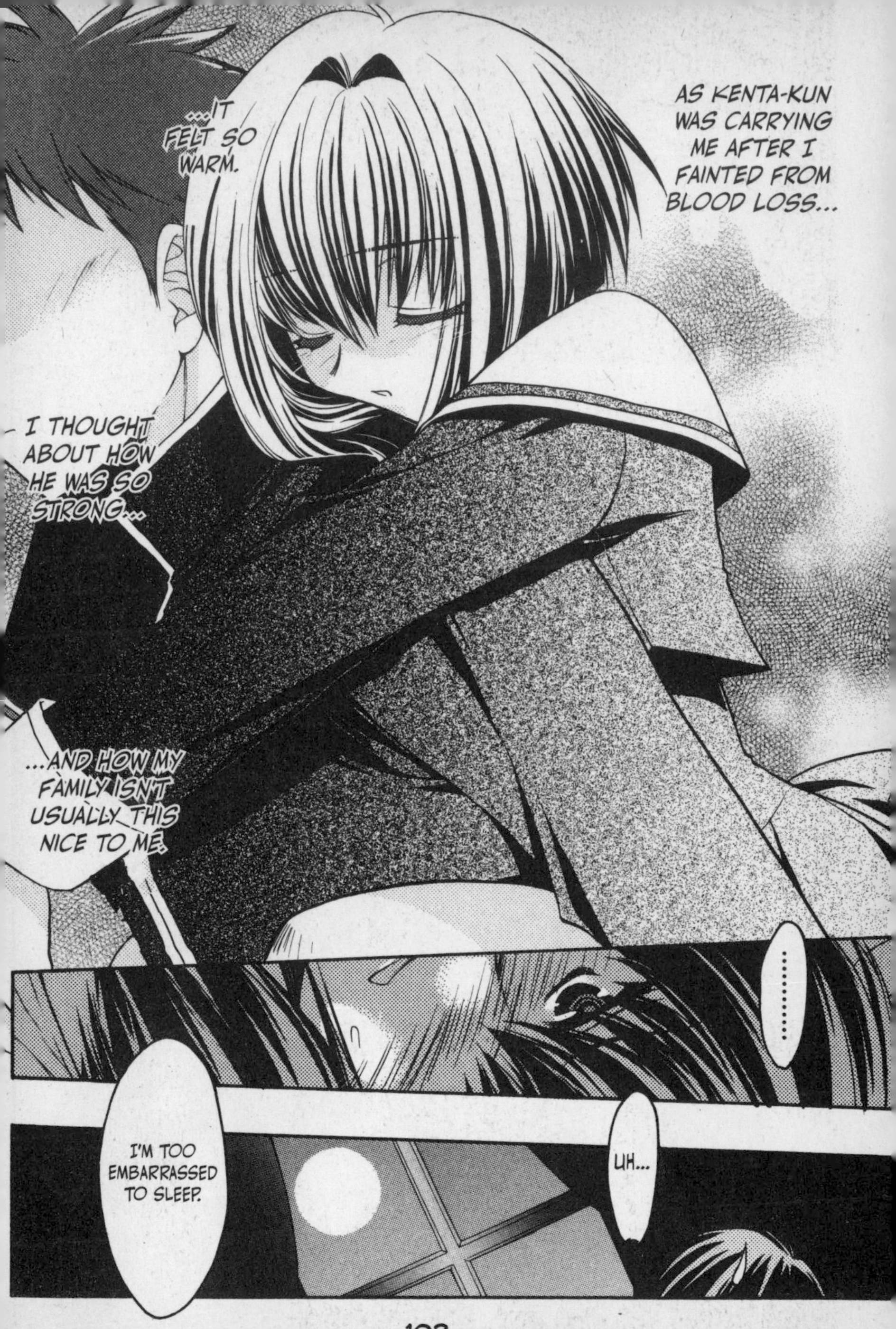
AS KENTA-KUN WAS CARRYING ME AFTER I FAINTED FROM BLOOD LOSS...
...IT FELT SO WARM.
I THOUGHT ABOUT HOW HE WAS SO STRONG...
...AND HOW MY FAMILY ISN'T USUALLY THIS NICE TO ME.
........
UH...
I'M TOO EMBARRASSED TO SLEEP.

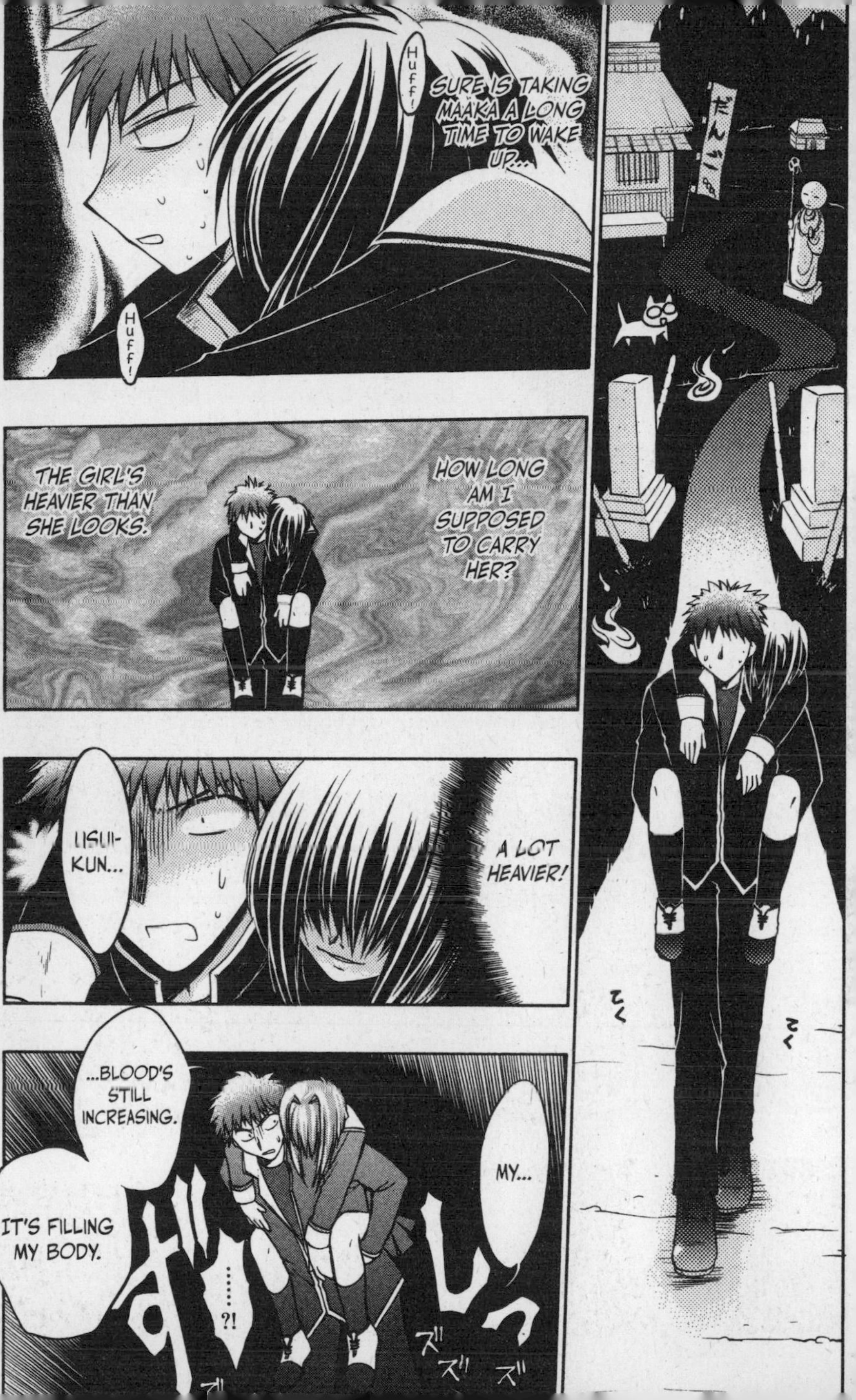
Huff!
SURE IS TAKING MAAKA A LONG TIME TO WAKE UP...
Huff!
HOW LONG AM I SUPPOSED TO CARRY HER?
THE GIRL'S HEAVIER THAN SHE LOOKS.
A LOT HEAVIER!
USUI-KUN...
MY...
...BLOOD'S STILL INCREASING.
IT'S FILLING MY BODY.
......?!
ずしっ
ズズズ

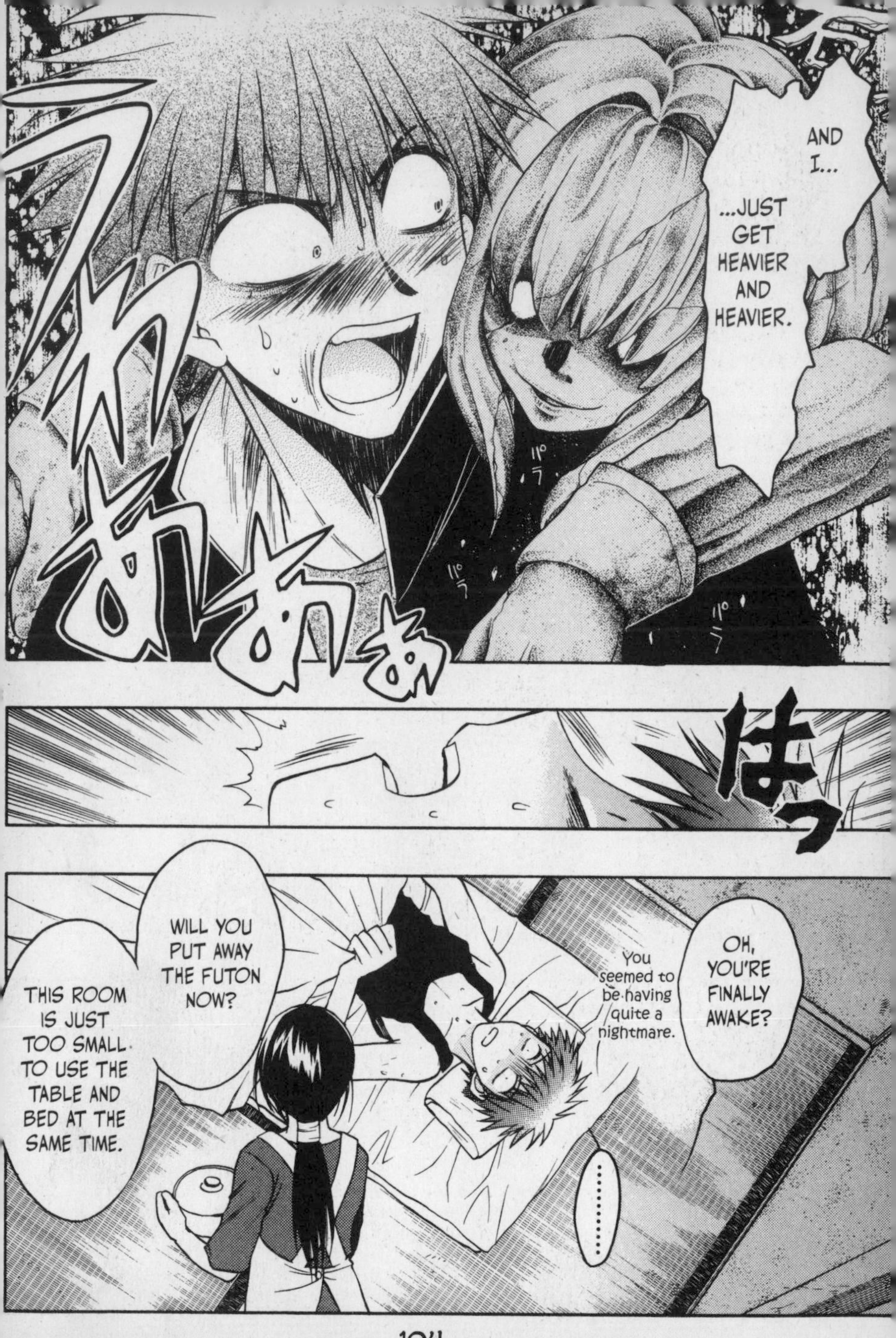
AND I...
...JUST GET HEAVIER AND HEAVIER.
はっ
OH, YOU'RE FINALLY AWAKE?
You seemed to be having quite a nightmare.
WILL YOU PUT AWAY THE FUTON NOW?
THIS ROOM IS JUST TOO SMALL TO USE THE TABLE AND BED AT THE SAME TIME.
......

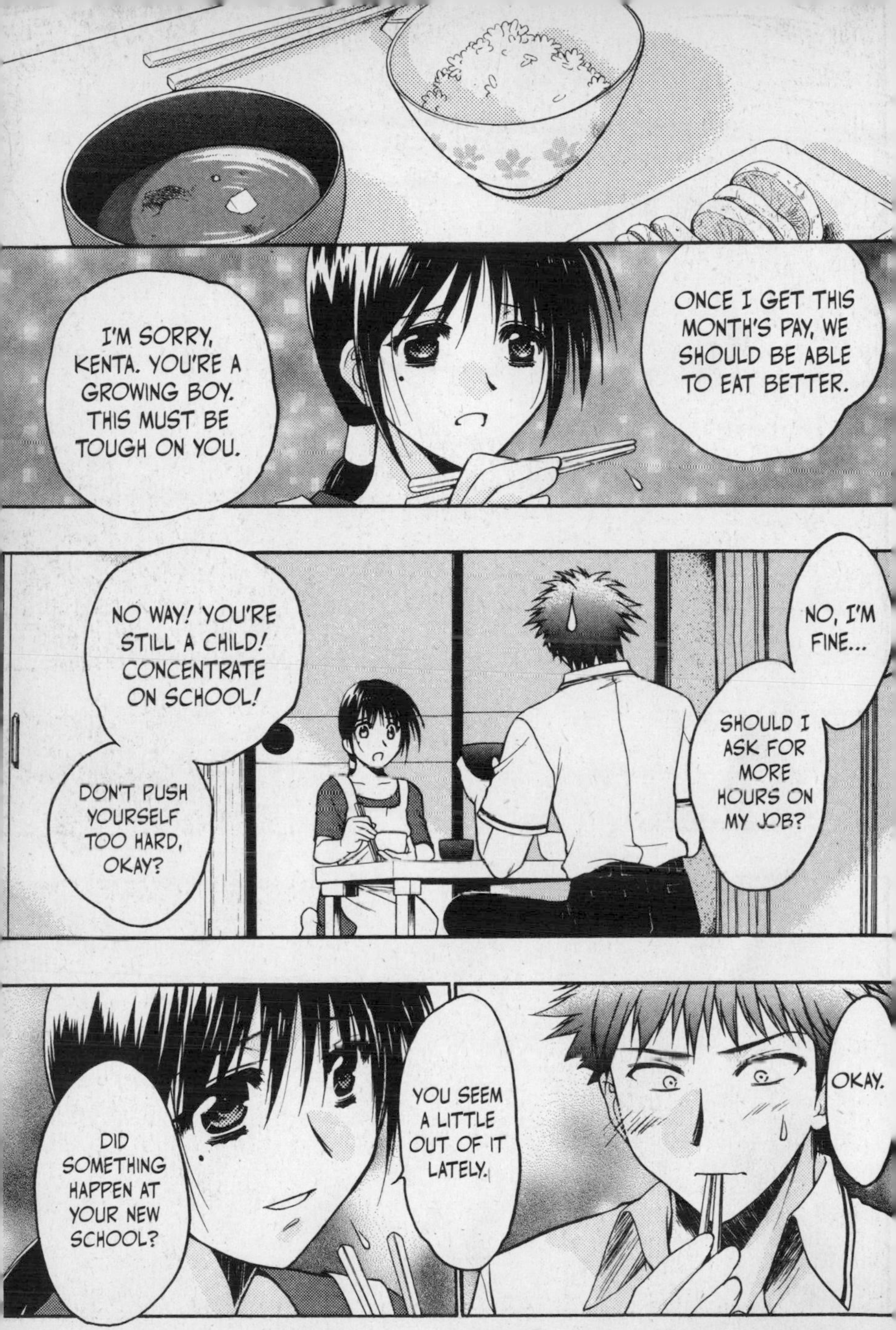
ONCE I GET THIS MONTH'S PAY, WE SHOULD BE ABLE TO EAT BETTER.
I'M SORRY, KENTA. YOU'RE A GROWING BOY. THIS MUST BE TOUGH ON YOU.
NO, I'M FINE...
SHOULD I ASK FOR MORE HOURS ON MY JOB?
NO WAY! YOU'RE STILL A CHILD! CONCENTRATE ON SCHOOL!
DON'T PUSH YOURSELF TOO HARD, OKAY?
OKAY.
YOU SEEM A LITTLE OUT OF IT LATELY.
DID SOMETHING HAPPEN AT YOUR NEW SCHOOL?

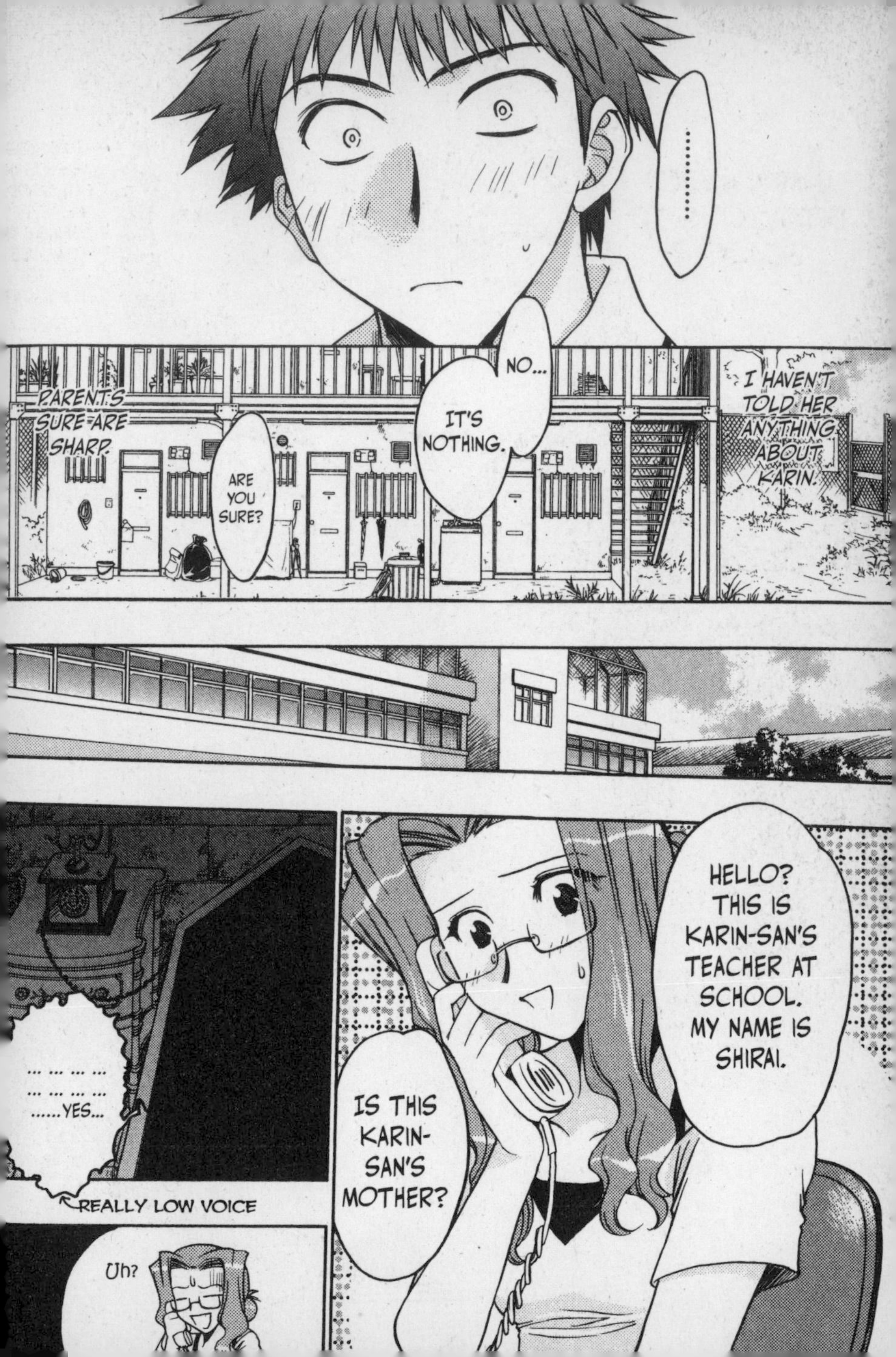
......
I HAVEN'T TOLD HER ANYTHING ABOUT KARIN.
NO...
IT'S NOTHING.
ARE YOU SURE?
PARENTS SURE ARE SHARP.
HELLO? THIS IS KARIN-SAN'S TEACHER AT SCHOOL. MY NAME IS SHIRAI.
IS THIS KARIN-SAN'S MOTHER?
... ... ... ...
... ... ... ...
......YES...
REALLY LOW VOICE
Uh?

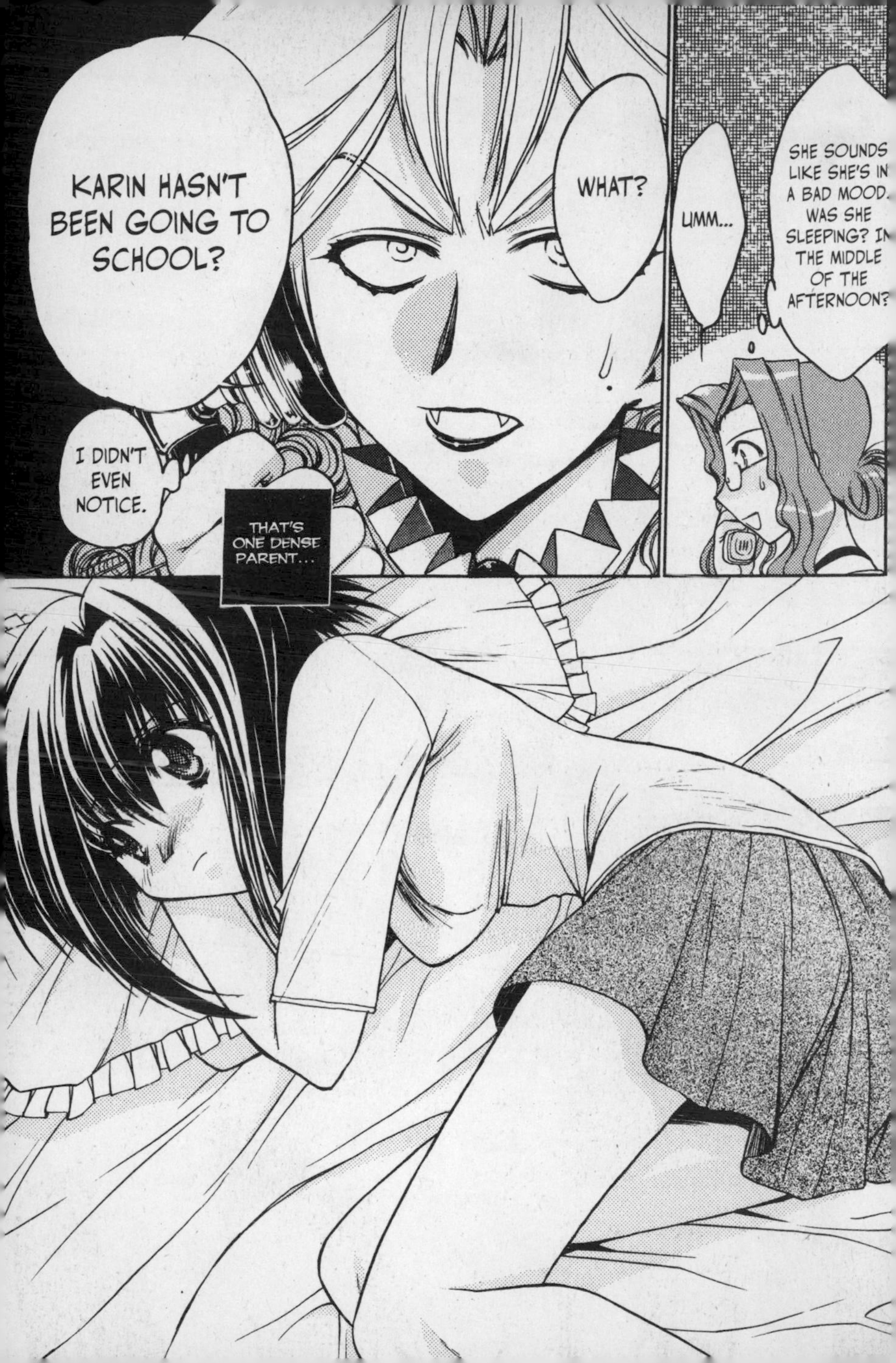
SHE SOUNDS LIKE SHE'S IN A BAD MOOD. WAS SHE SLEEPING? IN THE MIDDLE OF THE AFTERNOON?
UMM...
WHAT?
KARIN HASN'T BEEN GOING TO SCHOOL?
I DIDN'T EVEN NOTICE.
THAT'S ONE DENSE PARENT...

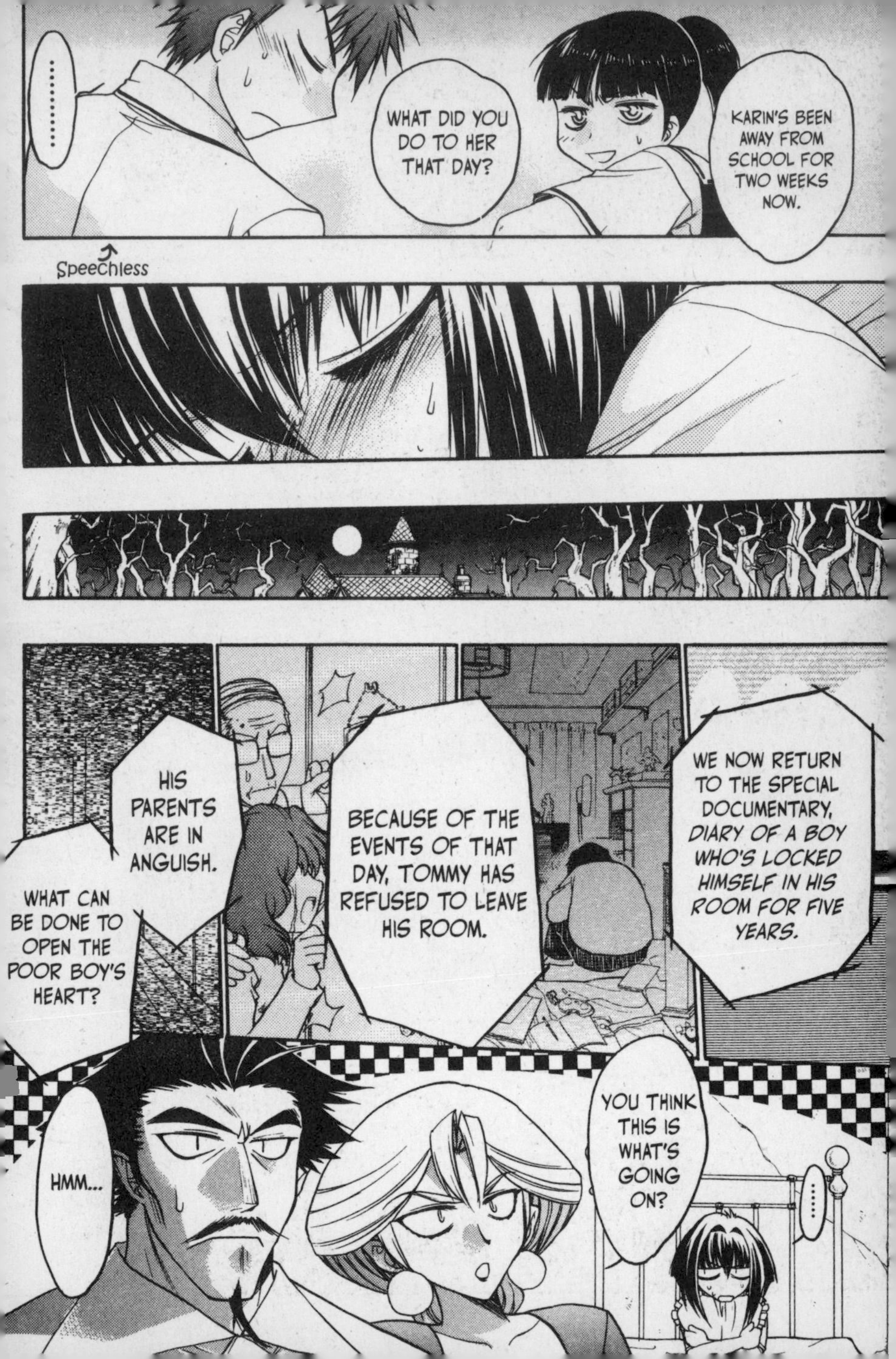
KARIN'S BEEN AWAY FROM SCHOOL FOR TWO WEEKS NOW.
WHAT DID YOU DO TO HER THAT DAY?
......
Speechless
WE NOW RETURN TO THE SPECIAL DOCUMENTARY, *DIARY OF A BOY WHO'S LOCKED HIMSELF IN HIS ROOM FOR FIVE YEARS.*
BECAUSE OF THE EVENTS OF THAT DAY, TOMMY HAS REFUSED TO LEAVE HIS ROOM.
HIS PARENTS ARE IN ANGUISH.
WHAT CAN BE DONE TO OPEN THE POOR BOY'S HEART?
......
YOU THINK THIS IS WHAT'S GOING ON?
HMM...

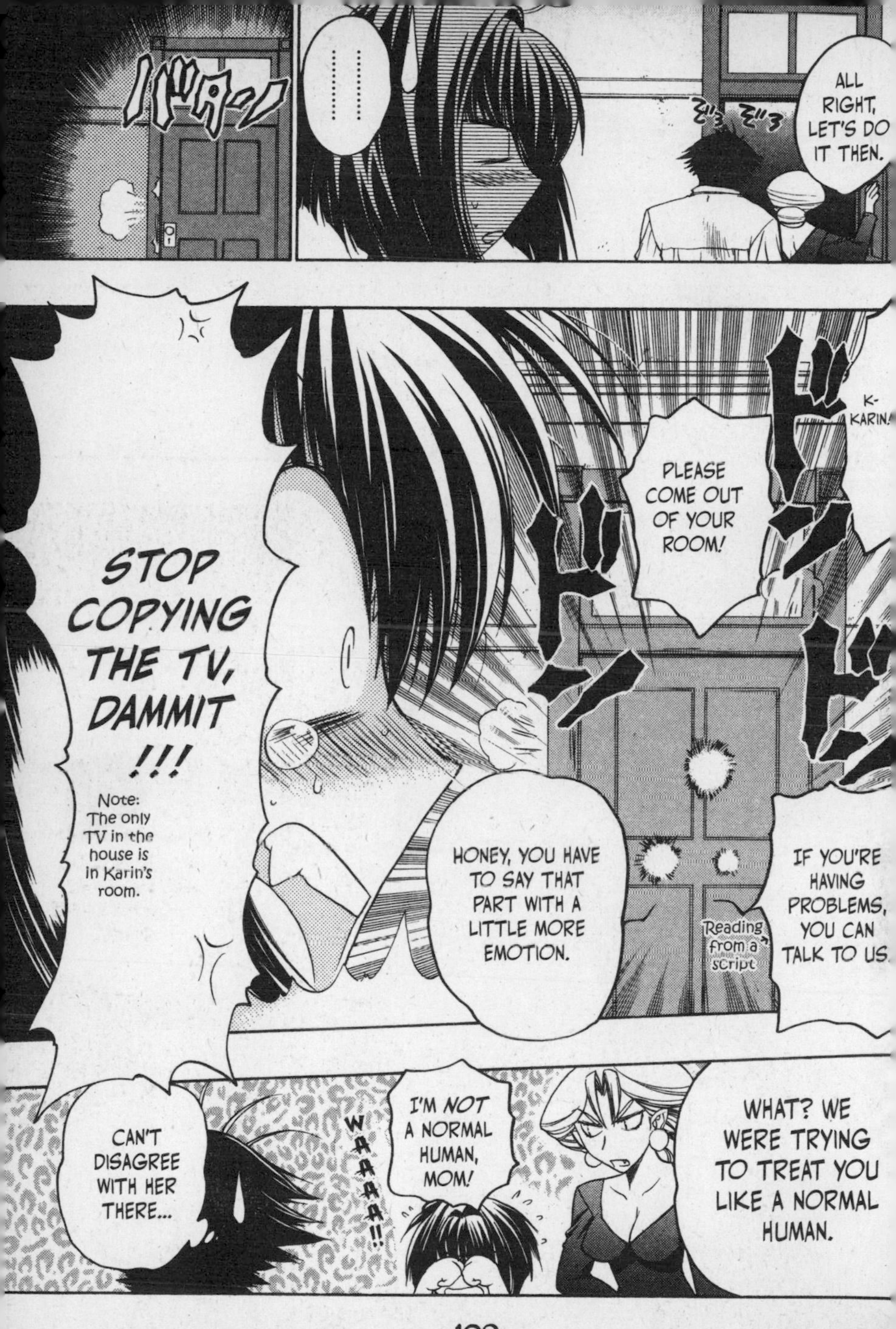
ALL RIGHT, LET'S DO IT THEN.
......
K-KARIN!
PLEASE COME OUT OF YOUR ROOM!
IF YOU'RE HAVING PROBLEMS, YOU CAN TALK TO US.
Reading from a script
HONEY, YOU HAVE TO SAY THAT PART WITH A LITTLE MORE EMOTION.
STOP COPYING THE TV, DAMMIT!!!
Note: The only TV in the house is in Karin's room.
WHAT? WE WERE TRYING TO TREAT YOU LIKE A NORMAL HUMAN.
I'M NOT A NORMAL HUMAN, MOM!
WAAAA!!
CAN'T DISAGREE WITH HER THERE...

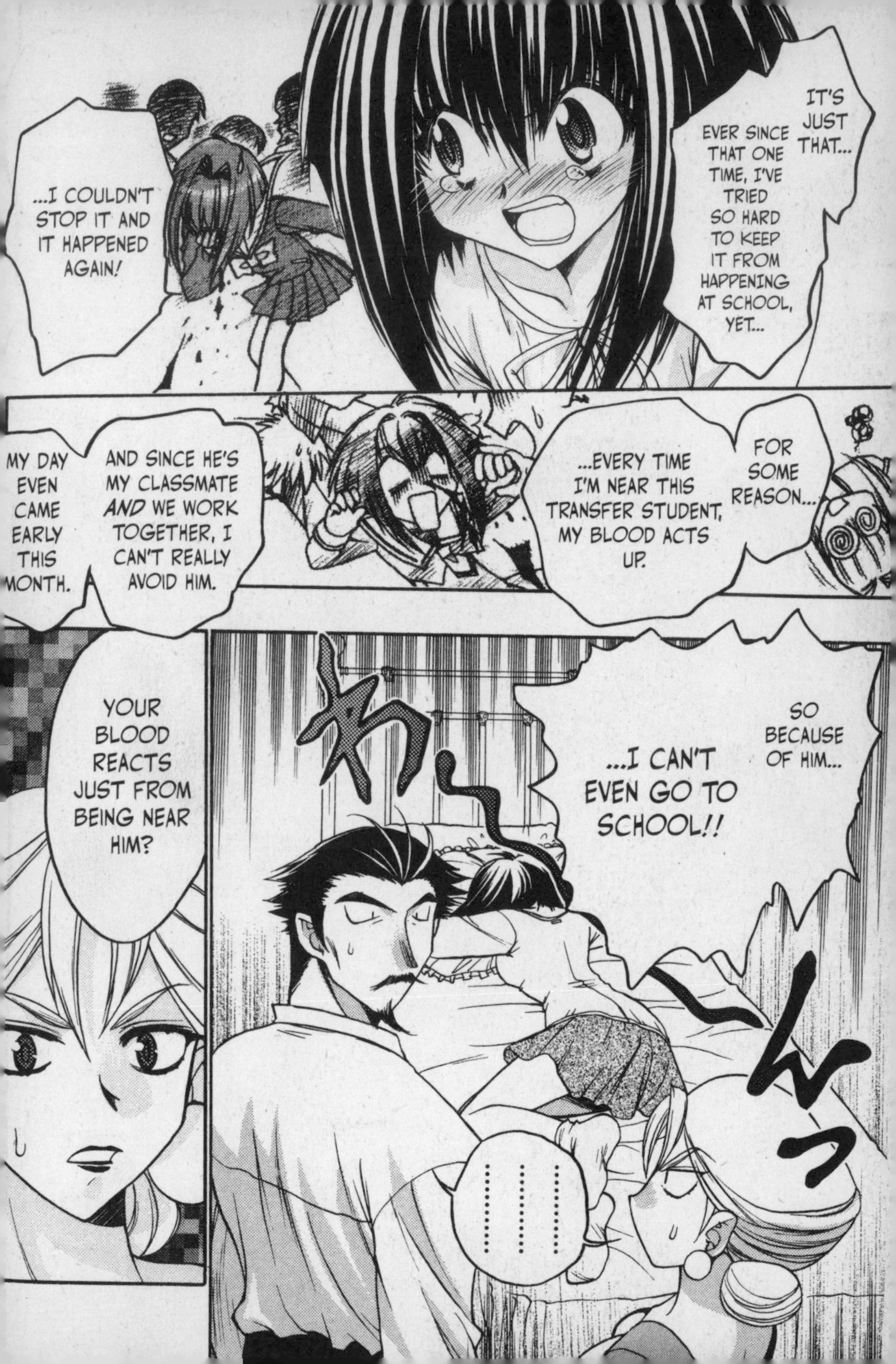

IT'S JUST THAT...
EVER SINCE THAT ONE TIME, I'VE TRIED SO HARD TO KEEP IT FROM HAPPENING AT SCHOOL, YET...
...I COULDN'T STOP IT AND IT HAPPENED AGAIN!
FOR SOME REASON...
...EVERY TIME I'M NEAR THIS TRANSFER STUDENT, MY BLOOD ACTS UP.
AND SINCE HE'S MY CLASSMATE *AND* WE WORK TOGETHER, I CAN'T REALLY AVOID HIM.
MY DAY EVEN CAME EARLY THIS MONTH.
SO BECAUSE OF HIM...
...I CAN'T EVEN GO TO SCHOOL!!
わ～んっ
......
YOUR BLOOD REACTS JUST FROM BEING NEAR HIM?

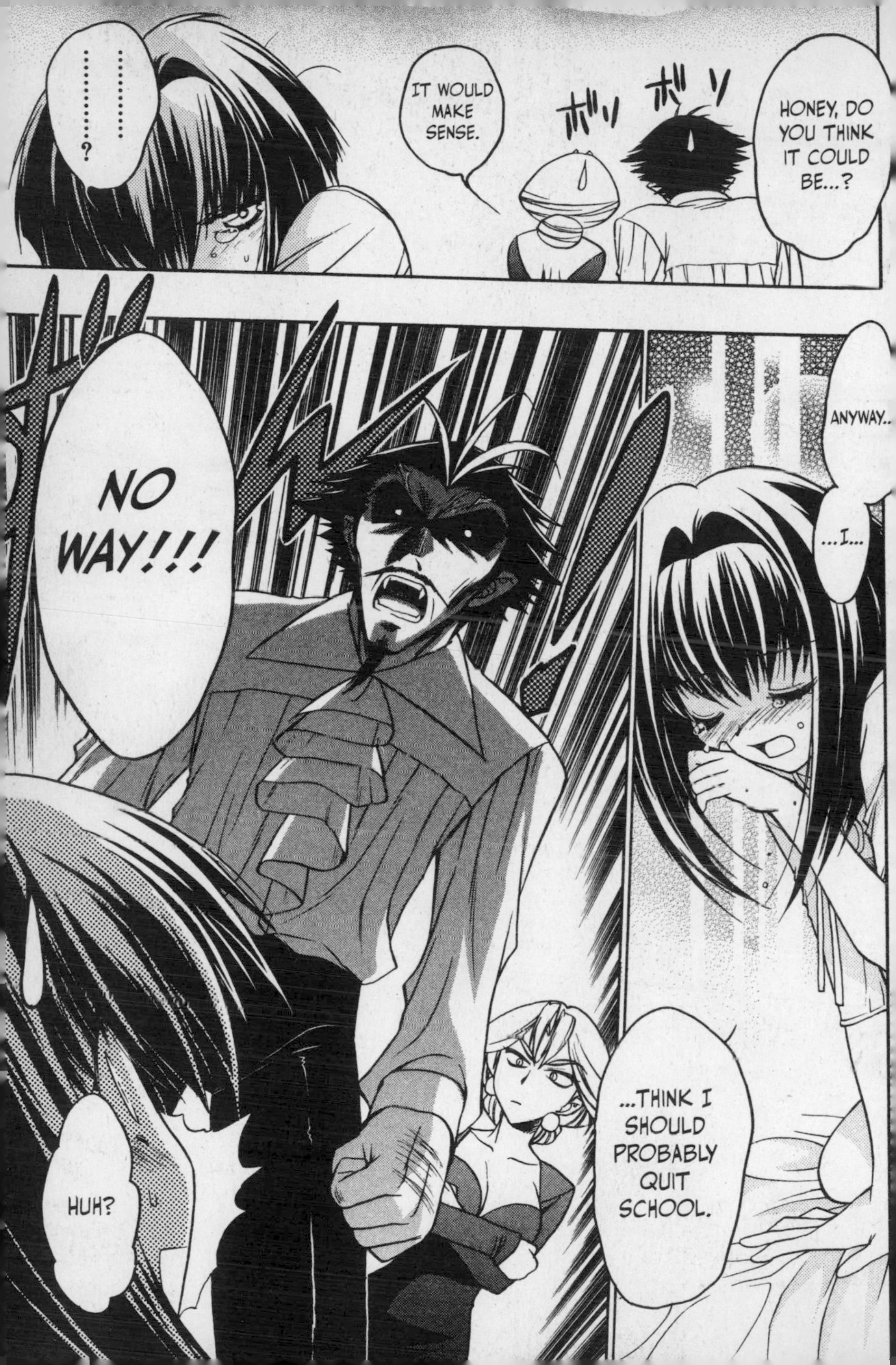

HONEY, DO YOU THINK IT COULD BE...?
ボソ ボソ
IT WOULD MAKE SENSE.
......?
ANYWAY..
...I...
...THINK I SHOULD PROBABLY QUIT SCHOOL.
NO WAY!!!
HUH?

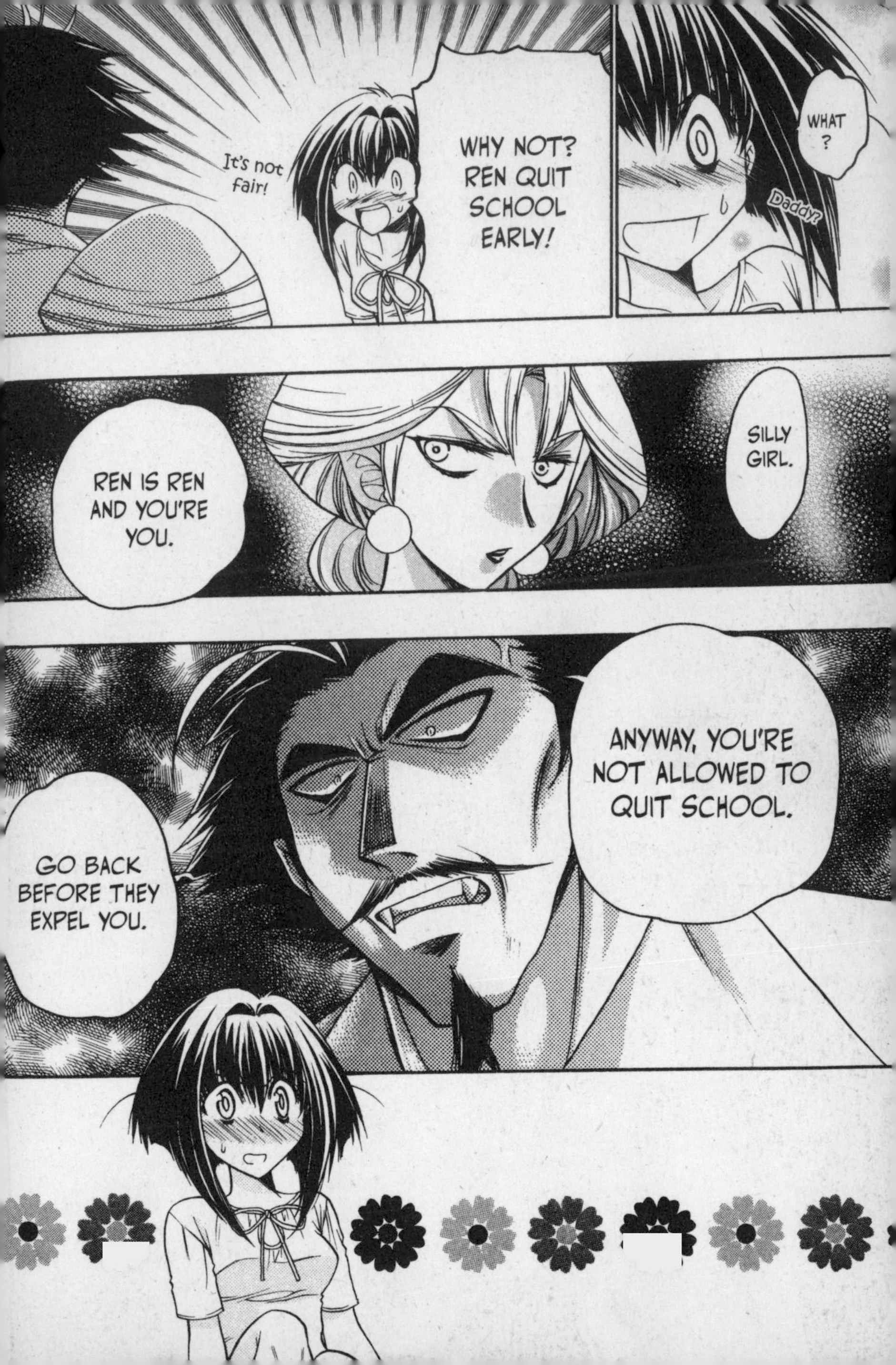
WHAT ?
Daddy?
WHY NOT? REN QUIT SCHOOL EARLY!
It's not fair!
SILLY GIRL.
REN IS REN AND YOU'RE YOU.
ANYWAY, YOU'RE NOT ALLOWED TO QUIT SCHOOL.
GO BACK BEFORE THEY EXPEL YOU.

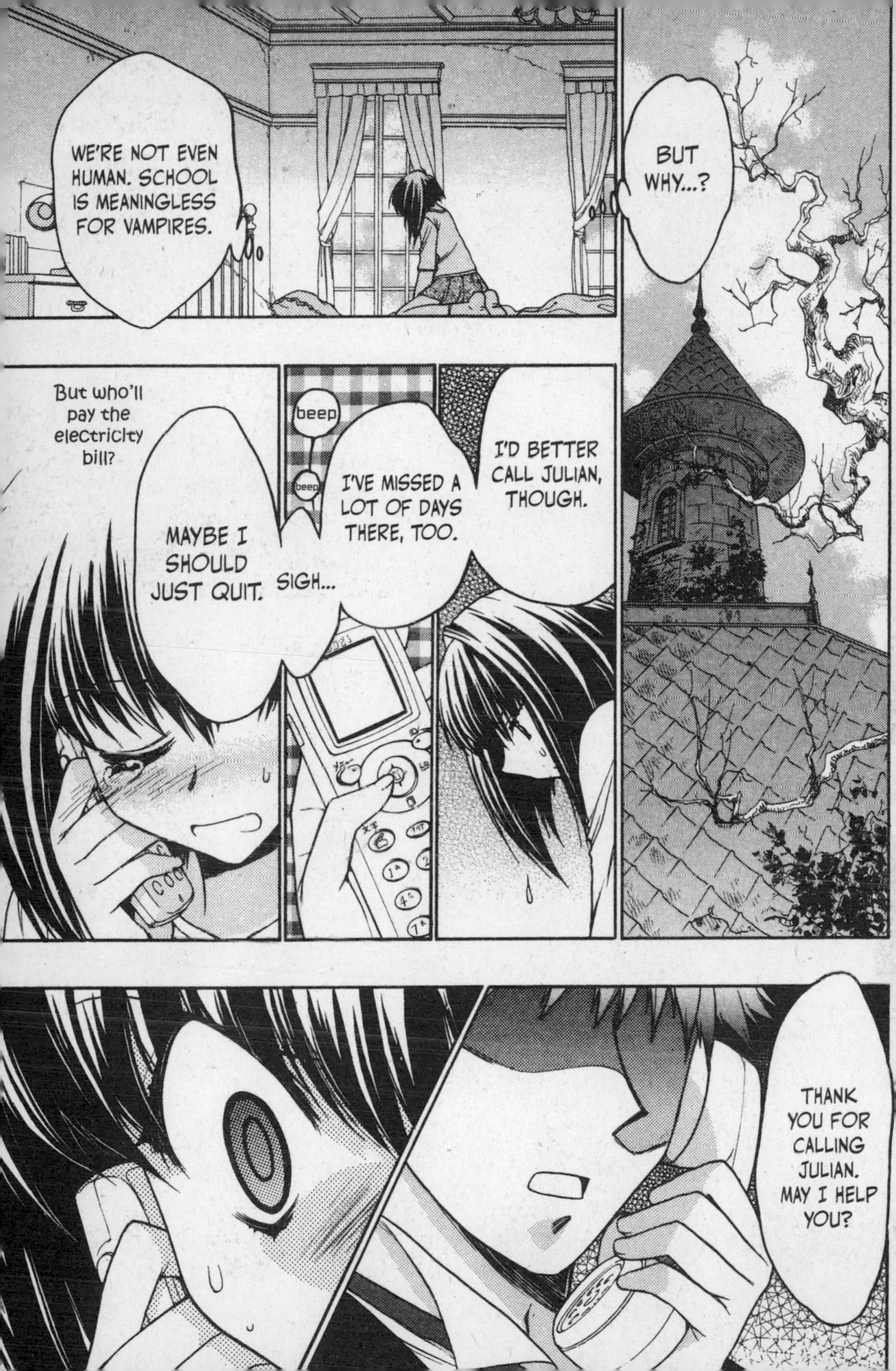
BUT WHY...?
WE'RE NOT EVEN HUMAN. SCHOOL IS MEANINGLESS FOR VAMPIRES.
I'D BETTER CALL JULIAN, THOUGH.
beep
beep
I'VE MISSED A LOT OF DAYS THERE, TOO.
SIGH...
MAYBE I SHOULD JUST QUIT.
But who'll pay the electricity bill?
THANK YOU FOR CALLING JULIAN. MAY I HELP YOU?

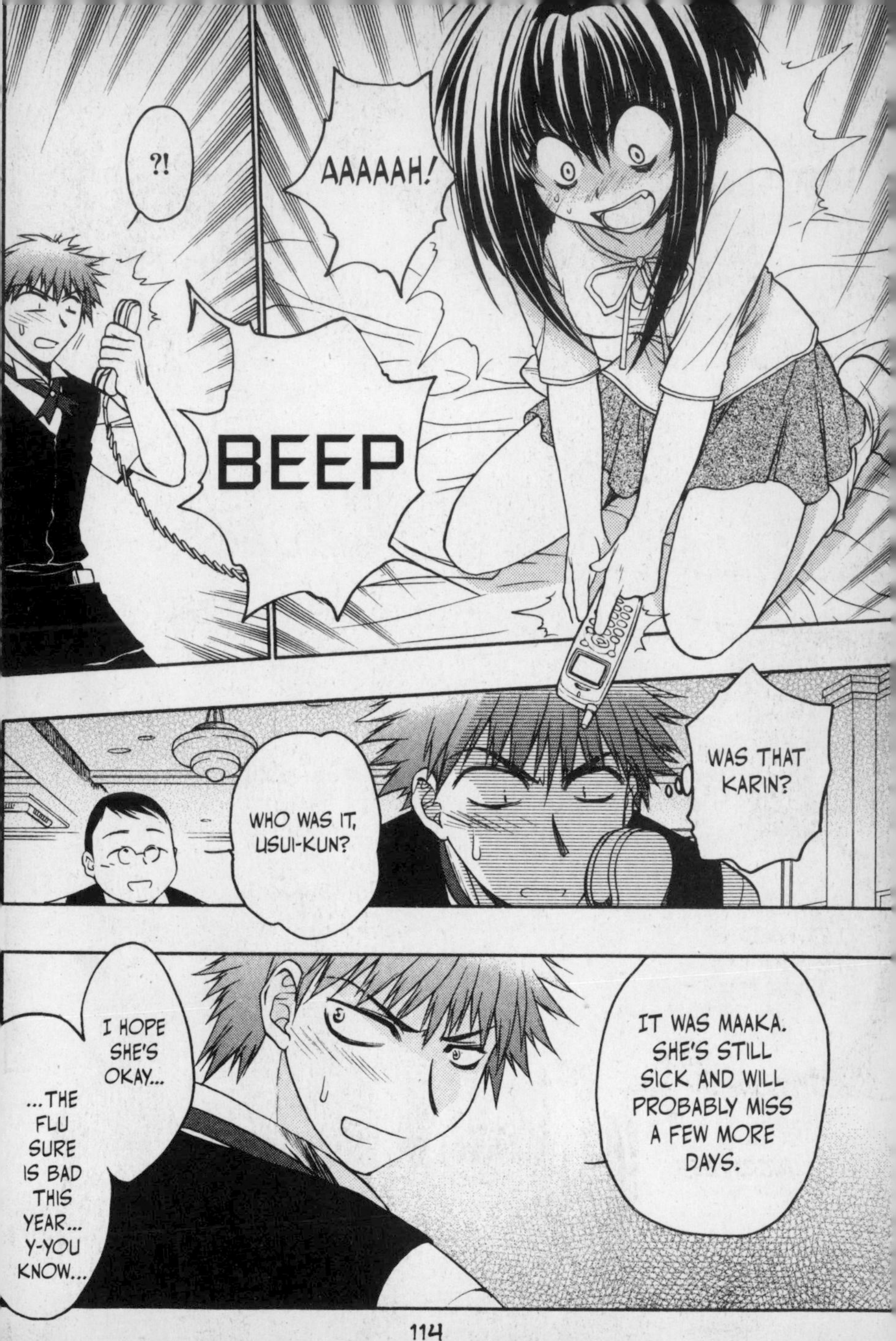
AAAAAH!
?!
BEEP
WAS THAT KARIN?
WHO WAS IT, USUI-KUN?
IT WAS MAAKA. SHE'S STILL SICK AND WILL PROBABLY MISS A FEW MORE DAYS.
I HOPE SHE'S OKAY...
...THE FLU SURE IS BAD THIS YEAR... Y-YOU KNOW...

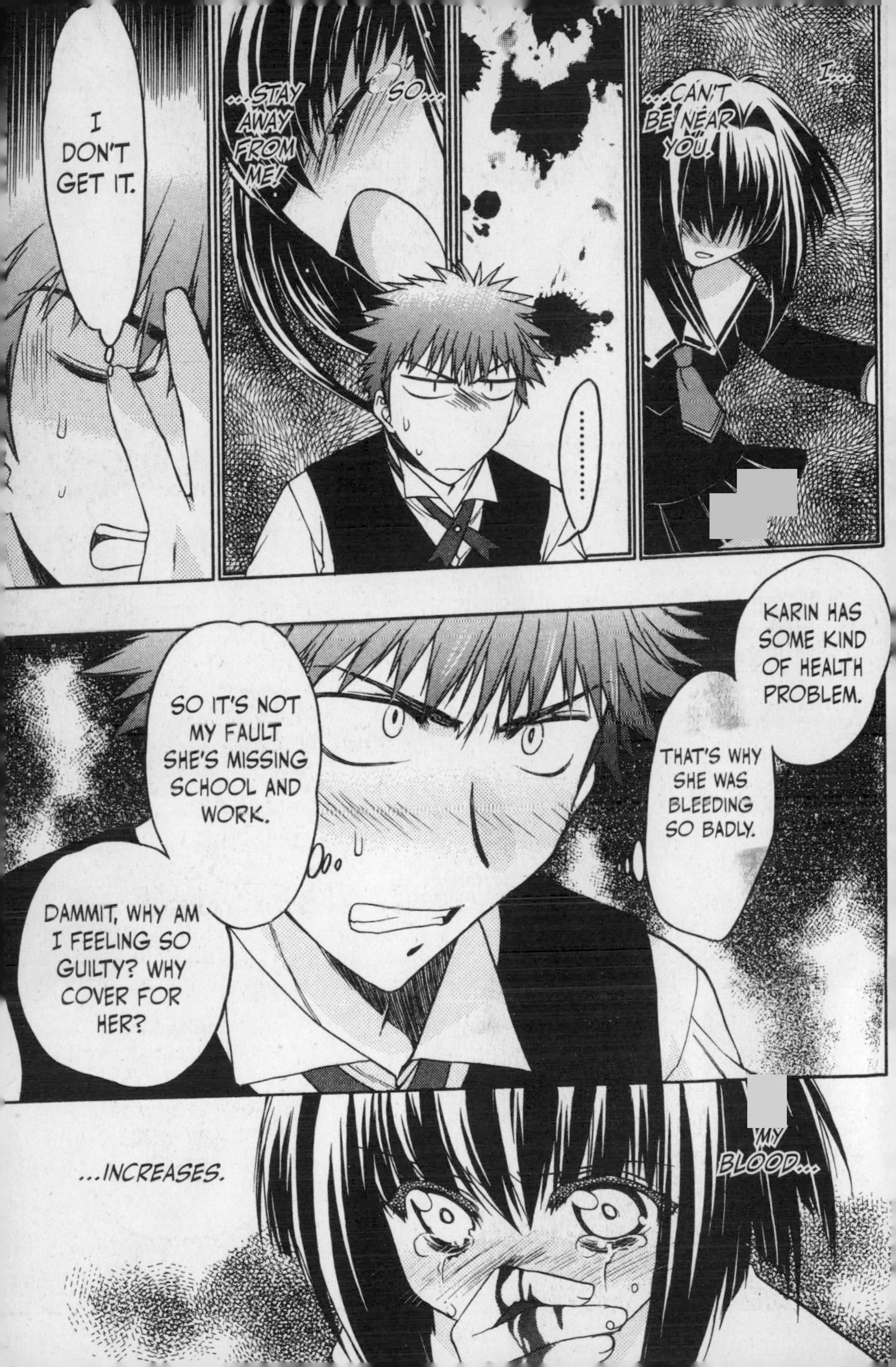
I...
...CAN'T BE NEAR YOU.
SO...
...STAY AWAY FROM ME!
......
I DON'T GET IT.
KARIN HAS SOME KIND OF HEALTH PROBLEM.
THAT'S WHY SHE WAS BLEEDING SO BADLY.
SO IT'S NOT MY FAULT SHE'S MISSING SCHOOL AND WORK.
DAMMIT, WHY AM I FEELING SO GUILTY? WHY COVER FOR HER?
MY BLOOD...
...INCREASES.

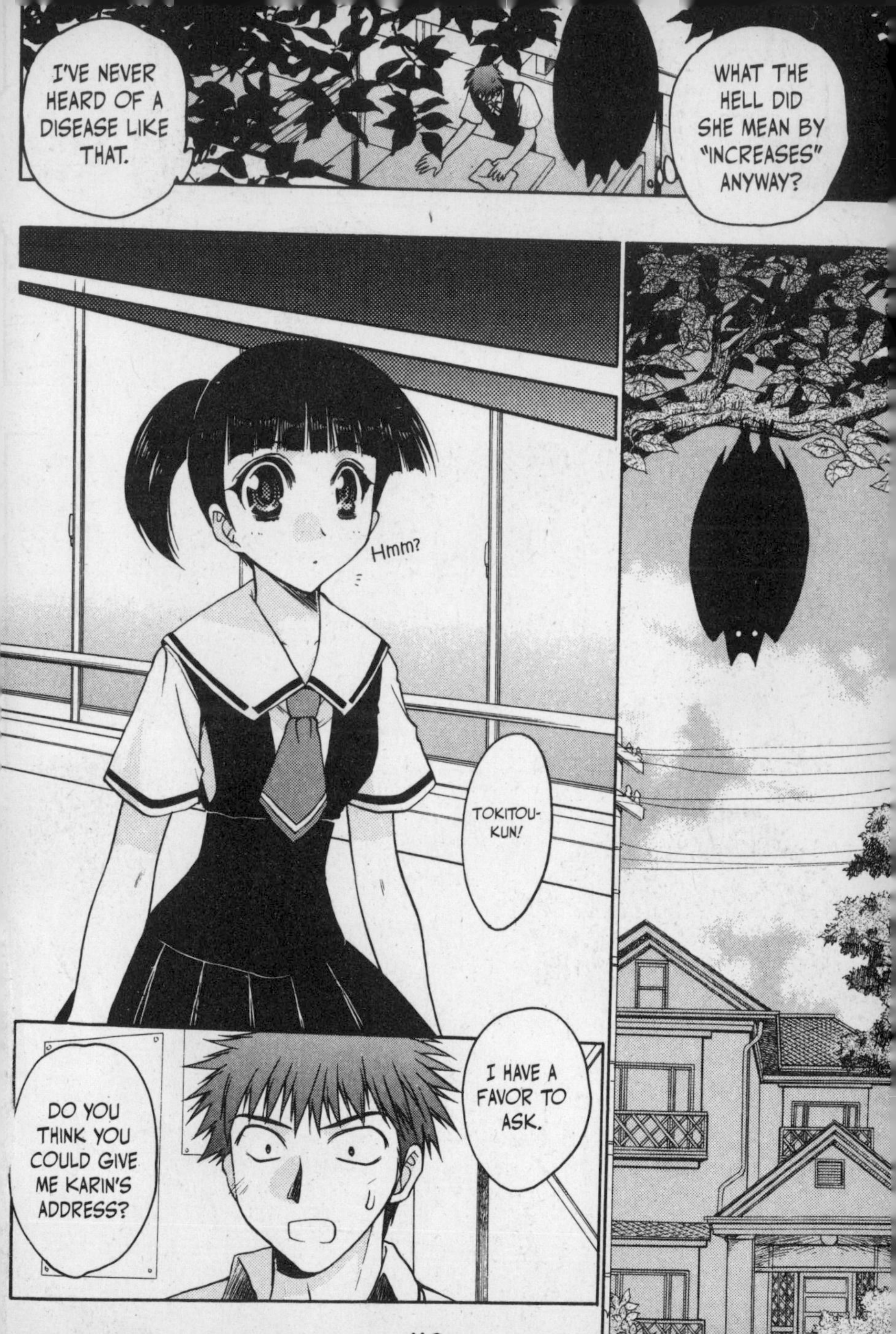
WHAT THE HELL DID SHE MEAN BY "INCREASES" ANYWAY?
I'VE NEVER HEARD OF A DISEASE LIKE THAT.
TOKITOU-KUN!
Hmm?
I HAVE A FAVOR TO ASK.
DO YOU THINK YOU COULD GIVE ME KARIN'S ADDRESS?

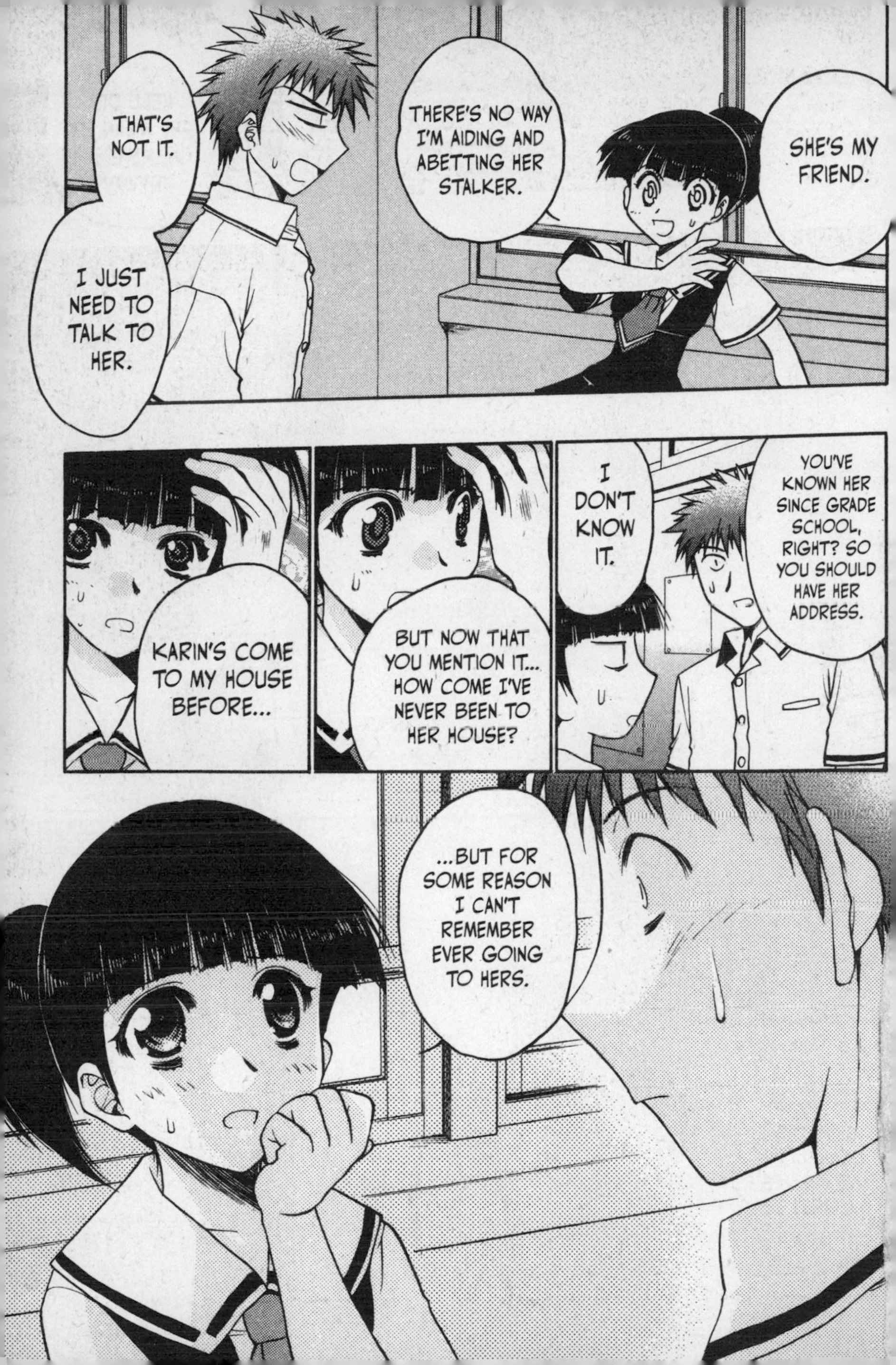
SHE'S MY FRIEND.
THERE'S NO WAY I'M AIDING AND ABETTING HER STALKER.
THAT'S NOT IT.
I JUST NEED TO TALK TO HER.
YOU'VE KNOWN HER SINCE GRADE SCHOOL, RIGHT? SO YOU SHOULD HAVE HER ADDRESS.
I DON'T KNOW IT.
BUT NOW THAT YOU MENTION IT... HOW COME I'VE NEVER BEEN TO HER HOUSE?
KARIN'S COME TO MY HOUSE BEFORE...
...BUT FOR SOME REASON I CAN'T REMEMBER EVER GOING TO HERS.

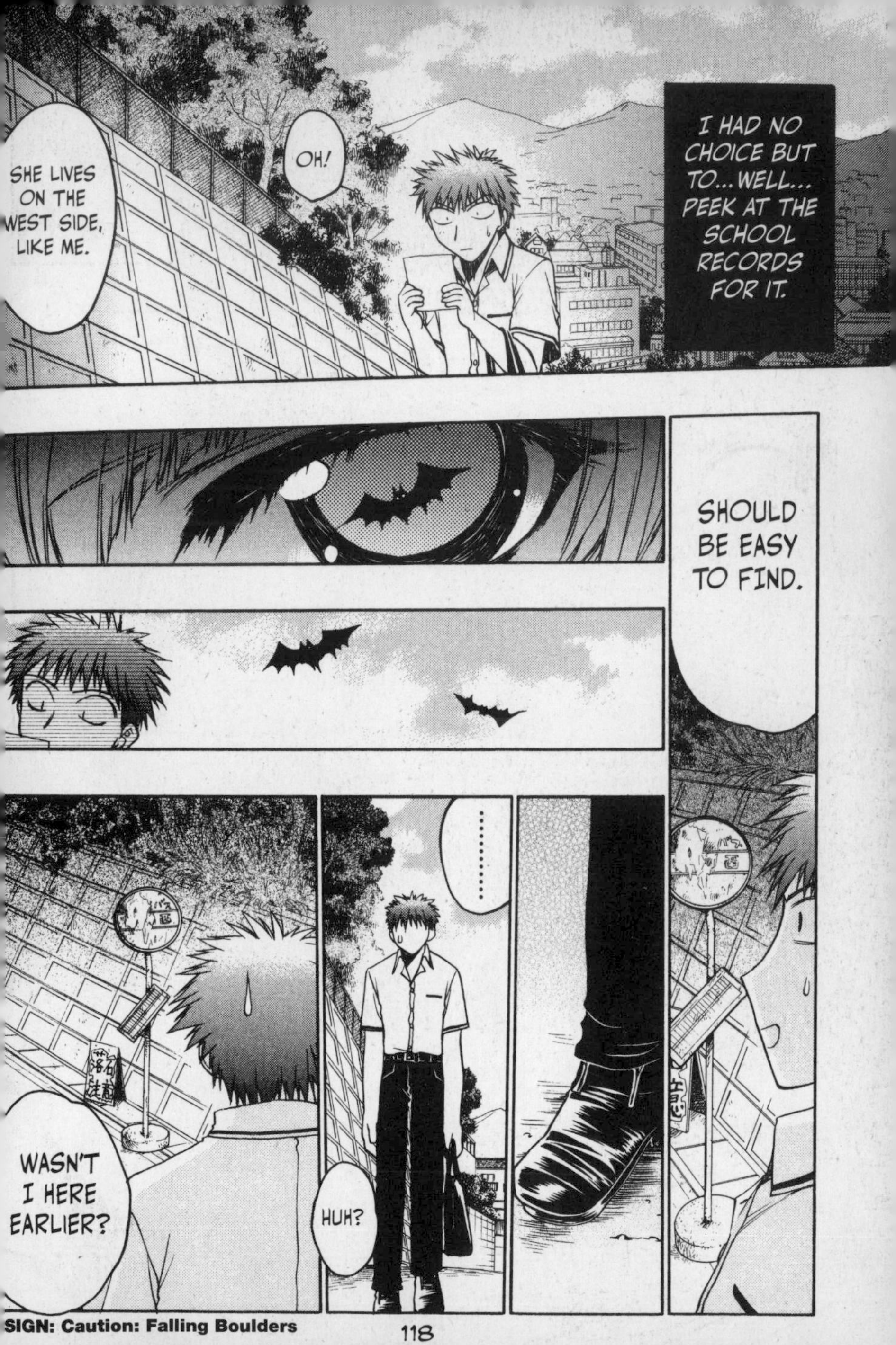
I HAD NO CHOICE BUT TO...WELL... PEEK AT THE SCHOOL RECORDS FOR IT.
OH!
SHE LIVES ON THE WEST SIDE, LIKE ME.
SHOULD BE EASY TO FIND.
.........
HUH?
WASN'T I HERE EARLIER?

**SIGN: Caution: Falling Boulders**

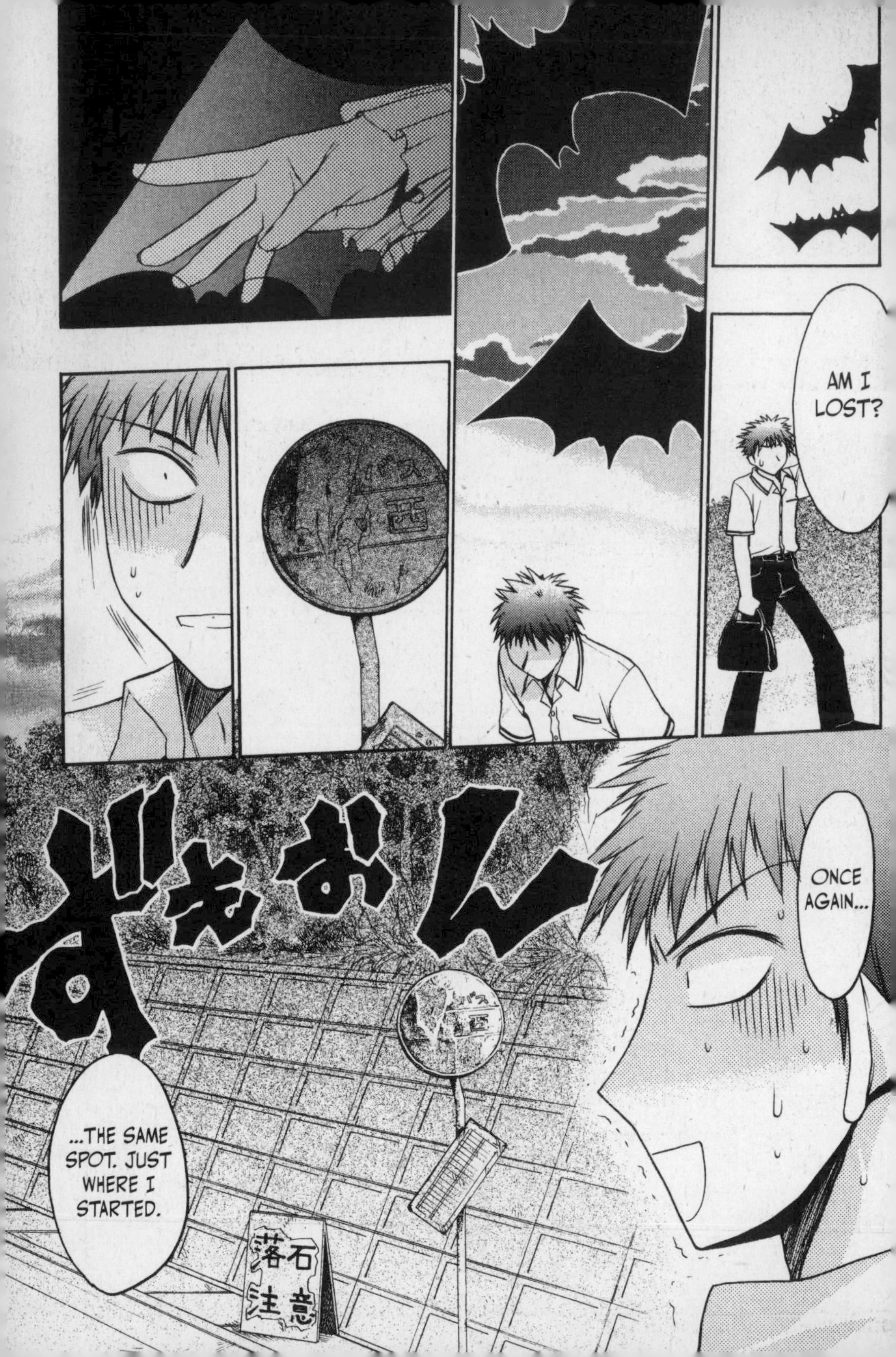
AM I LOST?
バス
西
ONCE AGAIN...
ずぉん
...THE SAME SPOT. JUST WHERE I STARTED.
落石注意

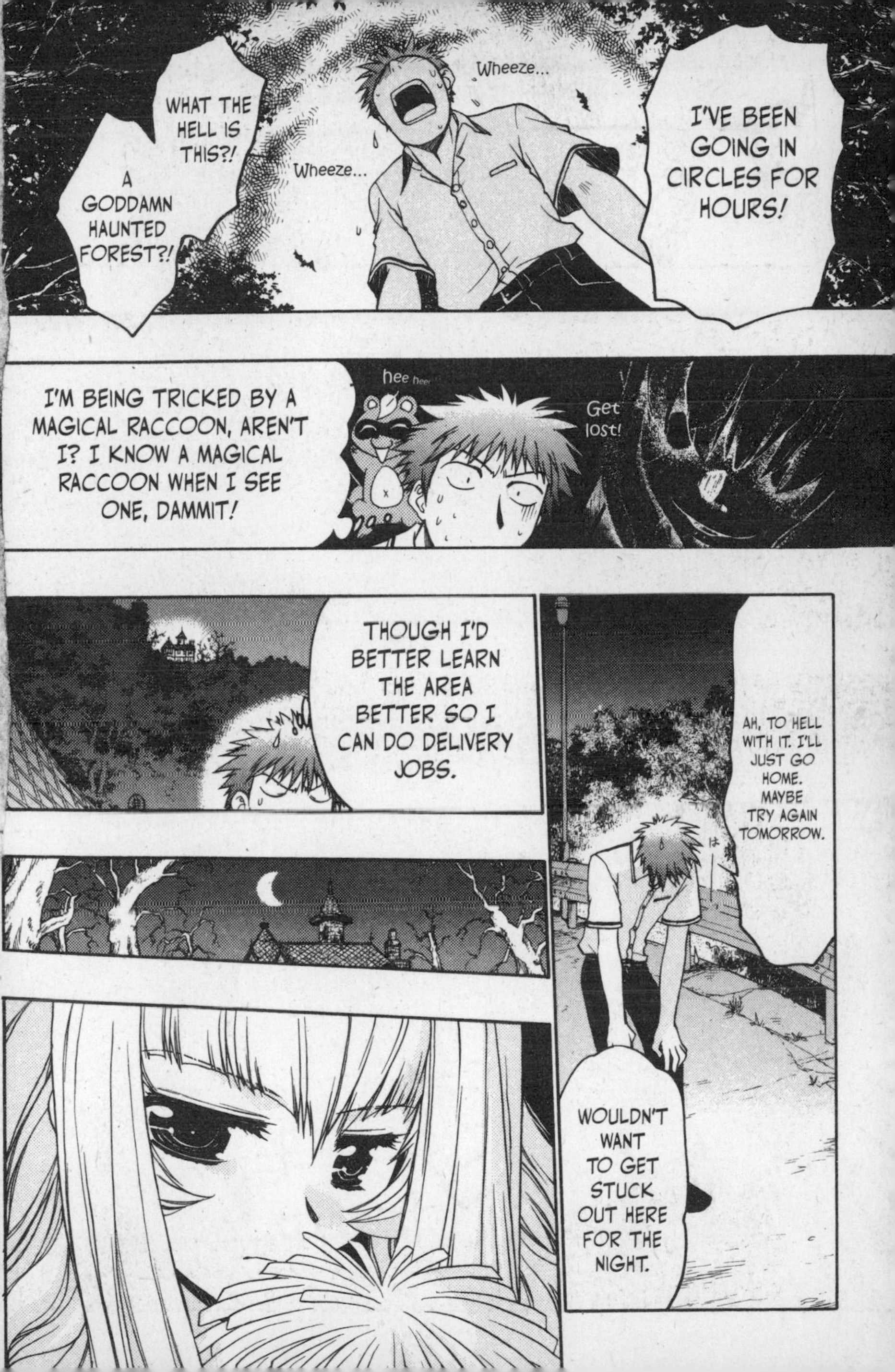
I'VE BEEN GOING IN CIRCLES FOR HOURS!
Wheeze...
WHAT THE HELL IS THIS?!
Wheeze...
A GODDAMN HAUNTED FOREST?!
Get lost!
hee
I'M BEING TRICKED BY A MAGICAL RACCOON, AREN'T I? I KNOW A MAGICAL RACCOON WHEN I SEE ONE, DAMMIT!
AH, TO HELL WITH IT. I'LL JUST GO HOME. MAYBE TRY AGAIN TOMORROW.
WOULDN'T WANT TO GET STUCK OUT HERE FOR THE NIGHT.
THOUGH I'D BETTER LEARN THE AREA BETTER SO I CAN DO DELIVERY JOBS.

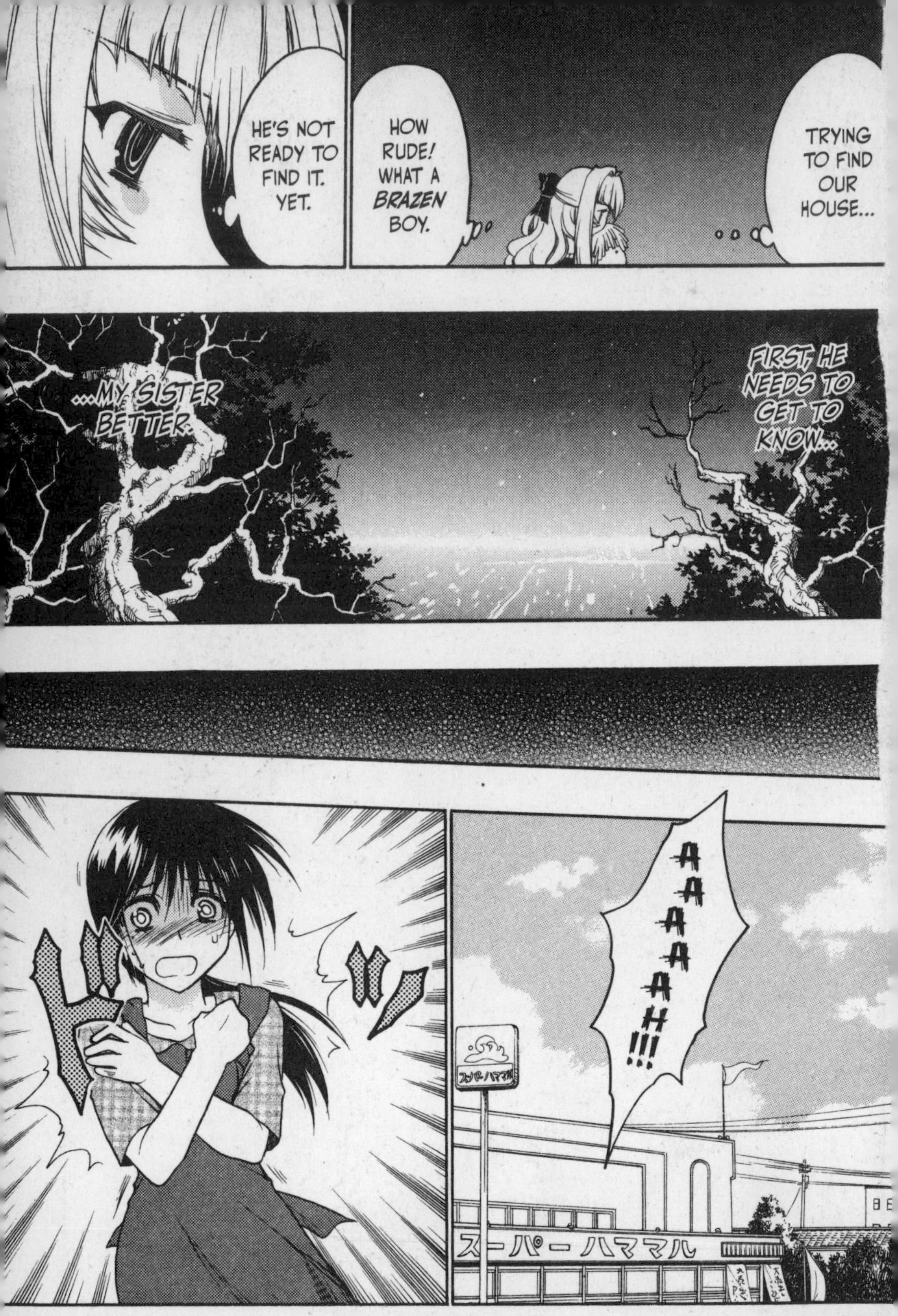
TRYING TO FIND OUR HOUSE...
HOW RUDE! WHAT A BRAZEN BOY.
HE'S NOT READY TO FIND IT. YET.
FIRST, HE NEEDS TO GET TO KNOW...
...MY SISTER BETTER.
AAAAAH!!!
スーパーハママル

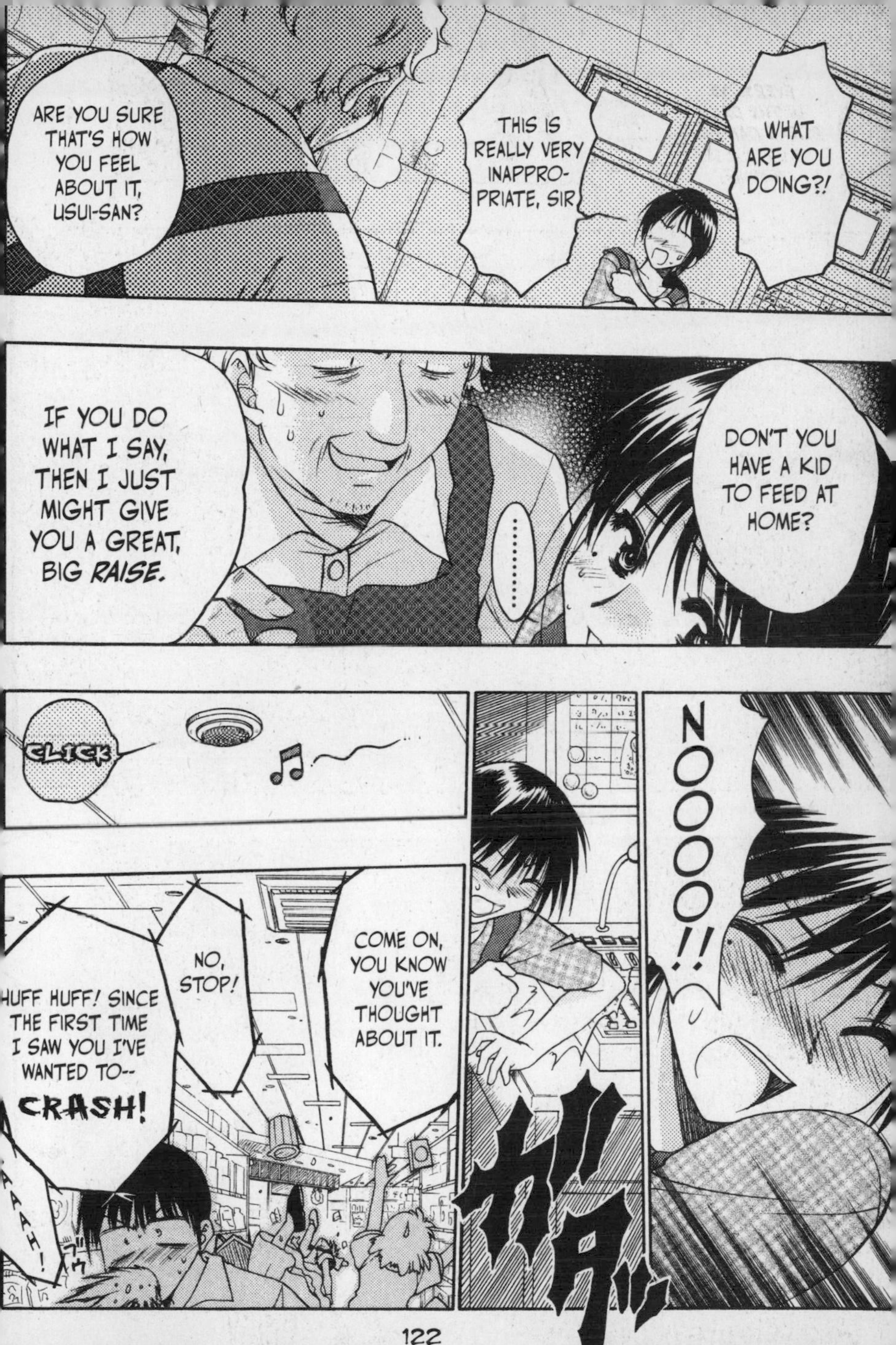
WHAT ARE YOU DOING?!
THIS IS REALLY VERY INAPPROPRIATE, SIR
ARE YOU SURE THAT'S HOW YOU FEEL ABOUT IT, USUI-SAN?
DON'T YOU HAVE A KID TO FEED AT HOME?
......
IF YOU DO WHAT I SAY, THEN I JUST MIGHT GIVE YOU A GREAT, BIG *RAISE.*
NOOOO!!
CLICK
COME ON, YOU KNOW YOU'VE THOUGHT ABOUT IT.
NO, STOP!
HUFF HUFF! SINCE THE FIRST TIME I SAW YOU I'VE WANTED TO--
CRASH!
AAAH!

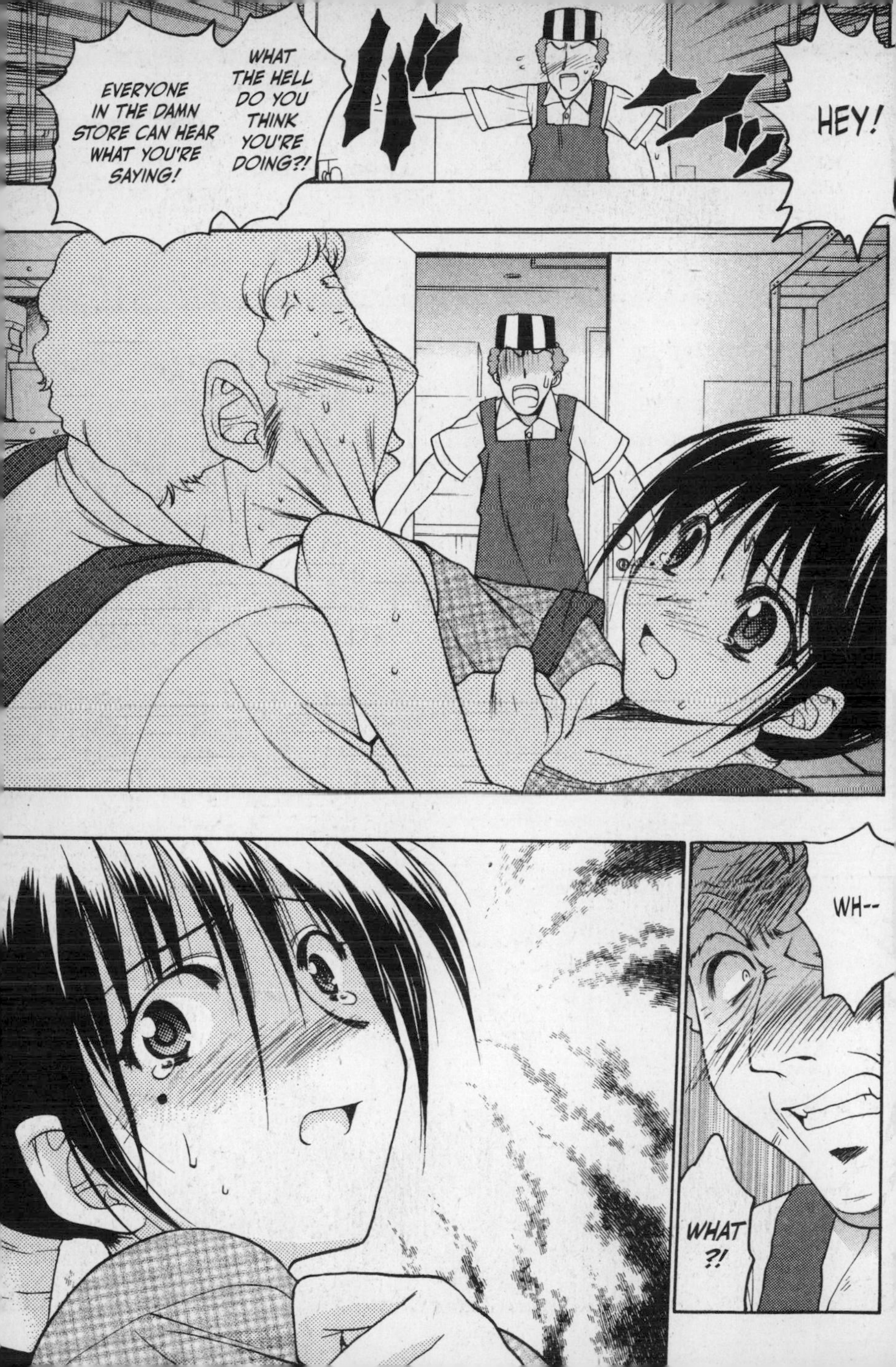
HEY!
WHAT THE HELL DO YOU THINK YOU'RE DOING?!
EVERYONE IN THE DAMN STORE CAN HEAR WHAT YOU'RE SAYING!
WH--
WHAT ?!

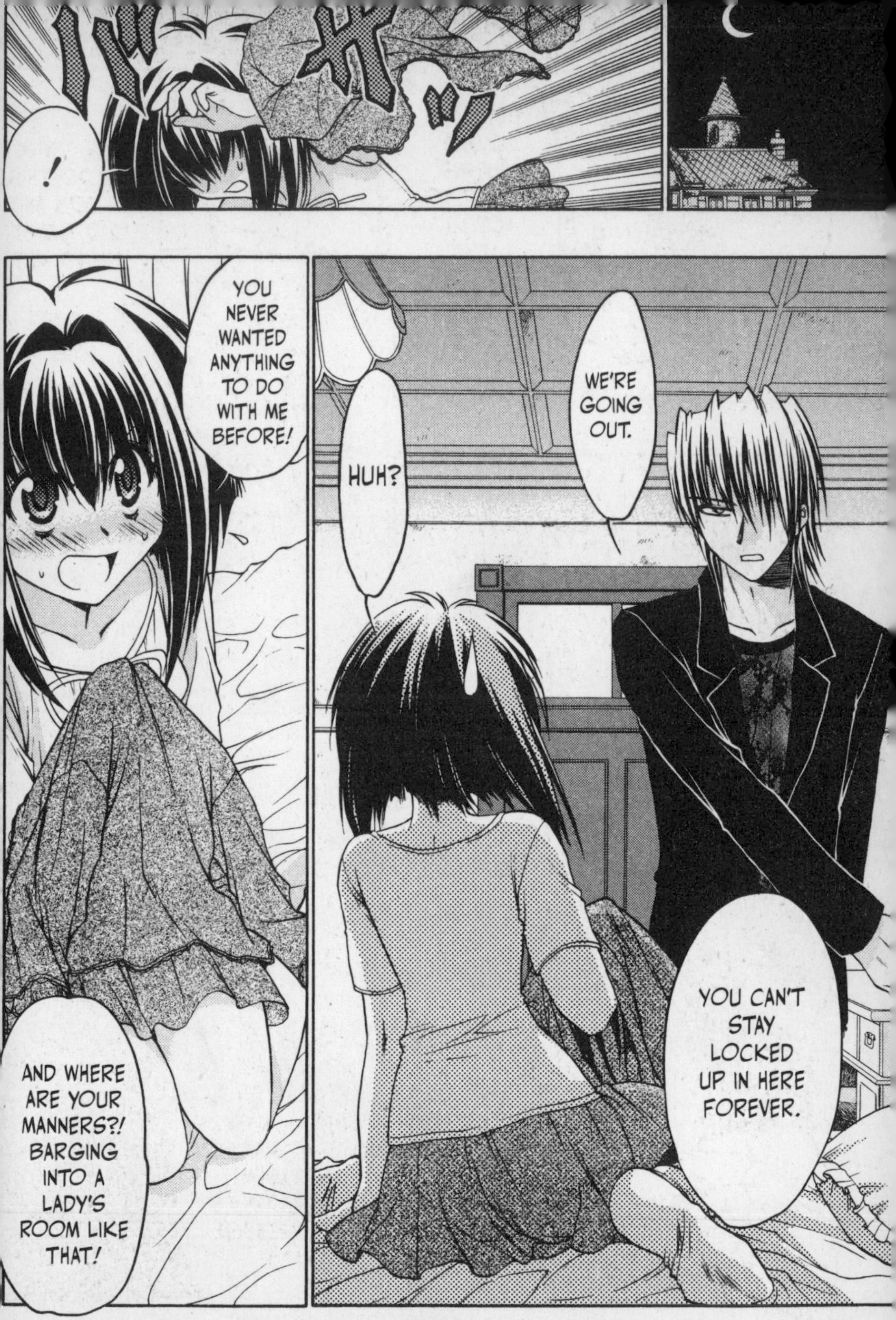
!
WE'RE GOING OUT.
HUH?
YOU CAN'T STAY LOCKED UP IN HERE FOREVER.
YOU NEVER WANTED ANYTHING TO DO WITH ME BEFORE!
AND WHERE ARE YOUR MANNERS?! BARGING INTO A LADY'S ROOM LIKE THAT!

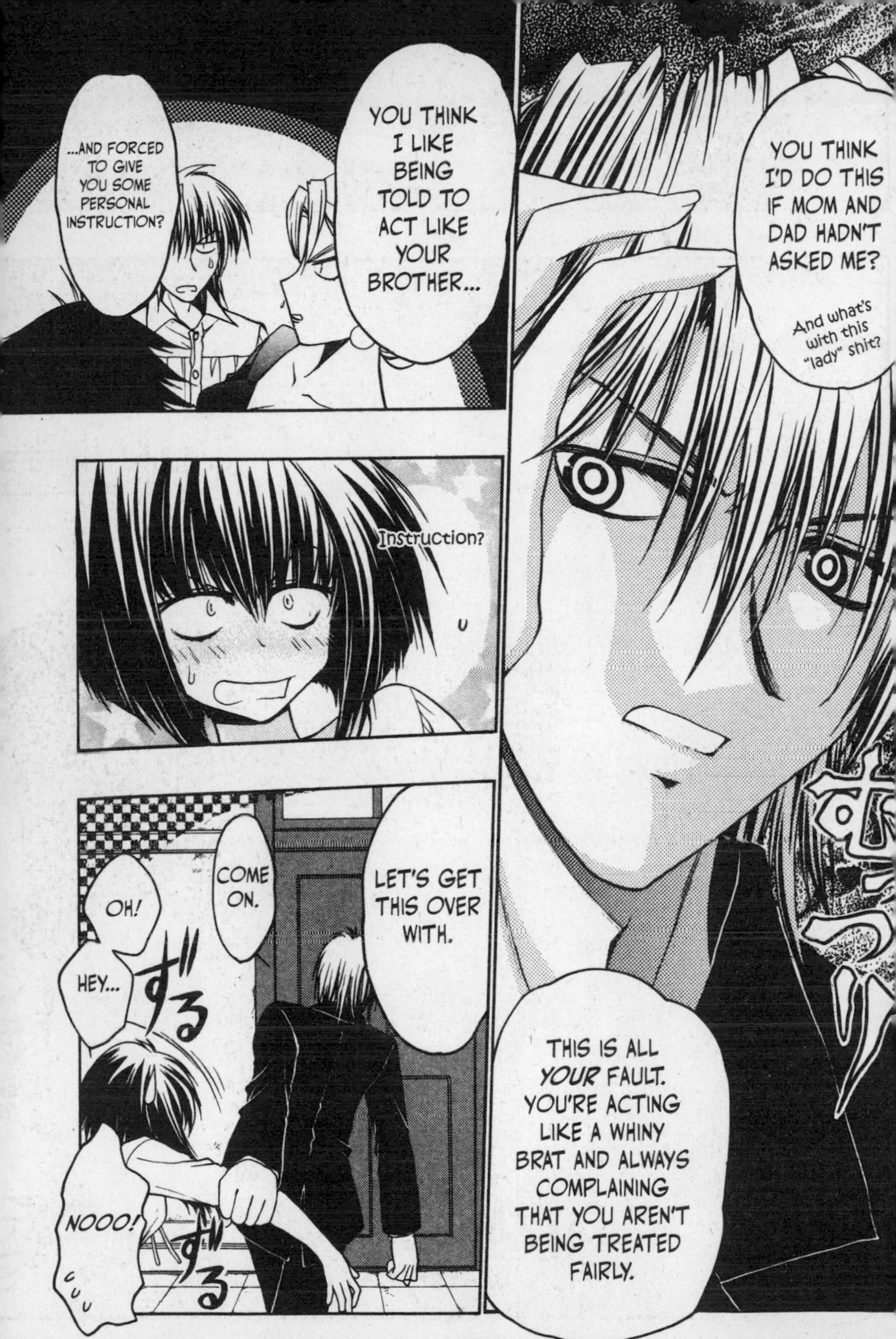
YOU THINK I'D DO THIS IF MOM AND DAD HADN'T ASKED ME?
And what's with this "lady" shit?
THIS IS ALL *YOUR* FAULT. YOU'RE ACTING LIKE A WHINY BRAT AND ALWAYS COMPLAINING THAT YOU AREN'T BEING TREATED FAIRLY.
YOU THINK I LIKE BEING TOLD TO ACT LIKE YOUR BROTHER...
...AND FORCED TO GIVE YOU SOME PERSONAL INSTRUCTION?
Instruction?
LET'S GET THIS OVER WITH.
COME ON.
OH!
HEY...
ずる
NOOO!
ずる

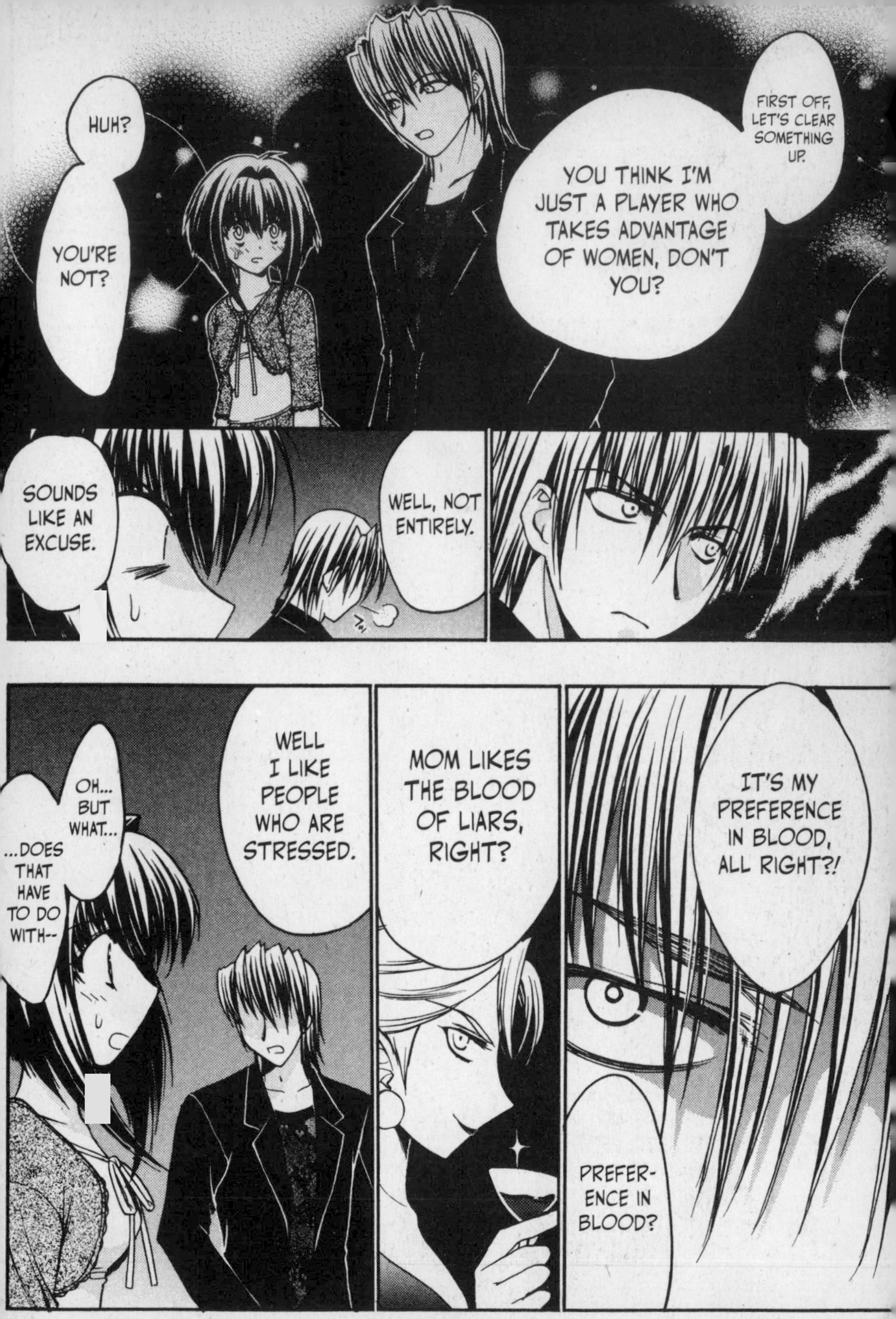
FIRST OFF, LET'S CLEAR SOMETHING UP.
YOU THINK I'M JUST A PLAYER WHO TAKES ADVANTAGE OF WOMEN, DON'T YOU?
HUH?
YOU'RE NOT?
WELL, NOT ENTIRELY.
SOUNDS LIKE AN EXCUSE.
IT'S MY PREFERENCE IN BLOOD, ALL RIGHT?!
PREFER-ENCE IN BLOOD?
MOM LIKES THE BLOOD OF LIARS, RIGHT?
WELL I LIKE PEOPLE WHO ARE STRESSED.
OH... BUT WHAT...
...DOES THAT HAVE TO DO WITH--

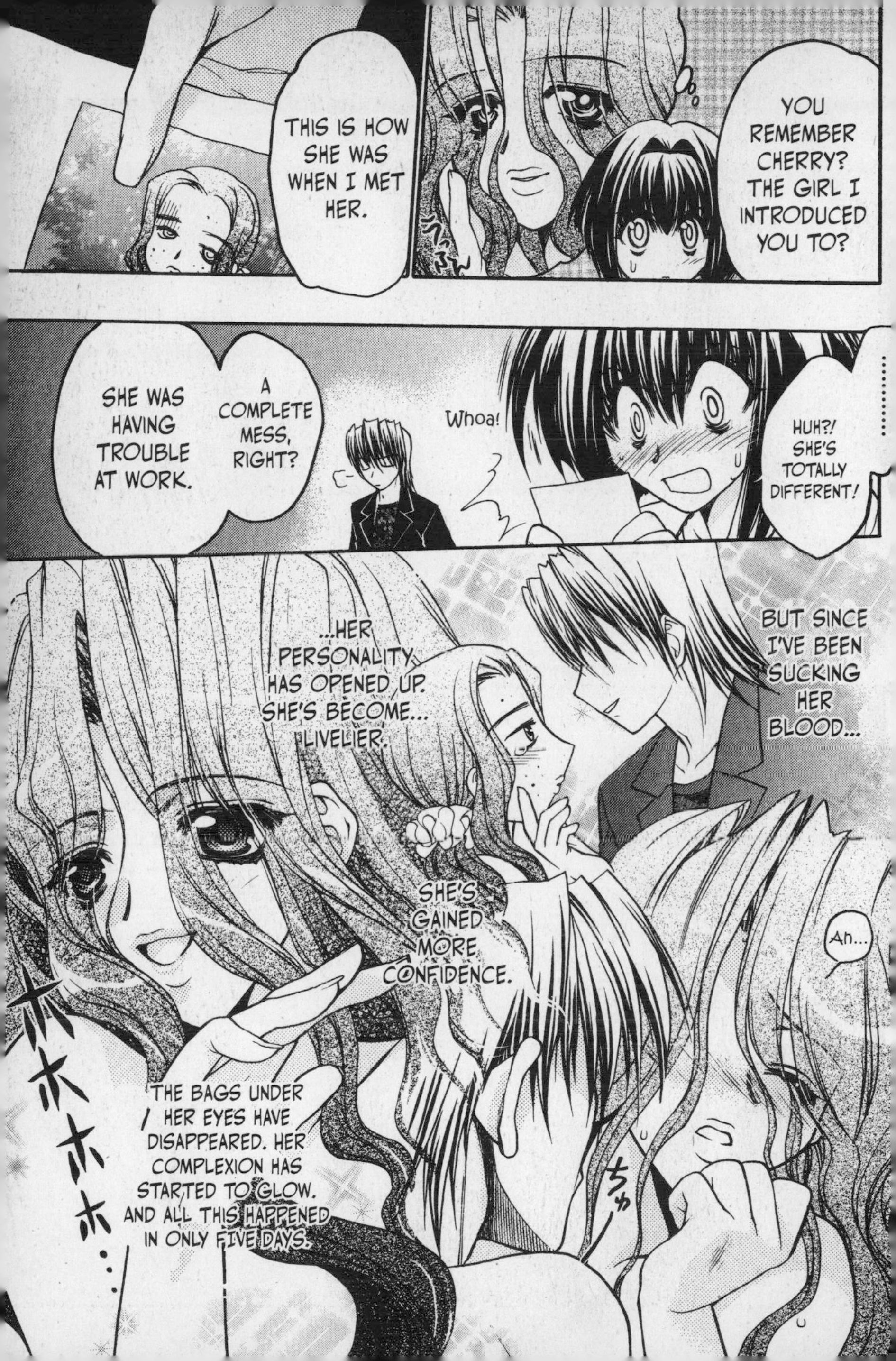
YOU REMEMBER CHERRY? THE GIRL I INTRODUCED YOU TO?
THIS IS HOW SHE WAS WHEN I MET HER.
HUH?! SHE'S TOTALLY DIFFERENT!
Whoa!
A COMPLETE MESS, RIGHT?
SHE WAS HAVING TROUBLE AT WORK.
BUT SINCE I'VE BEEN SUCKING HER BLOOD...
...HER PERSONALITY HAS OPENED UP. SHE'S BECOME... LIVELIER.
Ah...
SHE'S GAINED MORE CONFIDENCE.
ちゅ
THE BAGS UNDER HER EYES HAVE DISAPPEARED. HER COMPLEXION HAS STARTED TO GLOW. AND ALL THIS HAPPENED IN ONLY FIVE DAYS.
ホホホホ…

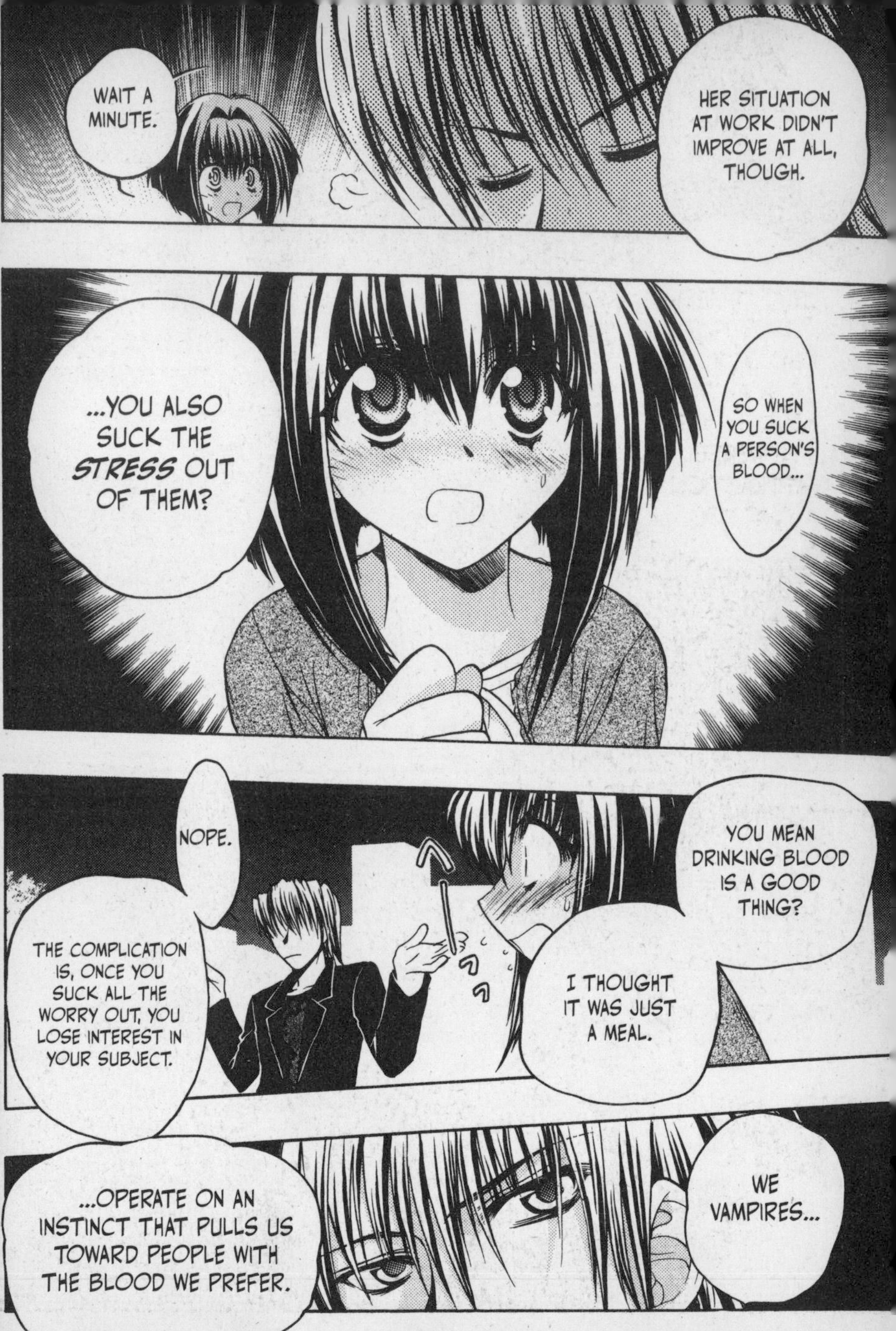
HER SITUATION AT WORK DIDN'T IMPROVE AT ALL, THOUGH.
WAIT A MINUTE.
SO WHEN YOU SUCK A PERSON'S BLOOD...
...YOU ALSO SUCK THE STRESS OUT OF THEM?
YOU MEAN DRINKING BLOOD IS A GOOD THING?
I THOUGHT IT WAS JUST A MEAL.
NOPE.
THE COMPLICATION IS, ONCE YOU SUCK ALL THE WORRY OUT, YOU LOSE INTEREST IN YOUR SUBJECT.
WE VAMPIRES...
...OPERATE ON AN INSTINCT THAT PULLS US TOWARD PEOPLE WITH THE BLOOD WE PREFER.

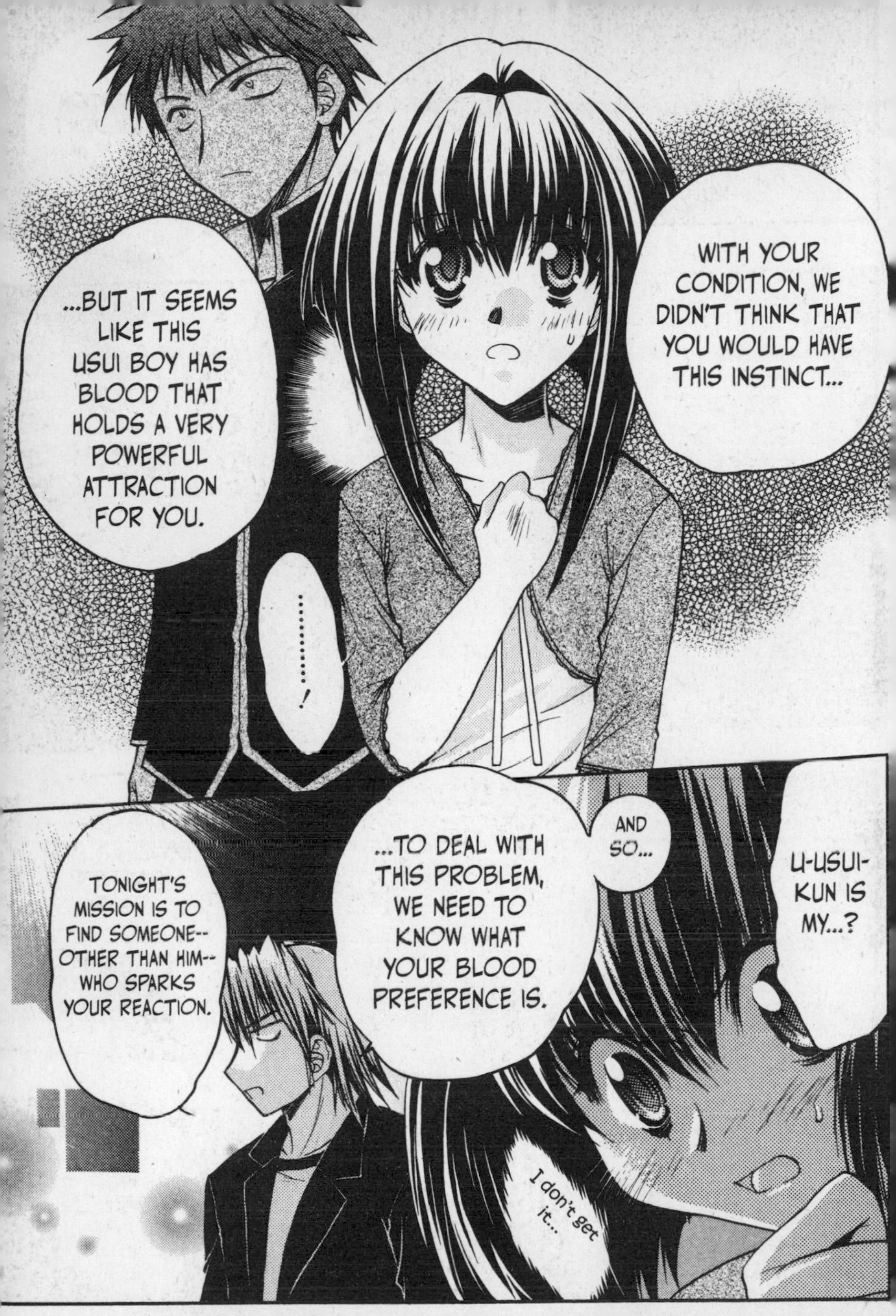
WITH YOUR CONDITION, WE DIDN'T THINK THAT YOU WOULD HAVE THIS INSTINCT...
...BUT IT SEEMS LIKE THIS USUI BOY HAS BLOOD THAT HOLDS A VERY POWERFUL ATTRACTION FOR YOU.
.........!
U-USUI-KUN IS MY...?
I don't get it...
AND SO...
...TO DEAL WITH THIS PROBLEM, WE NEED TO KNOW WHAT YOUR BLOOD PREFERENCE IS.
TONIGHT'S MISSION IS TO FIND SOMEONE--OTHER THAN HIM--WHO SPARKS YOUR REACTION.

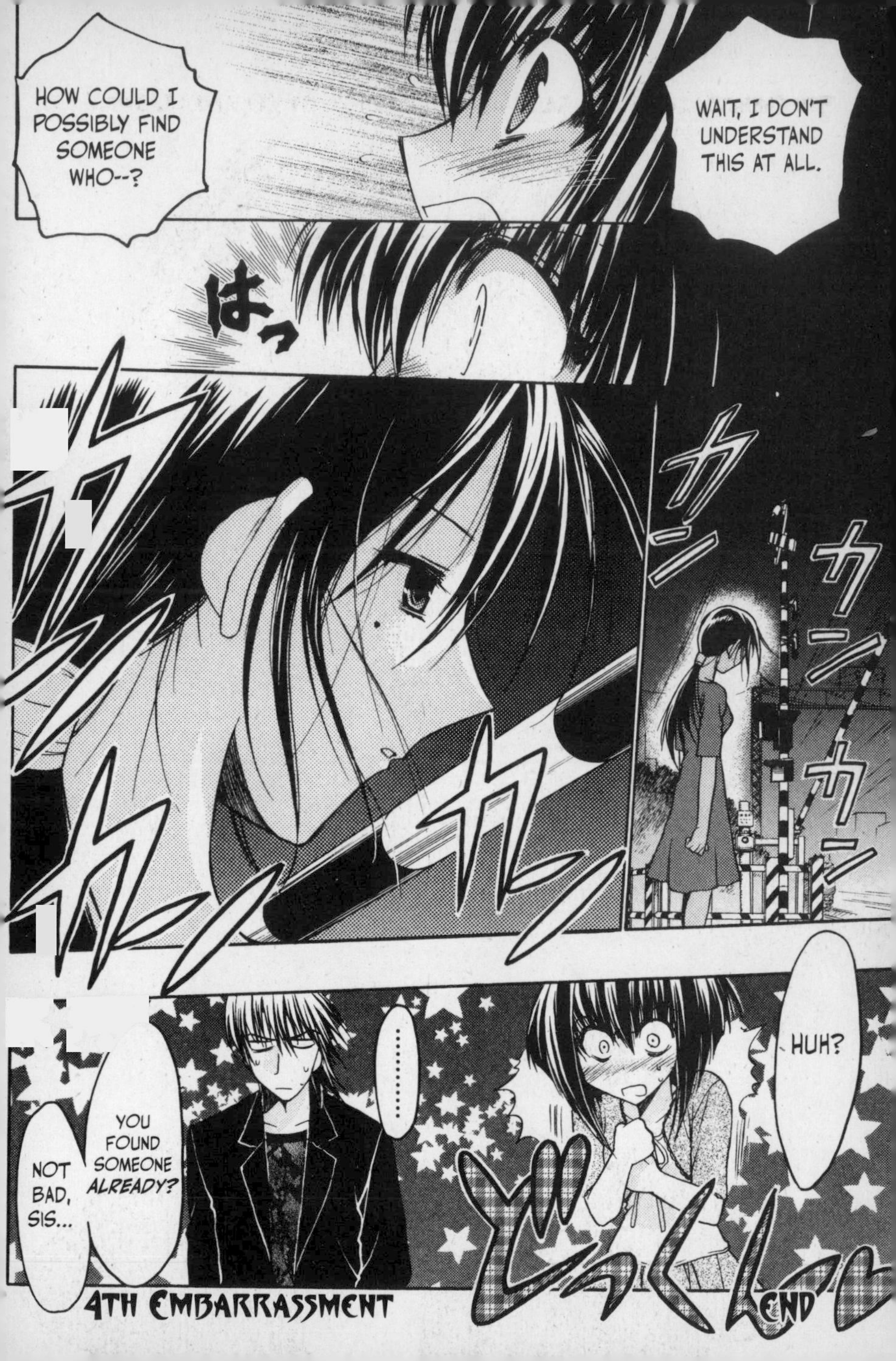
WAIT, I DON'T UNDERSTAND THIS AT ALL.
HOW COULD I POSSIBLY FIND SOMEONE WHO--?
はっ
カーン
カーン
カーン
カン
カン
HUH?
......
YOU FOUND SOMEONE ALREADY?
NOT BAD, SIS...
どっくん
END
4TH EMBARRASSMENT

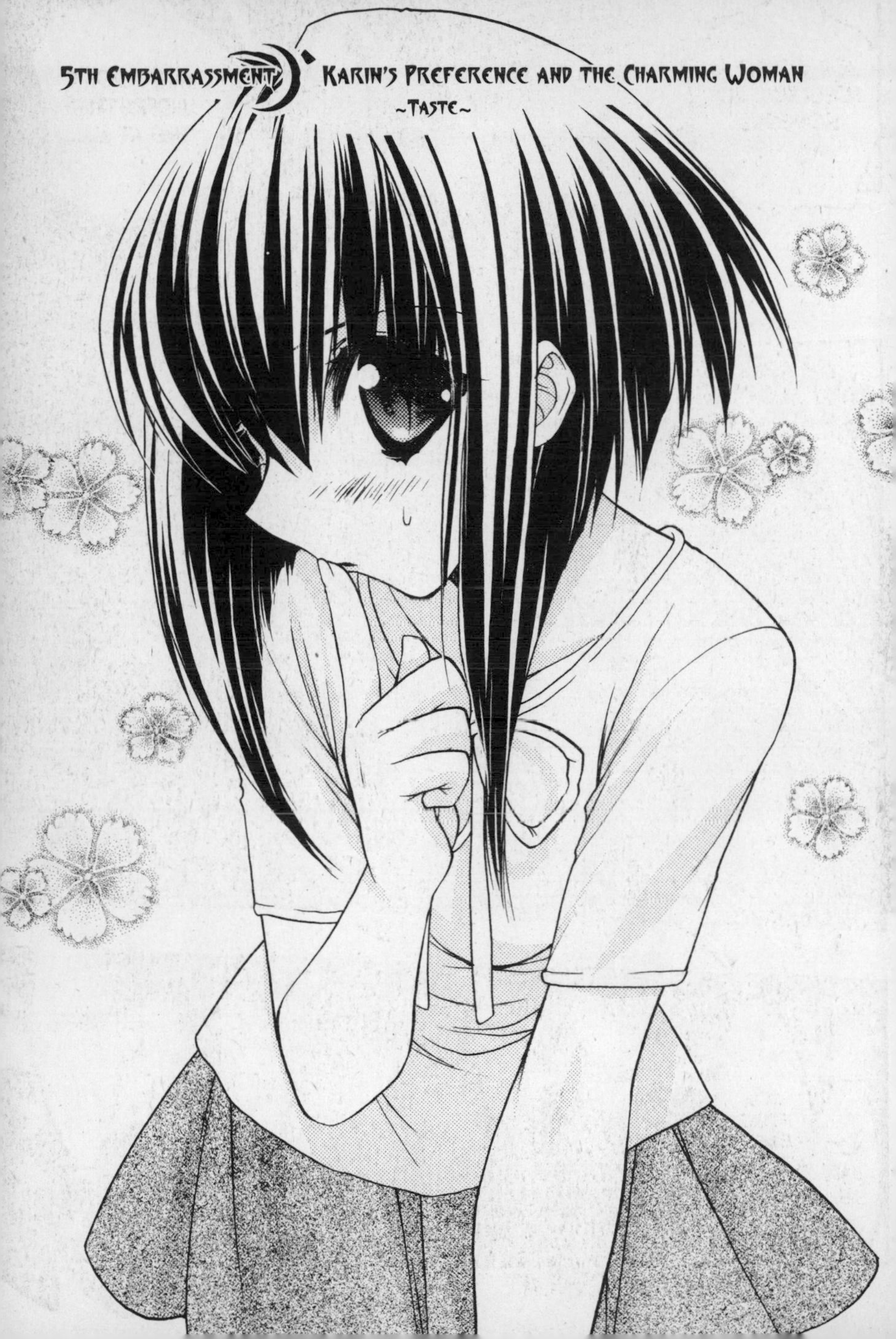
5th Embarrassment Karin's Preference and the Charming Woman
~Taste~

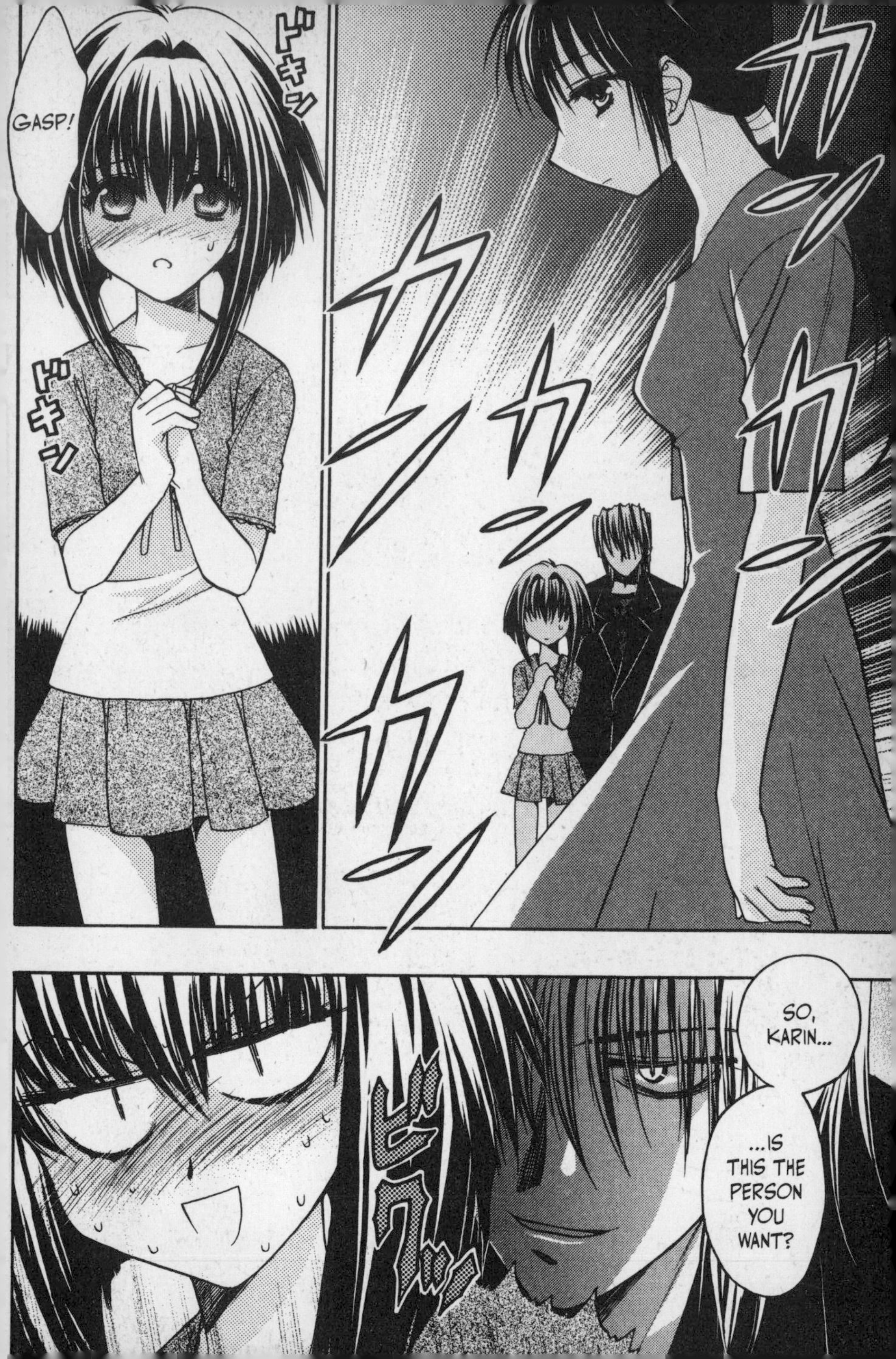
GASP!
ドキッ
ドキン
SO, KARIN...
...IS THIS THE PERSON YOU WANT?

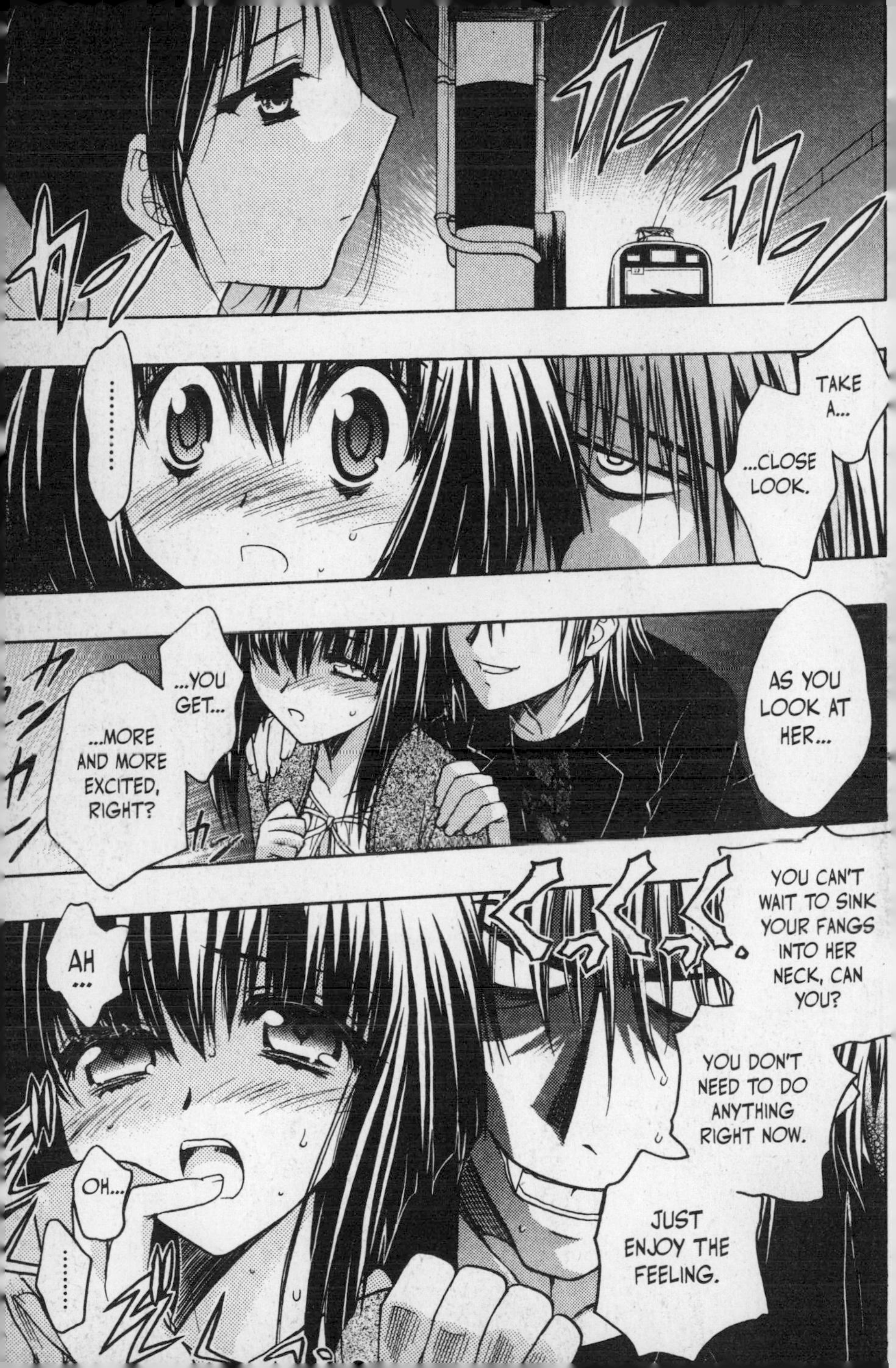
TAKE A...
...CLOSE LOOK.
......
AS YOU LOOK AT HER...
...YOU GET...
...MORE AND MORE EXCITED, RIGHT?
YOU CAN'T WAIT TO SINK YOUR FANGS INTO HER NECK, CAN YOU?
YOU DON'T NEED TO DO ANYTHING RIGHT NOW.
JUST ENJOY THE FEELING.
AH...
OH...
......

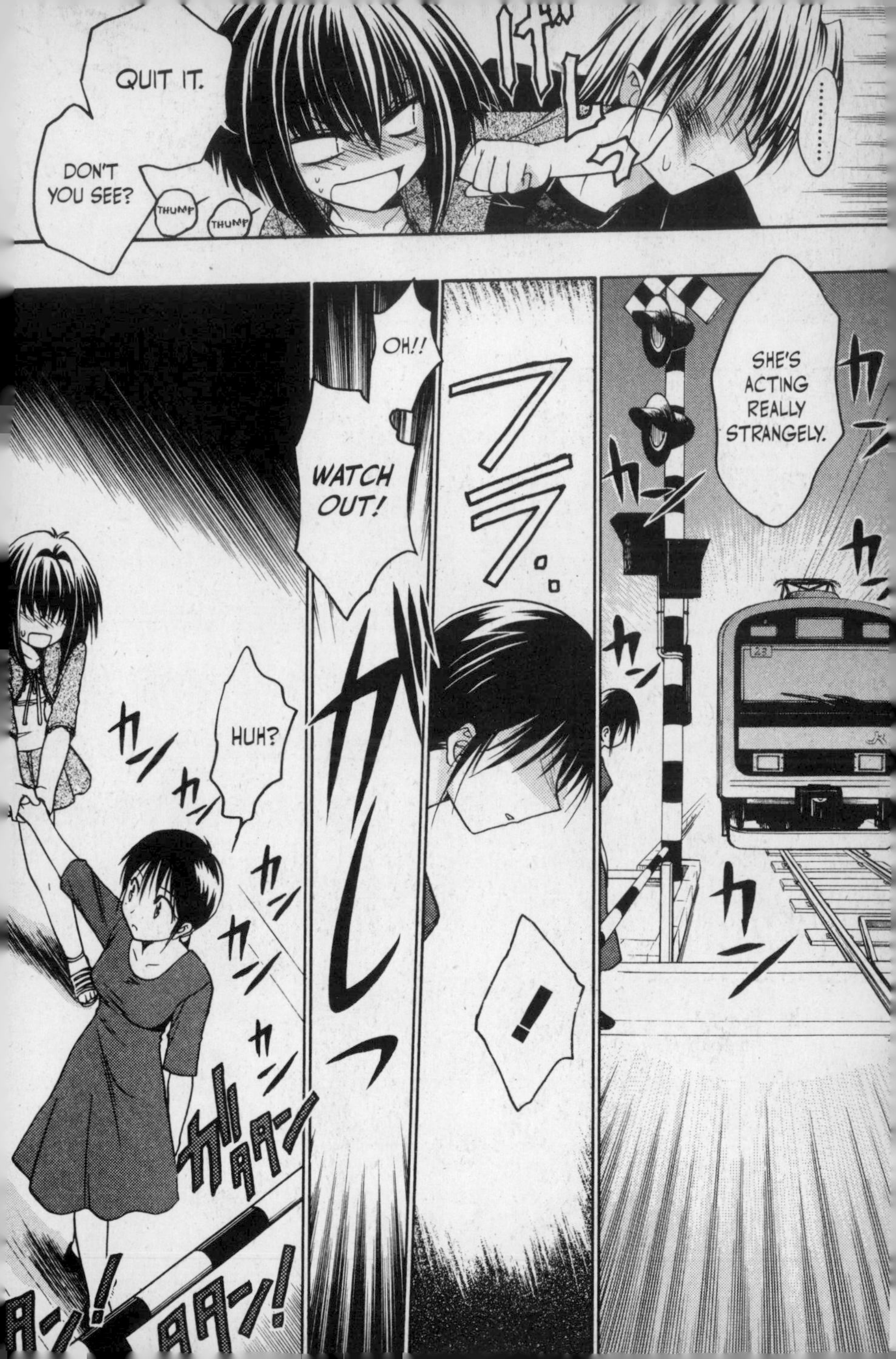
......
QUIT IT.
DON'T YOU SEE?
THUMP
THUMP
SHE'S ACTING REALLY STRANGELY.
!
OH!!
WATCH OUT!
HUH?

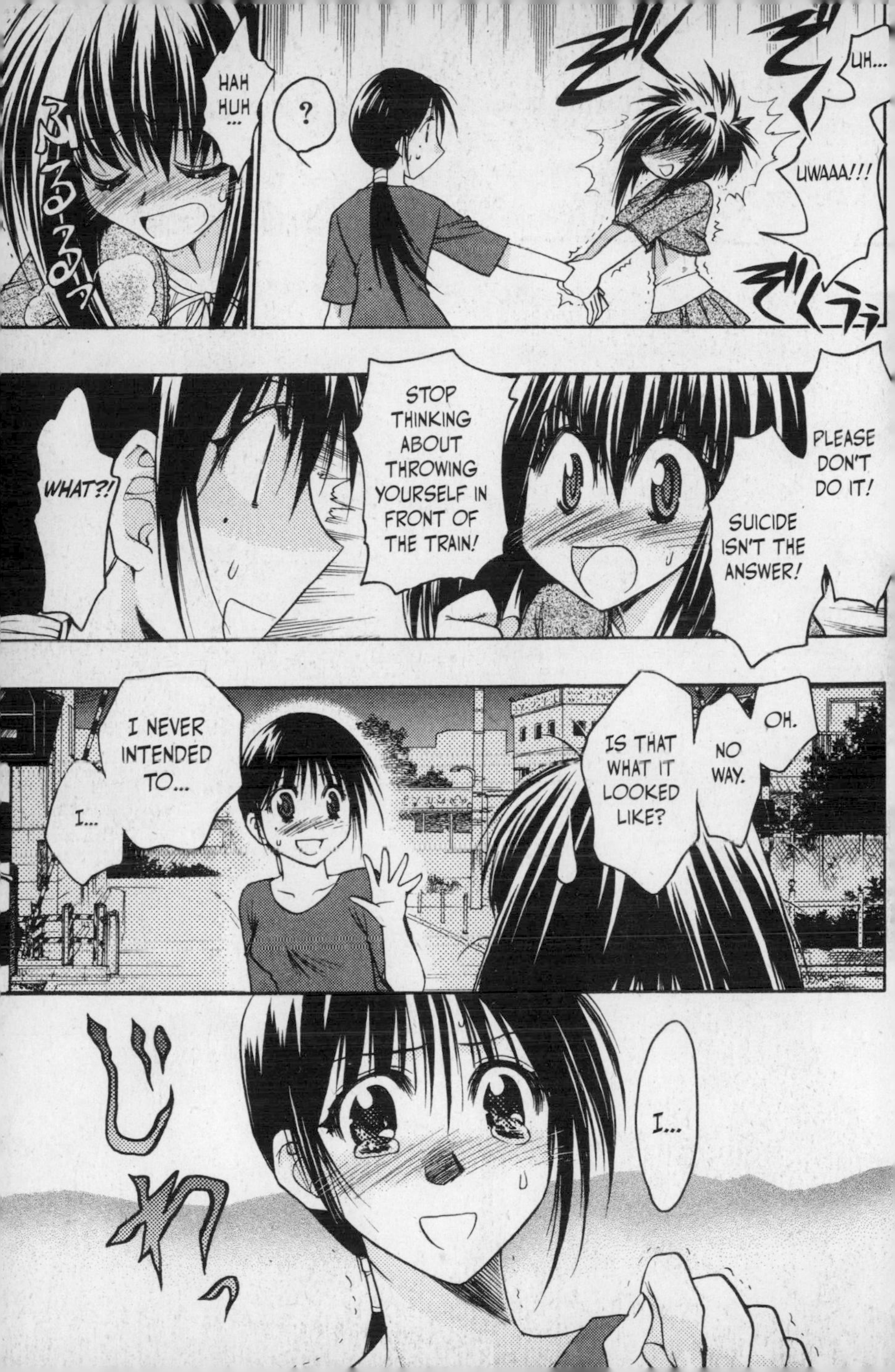
UH...
UWAAA!!!
?
HAH HUH ...
ぷるるるっ
PLEASE DON'T DO IT!
SUICIDE ISN'T THE ANSWER!
STOP THINKING ABOUT THROWING YOURSELF IN FRONT OF THE TRAIN!
WHAT?!
OH.
NO WAY.
IS THAT WHAT IT LOOKED LIKE?
I NEVER INTENDED TO...
I...
I...
じわっ

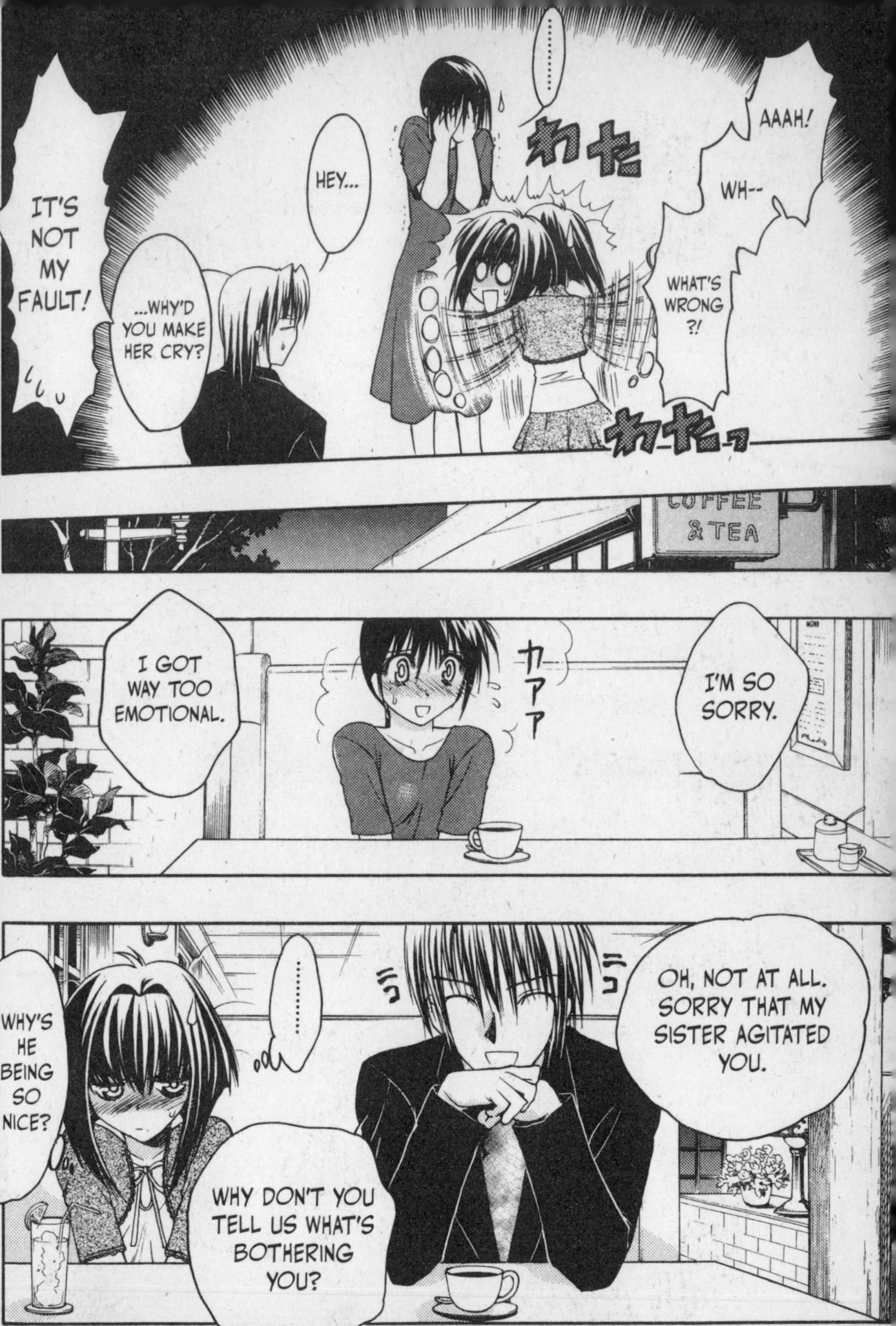
AAAH!
WH--
WHAT'S WRONG ?!
わた
わたっ
......
HEY...
...WHY'D YOU MAKE HER CRY?
IT'S NOT MY FAULT!
COFFEE & TEA
I'M SO SORRY.
カアア
I GOT WAY TOO EMOTIONAL.
OH, NOT AT ALL. SORRY THAT MY SISTER AGITATED YOU.
......
WHY'S HE BEING SO NICE?
WHY DON'T YOU TELL US WHAT'S BOTHERING YOU?

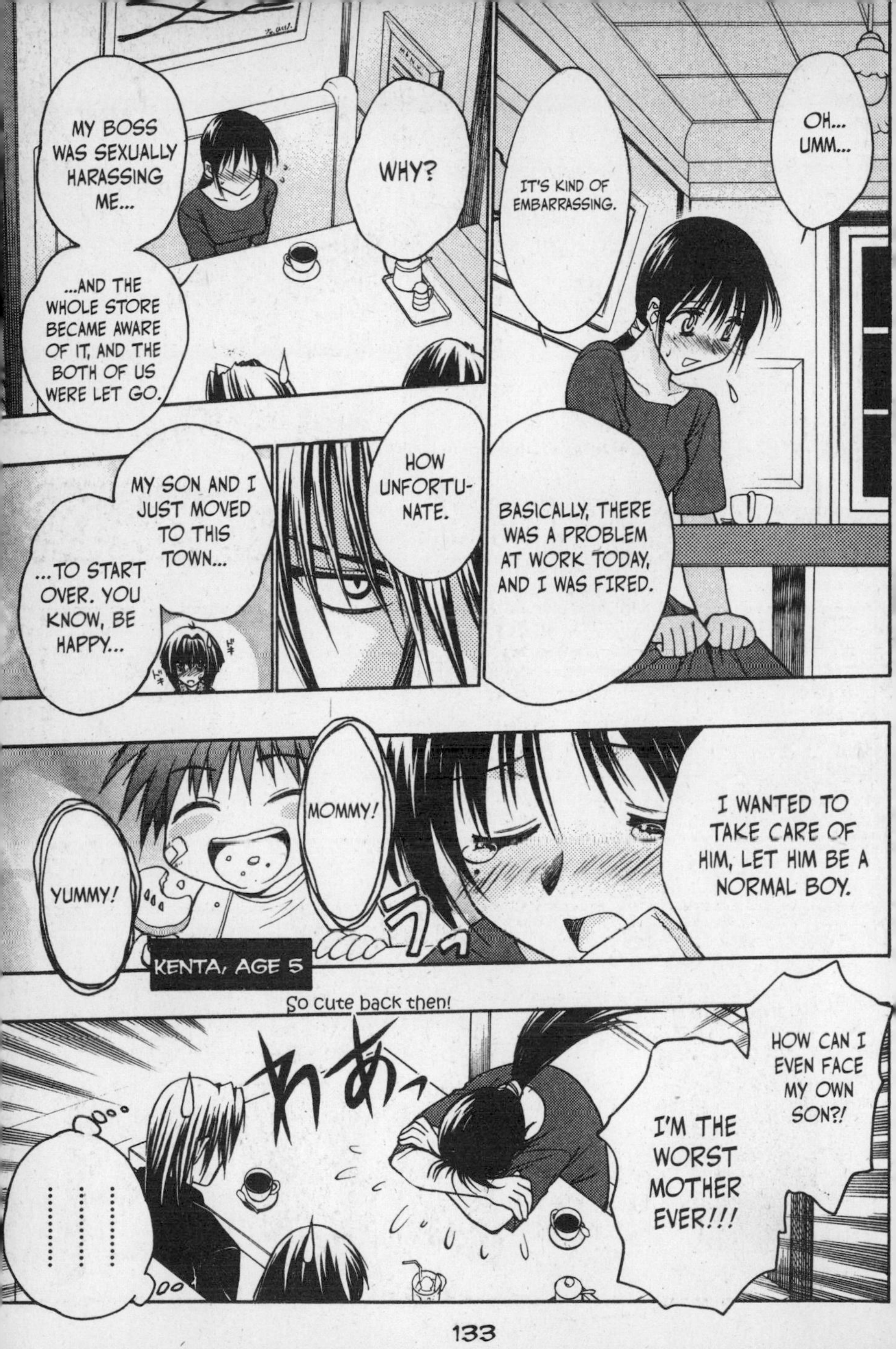
OH... UMM...
IT'S KIND OF EMBARRASSING.
BASICALLY, THERE WAS A PROBLEM AT WORK TODAY, AND I WAS FIRED.
WHY?
MY BOSS WAS SEXUALLY HARASSING ME...
...AND THE WHOLE STORE BECAME AWARE OF IT, AND THE BOTH OF US WERE LET GO.
HOW UNFORTU-NATE.
MY SON AND I JUST MOVED TO THIS TOWN...
...TO START OVER. YOU KNOW, BE HAPPY...
I WANTED TO TAKE CARE OF HIM, LET HIM BE A NORMAL BOY.
MOMMY!
YUMMY!
KENTA, AGE 5
So cute back then!
HOW CAN I EVEN FACE MY OWN SON?!
I'M THE WORST MOTHER EVER!!!
わあっ
......

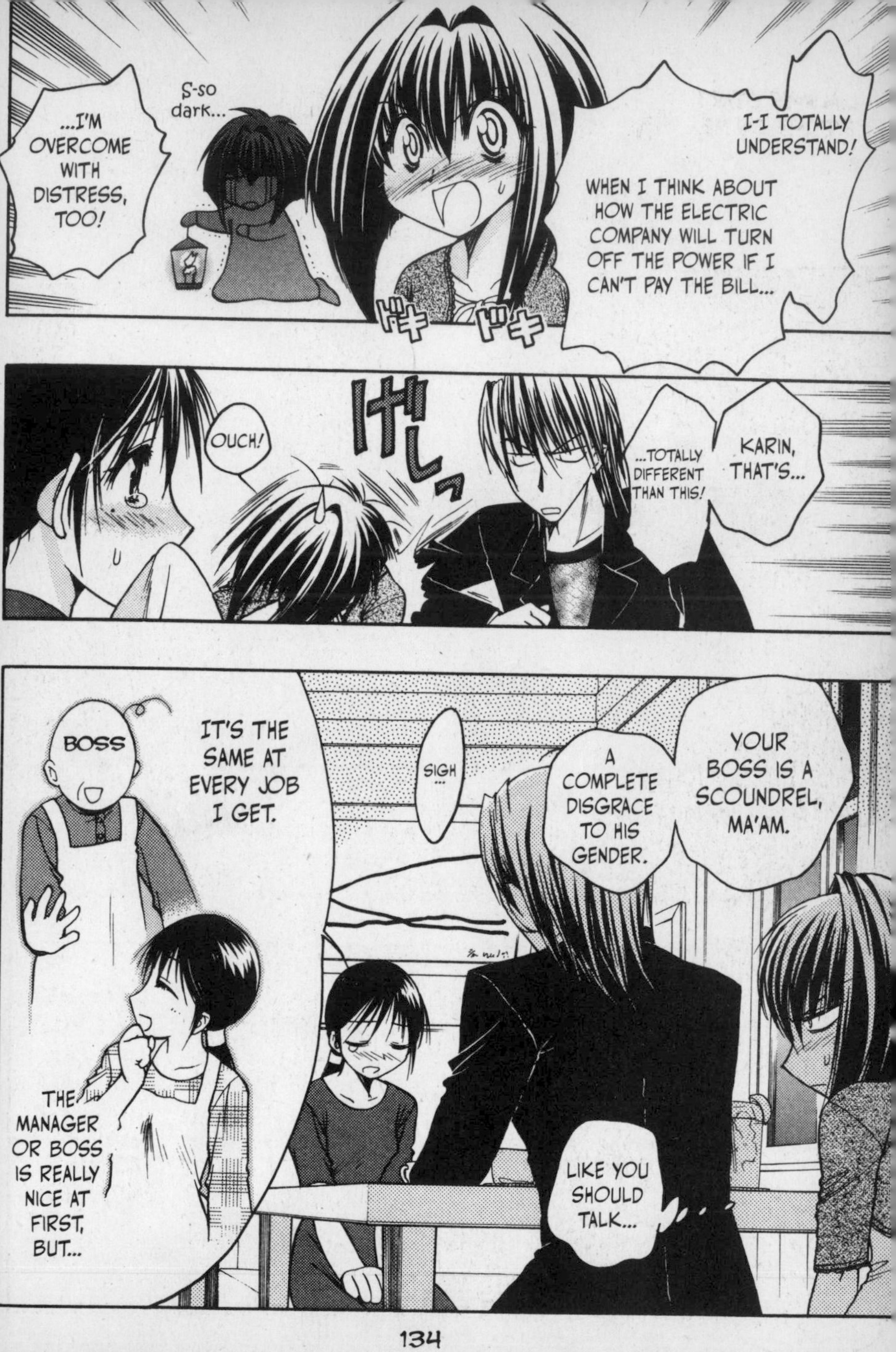

I-I TOTALLY UNDERSTAND!
WHEN I THINK ABOUT HOW THE ELECTRIC COMPANY WILL TURN OFF THE POWER IF I CAN'T PAY THE BILL...
ドキ ドキ
S-so dark...
...I'M OVERCOME WITH DISTRESS, TOO!
KARIN, THAT'S...
...TOTALLY DIFFERENT THAN THIS!
げしっ
OUCH!
YOUR BOSS IS A SCOUNDREL, MA'AM.
A COMPLETE DISGRACE TO HIS GENDER.
SIGH...
IT'S THE SAME AT EVERY JOB I GET.
BOSS
THE MANAGER OR BOSS IS REALLY NICE AT FIRST, BUT...
LIKE YOU SHOULD TALK...

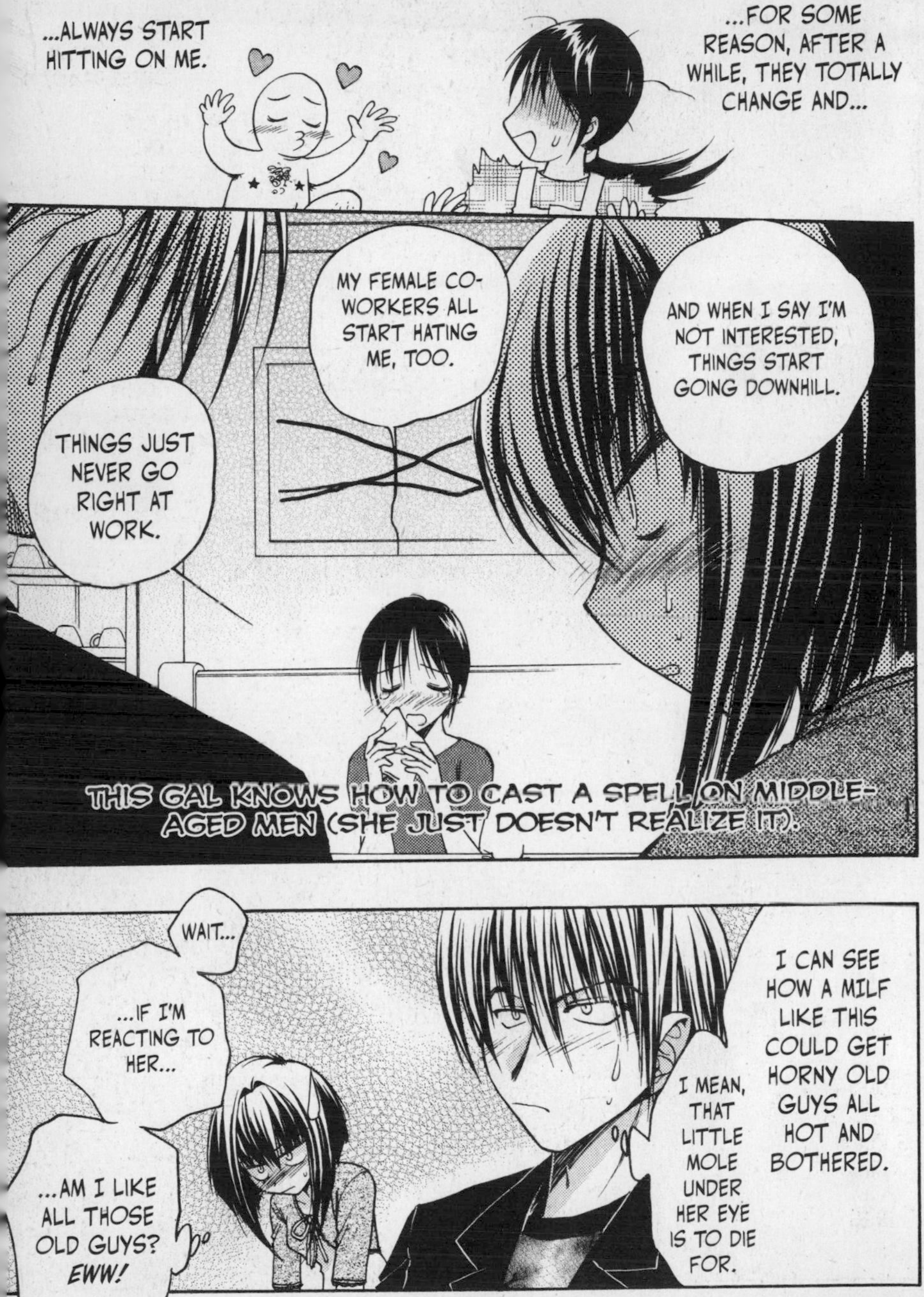
...FOR SOME REASON, AFTER A WHILE, THEY TOTALLY CHANGE AND...
...ALWAYS START HITTING ON ME.
AND WHEN I SAY I'M NOT INTERESTED, THINGS START GOING DOWNHILL.
MY FEMALE CO-WORKERS ALL START HATING ME, TOO.
THINGS JUST NEVER GO RIGHT AT WORK.
THIS GAL KNOWS HOW TO CAST A SPELL ON MIDDLE-AGED MEN (SHE JUST DOESN'T REALIZE IT).
I CAN SEE HOW A MILF LIKE THIS COULD GET HORNY OLD GUYS ALL HOT AND BOTHERED.
I MEAN, THAT LITTLE MOLE UNDER HER EYE IS TO DIE FOR.
WAIT...
...IF I'M REACTING TO HER...
...AM I LIKE ALL THOSE OLD GUYS? *EWW!*

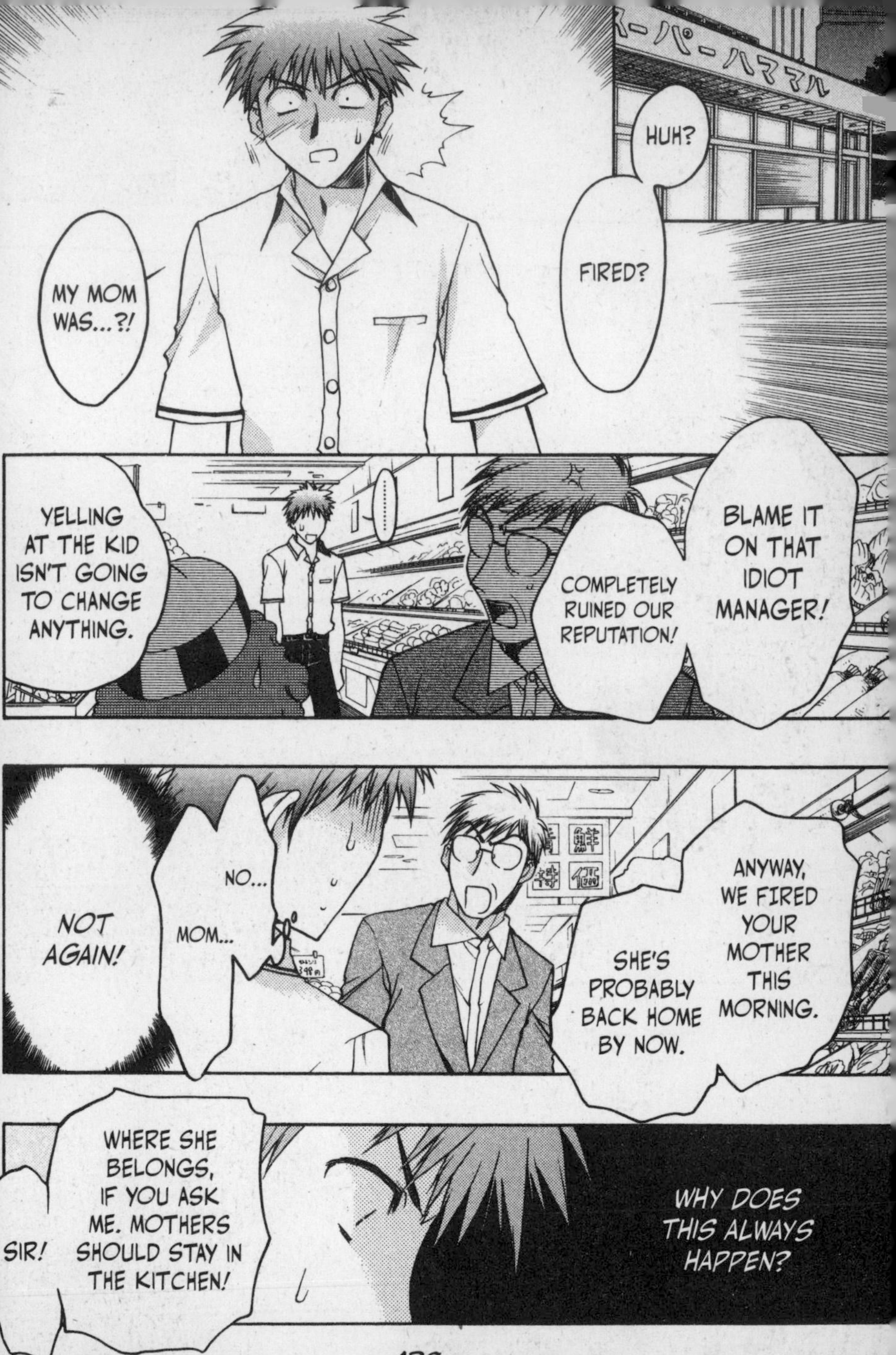
スーパーハママル
HUH?
FIRED?
MY MOM WAS...?!
BLAME IT ON THAT IDIOT MANAGER!
COMPLETELY RUINED OUR REPUTATION!
......
YELLING AT THE KID ISN'T GOING TO CHANGE ANYTHING.
ANYWAY, WE FIRED YOUR MOTHER THIS MORNING.
SHE'S PROBABLY BACK HOME BY NOW.
NO...
MOM...
NOT AGAIN!
WHY DOES THIS ALWAYS HAPPEN?
WHERE SHE BELONGS, IF YOU ASK ME. MOTHERS SHOULD STAY IN THE KITCHEN!
SIR!

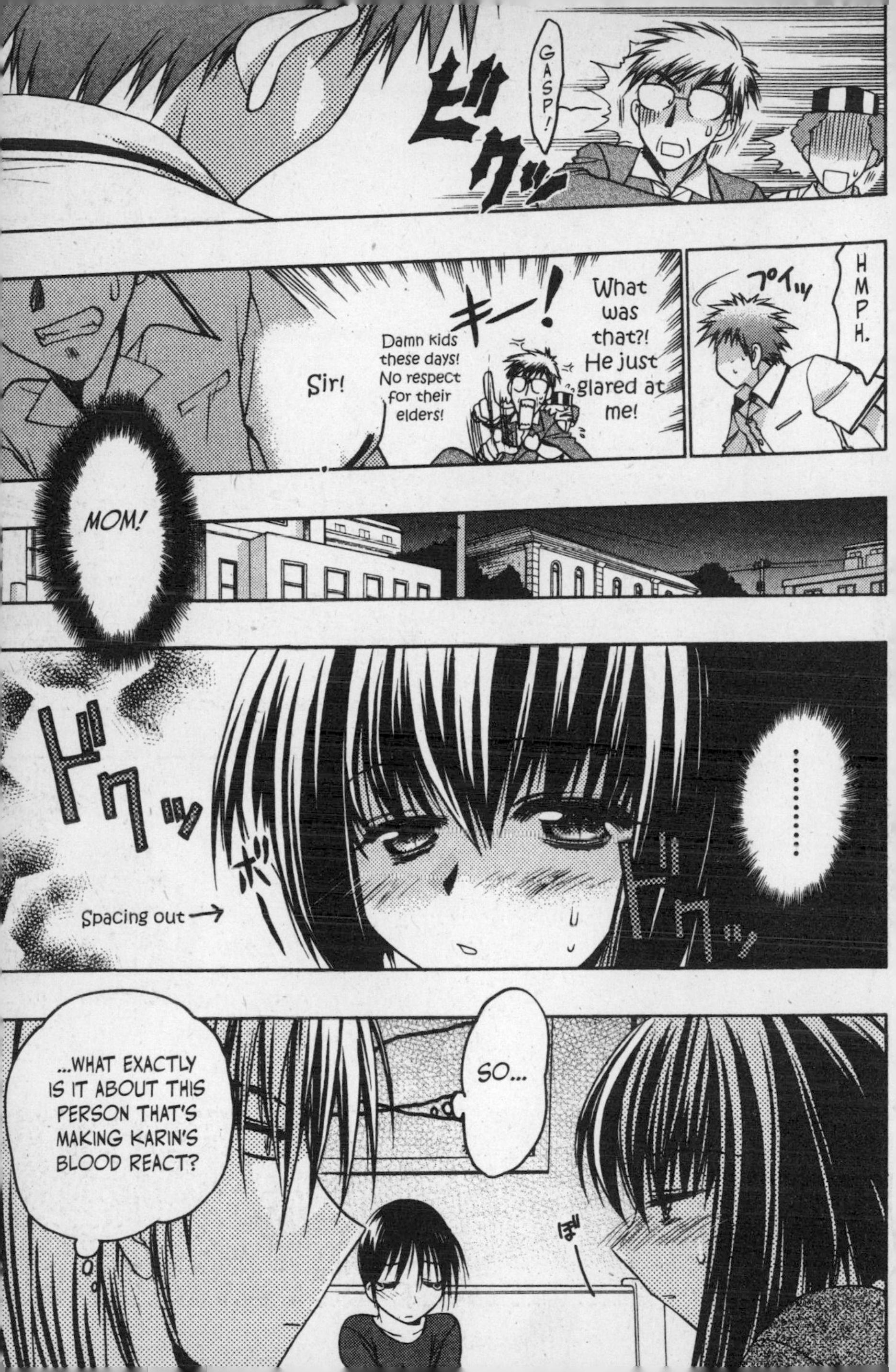
GASP!
HMPH.
What was that?! He just glared at me!
Damn kids these days! No respect for their elders!
Sir!
MOM!
......
Spacing out
SO...
...WHAT EXACTLY IS IT ABOUT THIS PERSON THAT'S MAKING KARIN'S BLOOD REACT?

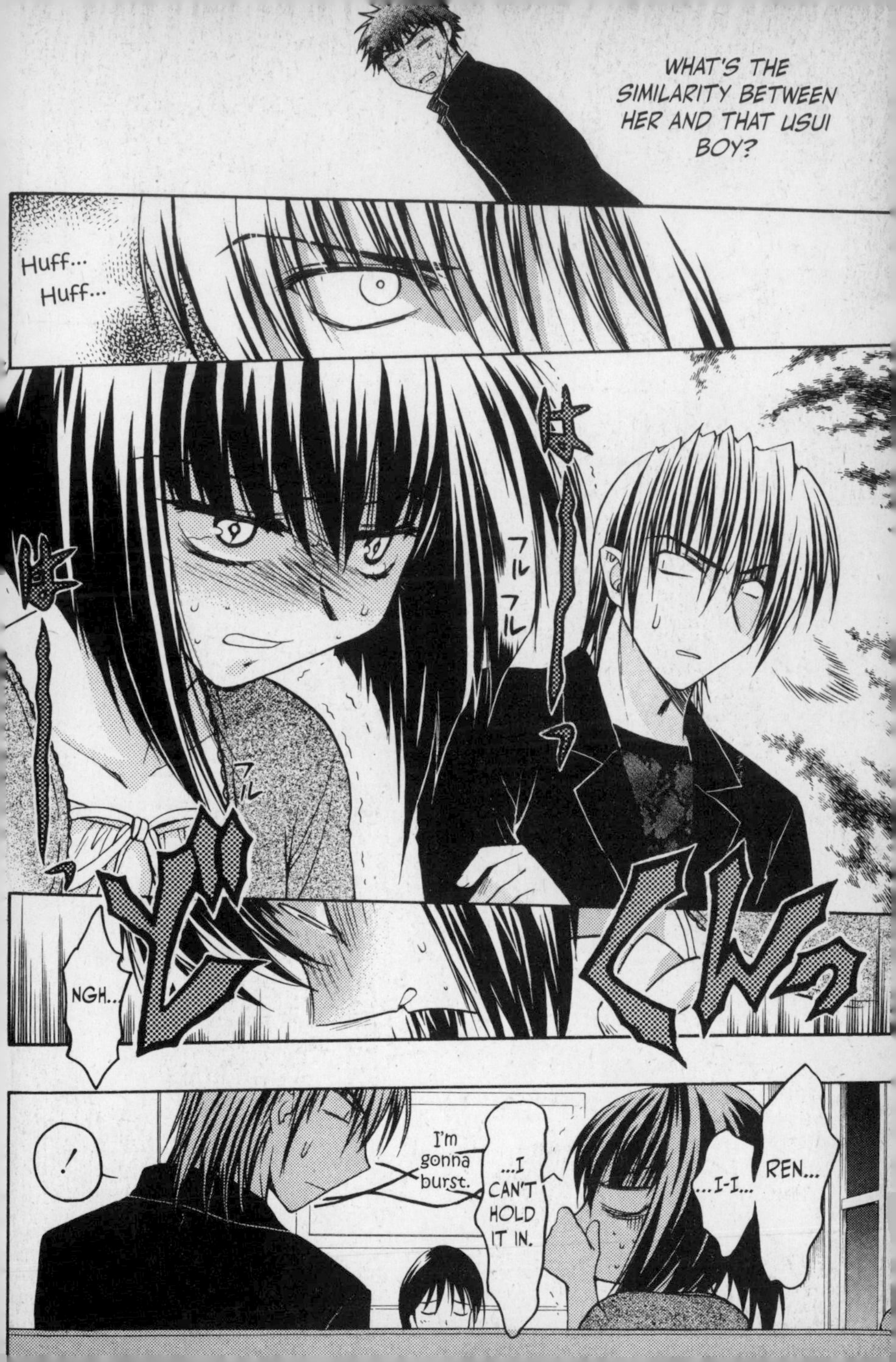

WHAT'S THE SIMILARITY BETWEEN HER AND THAT USUI BOY?
Huff... Huff...
フルフル
フル
NGH...
REN...
...I-I...
...I CAN'T HOLD IT IN.
I'm gonna burst.
!

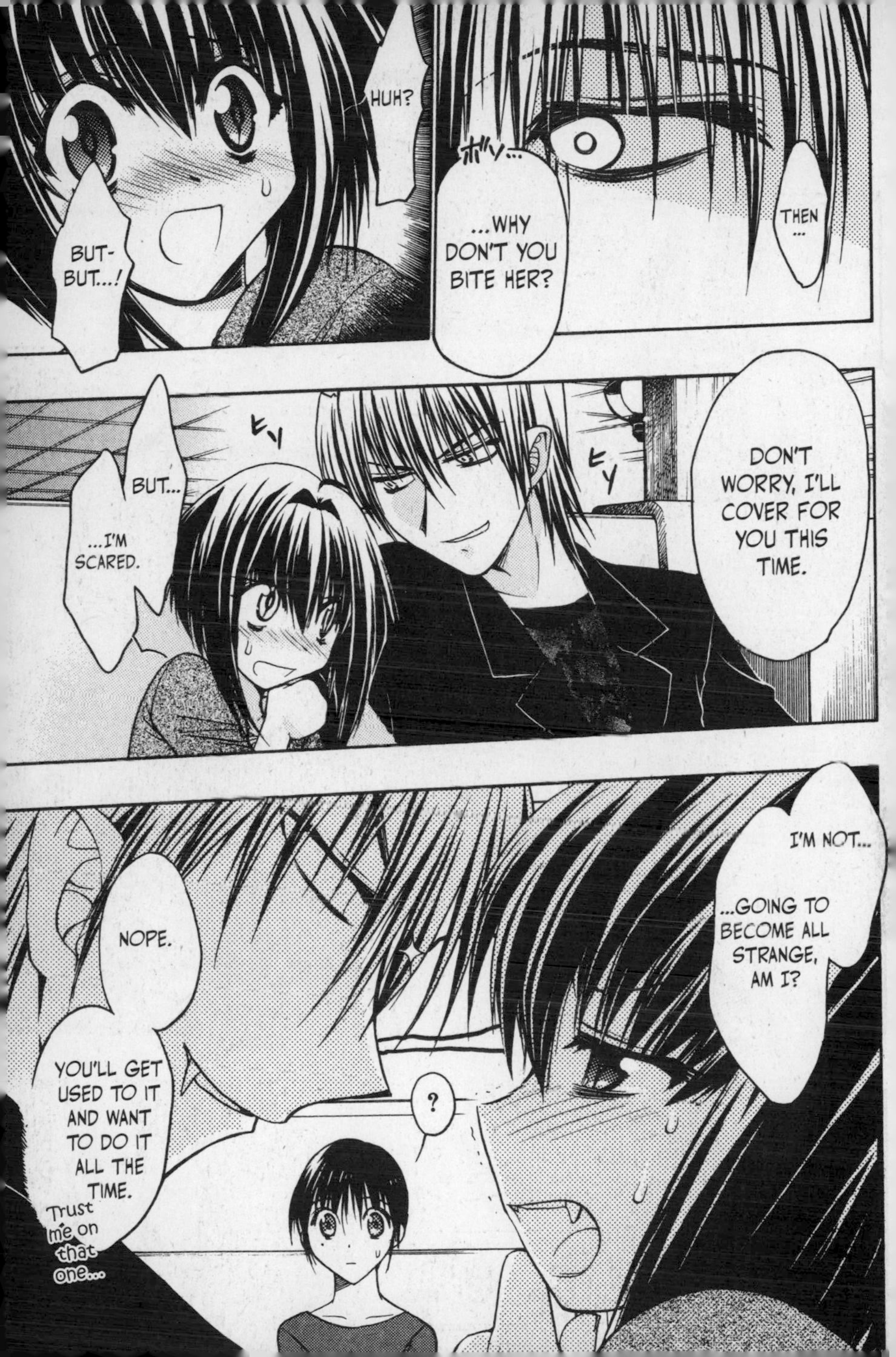
THEN...
ボソ...
...WHY DON'T YOU BITE HER?
HUH?
BUT-BUT...!
DON'T WORRY, I'LL COVER FOR YOU THIS TIME.
ヒソ
ヒソ
BUT...
...I'M SCARED.
I'M NOT...
...GOING TO BECOME ALL STRANGE, AM I?
?
NOPE.
YOU'LL GET USED TO IT AND WANT TO DO IT ALL THE TIME.
Trust me on that one...

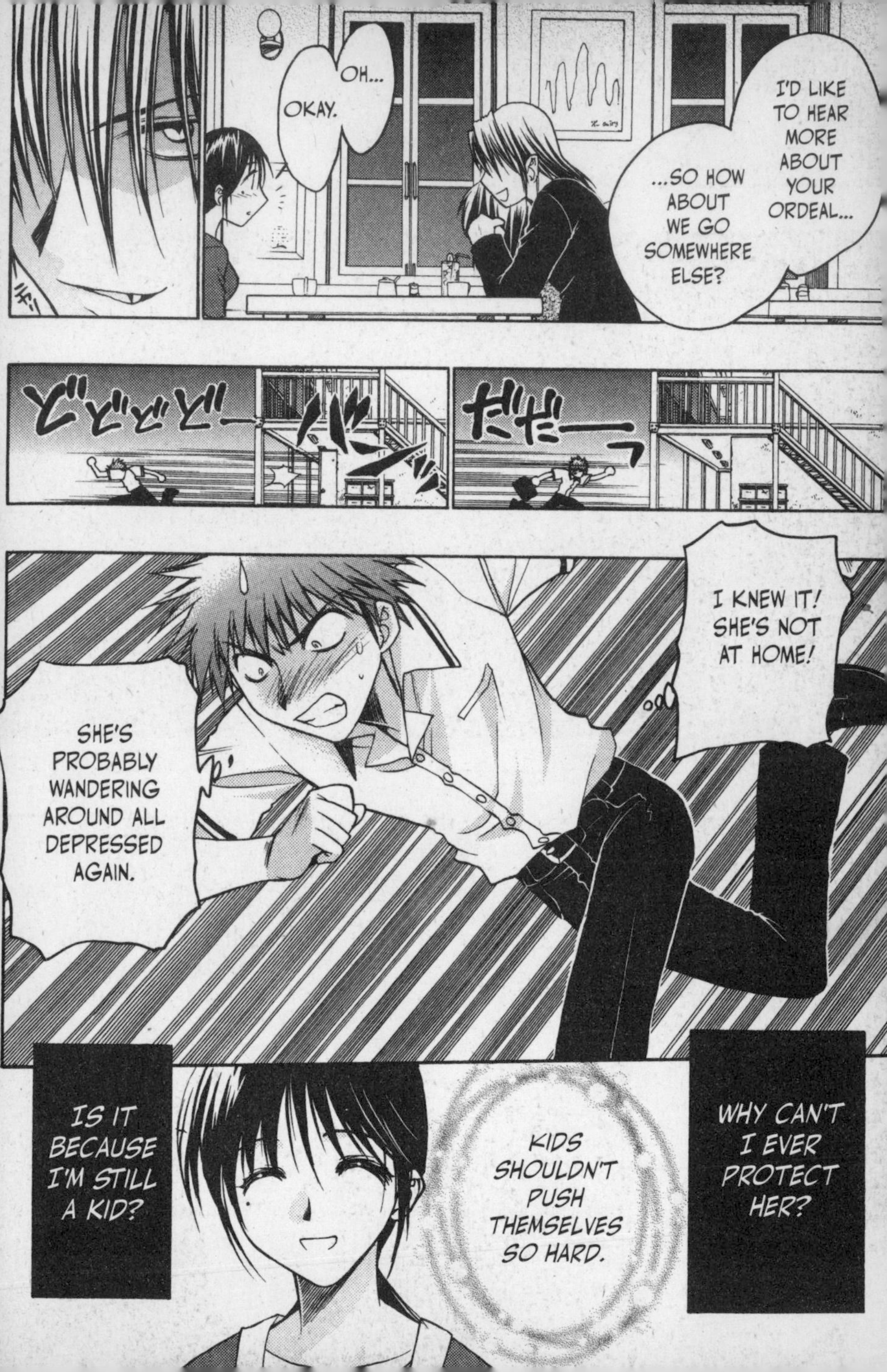
I'D LIKE TO HEAR MORE ABOUT YOUR ORDEAL...
...SO HOW ABOUT WE GO SOMEWHERE ELSE?
OH... OKAY.
だだー
バン
どどどど
I KNEW IT! SHE'S NOT AT HOME!
SHE'S PROBABLY WANDERING AROUND ALL DEPRESSED AGAIN.
WHY CAN'T I EVER PROTECT HER?
KIDS SHOULDN'T PUSH THEMSELVES SO HARD.
IS IT BECAUSE I'M STILL A KID?

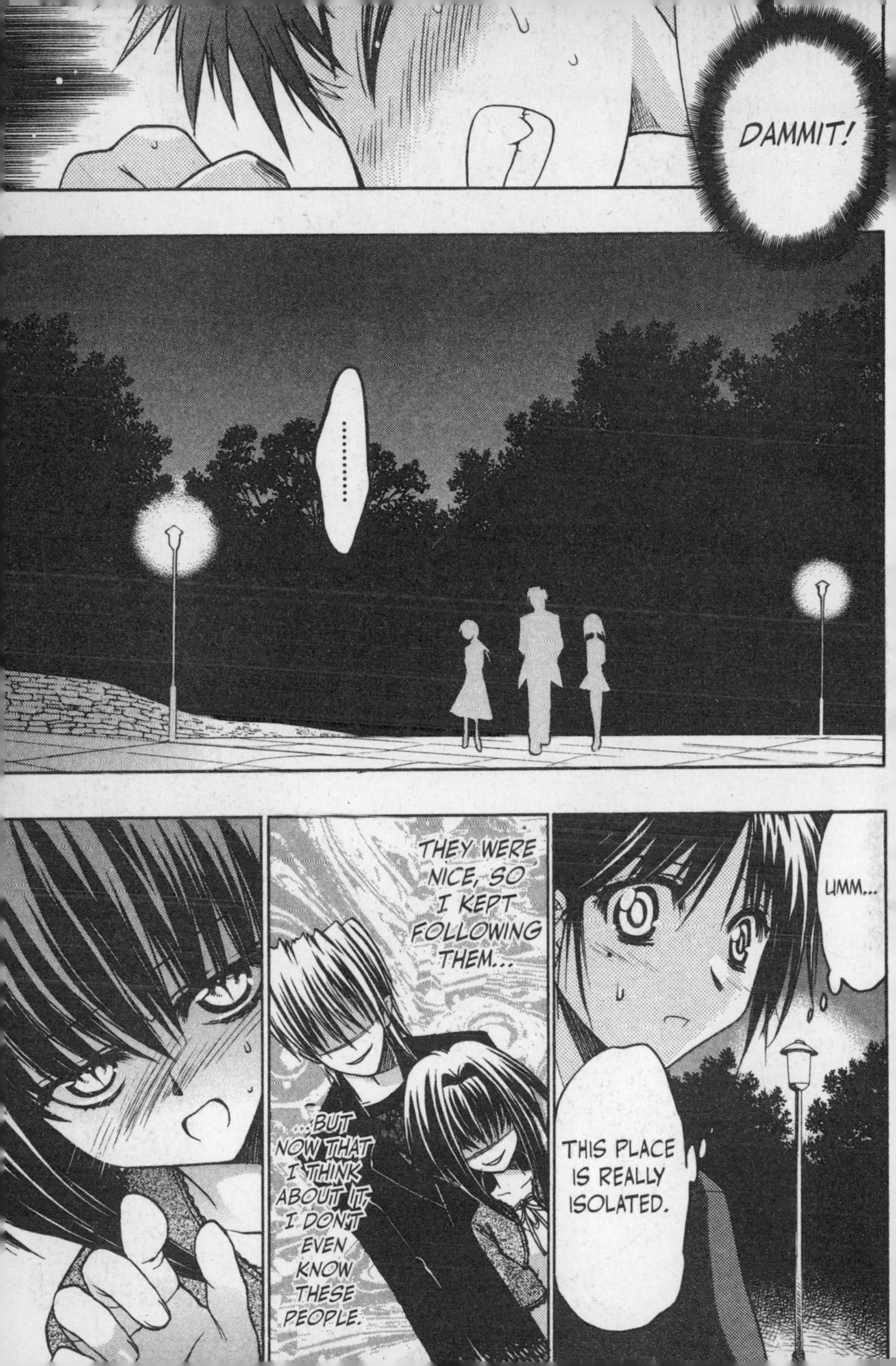
DAMMIT!
......
UMM...
THIS PLACE IS REALLY ISOLATED.
THEY WERE NICE, SO I KEPT FOLLOWING THEM...
...BUT NOW THAT I THINK ABOUT IT, I DON'T EVEN KNOW THESE PEOPLE.

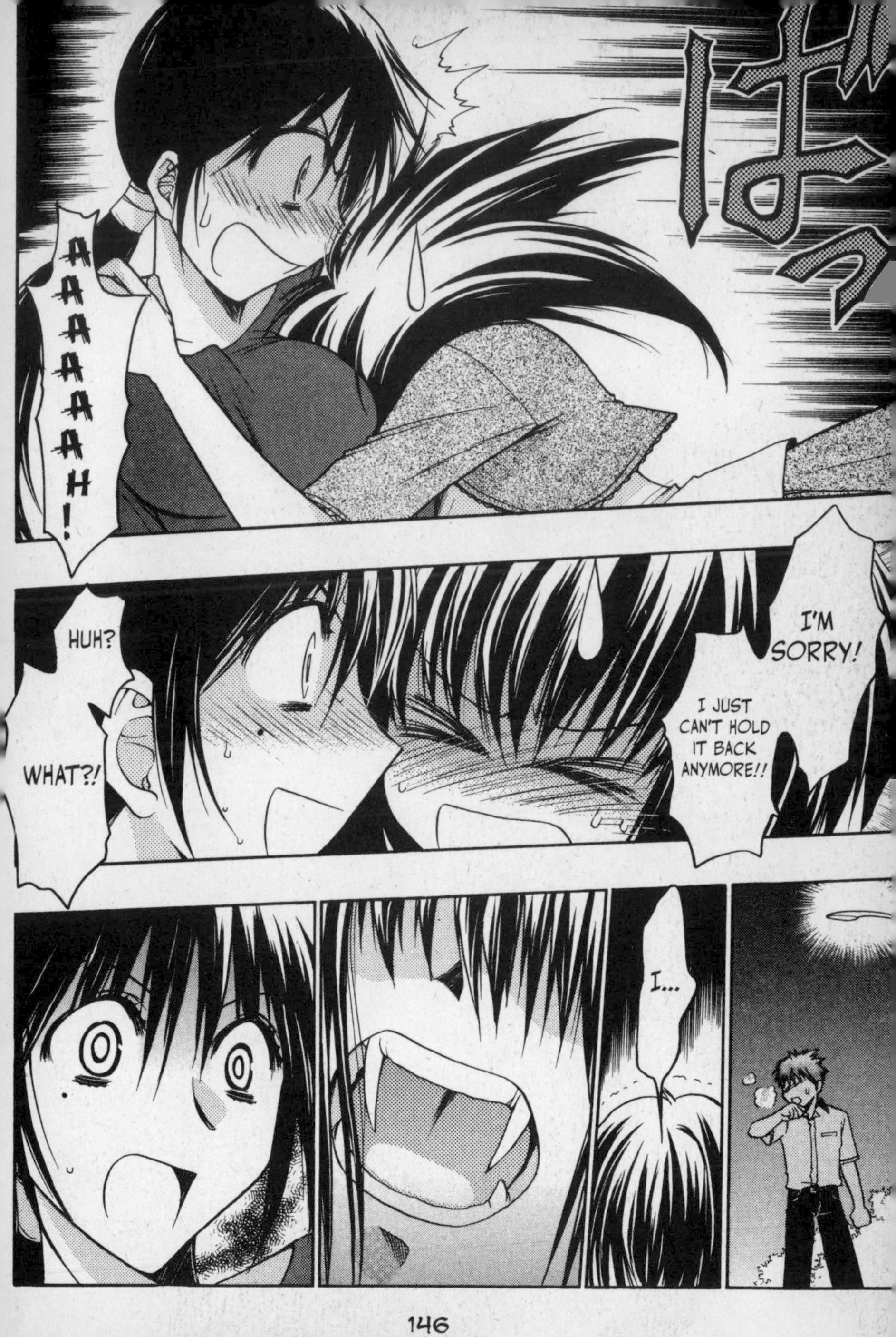
ぱっ
AAAAAAAH!
I'M SORRY!
I JUST CAN'T HOLD IT BACK ANYMORE!!
HUH?
WHAT?!
I...

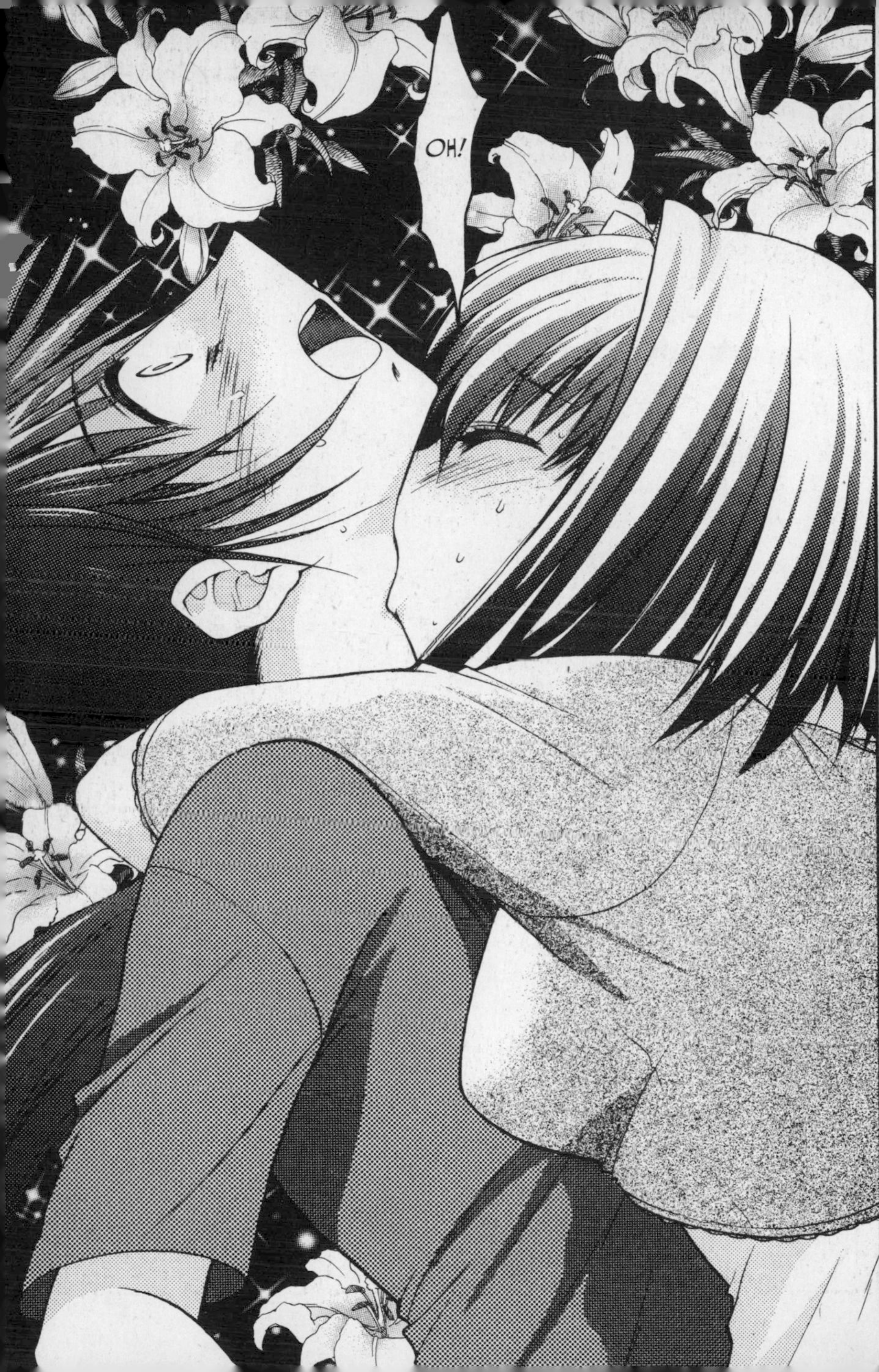
OH!

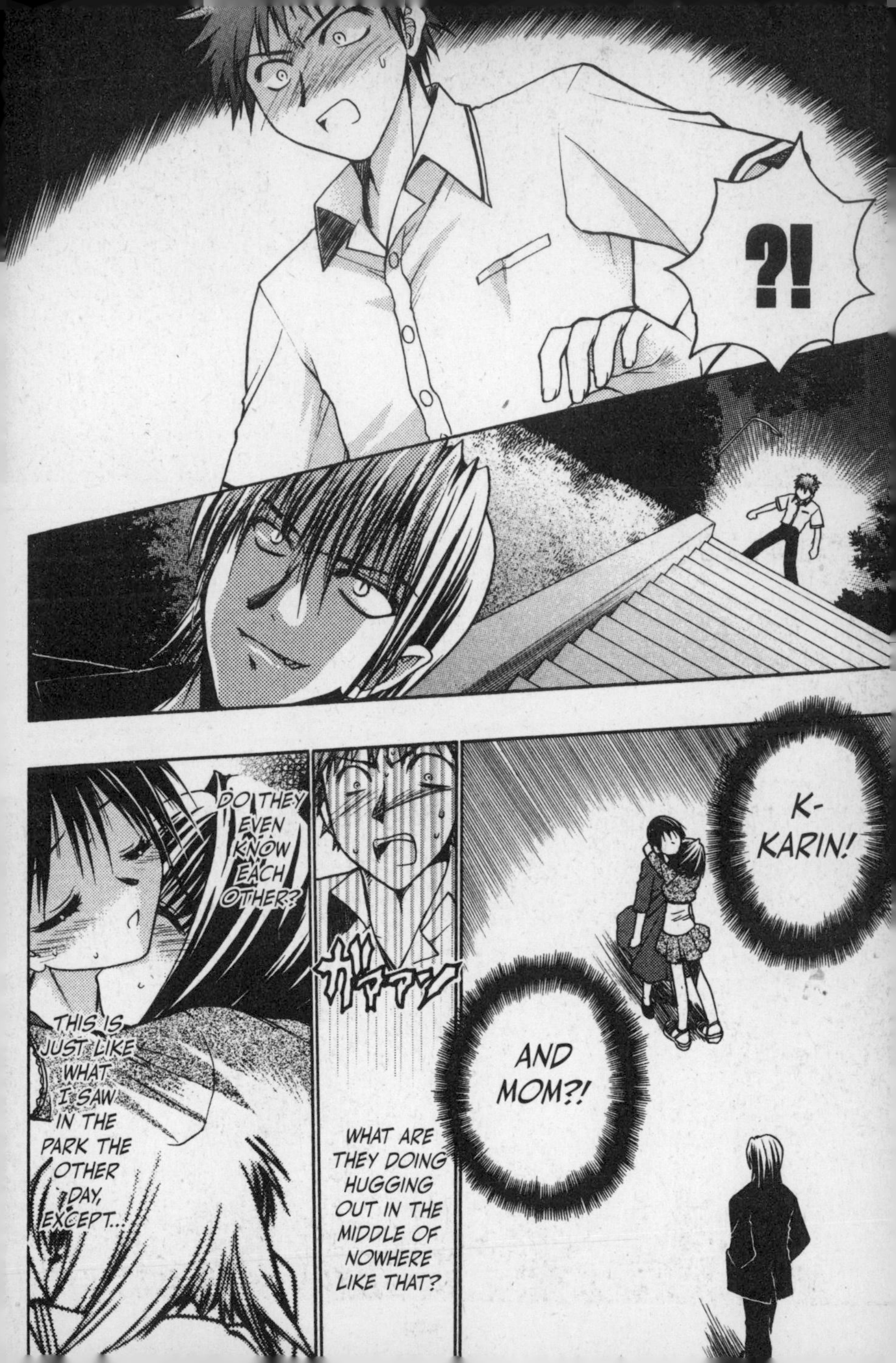
?!
K-KARIN!
AND MOM?!
WHAT ARE THEY DOING HUGGING OUT IN THE MIDDLE OF NOWHERE LIKE THAT?
DO THEY EVEN KNOW EACH OTHER?
THIS IS JUST LIKE WHAT I SAW IN THE PARK THE OTHER DAY, EXCEPT...

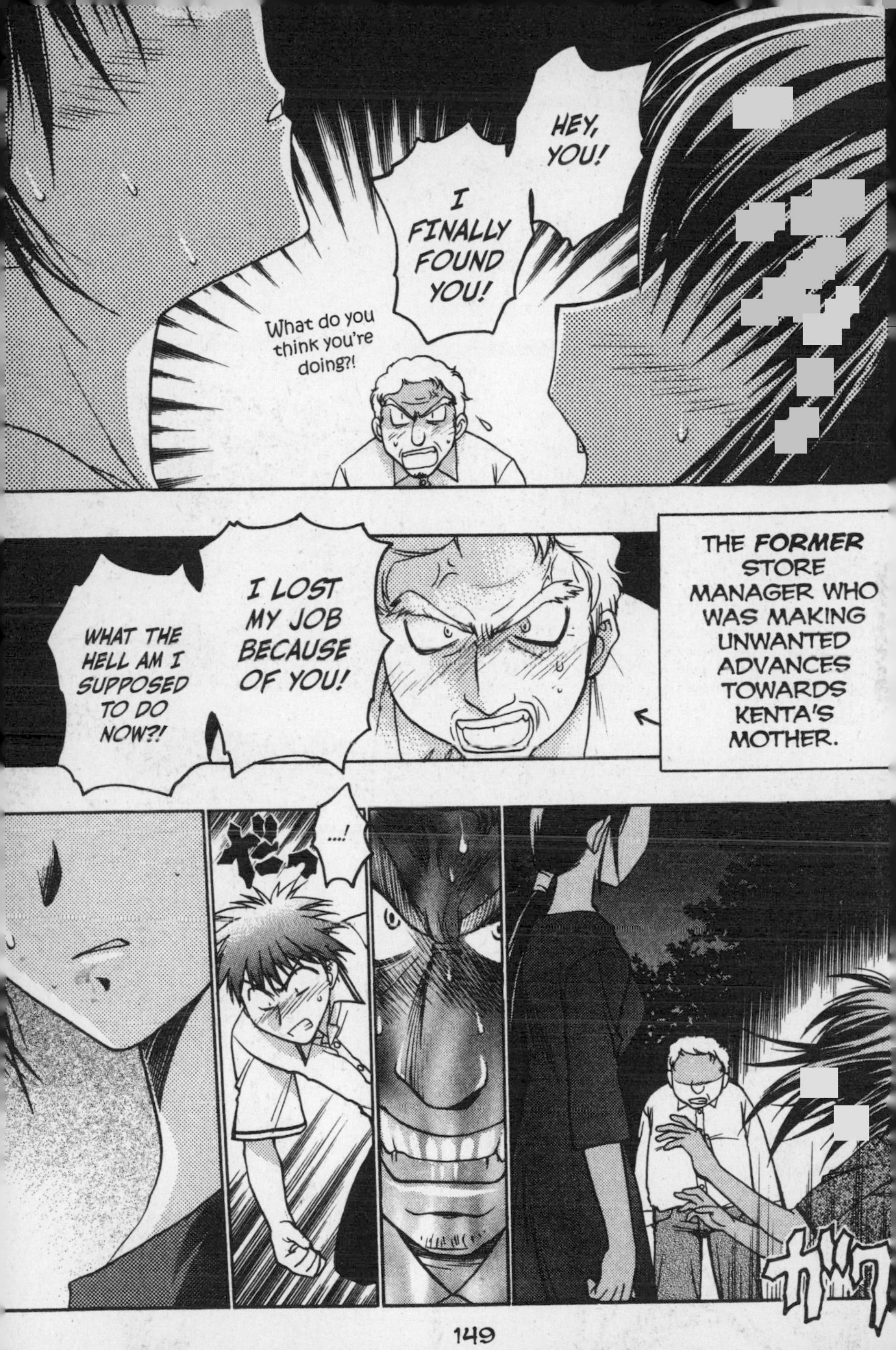
HEY, YOU!
I FINALLY FOUND YOU!
What do you think you're doing?!
THE FORMER STORE MANAGER WHO WAS MAKING UNWANTED ADVANCES TOWARDS KENTA'S MOTHER.
I LOST MY JOB BECAUSE OF YOU!
WHAT THE HELL AM I SUPPOSED TO DO NOW?!
...!

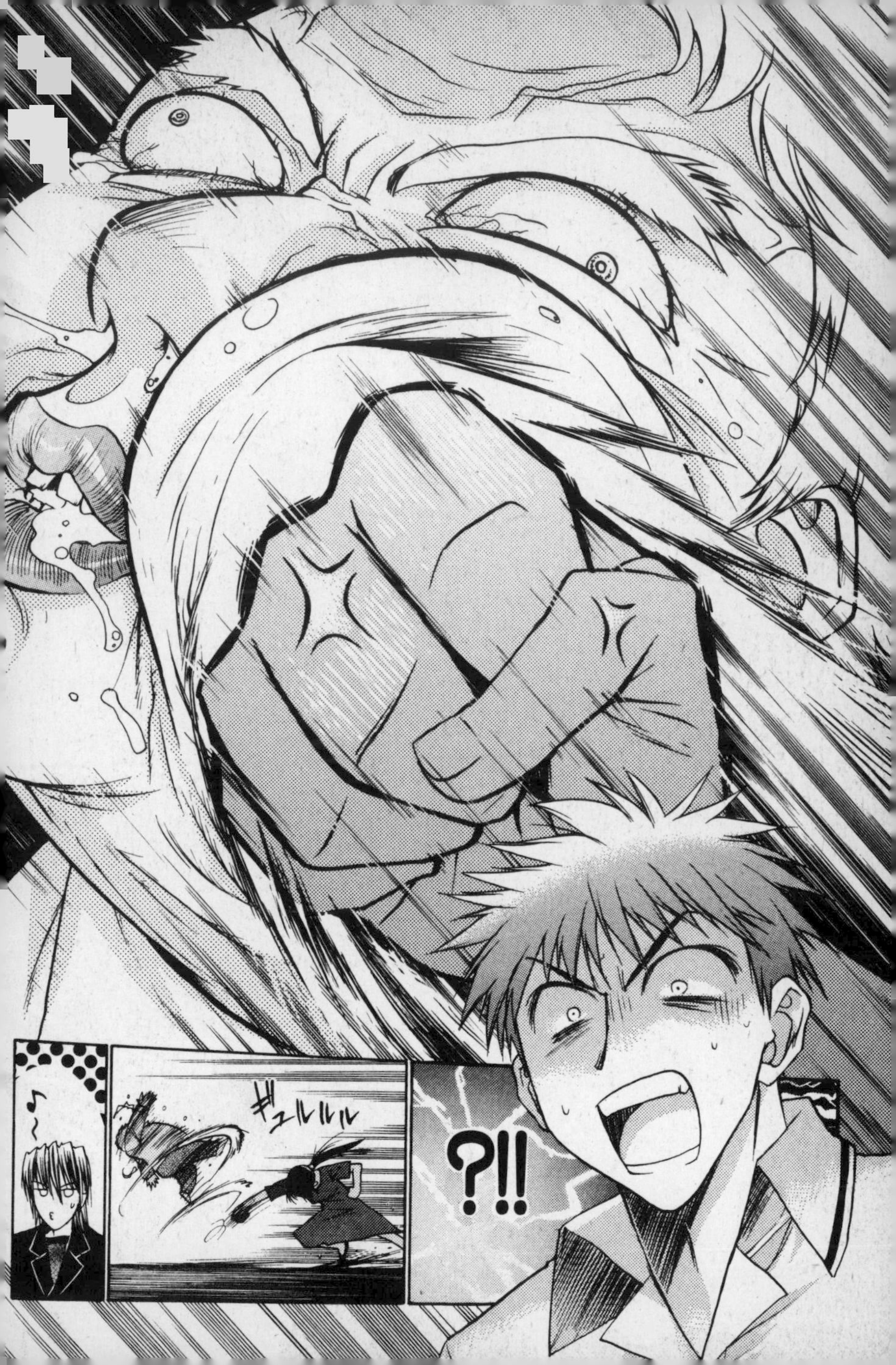
?!!
ギュルルル
♪~

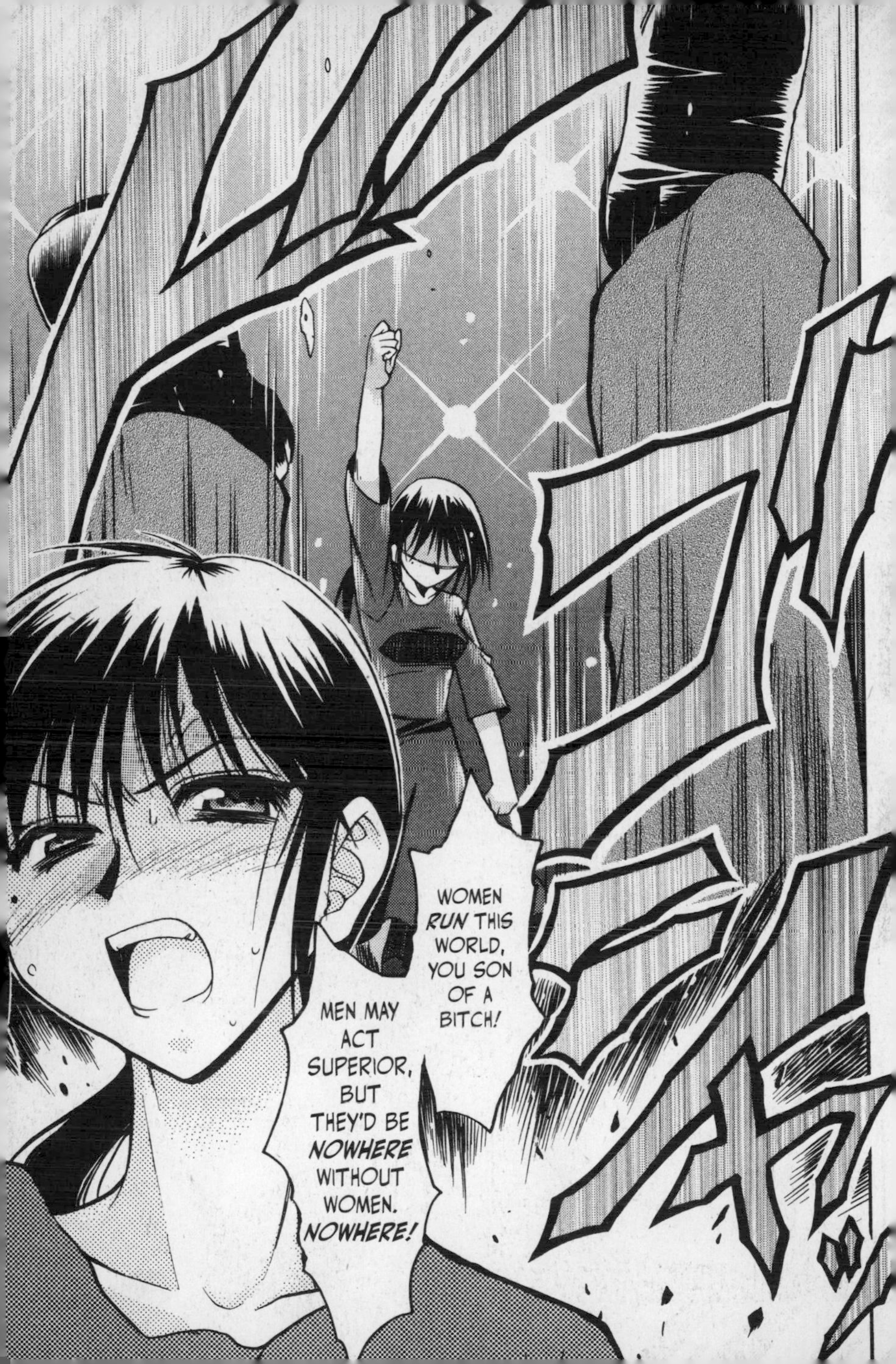
WOMEN *RUN* THIS WORLD, YOU SON OF A BITCH!
MEN MAY ACT SUPERIOR, BUT THEY'D BE *NOWHERE* WITHOUT WOMEN. *NOWHERE!*

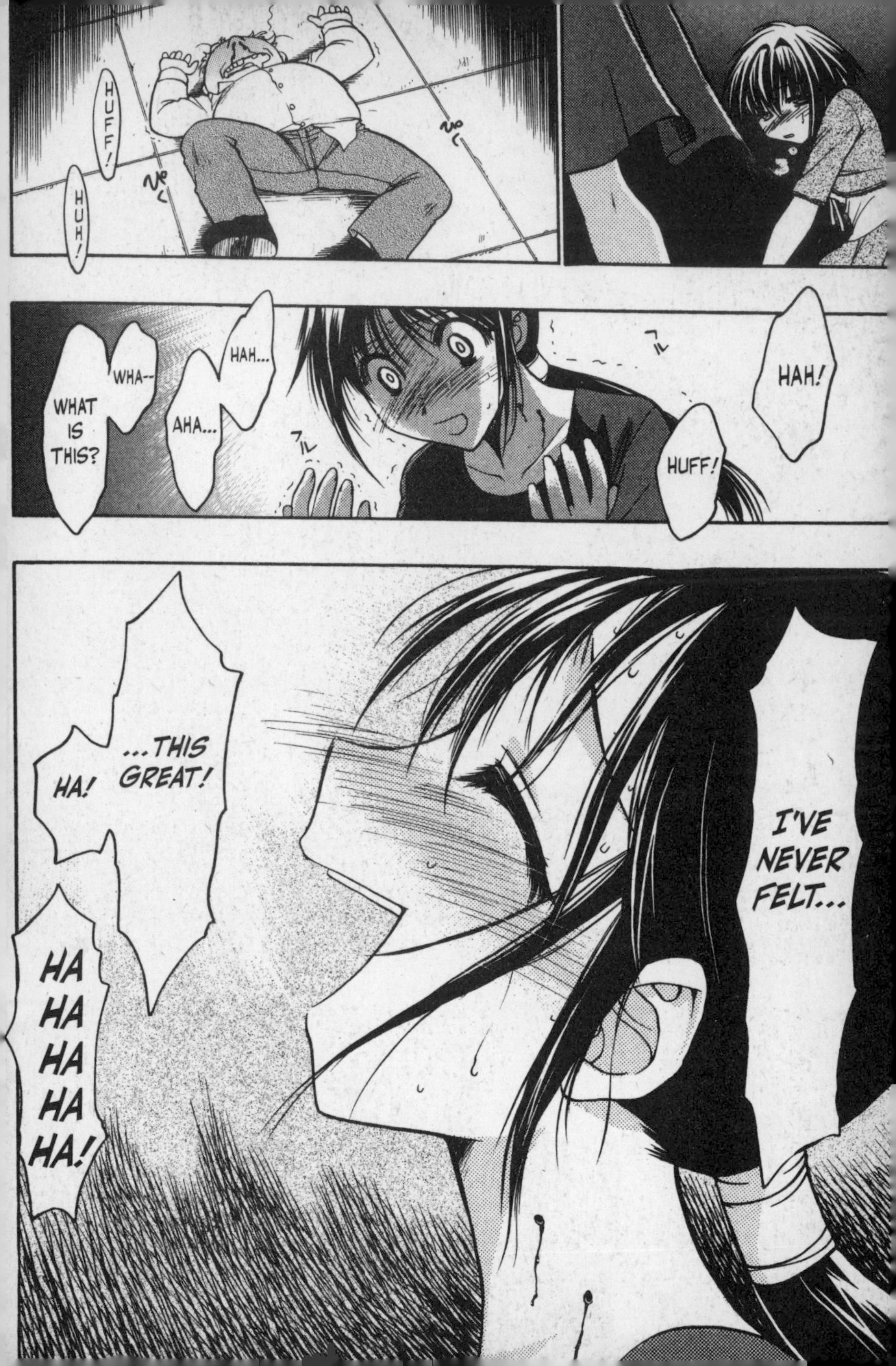
HUFF!
HUH!
HAH!
HUFF!
HAH...
AHA...
WHA--
WHAT IS THIS?
I'VE NEVER FELT...
...THIS GREAT!
HA!
HA HA HA HA HA HA!

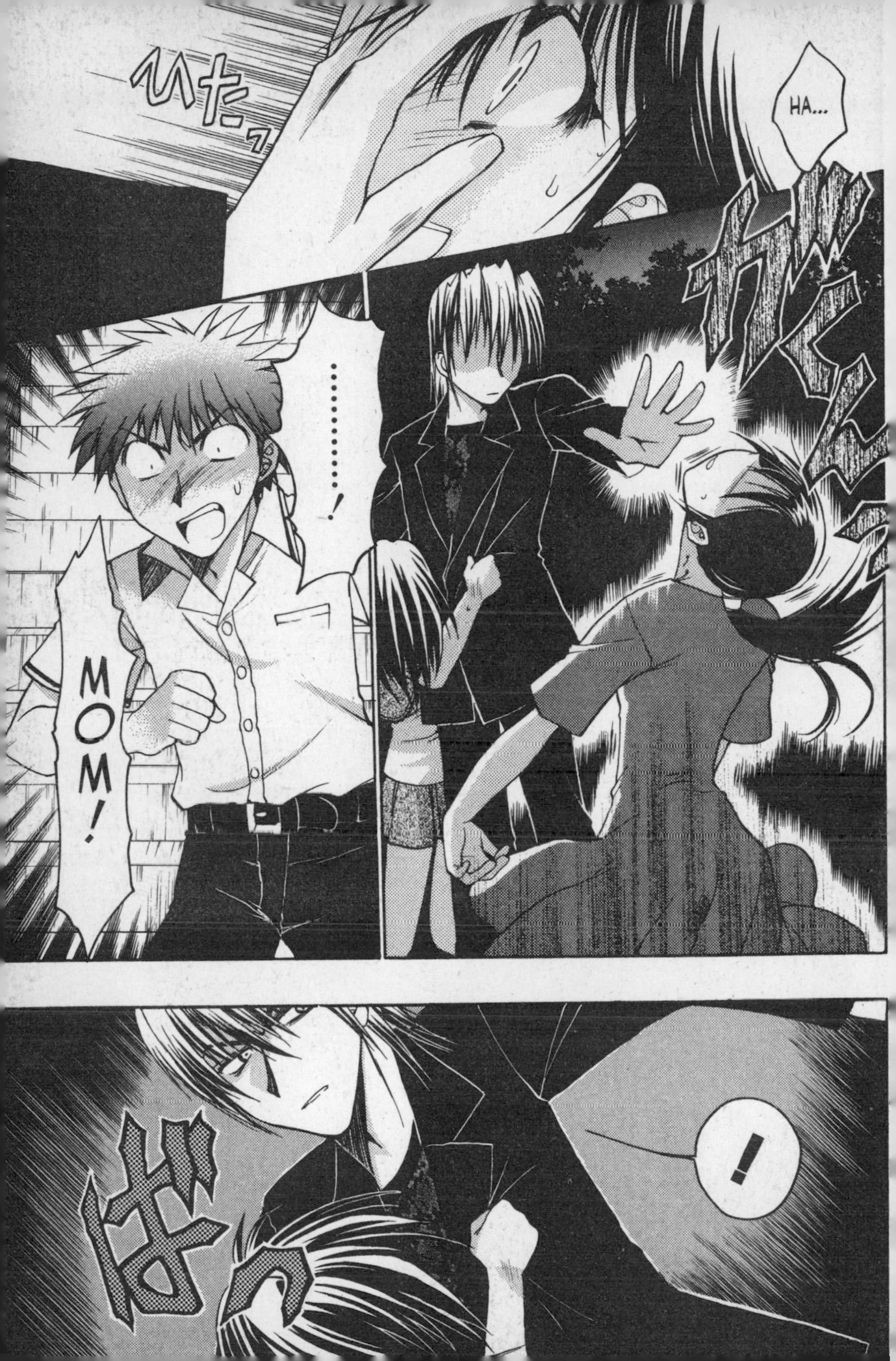
HA...
ひたっ
......!
MOM!
!
はっ

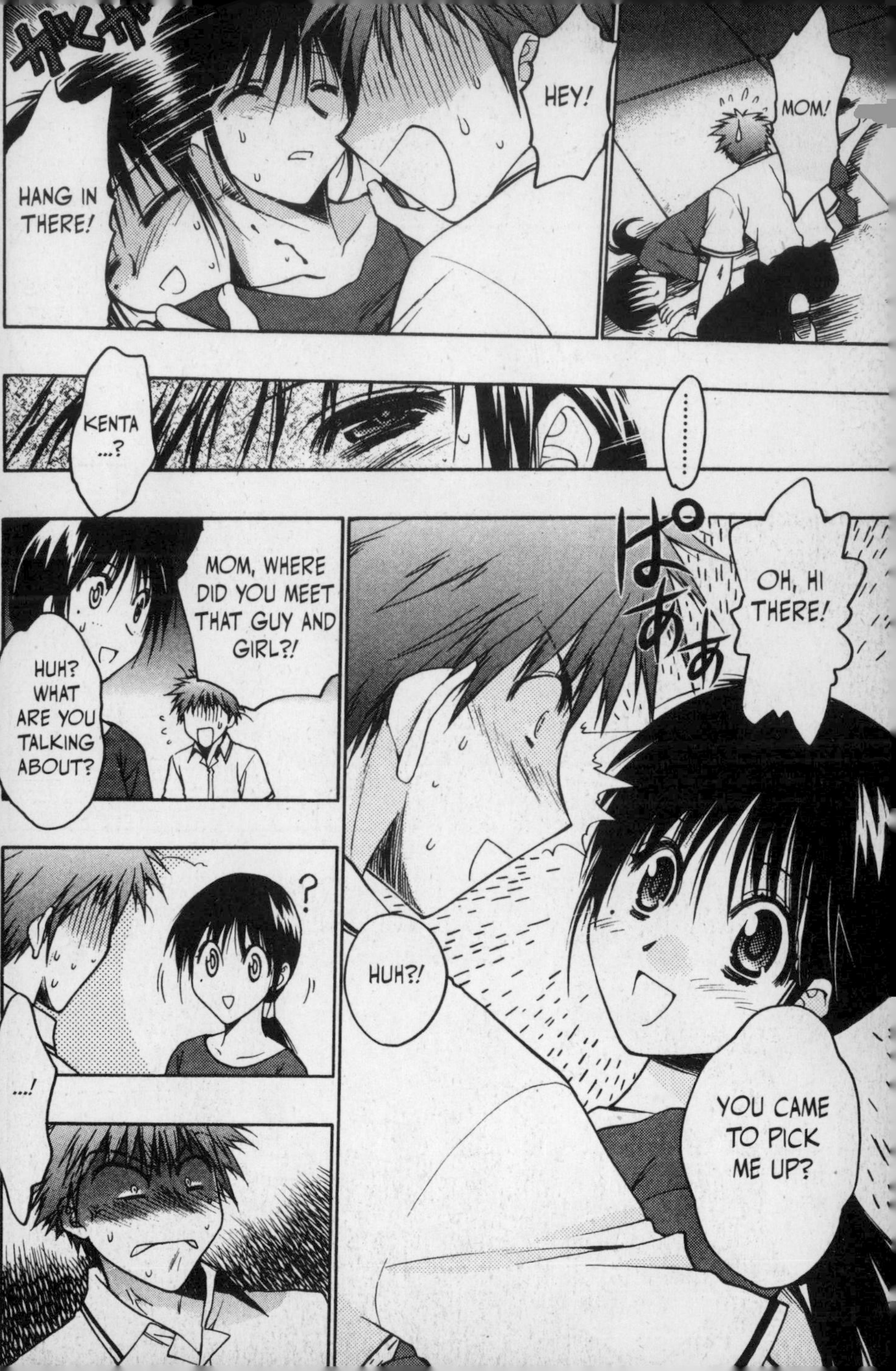
MOM!
HEY!
HANG IN THERE!
......
KENTA ...?
ぱあぁ
OH, HI THERE!
HUH?!
YOU CAME TO PICK ME UP?
MOM, WHERE DID YOU MEET THAT GUY AND GIRL?!
HUH? WHAT ARE YOU TALKING ABOUT?
?
...!

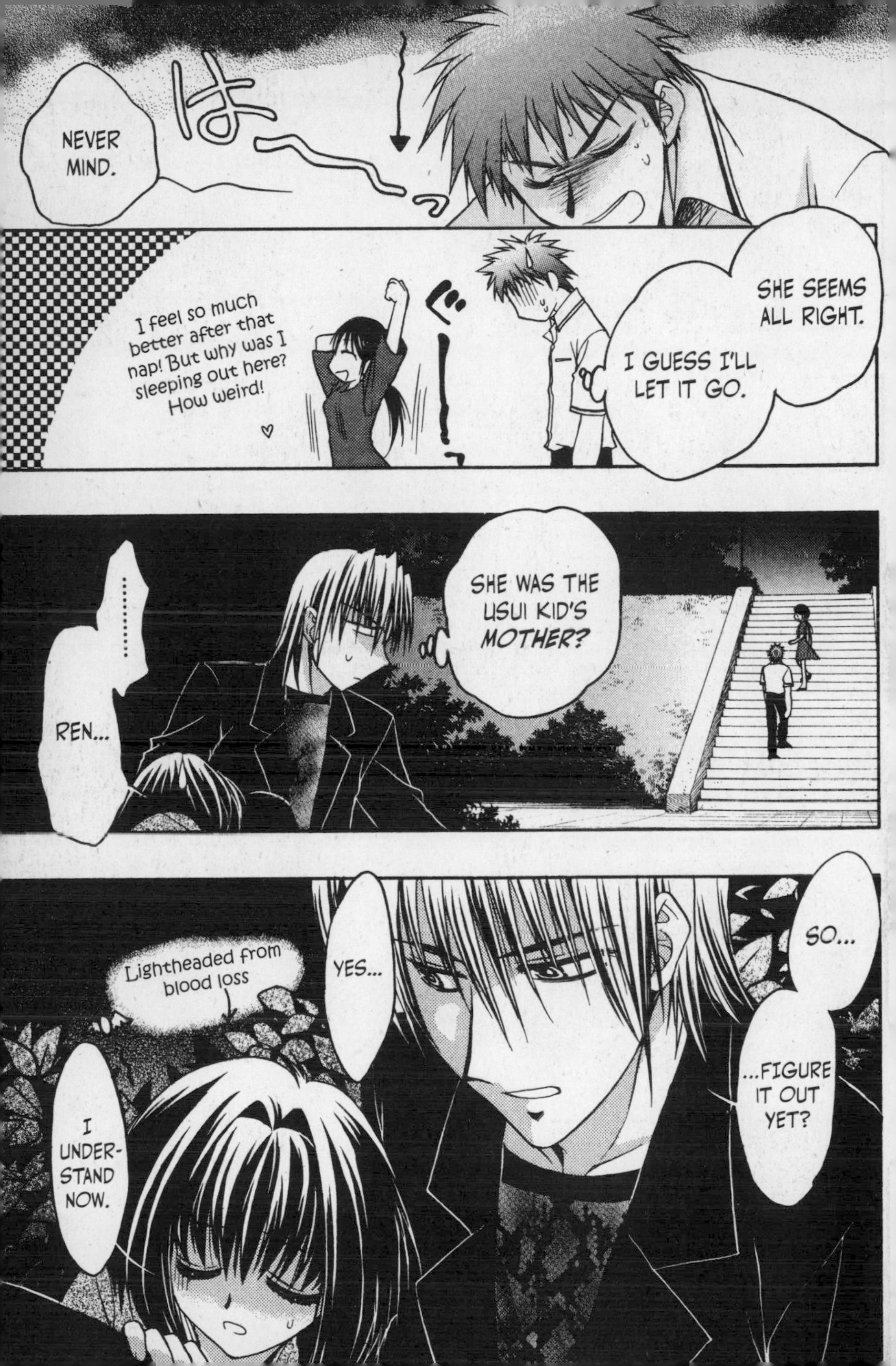

は〜っ
NEVER MIND.
SHE SEEMS ALL RIGHT.
I GUESS I'LL LET IT GO.
ぐーっ
I feel so much better after that nap! But why was I sleeping out here? How weird! ♡
SHE WAS THE USUI KID'S *MOTHER?*
......
REN...
SO...
...FIGURE IT OUT YET?
YES...
Lightheaded from blood loss
I UNDER-STAND NOW.

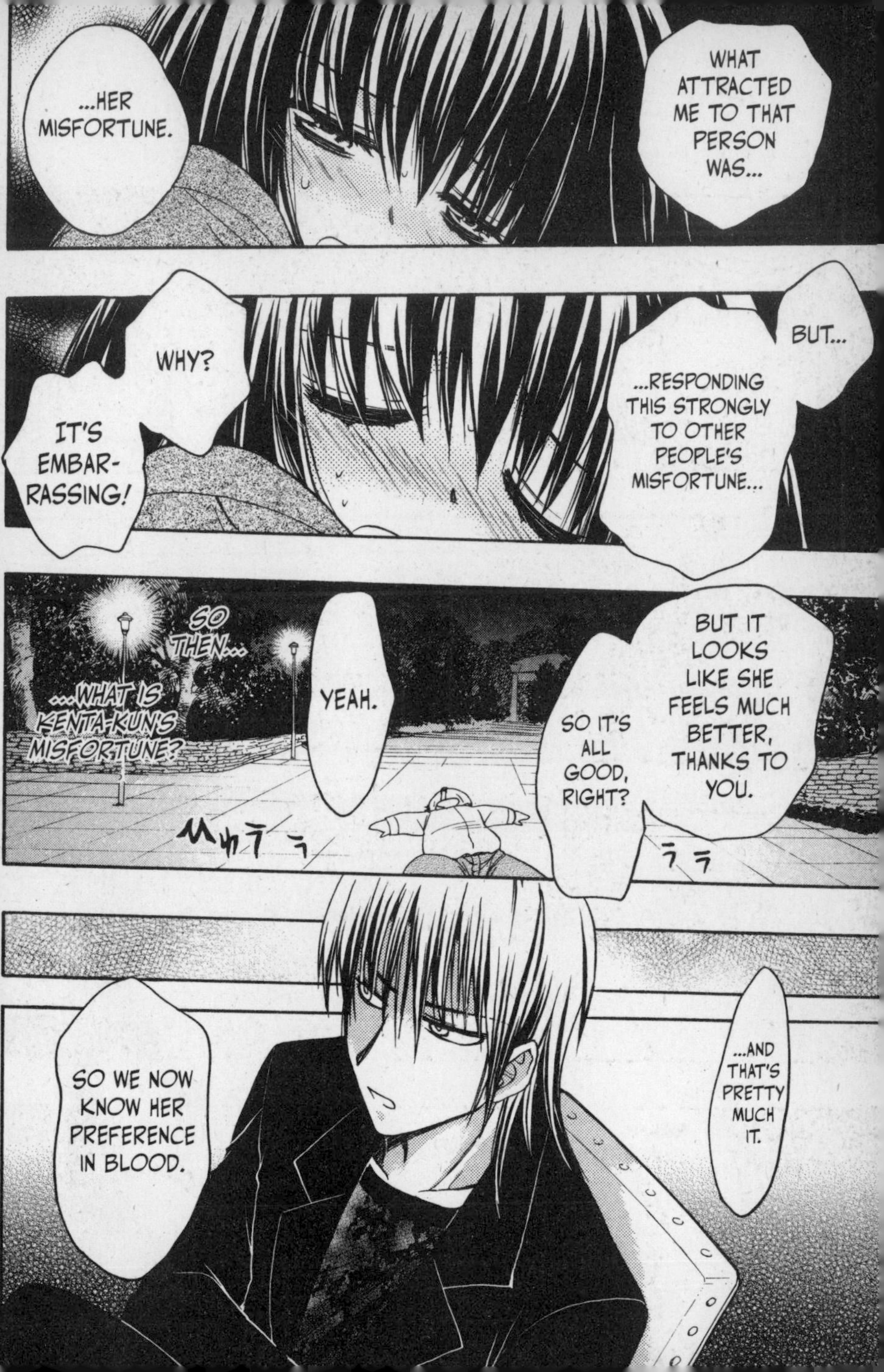
WHAT ATTRACTED ME TO THAT PERSON WAS...
...HER MISFORTUNE.
BUT...
...RESPONDING THIS STRONGLY TO OTHER PEOPLE'S MISFORTUNE...
WHY?
IT'S EMBARRASSING!
BUT IT LOOKS LIKE SHE FEELS MUCH BETTER, THANKS TO YOU.
SO IT'S ALL GOOD, RIGHT?
YEAH.
SO THEN...
...WHAT IS KENTA-KUN'S MISFORTUNE?
...AND THAT'S PRETTY MUCH IT.
SO WE NOW KNOW HER PREFERENCE IN BLOOD.

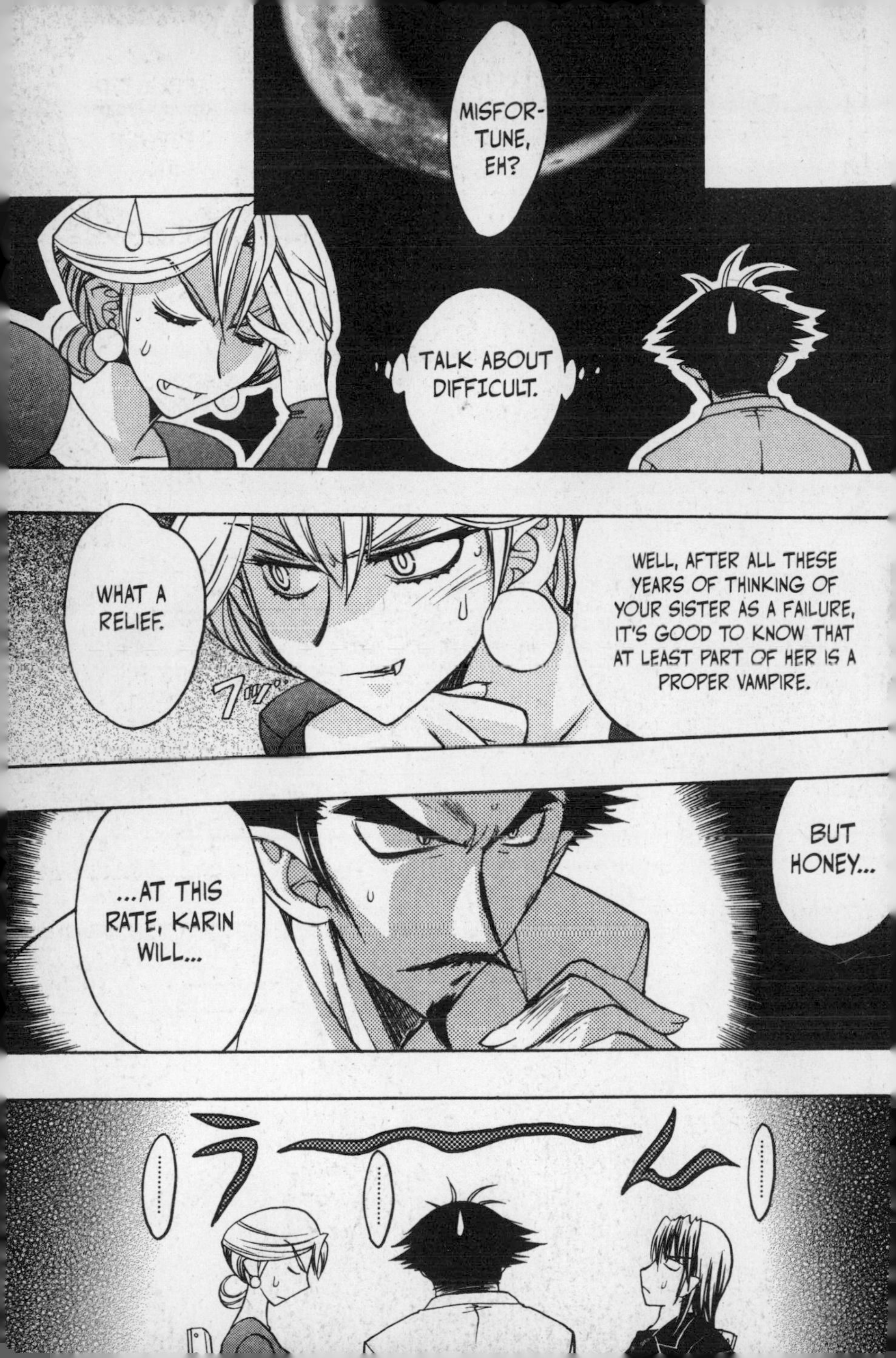
MISFOR-TUNE, EH?
TALK ABOUT DIFFICULT.
WELL, AFTER ALL THESE YEARS OF THINKING OF YOUR SISTER AS A FAILURE, IT'S GOOD TO KNOW THAT AT LEAST PART OF HER IS A PROPER VAMPIRE.
WHAT A RELIEF.
フッ
BUT HONEY...
...AT THIS RATE, KARIN WILL...
うーーーん
......
......
......

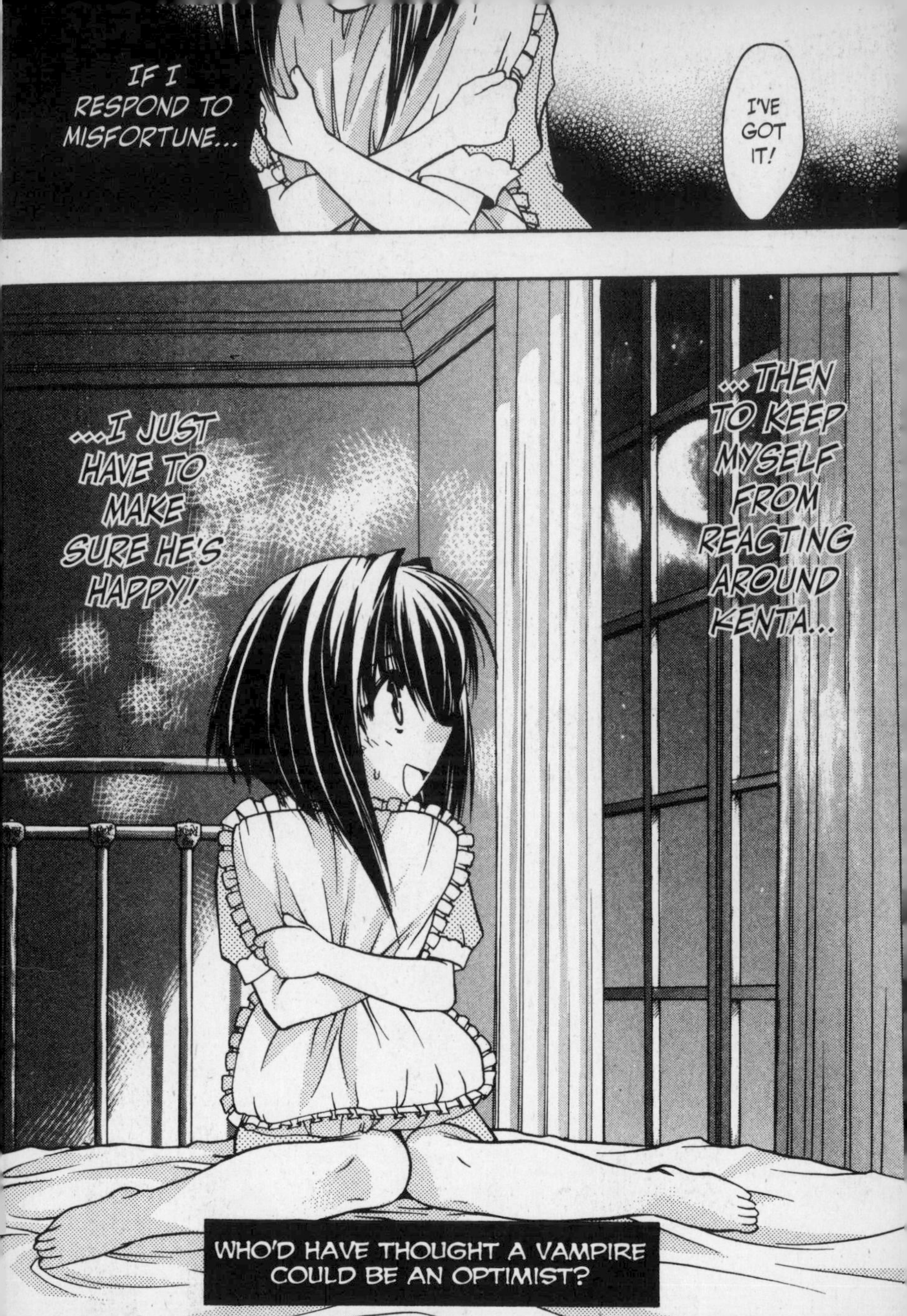
I'VE GOT IT!
IF I RESPOND TO MISFORTUNE...
...THEN TO KEEP MYSELF FROM REACTING AROUND KENTA...
...I JUST HAVE TO MAKE SURE HE'S HAPPY!
WHO'D HAVE THOUGHT A VAMPIRE COULD BE AN OPTIMIST?

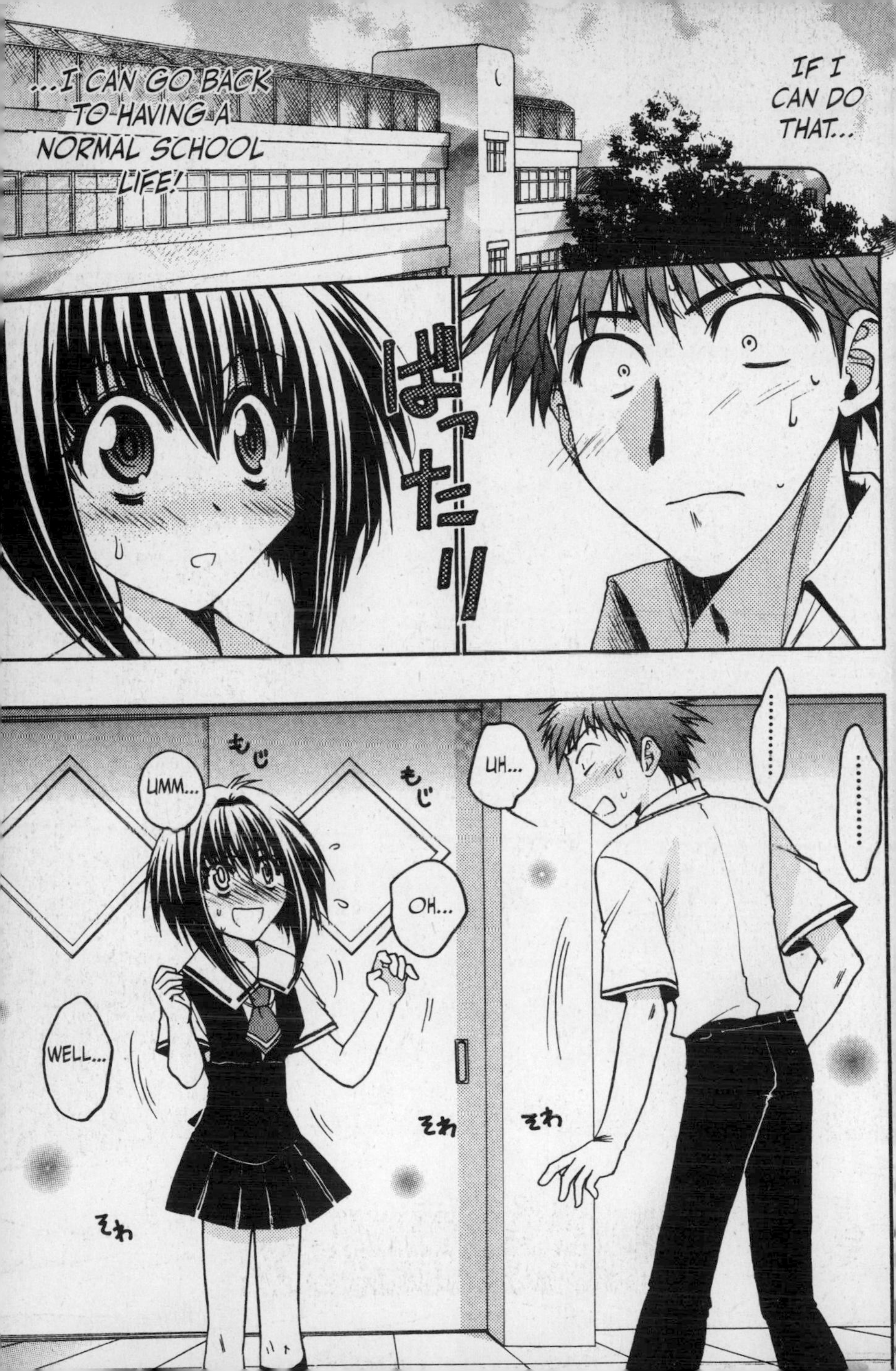

IF I CAN DO THAT...
...I CAN GO BACK TO HAVING A NORMAL SCHOOL LIFE!
ぱったり
......
......
UH...
もじ もじ
OH...
UMM...
WELL...
そわ そわ そわ

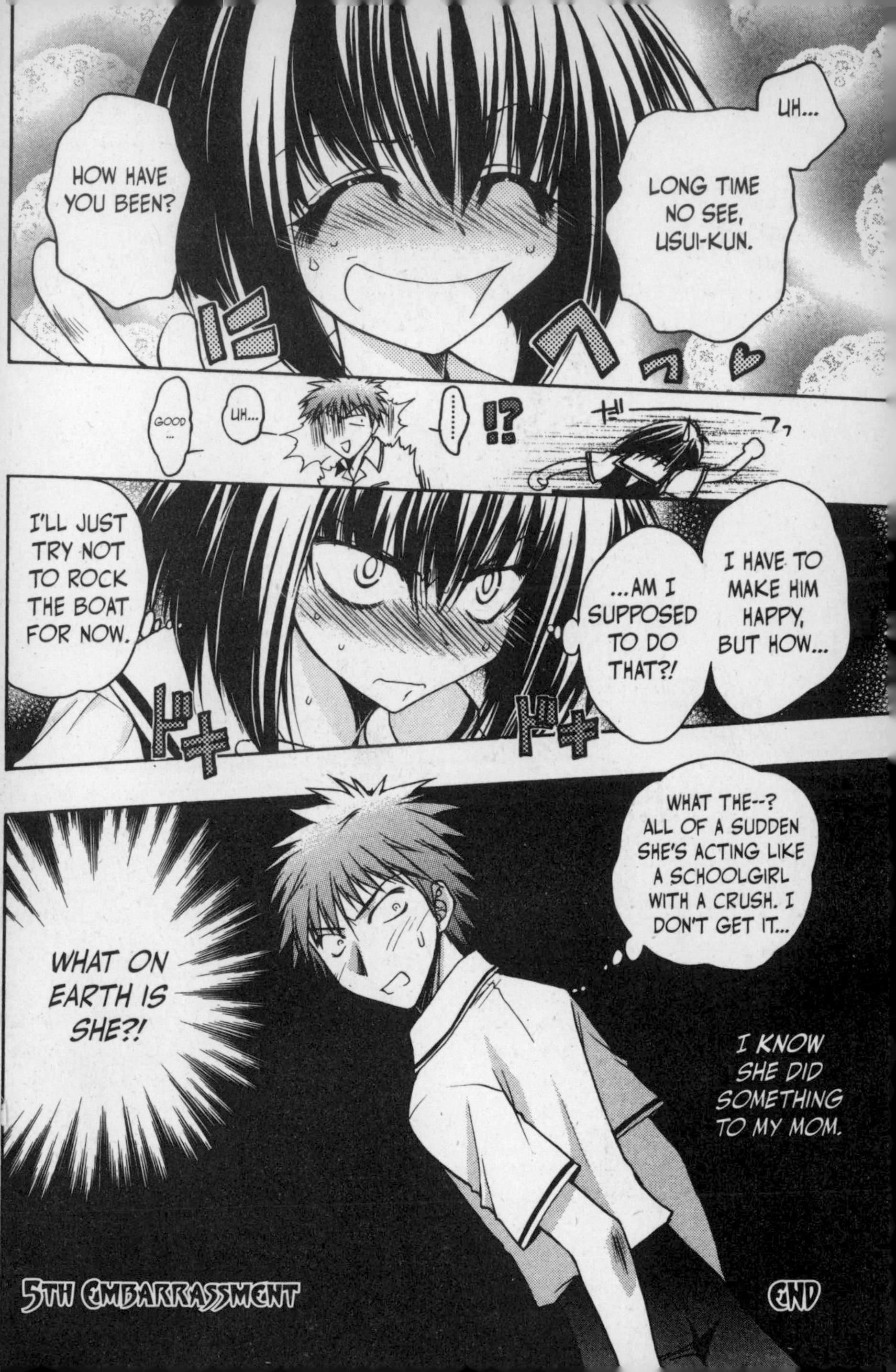
UH... LONG TIME NO SEE, USUI-KUN.
HOW HAVE YOU BEEN?
!?
......
UH...
GOOD ...
I HAVE TO MAKE HIM HAPPY, BUT HOW...
...AM I SUPPOSED TO DO THAT?!
I'LL JUST TRY NOT TO ROCK THE BOAT FOR NOW.
WHAT THE--? ALL OF A SUDDEN SHE'S ACTING LIKE A SCHOOLGIRL WITH A CRUSH. I DON'T GET IT...
I KNOW SHE DID SOMETHING TO MY MOM.
WHAT ON EARTH IS SHE?!
END
5TH EMBARRASSMENT

# EXTRAS

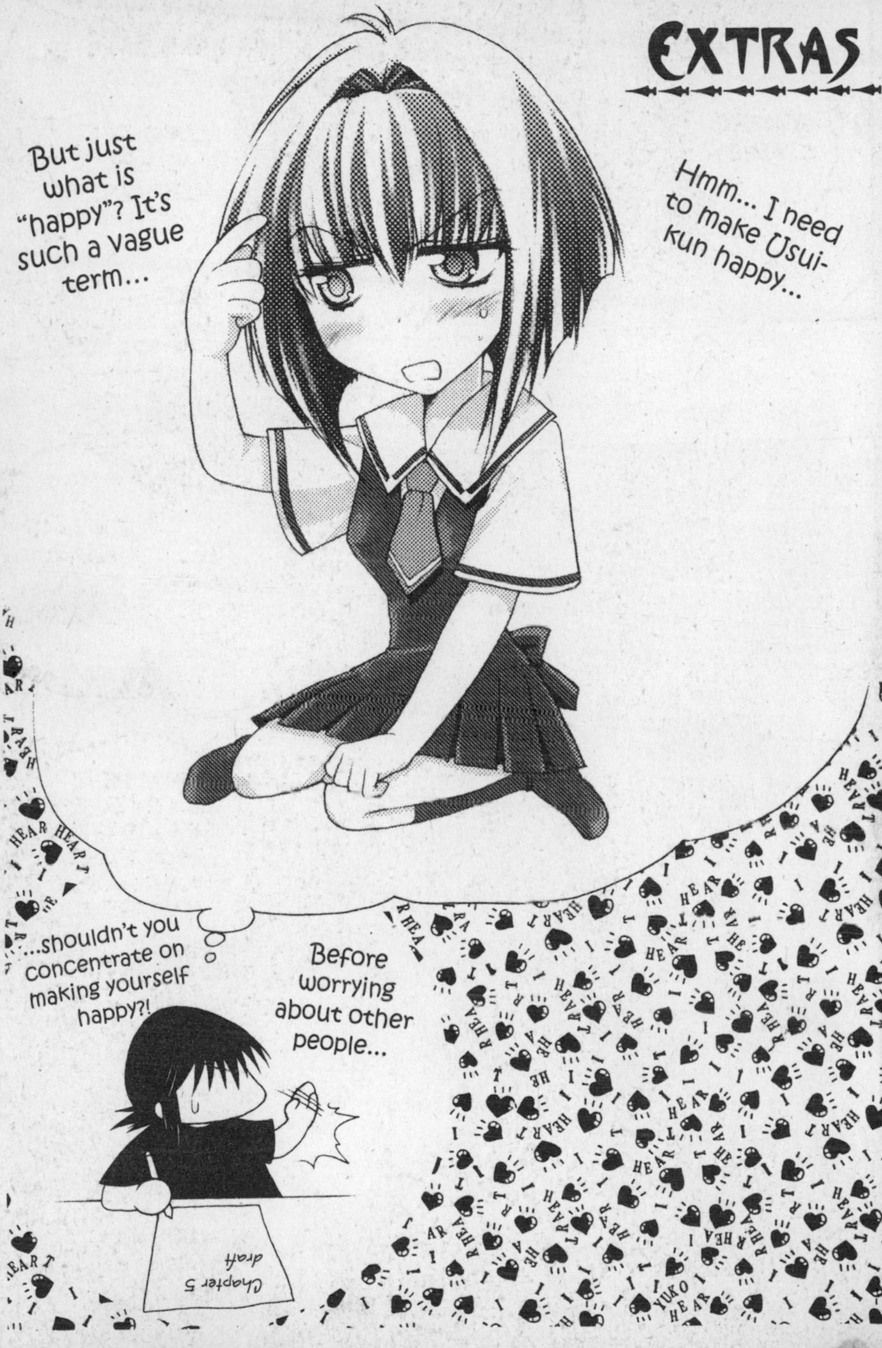
Hmm... I need to make Usui-kun happy...
But just what is "happy"? It's such a vague term...
Before worrying about other people...
...shouldn't you concentrate on making yourself happy?!
Chapter 5 draft

MEETING WITH MY EDITOR TO DISCUSS THE NEW SERIES. (THIS WAS AROUND MID-2002.)

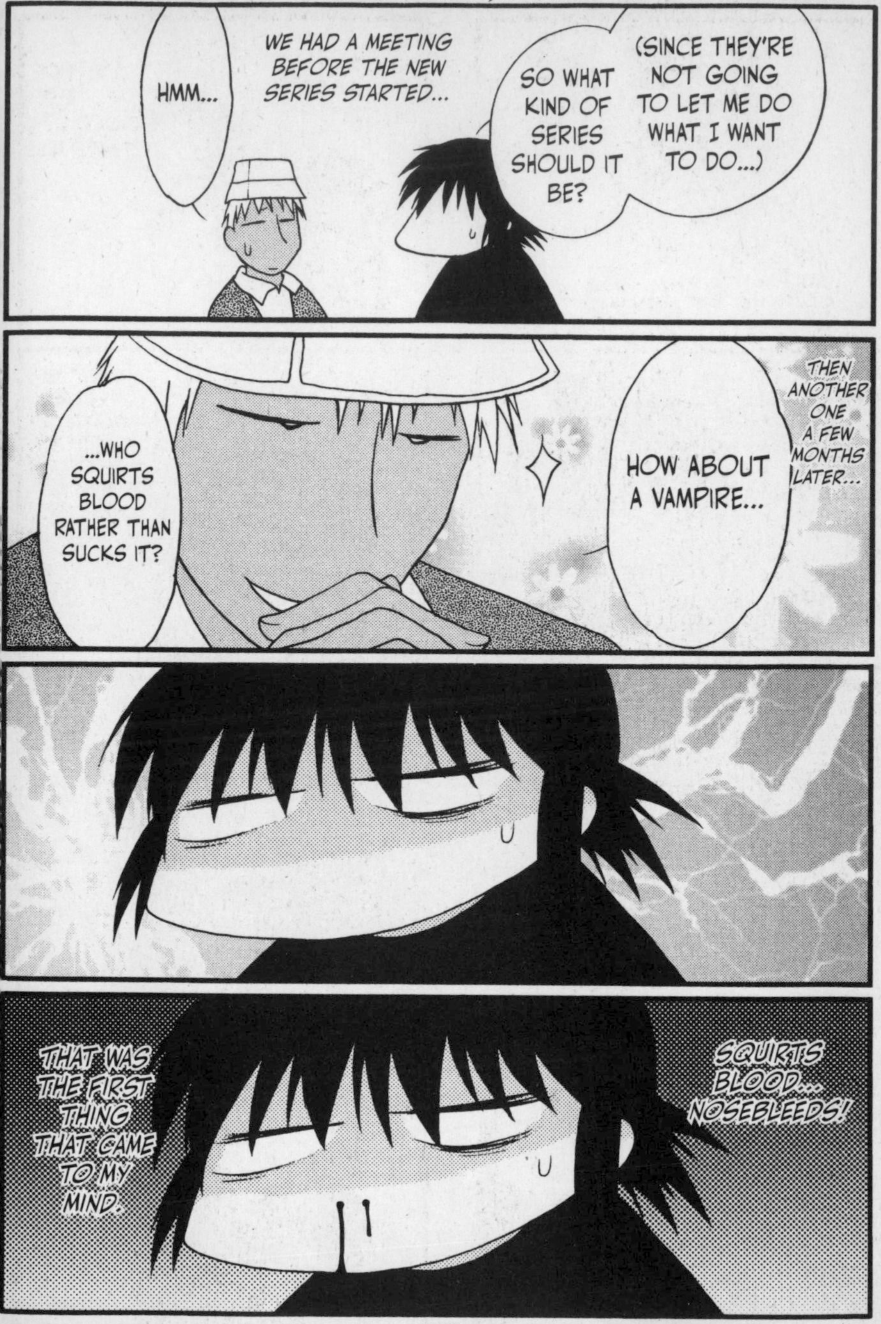
(SINCE THEY'RE NOT GOING TO LET ME DO WHAT I WANT TO DO...)
SO WHAT KIND OF SERIES SHOULD IT BE?
WE HAD A MEETING BEFORE THE NEW SERIES STARTED...
HMM...
THEN ANOTHER ONE A FEW MONTHS LATER...
HOW ABOUT A VAMPIRE...
...WHO SQUIRTS BLOOD RATHER THAN SUCKS IT?
SQUIRTS BLOOD... NOSEBLEEDS!
THAT WAS THE FIRST THING THAT CAME TO MY MIND.

## On a Roll 1

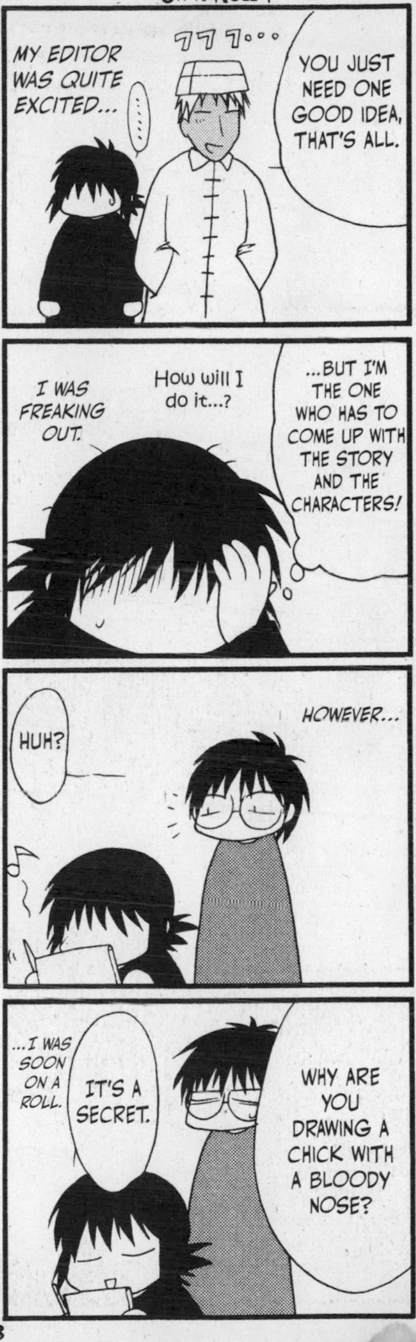

YOU JUST NEED ONE GOOD IDEA, THAT'S ALL.
MY EDITOR WAS QUITE EXCITED...
......
...BUT I'M THE ONE WHO HAS TO COME UP WITH THE STORY AND THE CHARACTERS!
How will I do it...?
I WAS FREAKING OUT.
HOWEVER...
HUH?
WHY ARE YOU DRAWING A CHICK WITH A BLOODY NOSE?
IT'S A SECRET.
...I WAS SOON ON A ROLL.


## On a Roll 2

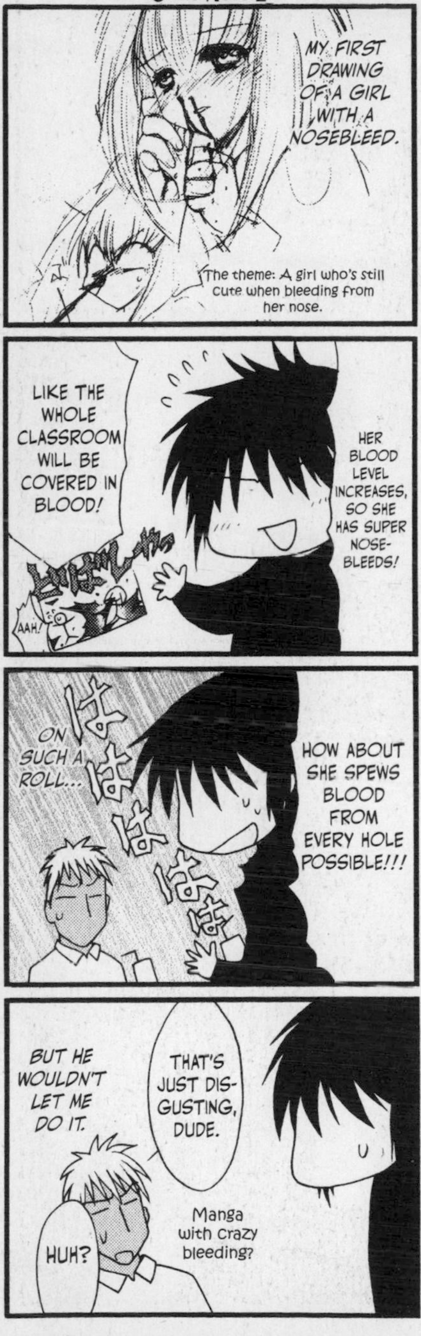

MY FIRST DRAWING OF A GIRL WITH A NOSEBLEED.
The theme: A girl who's still cute when bleeding from her nose.
HER BLOOD LEVEL INCREASES, SO SHE HAS SUPER NOSE-BLEEDS!
LIKE THE WHOLE CLASSROOM WILL BE COVERED IN BLOOD!
AAH!
HOW ABOUT SHE SPEWS BLOOD FROM EVERY HOLE POSSIBLE!!!
はははは
ON SUCH A ROLL...
THAT'S JUST DISGUSTING, DUDE.
BUT HE WOULDN'T LET ME DO IT.
Manga with crazy bleeding?
HUH?

GRAND ERUPTION

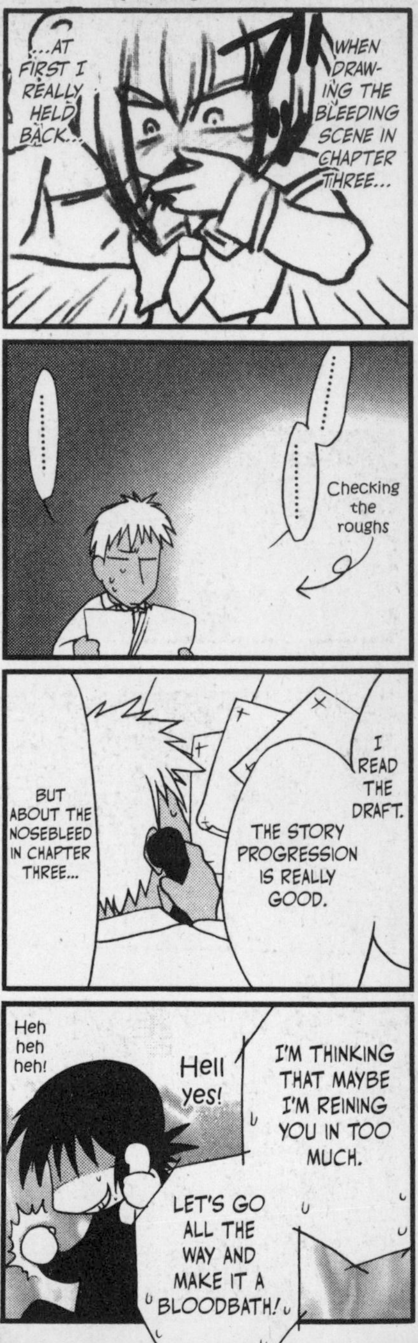
WHEN DRAW-ING THE BLEEDING SCENE IN CHAPTER THREE...
...AT FIRST I REALLY HELD BACK...
......
......
Checking the roughs
I READ THE DRAFT.
THE STORY PROGRESSION IS REALLY GOOD.
BUT ABOUT THE NOSEBLEED IN CHAPTER THREE...
I'M THINKING THAT MAYBE I'M REINING YOU IN TOO MUCH.
LET'S GO ALL THE WAY AND MAKE IT A BLOODBATH!
Hell yes!
Heh heh heh!

THAT'S NOT TRUE

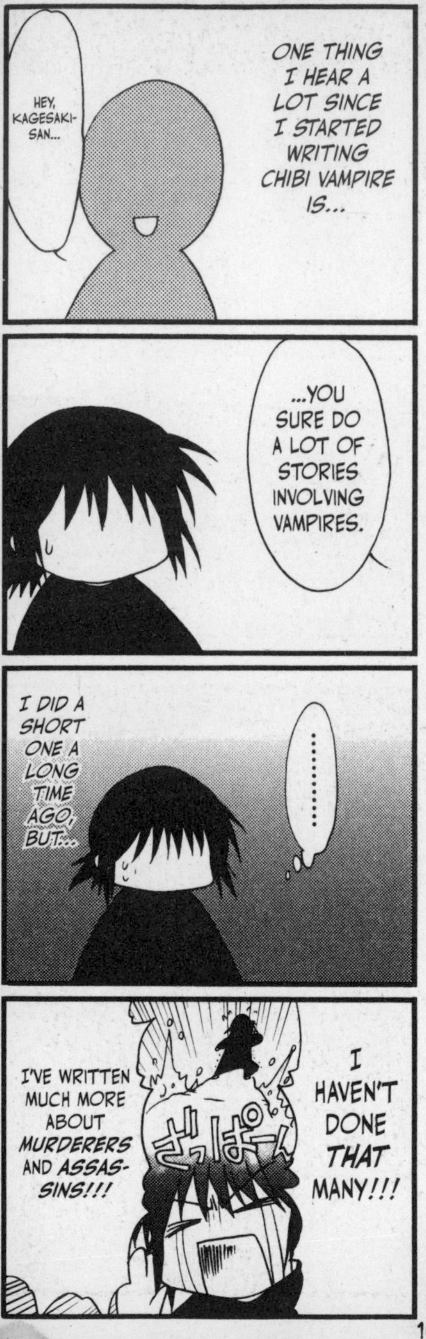
ONE THING I HEAR A LOT SINCE I STARTED WRITING CHIBI VAMPIRE IS...
HEY, KAGESAKI-SAN...
...YOU SURE DO A LOT OF STORIES INVOLVING VAMPIRES.
......
I DID A SHORT ONE A LONG TIME AGO, BUT...
I HAVEN'T DONE THAT MANY!!!
ざっぱーん
I'VE WRITTEN MUCH MORE ABOUT MURDERERS AND ASSAS-SINS!!!

# ANJU'S ROOM

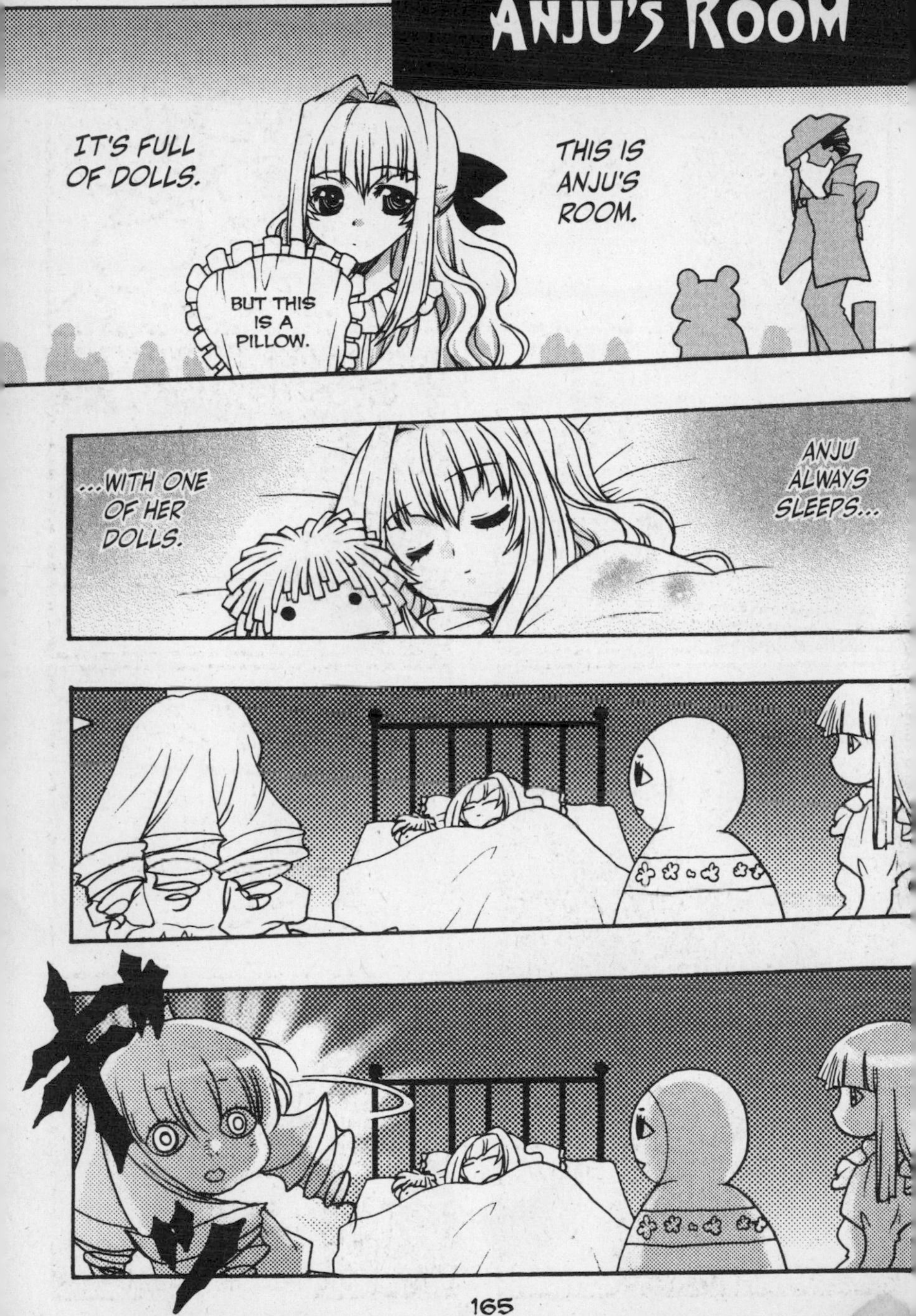
THIS IS ANJU'S ROOM.
IT'S FULL OF DOLLS.
BUT THIS IS A PILLOW.
ANJU ALWAYS SLEEPS...
...WITH ONE OF HER DOLLS.

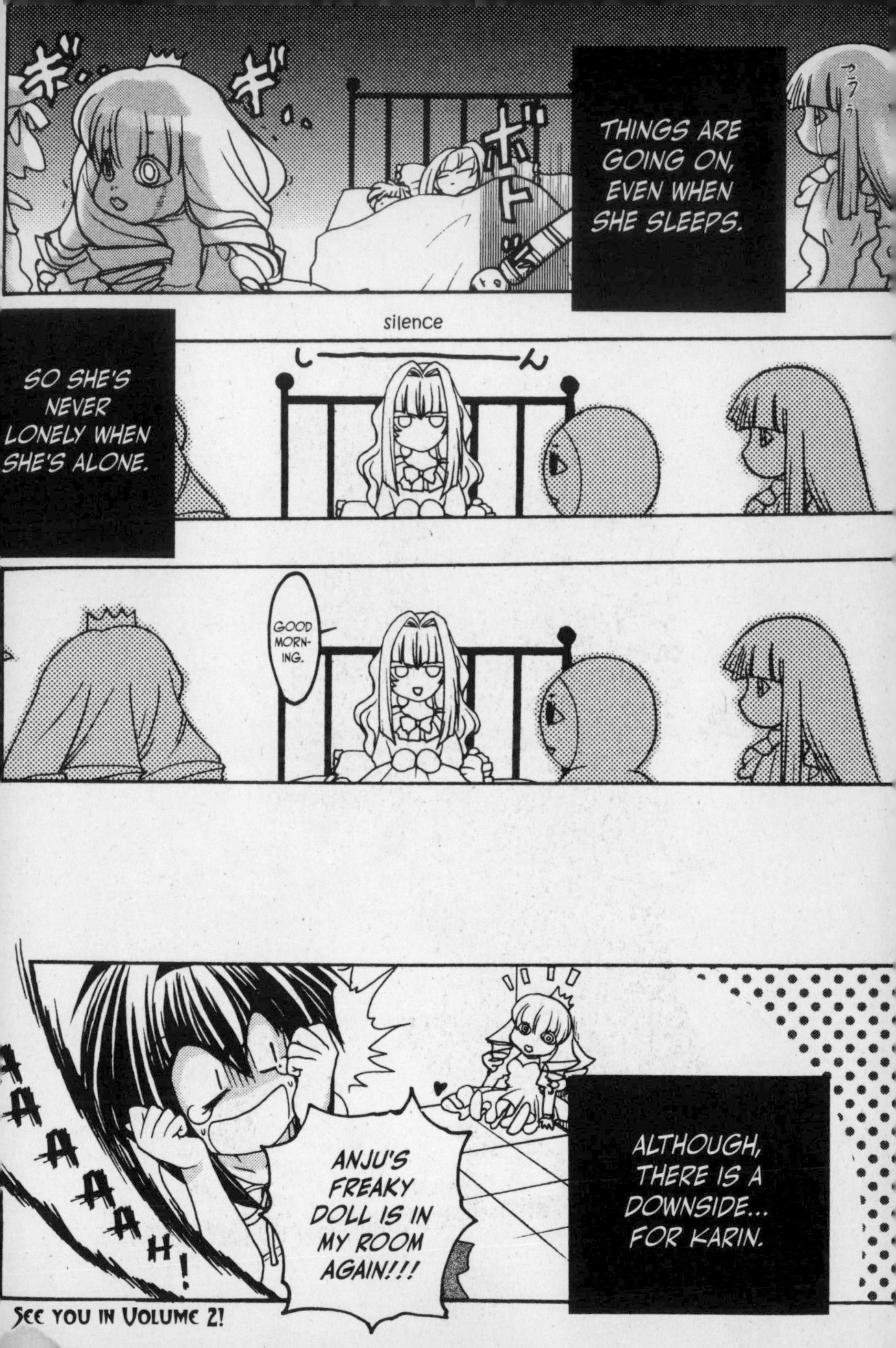
THINGS ARE GOING ON, EVEN WHEN SHE SLEEPS.
silence
SO SHE'S NEVER LONELY WHEN SHE'S ALONE.
GOOD MORNING.
ALTHOUGH, THERE IS A DOWNSIDE... FOR KARIN.
ANJU'S FREAKY DOLL IS IN MY ROOM AGAIN!!!
AAAAAAH!

See you in Volume 2!

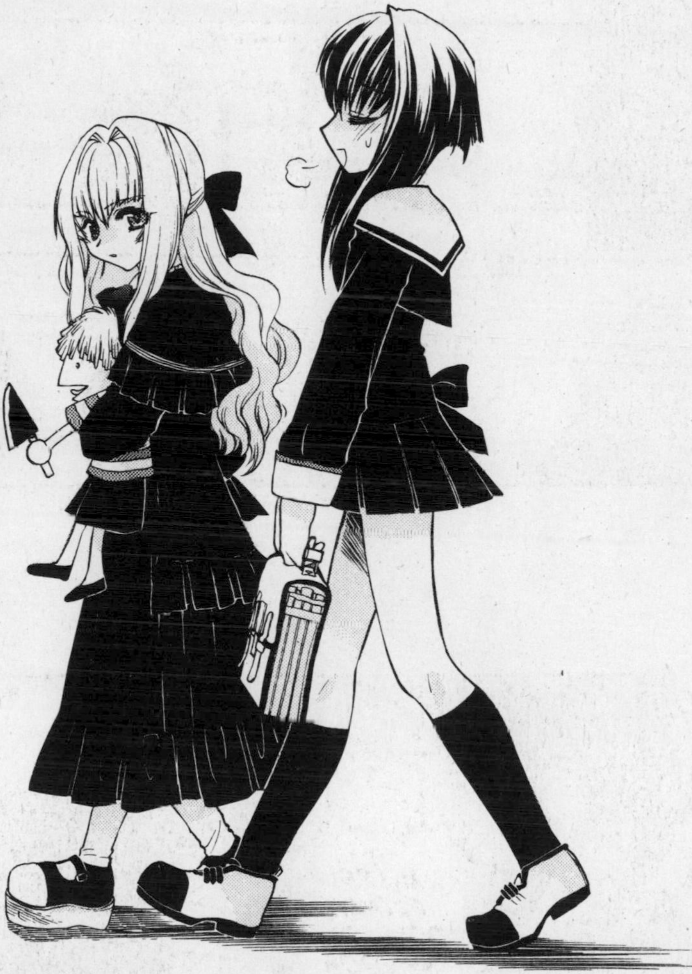

# In the next volume of

# Chibi Vampire

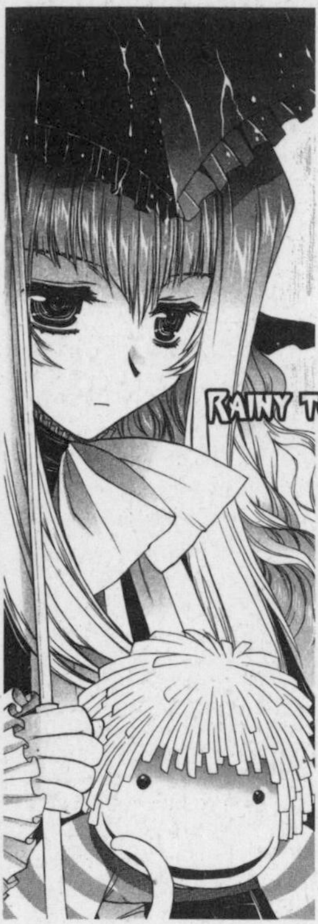

Rainy teen angst...

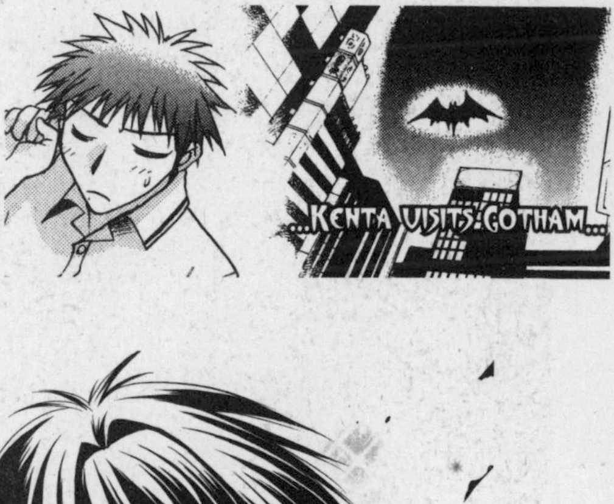
...Kenta visits Gotham...

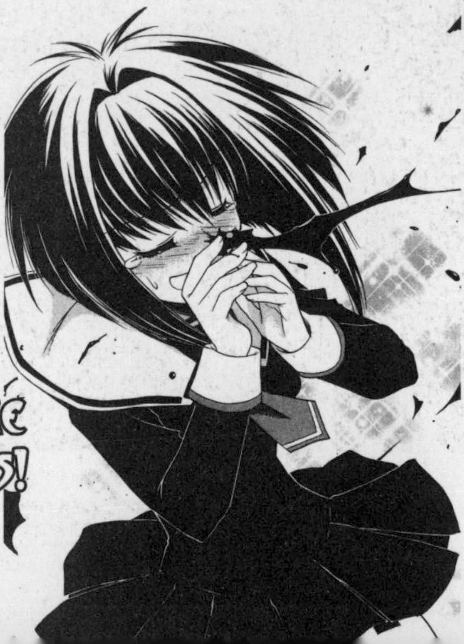

...And more nosebleeds!

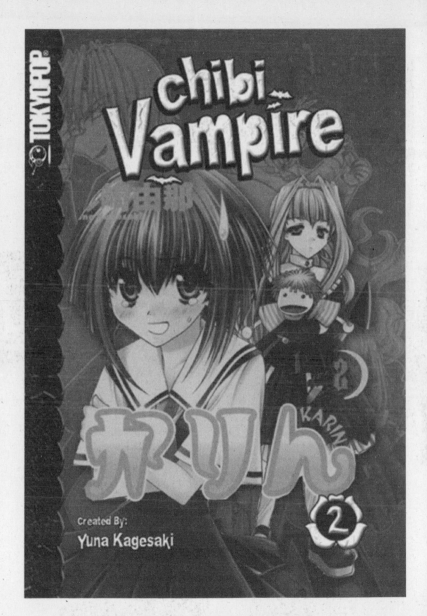

**AVAILABLE AUGUST 2006!**

# 4,000 YEN LUNCH

ON A COLD DAY IN FEBRUARY...
This is one steep hill...
...WE WENT TO A SMALL TOWN TO DO LOCATION RESEARCH FOR CHIBI VAMPIRE.
Wheeze! Wheeze
Wait!
THERE WERE ALL THESE HUGE HOMES...
...AND EVERY FIVE MINUTES, WE'D SEE A MIDDLE-AGED MAN ACTING YOUNGER THAN HE WAS.
THERE WAS A REALLY COOL-LOOKING WESTERN MANSION.
AND IN THE CITY, THERE WERE TONS OF RICH-LOOKING OLDER LADIES SHOPPING.
Off to get a new purse!
LA LA LA LA!
I THINK WE'VE FOUND OUR LOCATION...
...BECAUSE THIS PLACE IS SCARING THE HELL OUT OF ME.
Dumplings are good, though!
Because part of it's in China.
China Town
REALLY?

# TOKYOPOP SHOP

SPOTLIGHT TOKYOPOP MANGA SUPPLEMENT

# OFF*BEAT

BY JEN LEE QUICK

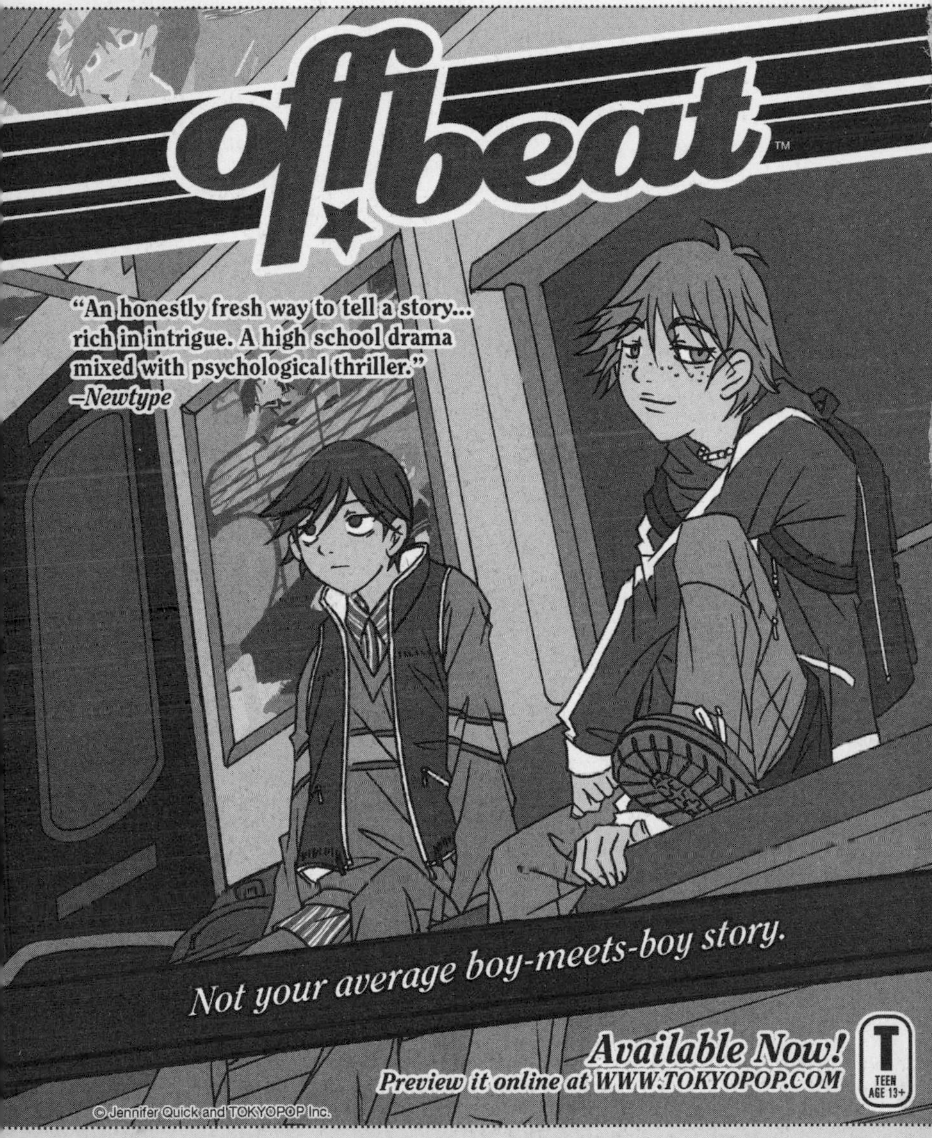
offbeat™
"An honestly fresh way to tell a story... rich in intrigue. A high school drama mixed with psychological thriller."
–Newtype
Not your average boy-meets-boy story.
Available Now!
Preview it online at WWW.TOKYOPOP.COM
T TEEN AGE 13+
© Jennifer Quick and TOKYOPOP Inc.

FOR MORE INFORMATION VISIT: WWW.TOKYOPOP.COM/OFFBEAT

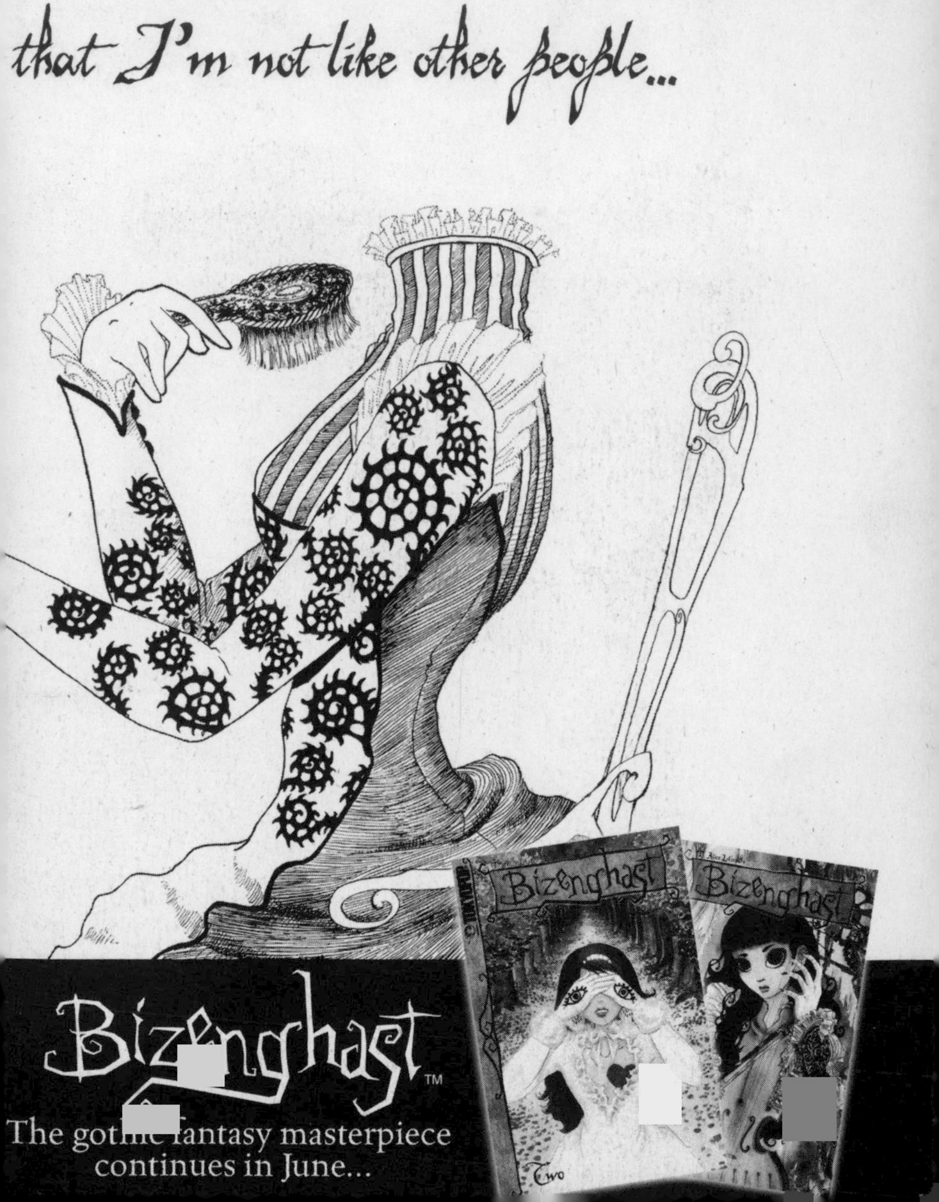
that I'm not like other people...
Bizenghast
Bizenghast
Two
Bizenghast™
The gothic fantasy masterpiece continues in June...